Teaching Mathematics
to the Learning Disabled

All my love,
Nancy
8/31/89

Teaching Mathematics
to the Learning Disabled
Second Edition

Nancy S. Bley   *Carol A. Thornton*

8700 Shoal Creek Boulevard, Austin, Texas 78758

Library of Congress Cataloging-in-Publication Data

Bley, Nancy S.
    Teaching mathematics to the learning disabled.

    Includes index.
    1. Mathematics—Study and teaching (Elementary)
2. Learning disabled children—Education—Mathematics.
I. Thornton, Carol A. II. Title.
QA135.5.B56 1989   371.9'0447   89-3922
ISBN 0-89079-200-3

8700 Shoal Creek Boulevard
Austin, Texas 78758
10 9 8 7 6 5 4 3 2 1   89 90 91 92

To our husbands, Michael and Denis,
our children,
Chris,
Stephanie, and Jennifer,
and to
Gail and Genny,
for their patient understanding and support
throughout this project.

CONTENTS

PREFACE

This second edition of *Teaching Mathematics to the Learning Disabled* is written in the belief that, though they may learn "differently," most learning disabled students can master important mathematical concepts and skills. This belief has evolved out of our own personal experiences with learning disabled students. Approaches and techniques that we have found most successful are interwoven in the suggestions given throughout the text.

After a brief overview of learning disabilities and their effect on learning elementary- and junior-high or middle-school mathematics, Chapter 1 focuses on 10 general techniques that can aid the planning and implementation of mathematics instruction for the learning disabled. The remaining 10 chapters deal with specific areas of school mathematics instruction. This edition contains new information on the use of calculators and computers with learning disabled students. In addition, it reflects emerging trends in school mathematics and suggests ways of helping learning disabled students deal with new curriculum content and new areas of emphasis. In particular, recurring themes include helping learning disabled students develop number and operation sense and build appropriate problem solving, estimation, and mental computation skills.

Rather than treat comprehensively all topics in the school mathematics curriculum, emphasis has been placed on these and other topics which, from the perspective of the *Curriculum and Evaluation Standards for School Mathematics* (National Council of Teachers of Mathematics, 1989), potentially can or do commonly cause learning disabled students the most difficulty. Background information at the beginning of each section summarizes standard approaches to the topic and points out particular problems learning disabled students may encounter with a given concept or skill. Then, in follow-up, a sequence of suggested activities and exercises is listed. Based on the assumption that teachers are familiar with standard approaches to handling the topics, these sequences are intended to highlight instructional alternatives to meeting special needs and to give instances where special visual, auditory, or kinesthetic support is appropriate.

Color coding, for example, is one of the visual cueing techniques that are consistently employed. In general, when using this approach, it might be suggested that students be checked for intact color vision. If they show any difficulty, similar techniques like bold print or underscoring might be used instead.

Cueing used during early instruction of a topic is gradually withdrawn as students become more confident and able to work independently. Indeed, that is the goal: to help students learn to compensate for any disability and to deal effectively with mathematics both in academic and everyday situations. Any inspiration we can provide towards accomplishing this goal comes primarily from the students with whom we have worked and from whom we ourselves have learned.

Nancy S. Bley
Carol A. Thornton

CHAPTER

Planning Instruction for Special Needs

Learning disabled children are unable to learn the way most children do. For this reason, there characteristically is a discrepancy between the children's learning potential and performance in mathematics. Probably, these children's single biggest obstacle to learning is their inability to perform well independently. This may be due to several reasons, including:

- They are unable to use critical thinking without specific training;
- They have visual perception difficulties that preclude seeing accurately what is presented to them;
- They have poor retention; or
- Auditorially, they misperceive words or parts of words.

Some learning disabled students have good study skills and are highly motivated. They are willing to learn and try to stay on task. Typically, this willingness decreases with age as problems, like those just mentioned, continually frustrate learning attempts. Students then often begin to misbehave, withdraw, or simply not attend.

This problem is compounded when learning disabled students are mainstreamed or taught in resource rooms along with children who have uniquely different learning styles, abilities, and interests. The mathematics teacher must somehow deal with each student's diverse learning needs. In some instances, the curricular goals set by the school district seem unrealistic for certain individuals. How does one adequately teach the expected content and still help those students who have legitimate learning difficulties?

In regular mathematics classes, even the best attempts to handle the different learning needs of learning disabled students through individual assignments or cooperative learning schemes are sometimes thwarted. Although the teacher may be able to spend some time working individually with a child or a small group, overall, the setting still demands considerable independent work skills. It cannot be assumed that learning disabled children possess these skills. Instead, they must specifically be taught and then monitored regularly, not just in the resource room but in the larger classroom setting as well.

An additional problem for the teacher is the need to use textual materials typically written for regular class students. Most commercial texts are visually confusing, with the result that children cannot copy and space out the work as intended. Lessons frequently are not sequenced to provide adequate transition between topics, and there usually is not enough review of important concepts and skills. For learning disabled students who cannot transfer concepts from the concrete to the abstract without teacher assistance, the use of manipulatives may be meaningless.

All these issues should be addressed in the context of emerging new thrusts in school mathematics. Students who entered kindergarten in 1988 can expect to graduate from high school in the year 2001. Yet, these students who will graduate in the 21st century still frequently face the computation-dominated curriculum which is more suitable for the 19th century. To address this inconsistency, the National Council of Teachers of Mathematics (NCTM) has issued its *Curriculum and Evaluation Standards for School Mathematics* (1989).

The position taken by leaders in mathematics education is that, while computation is still vital in the current information age, it is obvious that obtaining answers by standard paper-and-pencil methods is not sufficient. There is now a need to be flexible in choosing among available resources—calculator or computer, paper and pencil, or mental calculation methods. There also is an important need to be able to judge whether answers obtained are "reasonable"—perhaps by estimating or cross-checking using alternate methods.

Wise decision making and the ability to think critically is the key. This sometimes involves the ability to judge which operation should be carried out in a specific setting. Practical problem solving rooted in a good sense of number and relationships between number, as well as adequate understanding of each of the operations, is necessary.

The National Council of Supervisors of Mathematics (NCSM) has endorsed the position taken by NCTM. Thus, their official statement, the *Twelve Components of Essential Mathematics* (see Table 1-1), also summarizes the thinking NCTM expresses in its *Standards* document (1989). The full text of their position

Table 1-1
Twelve Components of Essential Mathematics

Problem Solving

Learning to solve problems is the principal reason for studying mathematics. Problem solving is the process of applying previously acquired knowledge to new and unfamiliar situations. Solving word problems in texts is one form of problem solving, but students also should be faced with non-text problems. Problem-solving strategies involve posing questions, analyzing situations, translating results, illustrating results, drawing diagrams, and using trial and error. Students should see alternate solutions to problems; they should experience problems with more than a single solution.

Communicating Mathematical Ideas

Students should learn the language and notation of mathematics. For example, they should understand place value and scientific notation. They should learn to receive mathematical ideas through listening, reading, and visualizing. They should be able to present mathematical ideas by speaking, writing, drawing pictures and graphs, and demonstrating with concrete models. They should be able to discuss mathematics and ask questions about mathematics.

Mathematical Reasoning

Students should learn to make independent investigations of mathematical ideas. They should be able to identify and extend patterns and use experiences and observations to make conjectures (tentative conclusions). They should learn to use a counter-example to disprove a conjecture and they should learn to use models, known facts, and logical arguments to validate a conjecture. They should be able to distinguish between valid and invalid arguments.

Applying Mathematics to Everyday Situations

Students should be encouraged to take everyday situations, translate them into mathematical representations (graphs, tables, diagrams, or mathematical expressions), process the mathematics, and interpret the results in light of the initial situation. They should be able to solve ratio, proportion, percent, and direct variation and inverse variation problems. Not only should students see how mathematics is applied in the real world, but also they should observe how mathematics grows from the world around them.

Alertness to the Reasonableness of Results

In solving problems, students should question the reasonableness of a solution or conjecture in relation to the original problem. Students must develop the number sense to determine if results of calculations are reasonable in relation to the original numbers and the operations used. With the increase in the use of calculating devices in society, this capability is more important than ever.

Estimation

Students should be able to carry out rapid approximate calculations through the use of mental arithmetic and a variety of computational estimation techniques. When computation is needed in a problem or consumer setting, an estimate can be used to check reasonableness, examine a conjecture, or make a decision. Students should acquire simple techniques for estimating measurements such as length, area, volume, and mass (weight). They should be able to decide when a particular result is precise enough for the purpose at hand.

Table 1-1. Continued.

Appropriate Computational Skills

Students should gain facility in using addition, subtraction, multiplication, and division with whole numbers and decimals. Today, long, complicated computations should be done with a calculator or computer. Knowledge of single-digit number facts is essential, and using mental arithmetic is a valuable skill. In learning to apply computation, students should have practice in choosing the appropriate computational method: mental arithmetic, paper-pencil algorithm, or calculating device. Moreover, there are everyday situations that demand recognition of, and simple computation with, common fractions. In addition, the ability to recognize, use, and estimate with percents must also be developed and maintained.

Algebraic Thinking

Students should learn to use variables (letters) to represent mathematical quantities and expressions; they should be able to represent mathematical functions and relationships using tables, graphs, and equations. They should understand and correctly use positive and negative numbers, order of operations, formulas, equations, and inequalities. They should recognize the ways in which one quantity changes in relation to another.

Measurement

Students should learn the fundamental concepts of measurement through concrete experiences. They should be able to measure distance, mass (weight), time, capacity, temperature, and angles. They should learn to calculate simple perimeters, areas, and volumes. They should be able to perform measurement in both metric and customary systems using the appropriate tools and levels of precision.

Geometry

Students should understand the geometric concepts necessary to function effectively in the three-dimensional world. They should have knowledge of concepts such as parallelism, perpendicularity, congruence, similarity, and symmetry. Students should know properties of simple plane and solid geometric figures. Students should visualize and verbalize how objects move in the world around them using terms such as slides, flips, and turns. Geometric concepts should be explored in settings that involve problem solving and measurement.

Statistics

Students should plan and carry out the collection and organization of data to answer questions in their everyday lives. Students should know how to construct, read, and draw conclusions from simple tables, maps, charts, and graphs. They should be able to present information about numerical data such as measures of central tendency (mean, median, mode) and measures of dispersion (range, deviation). Students should recognize the basic uses and misuses of statistical representation and inference.

Probability

Students should understand elementary notions of probability to determine the likelihood of future events. They should identify situations where immediate past experience does not affect the likelihood of future events. They should become familiar with how mathematics is used to help make predictions such as election results, business forecasts, and outcomes of sporting events. They should learn how probability applies to research results and to the decision-making process.

(National Council of Supervisors of Mathematics, 1988, Minneapolis, MN. Reprinted with permission.)

(NCSM, 1988) contained additional statements concerning (a) the need to promote a positive climate for mathematics learning; (b) the use of technology in school mathematics; and (c) implications for evaluation.

In the last section, a word of caution is expressed concerning the use of standardized tests which only emphasize computation. Recommendations, which are likely to impact new versions of standardized tests, include:

- More analysis of applied problem solving and critical thinking/reasoning in mathematics; and
- Allowing the use of calculators on the tests.

Clearly, the emergence of a mathematics curriculum which emphasizes the essentials summarized in Table 1 has implications for writing individual educational programs in mathematics for learning disabled students. These plans also should capture the spirit of NCTM (1989) and NCSM (1988), which emphasize ideas like the following:

- Young children typically learn mathematics best through manipulating concrete materials and interacting with their environment. That environment should be planned carefully to nurture the development of mathematical concepts.
- Written symbols/computational procedures typically should be introduced after or in conjunction with exploratory work which focuses on providing meaning to what is written.
- Problem solving should be integrated into all facets of a child's mathematics program.
- Internalization of mathematical concepts and development of language skills are two aspects of learning which can and should reinforce each other. Instructional activities should offer students opportunities to discuss their thinking, ask questions, and present their interpretation of a mathematical idea or computational procedure. As with independent study skills, many learning disabled students do not automatically develop the appropriate mathematical language; consequently, they must be taught the specifics involved.
- Students' feelings about themselves as learners and about their experiences with mathematics can greatly influence the level of their efforts and eventual success. By providing an environment that is accepting, encouraging, stimulating, and enjoyable, a program can foster a strong self-image and a positive attitude toward mathematics.

The following chapters will share techniques and ideas for incorporating these new thrusts into mathematics programs for learning disabled students in primary, intermediate and middle/junior high schools. These chapters will also illustrate, for selected topics and for new thrusts related to these topics, how specialized techniques can be used within traditional sequences of instruction.

The overriding goal of this text is to provide ideas for arranging instruction so that teachers *can* teach and children *will* learn. Sometimes it is necessary to alter the standard mathematics sequence to meet the individual needs of learning disabled students. At other times, it is better to circumvent difficulties, using specialized methods, so these students:

- Can learn in a way that is appropriate for them; and

- Will learn more general compensatory techniques which will enable them to continue to learn and use mathematics in ways that are best for THEM.

We hope the ideas suggested will act as a springboard for teachers to develop their own ideas for teaching learning disabled children.

Based on this perspective, the remainder of this chapter is devoted to:

- Providing the reader with an overview of learning disabilities as they relate to school mathematics through grade 8; and

- Suggesting general techniques that can aid classroom instruction and planning for learning disabled students.

LEARNING DISABILITIES AND THEIR EFFECT ON MATHEMATICS PERFORMANCE

Most mathematics teachers are familiar with at least some of the following situations:

- A homework assignment that is "wrong" because sloppy copying led to misreading or nonalignment of digits;

- The child who consistently receives high scores on quizzes of isolated basic facts, yet misses these same facts when doing larger computations or solving word problems;

- The child who never seems to pay attention during oral quizzes or explanations and cannot answer questions in class;

- The older elementary student who "refuses" to learn the basic facts;

- Children who add when they should multiply or skip steps in division problems.

The list is endless, and every teacher can probably pinpoint at least one child who matches each of these descriptions.

Such situations can be very frustrating for both teacher and student. While they may represent only a small percentage of the students in a class, the nature and magnitude of the problems may be large enough to affect presentation of material and overall instruction.

Each case could involve a learning disabled child. Since learning disabled children typically have average or above average intelligence, teachers may mistakenly think these students are not trying, that they are lazy, or just not paying attention. Because they are frequently misunderstood, many learning disabled students have mixed feelings about themselves. They do not look different. In many instances, they can participate competitively with peers in certain class activities, either due to the nature of the activity or due to compensatory techniques they have developed. They work just as hard as their classmates, take notes, and do their homework. But they still cannot achieve in mathematics. They still fail tests. Often learning disabled children do not study with others for fear they will appear dumb. They also feel they are missing out on a lot of fun. These type of children come in many variations. Enrolled in a resource room, they feel "marked." Even in mainstreamed situations they feel left out.

Understanding a child's disability sometimes helps teachers plan instruction to minimize frustrations and social pressure due to the handicap. Toward this end, the following paragraphs review common learning disabilities that influence success in mathematics. The major disabilities have been divided into several topics under the general headings of visual and auditory perception problems; spatial and temporal disabilities; and motor, memory, integrative, and behavioral deficits. Table 1-2 summarizes these topics. Comments on the implications of Piaget's developmental theory for teaching students with learning disabilities conclude the section.

Visual and Auditory Perception Problems

Figure-Ground Difficulties. Children with visual figure-ground difficulties may exhibit a variety of symptoms. These are the children who frequently lose their place on the page, do not finish all their work, or appear not to concentrate when copying problems from the book. Also, they tend to mix up parts of problems and often copy wrong symbols. Because most mathematics books present many problems on a page, learning disabled students may not differentiate between the problem number and the problem itself and may include neighboring digits in the computation. As a result, their work appears carelessly done.

The worksheet shown in Figure 1-1 illustrates some of these difficulties. The computation in the first problem is almost accurate, but includes the problem number in the final step. Problem 2 is started correctly. The answer to 12 subtract 6 is 6, but the answer is placed under problem 3. Since 7 subtract 1 is also

Table 1-2

Examples of Learning Disabilities Affecting Performance in Mathematics

	Visual Deficit	Auditory Deficit
Perceptual Figure-ground	— may not finish all problems on page — frequently loses place — difficulty seeing subtraction within a division problem — difficulty reading multidigit number (see Closure)	— trouble hearing pattern in counting — difficulty attending in the classroom
Discrimination	— difficulty differentiating coins — difficulty differentiating between or writing numbers (3 for 8; 2 for 5) — cannot discriminate between operation symbols — cannot discriminate between size of hands on clock — difficulty associating operation sign with problem (see Abstract Reasoning)	— cannot distingush between 30 and 13 (see receptive language) — difficulty with decimal numbers
Reversal	— reverses digits in a number (may also be a sequential memory problem) — difficulty with regrouping	
Spatial	— trouble writing on lined paper — difficulty with concept of *before/after*, so trouble telling time — trouble noticing size differences in shapes — trouble with fraction concept due to inability to note equal-sized parts — difficulty writing decimals — difficulty aligning numbers — difficulty with ordinal numbers — difficulty writing fractional numbers (may also be reversal)	— difficulty following directions using ordinal numbers

Table 1-2. Continued.

	Visual Deficit	Auditory Deficit
Memory Short-Term	— trouble retaining newly presented material — difficulty copying problems from the board (may be spatial)	— difficulty with oral drills — difficulty with dictated assignments
Long-Term	— inability to retain basic facts or processes over a long period — difficulty solving multioperation computation	
Sequential	— difficulty telling time — difficulty following through a multiplication problem — difficulty following through long division problems — difficulty solving column addition problems — difficulty solving multistep word problems	— cannot retain story problem that is dictated
Integrative Closure	— difficulty visualizing groups — difficulty reading multidigit number (see Figure-Ground) — difficulty with missing addends and missing factors — inability to draw conclusions, therefore, trouble noticing and continuing patterns — difficulty with word problems — trouble continuing counting pattern from within a sequence	— difficulty counting on from within a sequence
Expressive Language	— rapid oral drills very difficult	— difficulty counting on — difficulty explaining why a problem is solved as it is

Table 1-2. Continued.

	Visual Deficit	Auditory Deficit
Receptive Language	— difficulty relating words to meaning (may be spatial) — difficulty with words that have multiple meanings	— difficulty relating word to meaning — difficulty writing numbers from dictation
Abstract Reasoning	— inability to solve word problems — inability to compare size of numbers, using symbols — cannot understand patterning in counting — difficulty with decimal concept	

6, the student proceeded with this computation, not realizing that an entire problem had been skipped. In problem 5, the child is still adding, possibly because of the similarity of numbers in problems 4 and 5. Problem 6 was begun but not finished, without the student being aware of it.

Figure 1-1

Figure-ground deficits also interfere with the solution of multi-operation procedures, such as long division. Children may have difficulty sorting out the subtraction problem within the division computation. In the problem presented in Figure 1-2, the child recognized that subtraction was required but used the wrong numbers. Subtracting 6 from 6 left 0, and the child then continued to solve to the end. On other occasions, children may locate the right numbers but forget what they are to do with them. Rather than viewing a multidigit number as a whole, children with figure-ground difficulties tend to focus on individual digits and do not spontaneously group them. In the example of Figure 1-3, despite a firm understanding of place-value for three-digit numbers, the child may be unsure whether to say "sixty-one two" or "six hundred twelve." In such cases, if the teacher verbalizes alternatives for the number, the child can often associate correctly.

$$62\tfrac{1}{4}$$
$$4\overline{)269}$$
$$\underline{24}$$
$$09$$
$$\underline{8}$$
$$1$$

Figure 1-2

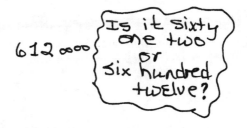

Figure 1-3

Children with auditory figure-ground deficits may have trouble attending in class. For example, they cannot sort out extraneous stimuli, such as the sound of chalk, from the teacher's explanation. Or they may seem to be daydreaming or disruptive when, in fact, they are trying to attend but simply cannot listen and learn simultaneously.

Auditory figure-ground difficulties can also interfere with a student's ability to hear counting patterns. Although place-value ideas form the basis of our number system, most young children learn to count by tuning in to repetitive patterns they hear. Even 5- and 6-year-olds learn to count by fives and tens, although they have no idea of place value. Learning to skip count often does not come easily to learning disabled children. Thus, they are often unable to discover the pattern (i.e., localize the repetitive part and repeat it) without a much stronger oral emphasis than is generally used.

Discrimination Problems. Visual discrimination errors may cause students to misread numbers. Very young children are often not developmentally ready to discriminate one number from another. As a result, they tend to write numbers backwards, especially 2, 3, or 5, often without even noticing the reversal. This difficulty is generally outgrown by the age of seven. Children with learning disabilities, however, may exhibit the problem more frequently or beyond the normal developmental stage. Because they do not perceive the numbers correctly, the task of writing numbers, copying problems from the board, or spontaneously writing them from dictation can be extremely difficult. By the time they have written a number, they may have lost their place or be so far behind in copying that the teacher may be ready to erase the board.

Telling time or recognizing coins can also be very difficult for children who are unable to discriminate size differences. The ability to recognize and differentiate between coins requires that a child notice discrete differences in size. Some children may recognize size differences in general but be unable to apply this skill to a practical situation. They may perform slower than classmates because of the perceptual deficit. Telling time, for example, takes these students longer because they must consciously locate the smaller hand on the clock while their peers locate it automatically.

As children encounter more and more symbols, perceptual problems become prominent. Figure 1-4 illustrates several perceptually related errors made by children who, in fact, knew how to handle the computation involved.

$$
\begin{array}{cc}
9 \\
+7 \\
\hline
13
\end{array}
\qquad
\begin{array}{cc}
\overset{1}{46} \\
\times\ 7 \\
\hline
294
\end{array}
\qquad
\begin{array}{cc}
\overset{1}{64} \\
+\ 8 \\
\hline
492
\end{array}
$$

Figure 1-4

In the first example, the child read 9 as 6. The computation for what was seen, however, is correct. In the next example, the computational process is right. The errors are due to interpreting the 6 as a 2. The third example shows what can happen when a child has trouble discriminating operation signs. At first the sign was correctly seen as a "plus" sign and addition was consequently performed. At the second step of the problem, however, the child perceived the sign as a multiplication sign and proceeded to use that operation.

Auditory discrimination problems are exemplified in the inability to hear numbers correctly. This, in turn, can affect a child's ability to count. Often children miss endings of words, leading to a counting pattern such as the following: ". . . 9, 10, 11, 12, 30, 40, 50, 60, 70, 80, 90, 20." The subtlety of this situation is that children, if asked to count aloud, may in fact *say the numbers correctly.* But internally they misperceive what they hear themselves say. Depending on the severity of the problem, these children may or may not be able to correct the pattern if the symbols for 13 through 20 are placed before them.

Reversals.   Another common perceptual difficulty results in reversals. Children with reversal tendencies not only make mirror images of individual digits as noted in the section on discrimination; they may also reverse the digits of a two-digit number when reading or writing. This problem naturally leads to errors in computation. For example, children may carry the wrong number when regrouping. The most common reversals occur in the teens: 21 for 12, 31 for 13, 41 for 14, and so on. An example of how reversals can affect multiplication computation is illustrated in Figure 1-5.

$$
\begin{array}{r} 13 \\ \times\ 9 \\ \hline 99 \end{array}
\qquad\qquad
\begin{array}{r} 58 \\ \times\ 9 \\ \hline 477 \end{array}
$$

Figure 1-5

The child read 31 for 13 in the first problem and consequently multiplied the 1 by 9. In the subsequent step, the digit "1" was correctly located in the 10s place and was multiplied next. Again, 9 was recorded in the product.

In the second problem, the digits were reversed when written down, thus accounting for the 7 in the ones place. The rest of the problem was computed accurately.

This last example illustrates the importance of teaching children, especially those with learning disabilities, first to write the number that is to be regrouped. More severe reversal and discrimination problems may require color coding or alternate methods of computing. Some of these approaches are discussed in Chapters 2 and 5.

Spatial and Temporal Disabilities

Spatial and temporal organization can greatly affect a child's mathematics performance and practical applications outside the classroom. Although children with temporal disabilities may be able to tell time by rote, their concept of time and, therefore, their general planning ability is often considerably impaired.

Other problems characterize the child with spatial disabilities. For example, difficulty locating position in space—knowing right from left or up from down—can make the task of number alignment almost insurmountable. Renaming in computation becomes even more difficult. Children with this handicap (a) need to understand *why* the regrouped number is placed above the tens digit, and (b) need visual and kinesthetic clues to help them locate and feel what "above" means.

Difficulties with spatial organization can prevent children from properly forming a number that they actually see accurately. They may reverse the position or invert it. Verbal cues such as "right" and "left" or "top" and "bottom" carry little meaning and are, therefore, no help in starting the number. Specific training involving motor activities, color coding, and continual integration with other skills is essential.

At the upper grade levels, spatial difficulties can interfere with the study of decimals, fractions, and word problems. Even when conceptual understanding is strong, difficulties may still arise. Locating where the decimal point belongs, determining the correct sequence of steps in a word problem, or properly placing the numbers in a fraction or a mixed number can be extremely difficult for a child with these deficits.

Motor Deficits

For many children, the process of writing numbers may be so difficult that it greatly affects their ability to succeed in mathematics. Children with perceptual-motor difficulties have trouble relating what they see to what they write. They cannot coordinate their eyes with the proper hand movements. As mathematical problems become longer and more involved, these children find it extremely difficult to complete written assignments because they expend so much time and energy retrieving the necessary finger movements for number formation that they forget what they are doing.

Memory Deficits

Although memory difficulties can be classified under perceptual deficits, we have chosen to separate them for purposes of remediation and planning. Many children seem to understand what is presented in class and may even accurately complete classroom assignments. But these same students may not carry through on homework. Or they may appear "lost" when the teacher continues a topic the next class day after only a short review. Initially, they may do quite well when a topic is presented. But, because there is only a limited review in the text, they quickly forget and appear never to have learned the material. These are the children who are often accused of not listening, of copying a friend's work, or of doing careless work.

In other cases, teachers may be baffled because, while students' classwork and homework are good, later they are unable to use the material as a basis for learning a new concept or skill. And when it comes time for a unit test on the material, they do poorly.

The difficulty in each of these examples may be due to specific short- or long-term memory problems that preclude retention of material over time. These children require training to acquire ways of remembering. They also need a considerable amount of overlearning before they are capable of retaining a concept or skill.

Short-term visual-memory deficits manifest themselves in several ways. For some, the process of copying numbers from the board or from a textbook is extremely difficult. The inability to retain visual images long enough to write them on paper causes slowness and errors. As a result, unlike their peers who can hold an entire problem in their minds (e.g., 48 + 63), these children must keep checking to see what they are to write. The time involved in this process greatly impedes the amount of work that can be done. Even when worksheets are provided, making it unnecessary for them to copy the problems, students may still be unable to retain enough information to perform accurate and quick computations.

Auditory short-term memory deficits often result in an inability to learn basic facts. For example, when presented with oral drills, children may not be able to retain the isolated numbers long enough to give an answer. In addition, visual-memory deficits may prevent retrieval of the correct answer, even if the problem is written down for the child.

Visual and auditory short-term memory problems can also hamper the ability to solve word problems. Although children may have no difficulty reading or comprehending the material, they may be unable to retain information long enough to solve a problem. This may be especially true of problems involving two or more steps.

For some children who may be able to learn visually from textbooks, the pace may be too fast. Often there is not enough review and skill incorporation for the necessary overlearning to occur. As a result, these students, although understanding the material when presented, may be unable to retain it or use it as a building block for future learning.

Many areas of mathematics require considerable sequencing ability. Obviously, students with sequential-memory deficits encounter special problems here. Most children, for example, learn to tell time by the age of seven or eight. But if they have trouble retaining a sequence, an otherwise simple task suddenly causes more trouble. Think for a moment of only the basic steps involved in telling time:

- Which hand do I look at first?

- What number does that hand refer to?

- What number should I say first?
- What number does the other hand refer to?
- How do I count by fives?

Assuming there is no spatial or temporal difficulty, the task of telling time requires that a considerable number of steps be sequenced properly. In order to use each step as a transition to the next, children with memory-sequencing problems must be taught each step to the point of overlearning.

Sequential memory also affects the ability to count money, to compute using the four basic operations, and to solve word problems. In addition, auditorially, it affects a student's overall ability to process and understand what is taught to the class as a whole. As a result, some children only retain isolated segments of what is said.

Figure 1-6 shows the work of a student whose primary disability is long-term and sequential memory. A close look will show that the child probably understands basic computation at the middle-grade level. But because the processes at this level are long and involved, they place great demands on the child's retention and sequencing abilities. This child is probably unaware that the problems are incomplete—only so much could be held in the memory at one time.

$$
5\frac{1}{2} = \frac{3}{6}
$$
$$
+3\frac{5}{6} = \frac{5}{6}
$$
$$
\frac{8}{6}
$$

$$
6\frac{4}{5} \times 2\frac{1}{2} = \frac{30}{5} \times \frac{5}{2} = 150
$$

Figure 1-6

Integrative Deficits

Learning disabled children often have trouble integrating what they learn. Some type of interference prevents them from pulling information together to draw conclusions, to make associations, or simply to use building blocks of information to learn material adequately. Following are some examples of common integrative problems.

Closure Difficulties. Children with closure problems may find it especially difficult to read multidigit numbers. They fail to group digits logically as they read the numbers. They may be able to count by rote or continue a sequence of four or five numbers and, yet, given a single number and asked what comes next, they may not be able to respond independently.

These same children have trouble with classification tasks. At a primary level, they have difficulty sorting shapes by one characteristic. Further, as they begin to use symbols, they may be unable to determine the similarity between a group of numbers (e.g., all even numbers). (Regardless of the specific disability, it is generally much harder for the learning disabled child to find similarities than to find differences.)

Word problems, too, involve closure. Most students, and many teachers, groan at the need to solve word problems. For learning disabled students there may be some legitimate reasons to groan. The ability to solve word problems greatly depends on developing an intuitive understanding of the different patterns which cause one to add, subtract, multiply, or divide. Learning disabled students find it much more difficult to build up this background of problem-solving patterns. Thus, they often need a "supply" box of examples as well as practice comparing words to symbols.

Counting on, a technique often taught early in the primary grades, can be very difficult for these students. Although they may have little trouble locating the starting point, eliciting the next number may be impossible. Counting on from within a sequence, especially when skip counting is involved, is extremely difficult and considerable drill and training is usually required to internalize the technique.

Mathematics educators today debate the merits of teaching missing addends to primary students. Retrieving the missing number involves many discrete tasks that must be tied together before the child is able to recall the answer. Specifically, the major tasks include:

- Number discrimination;
- Determining the correct operation for solving the problem;
- Mentally sorting out the correct response using visual imagery but no visual cues; and
- Eliciting the correct answer, either verbally or in writing.

For learning disabled children who have integrative deficits, carrying out these steps may be very difficult. Even if they can easily perform the first two steps, the final two require skills in which they are often weakest. There is simply too much to be retained and associated for the child to be able to sort out and express the answer.

Expressive Language Problems. Children with expressive language difficulties cannot verbalize clearly, if at all, what they obviously understand. These are the children who have trouble with rapid oral drills. As a result, they may not participate in class because they cannot express in words what they are thinking. They tend to do better on written homework or in situations where they receive visual cues and have enough time to respond. They cannot produce on demand. Therefore, timed tests, whether oral or written, only make this disability more apparent.

We commonly ask children to show that they understand a given concept by having them explain or apply it, either verbally or manually. Children with expressive language problems need visual cues to help them retrieve the words and sequence the steps once recalled. Often students can more easily distinguish between right and wrong processes than they can explain them. As a result, when a mistake occurs, they may recognize that something is not right, but be unable to correct it spontaneously unless given alternatives.

Reading and writing decimals can be difficult for children with expressive language difficulties. By comparison, fractions are easier. When one writes "2/100" or says "two one hundredths," it is clear that a "2" and a "100" are included among the digits for the fraction. Decimals lack this cueing. Hearing "two one hundredths" does not readily reveal the number of decimal digits in the number. Similarly, looking at ".02" does not automatically cue the response "two one hundredths."

Receptive Language Difficulties. "What do you mean?" "Please repeat that." "Can I have a clue?" These questions, and many others, are frequently asked by children with receptive language deficits because they have difficulty associating meaning with words. On occasion, all of us hear common words, perhaps in context, and temporarily "blank out" on the meaning. Usually the lapse is only temporary, a second or two. This is similar to what regularly happens to learning disabled children: they hear a word, recognize it as a unit, but fail to grasp the intended meaning.

In mathematics, this disability manifests itself in some or all of the following ways:

- Difficulty following directions;

- Difficulty understanding mathematical terms, especially those with multiple meanings, such as "sum," "times," "difference," and so on;

- Difficulty solving a computational problem set up differently than originally presented; and

- Difficulty solving word problems.

Children with receptive language deficits often appear very literal. They may not understand simple jokes and generally find it hard to make sense of much of what they hear or read. Although they can repeat the exact words and may go through rote processes that are similar, they often are unable to repeat the same process if presented with even the slightest variation.

Abstract Reasoning Problems.   One of the most difficult areas for children with learning problems, and for their mathematics teachers, involves abstract reasoning. As a general rule, new mathematical topics can and should be presented *concretely*. Many learning aids assist children in seeing, feeling, and dramatizing new concepts and skills. Presented in this hands-on manner and subsequently discussed, the concepts become a natural basis for the transfer of meaning to written symbols. Indeed, written symbols are typically associated with the models that illustrate the idea or process before being used alone.

Generally, when concrete aids are used, at least one of the following abilities is required:

- Verbalizing what has been learned or observed;

- Associating what is happening with symbolic representation; and

- Understanding, auditorially or receptively, what is being explained or shown.

Children who have trouble making associations because of poor abstract reasoning often find it impossible to perform any of the above tasks. These children need the immediate and repeated association of numbers, operation signs, and other mathematical symbols that we substitute for words to understand the concept.

For learning disabled children with this type of deficit, repetition and rote drill on a page help them feel comfortable with a given process or idea. They can then more easily begin to make associations that eventually will lend meaning to what they do. As a result of repeated drill and reassociation with concrete aids, the child develops:

- An understanding of the specific concept;

- The ability to reason and associate in general; and

- A stepping stone for later reasoning.

As noted earlier, children with learning disabilities require a considerable amount of overlearning to succeed. Most textbooks provide drills, especially in computation. However, for students with reasoning deficits, such pages may act as a hindrance. The repetition of a process relieves the need to make decisions. An entire page of addition with carrying does not help the child learn *when* it is necessary to carry, only *how* to carry. Instead, if the goal is, in fact, learning when to carry, it may be sufficient for the child to cross out all the problems that do not require carrying.

Behavioral Difficulties

Before we conclude this overview of learning disabilities, it is important to note those behavioral disabilities that can affect classroom performance and mathematics achievement. Following are the more common problems of this type.

Distractibility. Many learning disabled children are highly distracted either by external stimuli that most of us ignore or by internal stimuli of which we are often unaware. As a result, they find it difficult to stay on task—they seem to be in constant motion and never to be paying attention; the slightest sound or sight distracts them and they lose their place. Sometimes these children are unable to find their place again or do not even know they have lost it. They may appear purposely to be thinking about other things in order to avoid work. These are the children who are inordinately attentive to marks on a page or specks of dust. The mere sound of the chalk on the board may prevent them from listening to the teacher. In fact, they cannot sustain attention for a long period of time. When they appear to short-circuit, it is often necessary to let them change activities to allow them to regain their attention.

Perseveration. Perseveration (the continual repetition of an activity even though a change is required) also shows up in many ways. Children may perform the same operation throughout a page because they do not notice the signs have been changed. Or they may continue doing whatever was instructed in the first problem. Such behavior patterns are compulsive, not merely carelessness.

Figure 1-7 illustrates other ways in which perseveration can affect a child's computational work. In the first problem, 17 − 9, the child continued counting backwards, unable to stop at 8. Similarly, in the second problem the count was

$$
\begin{array}{r}
3\ 17 \\
\cancel{47} \\
-29 \\
\hline
17
\end{array}
\qquad
\begin{array}{r}
1 \\
46 \\
+35 \\
\hline
82
\end{array}
$$

Figure 1-7

extended further than necessary for 6 + 5. In other words, this child has no internalized means of stopping.

Once children have begun to attend, it may be extremely difficult for them to change activities unless they are reminded or physically drawn into doing so. In extreme cases, techniques such as handing children a clean sheet of paper on which to write or asking them to move from their seats to the board may help. Perseverations should be stopped whenever they are noted. Change is necessary to prevent perseverating from one academic subject to another.

Disinhibition and Impulsivity.   Children who exhibit disinhibition or impulsivity often have trouble making transitions from one topic to another during class. For example, turning the page of a book to a new topic may divert their attention from the introduction given by the teacher. These youngsters are usually quick to answer questions but often give irrelevant responses. Similarly, estimating answers is extremely difficult for them since they tend to guess wildly. Their thoughts are often triggered by some word they read or hear without them realizing that they made the association. As with perseveration, it is often necessary to change activities in order to refocus attention.

Reading Problems.   Although not ordinarily classified as behavior disorders, reading difficulties are included in this section because, when they interfere with mathematics performance, they can affect behavior. Most schools use state-adopted mathematics textbooks. Generally, these texts involve a lot of reading that often puts the learning disabled child at a severe disadvantage. In addition, most texts require a high degree of abstract reasoning and the ability to transfer and retain skills over time. They also require that the child demonstrate at least on-grade level reading. Many children with learning disabilities do not read at grade level. Yet, they are capable of performing on grade level or above in math if little reading is required. In the higher grades, mathematics becomes increasingly difficult for these learners due to its dependency on reading.

LEARNING THEORY AND LEARNING DISABILITIES

Most mathematics teachers, and primary-school teachers in particular, are aware of the implications of Piaget's developmental theory for mathematics learning. Children progress through certain developmental stages as they master mathematical concepts and skills. With learning disabled children who have difficulty making associations, however, it is often necessary to gear instruction (even at the middle- and upper-elementary levels) toward these stages as new and more abstract skills are learned. The purpose of the following paragraphs is to give the teacher an idea of how this type of instruction might be carried out with learning disabled children.

One-to-One and One-to-Many Correspondence

Most children begin developing the idea of one-to-one matching at the concrete level by the time they are 5 or 6 years old. Gradually, this skill develops to the point where the child can count and perform simple computational problems. This last step, though at a higher level cognitively, represents a one-to-many correspondence. As children begin to internalize their thinking, specific instruction usually ceases, and they are generally able to extend the simpler one-to-one matching skill to computational situations requiring one-to-many matchings.

In terms of one-to-many matchings, application to multiplication involving single or multidigit multipliers is apparent. Regardless of the presentation method, children ultimately must use one-to-many matching to be sure they have finished a given problem. Using the problem in Figure 1-8, it would not be unusual for the teacher to remind students to multiply all parts of the number 58 by 9. With learning disabled children, reviewing one-to-one and one-to-many matchings before teaching multiplication will make the process much simpler.

Figure 1-8

Classification

Classification involves the ability to group objects or ideas by a common characteristic. This skill can involve any of the following abilities:

- Spatial organization;
- Reasoning;
- Discrimination (visual or auditory); and
- Expressive language (verbal or manual).

As mathematics becomes more symbolic, concrete presentation of classification is generally de-emphasized. However, children learning about equivalent fractions and decimals need a high degree of internalized classification. Suppose, for example, these children are presented with different sizes and shapes—each having one of four equal parts shaded. On the basis of this common characteristic, the children must be able to classify each shaded part as the equivalent of one fourth.

Children with learning disabilities may find this task extremely difficult even though they are otherwise developmentally ready for it. For example, students with a reasoning deficit may not be able to determine the similarity without the help of specific tools, such as a flip chart (see Figure 1-9). Each page shows a different fractional relationship, and the child can match the concrete shapes to the pictorial representation and accompanying word. Children with figure-ground problems, in turn, may not see the four equal parts because they cannot properly focus their attention. These children would be aided by writing a number in each section, beginning with the shaded one. This would allow them to circle the number "1" in the shaded section thereby seeing more readily the 1-out-of-4 idea.

Figure 1-9

Flexibility

Children exhibit flexibility of thought when they show they can deal with:

- Multiple meanings;
- Different ways to express given sums or products; and
- Horizontal and vertical formats for basic facts.

In general, flexibility is the ability to classify by more than one characteristic. It also involves being capable of using those characteristics to solve more advanced problems.

How does flexibility apply to mathematics beyond the developmentally concrete stages? Figure 1-10 shows the work of an 11-year-old boy who failed to exhibit true flexibility of thought. When questioned whether he noticed the signs, he replied, "Sure, but you always change the bottom number when they're written this way." This child had been taught to multiply mixed numbers horizontally and to add them vertically. Although he readily recognized that the second problem involved multiplication, its vertical position confused him. In this case, it might be necessary to review briefly the horizontal and vertical multiplication of whole numbers before relating this idea to fractions. (Chapter 7 will offer further suggestions for how to handle problems of this nature.)

$$7\frac{3}{5} = 7\frac{6}{10}$$
$$+ 2\frac{1}{2} = 2\frac{5}{10}$$
$$\overline{9\frac{11}{10} = 10\frac{1}{10}}$$

$$4\frac{1}{2} = 4\frac{2}{4}$$
$$\times 2\frac{3}{4} = 2\frac{3}{4}$$
$$\overline{8\frac{6}{4} = 9\frac{2}{4} = 9\frac{1}{2}}$$

Figure 1-10

Seriation

Seriation involves discrimination as well as spatial or temporal organizational abilities—areas in which many children with learning difficulties in mathematics have disabilities. To be able to organize numbers in some specific order requires that one understand the concepts of "more" and "less," "before" and "after," as well as ordinal counting. Some children may understand these concepts and how to order numbers, and yet find it difficult to apply the seriation skill to more advanced mathematical topics, such as solving multistep word problems or ordering decimals and fractions. For example, when presented with the specific steps of a word problem (not necessarily in the right order) and some concrete aids, if needed, children may be able to explain what to do first, second, third, and so on. Yet, when asked to organize these steps spontaneously and without concrete aids or written (verbal) choices, these same children may be unable to do so. In other words, their learning deficits require that they be provided clues that other students might not need. Eventually, and with enough repetition, many learning disabled students learn to internalize these clues so they can begin to solve problems independently. Another way of helping with multistep word problems involves highlighting each step using a different color. The first step would be green and the last red, reminding students of traffic lights where you "go on green and stop on red." An accompanying worksheet would list the step numbers in matching colors.

Conservation

The ability to conserve implies the understanding that the basic value or amount of something does not change even though its shape or arrangement does. Some children are slow to learn how to conserve. Learning disabled children, in particular, tend to have difficulty applying the notion of conservation to advanced mathematical topics.

The early stages of conservation require that children recognize the invariance of quantity in spite of changes in shape. Similarly, the older child who is studying basic facts, using symbols only, needs to realize that 6×4 equals 4×6. By the time children learn to use a calculator for higher level computations, they need a solid understanding of the equivalence of fractions and decimals. Again, conservation emerges as the basis for understanding this equivalence.

The preceding examples illustrate the importance of carefully tuning in to a child's thinking at every level of mathematics. From the Piagetian perspective, the examples serve to emphasize the developmental readiness required to master particular concepts and skills. Thus, it may be necessary for the learning disabled child to review very basic ideas, often at the concrete level, before pursuing more sophisticated topics. Specific help, such as that just suggested, is critical in this process.

GENERAL TECHNIQUES FOR DEALING WITH LEARNING DISABILITIES IN THE MATHEMATICS CLASSROOM

J. is very attentive in class, seems to follow most presentations, and usually is able to answer the teacher's questions. However, his work is always sloppily done, answers to problems run into each other, and the teacher is generally unable to match his work with either the assignment or his solutions.

A. regularly gets 100% on weekly basic fact tests but can never seem to give the correct answers to facts when called upon to do so in class. She consistently makes fact errors when solving written word problems. And though she obviously knows *how*, she is often unable to complete a page of computation accurately.

Then there is P., who never seems to complete his work, especially classroom assignments. When given time during class to copy problems, he asks to get a drink, breaks a pencil, or otherwise wastes time. When he does manage to copy and finish an assignment, he makes many errors—his method of solving may be correct but his solutions are wrong.

These situations represent some of the problems a mathematics teacher might encounter and illustrate the demands placed on teachers to meet the needs of all students within the class. The children described, though seemingly covered by an umbrella of carelessness, may all be exhibiting learning disabilities with which they are inefficiently trying to cope. An overriding goal of the mathematics teacher is to plan and implement instruction so that all students in the class will benefit. What can be done to avoid spending an inordinate amount of time with one child to the exclusion of others, or vice versa? The techniques described in the remainder of this section are intended to help teachers in this regard.

Use Visuals and Manipulatives to Illustrate New and Important Ideas

Learning disabled children, like their peers in regular class mathematics, are basically concrete in their thinking. As a general rule, the use of simple or familiar objects to illustrate facts, ideas, and written symbols or processes promotes both understanding and retention.

Use Visual Cueing: Boxes, Circles, and Lines

Boxes. In an earlier section we showed how learning disabled children with figure-ground trouble may find it difficult to locate the assigned problems in standard textbooks; that is, they cannot visually separate the problems from each other. A useful, inexpensive tool for handling this difficulty is a geometric shape template. The template can be used to box the problems in the book so they can readily be found. Separating problems from each other prevents a child from seeing all of them as one.

Circles. Another common difficulty involves separating the problem number from the problem itself. In more and more textbooks, numbers are colored to differentiate them from the problems. Even then, however, they may be spatially so close to the problem that many children cannot see the difference. In addition, in some texts, they are still printed in the same black type as the problems to be solved. Circling the problem number before going on to solve the problem has proven a simple, yet very effective way to handle this difficulty.

More Circles and Boxes. Homework, especially from the text, can be a mammoth undertaking for a child with either fine-motor or figure-ground difficulties. Particularly at the intermediate and upper grade levels, it is not unusual for students to be assigned a page of 25 or 30 computational problems. Often these problems must be copied out of the book before they are solved. Many learning disabled children are so overwhelmed by the magnitude of the task that they do not do it at all. As a result, they are accused of being lazy or irresponsible.

Consider for a moment what is involved in a seemingly easy task of copying problems from a book. Children must be able to:

- Sort the problem number from the problem itself;

- Remember what they are copying and what the numbers look like so they do not have to trace them or continually look back at the page;

- Space the problems on the page so they can read the numbers and later solve without mixing one problem with another; and

- Align the numbers properly while copying to avoid errors in subsequent computation.

Due to this complexity, it may be necessary to shorten the task or split it into a two-night assignment. One night the student copies the problems, circles the problem numbers, boxes the problems, and sets up the worksheet. The second night the actual computation is done. Also, it may be necessary to help children use the shape template or a ruler to spatially organize their papers before beginning an assignment. Rather than lined paper, provide centimeter-square graph paper that can be boxed as shown in Figure 1-11.

Note: With the increased emphasis on the use of mental calculation, estimation, and calculators, it is hoped that teachers will begin assigning fewer computation problems, both in class and for homework. Such a decrease in paper-and-pencil calculation would especially benefit the learning disabled child besides allowing for more practical use of calculators, such as for checking answers.

Figure 1-11

Just Boxes, No Lines.   For some learning disabled children, the use of lined paper, even as an aid for number alignment, only adds further confusion. The added visual stimulus of the lines makes it hard for them to organize their work, especially if fine-motor deficits are involved. These students may have so much trouble staying on or within the lines and figuring out how to use them that their work becomes even more illegible than ever. In these cases, insist that the children use unlined paper. (Figures 1-12 through 1-15 show sample sheets teachers can keep in a file and draw upon as needed. Chapter 5 suggests more specific uses for pages of this type as an aid to computation.)

Planning ahead: Boxes, Circles, and Lines.   Before school starts each year, solicit the help of a parent, aide, or other volunteer to prepare textbook pages and different kinds of spatially formatted papers. The geometric-shaped template can be used to organize the pages spatially in the first chapters of the textbook. Problem numbers could also be circled. Important directions or examples may be underlined with bright colors or heavy lines. A file drawer containing special

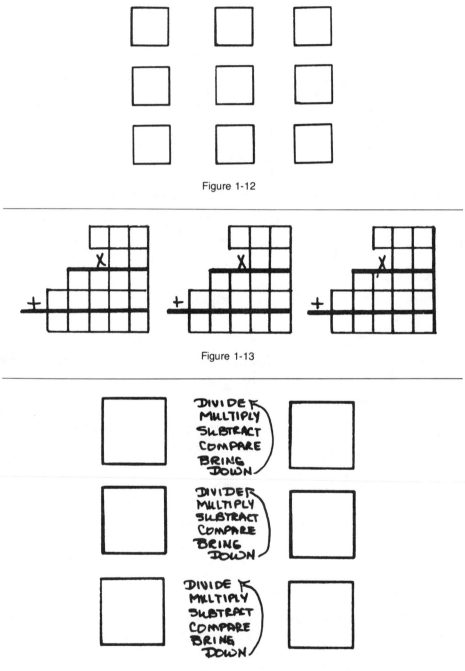

Figure 1-12

Figure 1-13

Figure 1-14

Figure 1-15

worksheet formats for children with spatial or perceptual difficulties could also be stocked at this time. (Figures 1-11 to 1-15 present samples of pages that may be useful. Chapters 2 through 10 provide other ideas along this line.)

Eventually, children should learn to perform some of these self-help skills themselves. Early in the school year, therefore, it may be a good idea to set aside 5 or 10 minutes each day for children with learning problems to learn how to box, circle, or underline as needed. Alternatively, this exercise may be equally important as a part of a specific assignment as the computation itself. Activities such as these are important, since they teach children ways of dealing with their handicaps. Compensatory techniques, such as boxing or otherwise delineating the material, allow the children to keep up and be more a part of the mathematics class. These techniques also have carryover to other subjects.

Assign Fewer Problems and Minimize or Eliminate Copying from the Textbook or Board

It is important to remember the goal of a mathematics lesson. Suppose the purpose is to review a computational skill. For students with severe spatial, motor, or perceptual deficits, teachers have a better means of evaluating performance if other difficulties are minimized. This may mean employing techniques like those described previously, or it might mean:

- Assigning only every fourth or fifth problem, rather than all the problems on a page; or

- Providing worksheets so children do not have to copy problems.

If students are highly distractible, it may be helpful to:

- Have them place an "x," a chip, or their fingers on the problem while computing so they do not lose the place;

- Create several standard formats for worksheets and provide construction paper masks that blot out all but one fourth or one third of the page at a time; or

- Cut a worksheet into fourths or thirds and assign only one small section at a time.

Use Visual Cueing: Color Code

Color coding, although it can appear confusing to those of us without memory or perceptual difficulties, can be an effective way to teach many learning disabled children. It provides them with any or all of the following:

- Ways of focusing attention;

- Ways of properly sequencing steps;

- Increased ability to recall information;

- Ways of identifying starting and stopping points;

- Cues to the appropriate response; and

- Increased ability to be independent.

As previously mentioned, it is generally advisable to code the first step green and the last step red. When using more than two colors, choose colors that are easily distinguished from each other. Do not make Step 2 orange and Step 3 red. For those few students who are color blind, use heavy lines instead of colors.

If students have auditory-memory or perceptual difficulties, try to keep verbal directions and explanations short and to the point. Reinforce them with visual cues. In the case of children with reading or language interference, present concrete examples or board illustrations that they can look at while explanations are given. The use of color to focus, delineate, or cue in illustrations and other visuals is also useful for students with visual perception or memory problems. Teachers can use colored chalk or marking pens during teaching sessions for this purpose. Later, using the same colors, they can make special follow-up worksheets for individual students. (Figures 1-16 and 1-17 present ideas for color-coded pages that can be kept on file and distributed as needed. Other ideas are included in subsequent chapters.)

Colors can also be used when boxing, circling, or underlining sections of a textbook. For example, directions ("Read these first.") might be underlined in green. This simple technique will prevent children from spending an inordinate amount of time searching for the directions or trying to separate them from the problems.

Alter, Adjust, or Reinforce the Standard Text Presentation when This Meets a Special Need

Most textbooks provide a standard sequence to be followed, but with some children it may not be appropriate. For example, more and more texts introduce decimals and decimal computation before fractional computation. For children with auditory discrimination, spatial organization, or abstract reasoning problems, a more careful review of basic fraction concepts and symbolism along with simultaneous presentation of fractions and decimals may be necessary. Even in written form, fractions are more "concrete" than decimals—they more graphically trigger the visual image of what is represented. The suggested review provides a basis for helping children learn decimal notation by associating it with fractions.

Basic facts can also be applied in other areas. If students have memory difficulties and are familiar only with certain basic facts, use these facts when presenting a new computational skill or topic. Controlling the class presentation with known facts will not cause learning disabled children to stand out from their peers; rather, it will allow them to learn along with their classmates. Additionally, this approach provides the overlearning which is so essential and eliminates the need for children, even those who are not learning disabled, to draw on weaknesses while trying to learn something new.

A final technique deals with homework assignments. Instead of assigning all problems on a given page, draw from several pages. Selectively list the problems and the order in which they should be completed. An assignment might look like this:

- Page 235: Problems 3, 7, 8, 5 (these problems may be three of one kind and a fourth that is slightly different)

- Page 182: Problems 2 and 14

- Page 203: Problems 1 through 4, and 7

- Page 182: Problems 7 and 1

Figure 1-17

Insist that the children solve the problems in the order presented as a means of avoiding perseveration, developing sequencing skills, and improving reasoning. This approach can be used with an entire class. (Note that it includes a review of previously learned material.)

Allow Children to Finger Trace or Use Other Tactile Cues

In some cases, seeing or hearing is not enough. More involvement is required. Standard procedures parallel those often used in reading: finger trace, say, then write. Sometimes children may be instructed to close their eyes while finger tracing a textured example. (Specific suggestions for using this general technique are described in the chapters that follow.) For reversals, it is recommended that students finger trace a textured numeral, then retrace the shape in midair or on paper before writing it.

Another technique can be used to reinforce retention of basic facts. Using the answer side of a flash card, children with visual-memory problems might finger trace both the problem and the answer. Upon turning the card over, they should try to give the answer immediately. If they forget, finger tracing the problem again often triggers the correct response.

Capitalize on Patterns and Other Associations to Promote Understanding or Retention

Many learning disabled children are helped by instruction that is based on using patterns or relevant associations. One technique is drawn from the area of basic facts. Often children can learn difficult facts by associating them with easier, known ones. The one-more-than idea is powerful in this regard. "$5 + 5 = 10$, so $5 + 6$ is one more (11);" or "$12 - 6 = 6$, so $13 - 6$ is one more (7)." (Three additional examples are illustrated in Figure 1-18. Other suggestions are detailed throughout the following chapters.)

Use Auditory Cueing

Children with visual, perceptual, or memory disabilities generally require a high degree of auditory reinforcement. At times, for example, it may be helpful for children to close their eyes to block out distracting visual stimuli and just *listen*. They might read a basic problem and its answer into a tape recorder, then listen to the playback for reinforcement. Examples of this basic approach are presented throughout the following chapters.

Make Samples for Students Who Need Them

Number Charts.   In many classrooms wall charts stretch all the way around the room, often showing manuscript or cursive letters. Be sure to include a number chart as well, even at the upper grade levels. It will help students who are capable of proceeding mathematically, but lack visual memory or other capabilities to put the skills into practice. The chart will serve as an unobtrusive aid and will minimize the chance of students with learning difficulties being teased by others in the class.

Charts for Special Topics.   Figure 1-19 presents a useful chart for children with receptive language deficits. Similarly, the technique pictured in Figure 1-20 has

CLOCK TIMES AND 5's:

2:30

$$\begin{array}{r} 6 \\ \times 5 \\ \hline 30 \end{array}$$

8
0

5's are easy
when you think
of the clock

Size cues for fractions:

$$\frac{1}{2} \quad \frac{1}{3} \quad \frac{1}{4} \quad \text{piece of cake}$$

Long division: Maximum of drill with minimum of frustration

$60\overline{)288} \qquad 61\overline{)288} \qquad 62\overline{)288}$

Figure 1-18

Add   =   Plus   =   ⊕

Subtract   =   Take Away   =   ⊖

Multiply   =   Times   =   ⊗

Divide   =   Divided By   =   ÷ or ⟌

Note: A different color is used for each line of
the chart. Equals signs and circles
are black.

Figure 1-19

proven helpful to many students with learning difficulties in mathematics. Charts like these are necessary references for many children with special problems while also being helpful to the rest of the class.

Other Techniques. To help children who confuse or forget the sequence of a computation, techniques like those illustrated in Figure 1-21 might be employed:

The short of it for Long division:

1) Divide
2) Multiply
3) Subtract
4) Compare
5) Bring Down

Figure 1-20

Figure 1-21

- Visual directional clues in a sample problem;
- Flip charts for a sample problem, with a separate page for each step; and
- A sample problem, completed step by step, at the top of a worksheet.

Carefully Sequence Instruction in Small Steps, with Adequate Provision for Practice and Review

Proper sequencing of instruction is critical for students with learning disabilities along with extra developmental and practice time for both understanding and retention of concepts and processes. In addition, breaking instruction into small, meaningful segments makes learning possible rather than overwhelming for these students. Specific suggestions for how to apply this technique are outlined for selected topics in each of the chapters that follow.

Sometimes teachers find it helpful to think of each of the following elements when planning a mathematics lesson:

- Daily review;
- "Look Ahead" activity (to teach/review concept or skill embedded in an upcoming lesson);

- Major thrust for the day; and

- Minimath (connected with or separate from the lesson itself, and focusing on concepts or skills that are best developed over time rather than in 2-week units, such as counting skills, calendar math, time, problem solving, estimation, mental math).

Sometimes, in conjunction with one or more of these aspects of a lesson, learning packets with special practice pages can be prepared in advance to satisfy the need for smaller increments and more review. A tape recorder also can be used to provide extra practice for those requiring auditory learning. In addition, a tape recorder is often helpful for students with visually based difficulties who are strong auditorially.

Many motivating games can be used to reinforce the learning of each small step. However, students must transfer learning from games to paper-and-pencil work. Many learning disabled students cannot make this transfer independently. For example, some children can play basic-fact dice games very easily. They can recognize the groupings and may be able to give answers without counting. However, they may not be able to perform the same computations on paper or mentally. They simply do not make the associations independently. For these children, it may be necessary to keep pages such as those illustrated in Figure 1-22 to aid the transition from games to class assignments.

It is often possible to make assignments or plan activities that build perception, auditory association, visual memory, or other processing skills. For example, students with perceptual difficulties might be assigned numbers or number sentences to copy, just as other children practice handwriting. If this task is perceptually too difficult, keep strips with number sentences on them for the children to copy during study or learning-center time. Alternatively, prerecord number sentences on tape for children to write or match with problems.

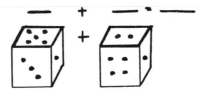

Figure 1-22

DISCUSSION

This chapter has focused on several important aspects of planning effective mathematics instruction for students with specific learning disabilities. It first presented an overview of the major disabilities from the perspective of their effect on mathematics performance. Knowing and understanding a handicap is a pre-requisite for effectively dealing with it during instruction. Ten general techniques for meeting the needs of learning disabled students in the mathematics classroom were then discussed. More detailed applications of these techniques to selected mathematical topics appear in the chapters that follow.

No attempt will be made to deal here with the content of the entire elementary school mathematics curriculum. It is assumed that teachers are familiar with standard sequences and approaches to presenting topics basic to that curriculum. Instead, the emphasis is on selected topics that commonly cause learning disabled students difficulty. For each topic, instructional sequences that incorporate special techniques and adaptations for meeting special needs will be outlined. Most of these suggestions can be carried out in regular classrooms as well as in resource, clinical, or self-contained settings. We hope the sample sequences and accompanying teaching ideas will encourage teachers to apply similar approaches to other mathematical topics.

CHAPTER

2

Number and Place Value: Developing "Number Sense"

Number and place value topics play an important role in primary-school mathematics instruction. In the beginning, children deal only with the numbers 1 to 10 or 12. They count groups of objects and record the number counted; they see and record clock times; they measure and record inch or centimeter measures; they use these numbers in early addition and subtraction work. Once mastered, these topics can be used to help students extend their understanding and ability to deal successfully with 2-, 3-, and higher digit whole numbers.

Each step should begin by modeling the numbers and building accurate and efficient counting techniques. Then, when children can both read and write the associated numerals, number comparisons and sequencing tasks are introduced. Since number words are used in writing checks, these normally are dealt with as soon as a child's reading skills are developed well enough to handle them. Throughout, the overriding goal of developing "number sense" is achieved by providing experiences that nurture a "good feel" for the size of number, for operations on numbers, and for relationships between numbers.

It is assumed that teachers and educators using this book are familiar with standard sequences and techniques for developing these topics, as well as with the renewed curricular emphasis on developing "number sense." From the perspective of the learning disabled child, however, standard approaches often fall short of meeting specific learning needs. This chapter focuses on eight areas within the early number and place value program that typically are troublesome to learning disabled students:

1. Counting in Early Number Work

2. Reversals: 1-Digit Numbers

3. Reversals: 2-Digit Numbers

4. Counting and Skip Counting: 2-Digit Numbers

5. Comparing Numbers

6. Rounding Numbers

7. Extended Counting Skills: Prerequisites for Mental Math

8. Reading and Writing Larger Numbers

For each of the eight sections, typical disabilities contributing to the problem are identified, and a carefully structured sequence of learning activities and exercises is suggested. Special techniques, such as finger tracing and visual or auditory cueing, are also illustrated.

In a ninth section, "Developing Number Sense," more general suggestions for developing number sense over time are presented. Most ideas can be carried out in regular education classrooms as well as in resource or clinical settings. A concluding section, "Using a Hand Calculator," outlines ideas to help learning disabled students with number and place-value topics.

COUNTING IN EARLY NUMBER WORK

Problem area: Inability to count on or back two or three numbers; inability to visually recognize the number of objects in a 10-frame; inability to recognize whether two or three numbers have been said in a vocal count.

Typical disabilities affecting progress: Difficulties with visual or auditory association, closure, figure-ground, expressive language.

Background: The early number program has its roots in counting. Children refine and rely heavily on this skill as they begin addition and subtraction. When the instructional goal shifts to memorizing basic facts, four extensions of counting contribute significantly to a child's success in quickly and accurately deriving answers to *unknown* facts:

- Counting on (2 + 7: "That's 7—8, 9." The child starts with the greater addend and counts on two. The answer or sum is 9.)

- Counting back (9 − 2: "That's 9—8, 7." The child starts with the total and counts back two numbers to 7.)

- Visual recognition of the 10-frame (6 and 4 fill the frame [see Figure 2-1]; 6 + 4 = 10. The 10-frame reference is useful for sums of 10 and related differences.)

Figure 2-1

- Auditorally recognizing when two or three numbers have been said. (11 − 9: "That's 9,—10, 11." The child counted up *two* numbers. The answer is 2.)

Each of these skills involves an extension of counting that can and should be developed in the early number program *prior to* any work with number facts. Otherwise, we ask children to learn two things at once: (a) the number facts; and (b) the counting skills for answering many of the easy number facts quickly. Rather, the goal is to assure that the extended counting skills are intact before we ask children to apply them in early addition-subtraction. After children learn to count linearly in sequence from one, we turn to developing these four useful extensions of counting.

Auditory Patterning

Counting, especially in the early stages, often involves the ability to recognize an auditory pattern. If students can recognize the pattern they still may finger count in order to process it. Is it necessary for children to finger count as they count on to add or count back to subtract 1, 2, or 3? Experience has shown that the following activities, started early, help students internalize these short counts, eliminate the need to finger count, and assist the counting on or counting backwards skills. The activities sensitize children to the differences between the auditory patterns which accompany the beats of two claps and three claps; the processing of two vs. three numbers.

Note: For children with auditory deficits, tap on the child's shoulder or back instead of clapping (Activity 1) or while saying the numbers (Activity 2).

Suggested Sequence of Activities and Exercises

1. **How many claps do you hear?** Clap 1, 2, or 3 times and ask students to tell how many claps they heard. *When children become comfortable with this activity, proceed to the following activity.*

2. **How many numbers do you hear?** Say two or three numbers in sequence (forwards or backwards), and ask students to tell how many numbers they heard.
   Examples: "6, 7, 8." ("Three numbers.")
   "11, 10." ("Two numbers.")
   Repeat this activity frequently. The pay-off comes later in the addition-subtraction program. Given 5 + 3, for example, students tend to begin to recognize (without finger counting) when they have counted on **3** more: "5,—6, 7, 8." Or, for problems like 11 − 2, they tend to recognize (without finger counting) when they have counted back **2**: "11,—10, 9." The following activities involve body movement and further reinforce the auditory patterning for two or three.

3. **Say and stand.** Sit, hands on knees. Say a number (e.g., 9). *Count on two* before you stand. Say the number. Children repeat. Continue, using other numbers. When children are comfortable with the "two more" pattern, carry out the same activity but with the challenge to *count back* two before standing: "8,—7, 6."

4. **Toe touch.** Have children stand, both hands above their head. Say a number (e.g., 8). *Count on three* before you touch your toes. Children repeat. Continue, using other numbers. When children are comfortable with the "three more" pattern, carry out a similar activity in which the challenge is to *count back* three before touching toes.

Counting On

Counting on involves two skills which potentially are especially difficult for learning disabled students: (a) visualizing groups of objects as a whole; and (b) eliciting a number from midpoint. To assist students, ensure that first activities include countable objects and flash cards to reinforce sight groups less than five. Practice eliciting the number after using visual cues as needed. Later, the transition to numbers greater than five is made. Generally, the teacher's immediate goal should be to provide many opportunities in which the first vocal number in a count is *not* "1." These ideas are central to the following sample instructional sequence for children with learning deficits.

Suggested Sequence of Activities and Exercises

Recognizing Sight Groups

1. **Is this two?** (For individuals or small groups; adapt to large-group instruction by using an overhead projector.) Place two small objects under each of five boxes on a table. Give each child a numeral "2" card showing two spots. One by one, lift each box so that children can have a quick peek before it is put back. Ask: "Is this two?" Start as a group activity, then call on individuals to respond. Check by allowing the children, in turn, to place each object over a spot on their "2" card. Repeat, but vary the arrangement of objects under the boxes. Sometimes place only one object under a box. In some cases, it may be necessary, at first, to use one color for all "2" clusters. Gradually, however, this cue is eliminated.

   - *Example:* Let green be the cueing color. At first use only green objects for the "two" clusters: two green sticks under one box; two green beads under another; and so on. As a next step, use objects of different colors for the "two" clusters, but place them inside a green loop, such as that drawn with crayon on paper. Gradually fade the loop out of the picture.

   - *Follow-up Activity:* Have children paste cloth scraps or construction paper pieces, by twos, on cards. "See how many different ways you can make two." Later use the cards, along with others, showing only one item, in an "Is This Two?" flash card activity.

     Note: With some children, especially those having expressive language deficits, it helps to associate the numeral 2 with the "two" clusters during early phases of the activity. The additional visual cueing provides a handle which helps students elicit the appropriate response and promotes over-learning as well.

   - *Example:* After students have pasted the cloth scraps on cards, by twos, have them match each card with a green numeral 2. As the cards showing one item are added as distractors, the green "2" cards may still be used (see Figure 2-2). The color cue, then the numeral itself, would gradually be eliminated.

2. **Is this three?** Adapt the previous activity to sight group recognition for three. Place the three objects before introducing other distractors (one or two items). Use a different color (e.g., black) if cueing is necessary.

3. **Say what you see.** Use flash cards made by the children in the previous follow-up activity (cards showing two or three objects). Include others show-

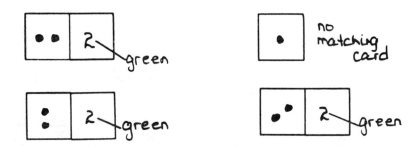

Figure 2-2

ing only one item. Flash the cards, asking students to tell how many they see. Use a thin underscore (e.g., green for two, black for three) *only* if necessary, and plan systematically to fade the prompt.

> *Note:* If possible, cover the cards with contact paper or acetate. Then, if underscoring is necessary for only some students, the cards can more easily be wiped clean and reused with others.

4. **Crayon up! Crayon down!** Pass out worksheets like that shown in Figure 2-3, containing one, two, or three items in each box. Sheets should be kept face down on students' desks until a turn-over signal is given. Tell the children: "When I say 'crayon up,' I want you to turn the sheet over and circle all groups of three with a black crayon. I will give you a very short time, then I will say 'crayon down.' It's all right not to finish. Just find all the threes you can." Later, the children can count from one within each box to check.

   • *Variation:* Flash a "2" or "3" numeral card, and have the children circle the appropriate number of objects. Initially, use colored numeral cards (e.g., a green "2"; a black "3"). Gradually eliminate the color cue.

5. **Adapt Activities 2, 3, and 4 to sight group recognition for four.**

Suggested Sequence of Activities and Exercises

Counting on

1. **Small handful.** (Materials: 12 small counters in a box with lid.) Have a child take a small handful of counters (e.g., 5) from the box, count how many are taken, and place them into the lid of the box. Hold the box lid high, so no

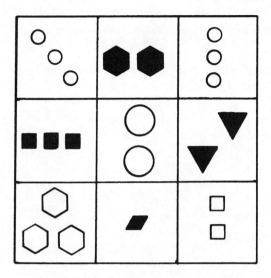

Figure 2-3

one can peek. "Let's put more counters into the lid. Count with me." "How many in the lid?" (5) "Now . . . (as, one by one, three additional counters are dropped into the lid) . . . there's 6, 7, 8." *If it seems to help, allow children to recount from 1 to check.* Then return all counters to the box and repeat for other "wee handfuls." Each time, have children *count on aloud* from the number of counters in the lid as, one by one, 1, 2 or 3 additional counters are dropped into the lid.

2. **Say, unfold, and count on!** (Materials: folded number/dot cards as shown in Figure 2-4. Use numbers 4–9 and one, two, or three dots on the cards.) Children say the number, unfold, and count on.

Figure 2-4

- As children become comfortable with the auditory patterning activities, the dot card can be replaced with a numeral card for 1, 2, and 3.

3. **Turn over.** Line up large numeral cards along the chalk tray (Figure 2-5). Let children see you turn one card over (e.g., the "7" card in Figure 2-5). Point to the card in front of the "7" and say, "Read this card, Amy." (6) "What comes after 6?" (7) Turn the card over to check.

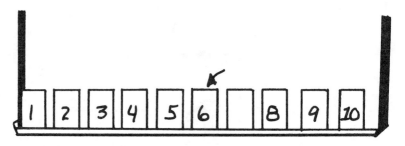

Figure 2-5

Note: It might help some children to say a number, finger trace and say the next few numbers after, then close their eyes while they repeat the sequence. If it seems helpful, allow children to recount from 1, emphasizing the last few numbers of the sequence.

- *Follow-up Activity 1:* As in Activity 3, but use a large-scale ruler or number line, decide on a number and cover all numbers to the right of it with an arrow card (Figure 2-6). "What's the arrow pointing to?" (6) Have children count on from the last number shown until you give a signal to stop.

Figure 2-6

- *Follow-up Activity 2:* As before, but encourage the children to study the ruler or card sequence so they remember "in their heads" where the numbers are. Then have them close their eyes while you turn over a numeral card.

4. **Walk on!** Use a large walk-on number line. Have children close their eyes and walk on the number line until told to stop, silently counting their steps. Use shelf paper to cover up extra numbers. When the children stop and open their eyes, call on someone to tell you quickly the number after the next one showing. As a follow-through, have the child stand on one number (e.g., 6) and show that just one more step takes you to the number after (7).

5. **Two more.** This activity prepares children to count on in addition problems with 2 as an addend (e.g., 6 + 2, 2 + 5, 7 + 2). Emphasis is on the auditory

patterning involved. Use the ruler and arrow card from Follow-Up Activity 1 for *Turn Over*. Point the arrow to a numeral (4 to 9) and have the children tell you the number 2 more. Orally emphasize the auditory pattern that makes this activity easy.

Example:

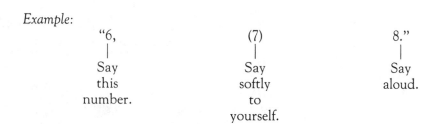

Repeat with other numbers, and later extend to addition problems having 3 as an addend. Some children with auditory deficits or perseveration tendencies may have difficulty saying the middle number(s) softly. These children might be taught to tap the table while speaking softly.

6. **Come again:** Prepare two card decks:

• Deck 1: 24 cards, four of each numeral, 4 through 9.

• Deck 2: 24 cards, twelve "2" cards, twelve "3" cards. In turn, the children draw a card from each deck. A "2" draw from Deck 2 means "quickly tell the number 2 more than" that drawn from Deck 1. A "3" draw means "quickly tell the number 3 more than" that drawn from Deck 1. Students keep both cards if they answer quickly and correctly. (It should be obvious when children are counting on rather than counting from 1.)

Counting Back

Many special children find it difficult to count backwards, even for short counts. Because about one fourth of the subtraction basic facts can be quickly answered by counting backwards, this skill deserves greater and *earlier* emphasis in work with numbers through 10 or 12. Too many school programs fail to develop this skill specifically, leaving children to learn the skill while trying to apply it when answering unknown subtraction facts like 9 − 2, 8 − 3, 11 − 2, and others. Children with learning deficits are among the first to be frustrated and fail in these situations. To acquire the skill level necessary to be able to count back two or three numbers in subtraction, ideas like the following have proven helpful.

1. **Up and back.** Have children use two body motions: clap hands while counting up to a number; clap knees while counting back from that number. Later, count up (teacher only) and let children count back.

   Example:
   > Teacher says: "1, 2, 3, 4" (while all clap hands).
   > Children respond (while all clap knees): "4, 3, 2, 1."

   In a final phase, count forwards silently and say just the last number (e.g., "4"). Children count backwards, starting with this number ("4, 3, 2, 1"). *Be sure children can count back from four before extending the backward count pattern to five. Then master that count pattern before extending further, and so on.*

2. **Break away!** (Materials: 16 interlocking cubes.) Taking turns, children make an interlocking cube train (e.g., a "9" train) and count backwards as, one by one, they break a cube away from the train (Figure 2-7). For students with expressive language difficulties, it may help to have numbers on each cube, initially. Once they feel confident with the auditory pattern and have developed a visual image to assist them, the numbers can be removed.

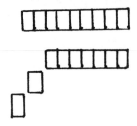

Figure 2-7

Visual Patterning Based on the 10-Frame

Good visual imagery for the 10-frame is an important skill. One example of 10 things, or six or seven is that number of objects "in the frame" (see Figure 2-8). The following two basic activities help build visual imagery for the 10-frame.

Figure 2-8

Suggested Sequence of Activities and Exercises

Prerequisite skills:
    a. Sight recognition for groups less than 5
    b. Sight recognition for group needed to make 5
    c. Understanding of "top" and "bottom"

1. **10-frame flash.** (Materials: A set of 10-frame cards similar to those shown in Figure 2-9.) Flash each card briefly, then remove it from sight. "How many stars did you see?" Repeat, emphasizing 6–9 stars in the frame. It often is helpful to make comments like: "Nine stars—that must be *all but one* filled. Let's check." "Seven stars—that must be the top row and two more: 5,—6, 7. Let's check."

Figure 2-9

2. **Frame fill.** (Materials: 10-frame cards, as in Activity 1.) Flash as before, then ask children to close their eyes. "Can you see the stars in the frame? How many would it take to fill the frame? . . . Let's check."

> *Note:* Good mental imagery for the 10-frame paves the way for success later with 10 sums and for subtracting any number from 10. It also is basic to using 10 as a bridge for adding facts like 6 + 8 and 7 + 5; for subtracting 13 − 8, 12 − 4 and other "harder" facts.

Once children have been introduced to each of these types of activities, it is possible to provide a sample of each activity type (counting on, counting back, how many numbers heard [two or three] and 10-frame work) during a 5-minute "Quick Math" period some time during the day. Until children have mastered the number facts which rely on these skills, they should be treated in daily or at least biweekly mini-math sessions.

REVERSALS: 1-DIGIT NUMBERS

Problem area: Number reversals (Ɛ for 3, 6 for 9), disorientations (⅃), and other disfigurations.

Typical disabilities affecting progress: Difficulties with visual discrimination, spatial organization, and visual-motor integration.

Background: Before children begin writing numerals, at least two prerequisites should be met:

1. Children should be able to count out the correct number of objects for each numeral written.

2. If children demonstrate motor coordination difficulties, provide preliminary work at the gross-motor level. In extreme cases, this may include movement exercises such as hopping, crawling, jumping, and ball catching. Activities such as the following also may be used. Note the continued reference to the number of objects named.

   - *Trace.* Draw large numerals on the chalkboard so children can use a finger or wet sponge to trace over them. Guide each child's hand and give verbal cues to prompt correct formation, if necessary. For example, "Down, around, the 6 curls up; the 6 sleeps sound."

     After making several 6s, have the child draw six balls to show "how many" the numeral stands for.

     If a child is confusing two numerals, such as 6 and 9, give verbal cues for only ONE of the digits. If the "curl around, sleep sound" cue is given for 6, then 9 is just referred to as the "other one." When cues are given for both numerals, children start confusing cues.

   - *Finger play.* Have children form numerals in damp sand. If necessary, make patterns for them to trace over and use verbal cues, as before.

It sometimes helps to have children close their eyes as you guide their formation of a numeral. "Feel the 6 go down, around. Now you make it." (First with eyes open, then with eyes closed.) Have the children make six anthills (or other sand objects) to illustrate 6.

If a child has severe spatial organization problems, it is helpful to confine all writing activities to a horizontal plane, even at this early stage. The down stroke on the 4 made by a child sitting at a desk, for example, has a different orientation to the body than that made while standing. It may be necessary in cases such as this to teach an alternate pattern for writing a 4 and a 5—one which involves only one stroke (see Figure 2-10). These patterns have also helped children with severe reversal tendencies. If children still have difficulty with reversals, the following basic sequence may help.

"One-stroke" patterns for 4 and 5

4 green

5 green

Figure 2-10

Suggested Sequence of Activities and Exercises

1. **Stencil in.** Provide stencils children can use to write given numerals. Place a green dot on the stencil to indicate the starting place. In Figure 2-11 the loop is outlined in red. This helps distinguish the 6 from a 9. When necessary, have children finger trace before starting, and use verbal cues.

Figure 2-11

2. "Get the feel."

- *Variation 1:* For children who confuse two numerals (e.g., 6 and 9). Have children use stencils to form both numerals. Use green dots for both numerals to show the starting place. Orally name both numerals, but for one use additional color and verbal cueing, as before, to emphasize its shape. For this number, have the child use objects to show "how many" are represented. Then tell the child, "Close your eyes. I'll move your hand. Am I making a 6?" (If no, ask "Am I making a 9?") If the child is not ticklish, write one of the numerals on the child's back. "Tell me what I'm writing . . . Yes, 6. Go to the chalk tray and pick out a picture card showing six things."

- It often helps to have textured numerals in front of the children while you finger trace on their backs. Felt numbers are better than sandpaper because they are less abrasive. While you trace, have the children look at the numerals to help fix the association. When finished, have them trace over the numeral they think you made. If correct, and if they are able to write numerals, they can be requested *immediately* to do so on the chalkboard, on paper, or in sand.

- *Variation 2:* For children who make mirror images of given numerals (see Figure 2-12). Move the hand or write on the back so the child can "feel" the numeral being written. Then have the child form the numeral in the air (on the desk). This can be done as you write the numeral on the child's back.

MIRROR   IMAGE EXAMPLES

Commonly recognized

E for 3

_____

Ɛ for 5

More subtle--not so
readily noted by teachers

ƨ for 6

4
+ ƨ °°°
10 °° (The ƨ is
           read as
           a 6.)

Figure 2-12

3. Count and trace.

- *Variation 1:* For children who confuse two numerals, such as 6 and 9. Have them count and complete the numeral to show how many, as in Figure 2-13. If necessary, use a green dot to show the starting place, and have children trace the numeral before writing it. "Does it feel like the 6? Does it circle round 'to sleep sound'?" Use red outlining on the loop, as in the following variation, if this helps.

- *Variation 2:* For children who make mirror images of given numerals. Children count and write a row of the numeral showing "how many." Use color coding to start the numeral. In Figure 2-14, the top curve is green. First solid lines are used, then dotted. Children may need to finger trace a few numerals before using pencil. Prompt with verbal cues when necessary. We prefer not to include incorrect mirror images. In our experience, emphasizing correct models has more quickly remedied the problem.

- *Follow-up Worksheet* (Figure 2-15): Children tend to revert to former reversal patterns. Though correctable, it does take time to resolve this problem. Worksheets like this, requiring only occasional independent writing of a numeral, provide self-correction when children forget the proper writing movement. As children trace over given samples, teachers might ask: "Do you feel you do it the same way when you write it?"

- *Optional Follow-Up:* For children who have been introduced to addition (or other operations and related basic facts), it may be necessary to help

Figure 2-13

Figure 2-14

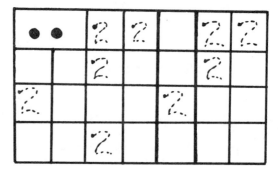

Figure 2-15

transfer the numeral recognition skill to problem situations. Figure 2-16 suggests a way of doing this. Children are asked to state the correct answer, complete the correct numeral, and cross out the wrong one. *Children can also be helped to transfer number recognition to printed numerals.* Have them find and circle given numerals appearing in newspaper ads, for example.

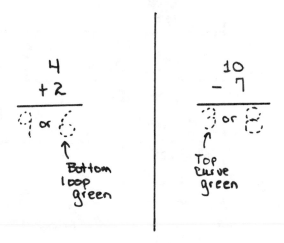

Figure 2-16

4. **You do.** As children need less structured cues to write "problem" numbers on paper, use a green dot to show where to start (Figure 2-17a). Children count the objects, trace the solid numeral, and use it as a pattern for writing other numerals in that row. If necessary, a yellow highlighter can be used when dotted lines no longer appear to guide correct formation. Eventually, numeral patterns are given only at the top of the worksheet (Figure 2-17b). In these examples, color outlining of the 6 loop is used if needed, but it would be eliminated gradually.

• *Optional Follow-Up:* Simple number combinations involving the numerals being worked on are again given. This time, however, the dotted numerals used in Figure 2-16 are not shown. Instead, Figure 2-18 illustrates a way of making the activity self-checking. Write problems on the bottom part of a sheet of construction paper, as shown. Cover this part with contact paper to allow use of a washable marker when answering. Children can fold the top part down over the problems and compare their answers with those given.

Figure 2-17

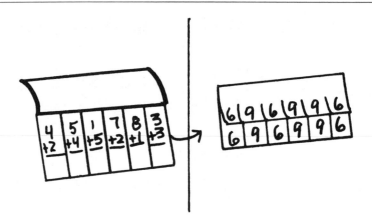

Figure 2-18

5. **Hand numbers.** Children can be taught to use their right hand to check the shape of many numerals. The curve of the 2, 3, and 5 all coincide with the shape formed by cupping the right hand. The numerals 7 and 9 can be "made" with the right hand and forearm, as in Figure 2-19. Left-handed children are at an advantage in this hand check—they do not even have to put their pencils down!

Figure 2-19

Activities and exercises similar to those in the preceding sequence can be used to help children who demonstrate other writing problems, including disorientation and disfiguration of numerals. Have model numbers available to which children can refer.

REVERSALS: 2-DIGIT NUMBERS

Problem area: Writing 23 for 32; 41 for 14, and so on.

Typical disabilities affecting progress: Difficulties with visual memory, visual discrimination, visual or auditory sequential memory.

Background: Four basic steps to instruction normally ensure successful understanding and use of two-digit numbers:

1. Children group objects such as popsicle sticks or chips by tens and then *tell* the number of tens and the number of extra ones.

2. Children count orally by tens and use objects to show the count: "2 tens, twenty; 6 tens, sixty," and so on. When multiples of 10 are established, extra ones are included: "2 tens and 3: twenty-three." Because of naming irregularities, teens are dealt with last. This way a child's first experience with 2-digit numbers is less likely to invite reversals.

3. Children group objects by tens and record the grouping. The tens-ones labels, used in early stages, are gradually eliminated (Figure 2-20). (Chapter 1 discussed how reading difficulties can interfere with successful mathematics performance. Figure 2-20b illustrates a format for children who are afraid of reading or who have deficits in this area.)

4. Children use objects (tens and ones) in early stages to help compare and sequence numbers.

When these four steps are followed, most children understand the tens-ones placement of digits within numbers. Sometimes the teens cause reversals, even among children who otherwise exhibit no particular reversal tendency. In such instances, the reminder that, "Teens are different. Remember that they are back-to-front numbers: What you hear first you write last," often helps correct the problem. Sometimes recounting from one, following the page numbers of a book and comparing with what has been written helps highlight and correct the difficulty. Children showing consistent reversal tendencies require more specialized programming, such as that outlined in the following section.

Figure 2-20

For children making mirror image digits (e.g., ℰ9 for 39), refer to the suggestions in Counting and Skip Counting on page 66.

Suggested Sequence of Activities and Exercises

1. **Tens and ones.** Use colored chips or graph paper pieces (see Figure 2-21a). Give the child 2 tens and 4 ones. "How many stacks of 10?" (2) Have child place a green textured numeral beneath the 2 ten-stacks. "How many ones?" (4) Position these to the right of the ten-stacks, and have the child place a

red numeral beneath the 4 ones (Figure 2-21b). "Two tens and 4, that's twenty-four. Finger trace the 24 so you get the feel of it. Start with tens." The child should say the number aloud as it is traced.

- *Follow-Up Discussion:* "Think of a traffic light. Suppose you want to walk across the street. When can you start walking?" (When the light is green.) "Yes, green means start. Red means stop. Look at the numerals we used. When you read or write numbers like this (point), you *start* with tens, the green one, and *stop* with ones."

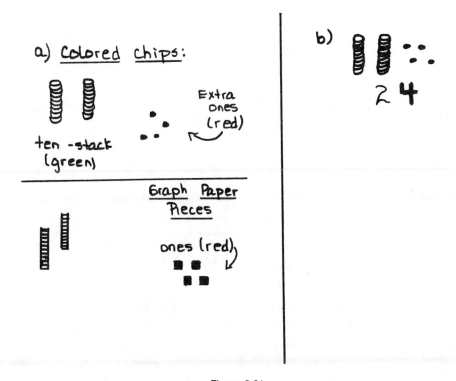

Figure 2-21

If the child has any difficulty relating 2 tens to twenty, 4 tens to forty, and so on, take time to reinforce this relationship. Use ten-stacks to dramatize the counting by tens. Capitalize on any phonetic similarities (e.g., *six* tens, *sixty*; *five* tens, *fifty*). Repeat the activity with other numbers. Omit teens until later, when naming irregularities can again be pointed out.

2. **Start with tens.** Give the child 2 tens and 4 ones as in the preceding activity. "Let's write how many chips you have. Where do we start?" (Tens—2 tens.)

"Write the '2' in green." "How many ones?" (4) "Write it in red (Figure 2-22a). What number did we write?" (Twenty-four.) "Finger trace the number as you say . . . Now close your eyes and picture it while I say it . . . Open your eyes. Is this what you saw?" (refer again to Figure 2-22a). Prompt the child, as necessary, throughout this dialogue.

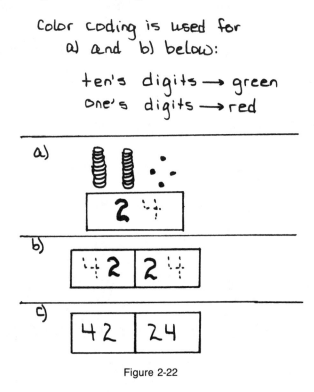

Color coding is used for
a) and b) below:

ten's digits → green
one's digits → red

a)

b)

c)

Figure 2-22

- Show the child Figure 2-22b. "Which of these say 24?" (Last one.) "How do you know?" (It starts with 2 tens.) Have the child finger trace, as before.

- Show the child Figure 2-22c. "This time there's no color. Can you remember which says twenty-four?" (First one.) "How do you know?" (It starts with 2 tens.)

Repeat with other 2-digit numbers. A worksheet similar to that of Figure 2-23 can be used in conjunction with the activity. Boxes can be filled in during discussion with the child. Note that:

- It may be sufficient merely to underline the tens digit in green and the ones digit in red.

- The separation of tens-ones columns into individual boxes has been avoided. When this is done, some students, with closure problems, do not see "24." Instead, they see a 2 and a 4. In our experience, these same students accept and profit more from the color distinctions.

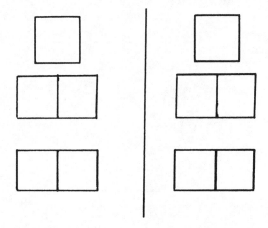

Figure 2-23

- *Follow-Up Worksheets:* Worksheets similar to that in Figure 2-24 are common in commercial workbooks. Sometimes it may be necessary, particularly for children with sequential-memory deficits, to color code these pages. In Figure 2-24a, for example, one could underscore the tens groups in green and the ones groups in red.

Figure 2-24

Similarly, in Figure 2-24b, the response line could be highlighted in green (tens place) and red (ones place). The first problem on a page could be marked as in Figure 2-25, serving as an example for how to complete the remainder of the page. No color coding would be used, except in the example. Rather than altering individual worksheets, some teachers may prefer to make cards, similar to those of Figure 2-26, to which children can refer while completing these types of pages. The cards would show materials commonly used by children and displayed on their worksheets.

Figure 2-25

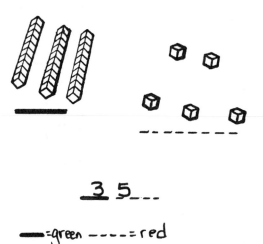

Figure 2-26

3. **Write and show.** Prerecorded cassette tapes are excellent for practice activities. Script suggestions include, "I'll say a number. You write it. Remember

to start with tens. Here's the first number: twenty-four." (Tape off while the child writes.) "Now use tens and ones to show twenty-four." (Tape off while child selects the ten-stacks and ones needed.) "You should now have two tens and four ones, twenty-four. Check it out. Turn to page A of the answer book" (see Figure 2-27).

Figure 2-27

Providing paper with predrawn boxes for children's responses helps avoid random placement of numbers. Also, *if a child is highly distractible*, setting up a definite workspace is beneficial. Use a plain sheet of paper, a plastic mat, or a piece of smooth plastic tablecloth for this purpose. Use the workspace to focus the child's attention. For example, "Use tens and ones to show me twenty-four in your workspace. . . . Good! Now clear your workspace."

- *Variation:* Provide a worksheet that is correlated to the cassette tape. Have the child circle the correct number: 24 or 42. For the first part of the tape, the tens digit could be color coded.

4. **Dot-to-dot.** Provide a prerecorded tape that dictates 2-digit numbers, with a pause between each. (If necessary, the tape can be turned off between each number.) Correlate a dot-to-dot pattern with the tape, so that a picture is formed if the child connects dots between each number dictated. The tape could begin with the reminder to "start with tens." If necessary, the tens place of each 2-digit numeral on the dot-to-dot sheet can be written or underlined in green.

5. **Secret message** (optional). Ask the child to number a paper 1 through 9. Now dictate a 2-digit number to be written beside each, as in Figure 2-28. Tell the child the 2-digit numbers are page numbers in a book. Instruct the child to use the book to find the penciled letter written beside each page number. "Look up number 1 (page 32). Do you see an 'A?' Write 'A' in the

number 1 box on your worksheet" (Figure 2-29). "Do the same for the others. See if you can answer the riddle. Remember to start with tens when looking for pages."

1. 32   4. 28   7. 81

2. 64   5. 73   8. 35

3. 45   6. 54   9. 93

Figure 2-28

What room has no walls
                    or doors?

A
1   2 3 4 5 6 7 8 9

Figure 2-29

This has proven a very motivating activity for students with auditory-memory problems, and one that can be constructed quickly. (Use a riddle book from a public library to help.)

- Children with spatial or severe visual-perception difficulties may have trouble completing worksheets of this nature. The numbers 1 to 9 may "run together" with others written from dictation. It may be necessary to provide prenumbered sheets for the numbers 1 to 9 (numbers written in a distinctly different color than that to be used by the child during dictation). If lined paper is used, skip a line between numbers. Or provide centimeter strips (see Figure 2-30) and have the children write a dictated number in alternate squares. For severe cases, it may be necessary to omit worksheets of this type.

6. **Terrible teens!** The naming irregularities of the teens should be pointed out to students:

> 2 tens and 4: "twenty-four" (24);
>
> 4 tens and 6: "forty-six" (46); and

But→   1 ten and 7: "seventeen" (17).

Figure 2-30

We still start with tens to write teens, but the verbal naming pattern does not hold. We must listen carefully to determine whether the ending is "teen" or "ty." (11 and 12 are in categories all their own!) Worksheets like those of Figure 2-31 can help children focus on the ending.

> **Note:** The "teen" and "ty" endings are written in red. The "6teen, 6ty" technique is effective even with nonreaders because the difference in configuration makes it easy to "read" the two forms.

Which is it?

6 <u>teen</u>.⋅⋅ 16 6 t<u>y</u> .	9 <u>teen</u>. 90 9 t<u>y</u> .
thir<u>teen</u>. 30 thir<u>ty</u> .	fif<u>teen</u>. 15 fif<u>ty</u> .
7 <u>teen</u>. 17 7 t<u>y</u>.	8 <u>teen</u>. 18 8 t<u>y</u> .

Figure 2-31

COUNTING AND SKIP COUNTING: 2-DIGIT NUMBERS

Problem area: Not understanding the patterning for counting, even though basic numeration concepts are well established.

Typical disabilities affecting progress: Difficulties with abstract reasoning, closure, visual or auditory association, and expressive language.

Background: It is often assumed that a child with adequate numeration understanding for 2-digit numbers can use these numbers to count. However, this is not always the case. Some children, such as those with the type of disabilities listed here, may be able to use objects (tens and ones) to illustrate given written numerals. Upon hearing a 2-digit number, they may also be able to write it and use objects to picture it. Yet, these same children may be unable to extend correctly a counting sequence of 2-digit numbers. And quite often they fail at even simple skip counting, such as counting by 5s or 10s.

These children characteristically lag behind peers, who rote count with 2-digit numbers even before they formally study them. In all likelihood, children with learning problems do not yet possess skip counting skills that are useful for early multiplication and daily situations involving time or money. Suppose brownies should bake 25 minutes. These children may have difficulty counting on from the present time (by 5s) to determine when the brownies should be taken from the oven. Likewise, they may be unable to count by 5s or 10s to tell the value of given coins or to check change received.

These children have difficulty making associations and recognizing patterns that ordinarily make counting and skip counting a reasonably simple task. Therefore, special instruction, such as that outlined in the following activities, is required. Rather than basing an activity immediately on number, the sequence first involves the child in *patterning*—the root of the presenting problem. At first, the child is given simple shapes and visual/auditory cues to help in recognizing and extending a pattern. Then, when the child is successful with number sequences (easily distinguishable numerals), color-coded counting charts are introduced.

Suggested Sequence of Activities and Exercises

1. **Finish the pattern.** Use wood or construction paper circles and squares (circles one color, squares another). Lay out a simple repeating pattern with the blocks. On two slips of paper, trace (same color as actual shapes) the dotted outlines of the next two blocks in the pattern (see Figure 2-32). Have the child name

the shapes, in order, so that the "square, square, circle, circle" auditory pattern is heard. Then ask the child to find the missing blocks and finish pattern. When all blocks are in place, have the child "read" the pattern (name all the shapes displayed, in order). Finally, ask the child to use blocks to copy the completed pattern.

   • *Follow-Up:* Repeat with other patterns, gradually omitting the dotted cue.

2. **Draw it in.** As in *Finish the Pattern,* but draw the repeating shape patterns on worksheets. At first, use two different colors and include the dotted outlines. Ask the child to "read" and complete each pattern. Then ask that the entire pattern again be read aloud. Provide space (and templates, if necessary), so that the child can copy the completed pattern. Gradually use more difficult patterns, fade the color cueing, and omit the dotted outlines. See if the child can add the next two or three shapes to the pattern without extra prompts. This is usually possible when pattern difficulty is gradually incremented along with gradual fading of prompts.

Figure 2-32

3. **What's next?** Follow the same "read, complete, read again, copy" format of the two preceding activities, but this time use numerals that can be readily

distinguished (e.g., Figure 2-33). Similar cueing techniques can also be used if necessary.

Figure 2-33

4. **An easy one!** Show the child Figure 2-34. "This is an easy one. Tell me what's alike in the numbers." (All end in 0.) "Read the numbers." (To hear the auditory pattern.) "What comes next?" (70). "How do you know?" (7 comes after 6). Have the child finish the sequence and read it aloud. "Look at the numbers so you can remember them in your head. . . . Now close your eyes and tell me the numbers." Prompt, as necessary, throughout the dialogue. Repeat parts of the dialogue, as necessary. If more patterning work is needed, adapt Activity 7 to provide practice.

Figure 2-34

5. **Count on.** Provide dimes the child can use for counting by 10s. If necessary, use a counting chart as in Figure 2-35, on which the child lays the dimes while

counting. (If a child's money concepts are too weak for this activity, refer to the Chapter 3 suggestions.) Eventually, the child should be able to count by 10s independently of the chart.

- *Variation* (to prepare for counting money amounts and checking change received): Lay four dimes ($.40) on the counting chart and ask the child to count on by 10s from $.40. Repeat, but vary the number of dimes initially laid on the chart.

Figure 2-35

6. **To 100.** (Prerequisite: The child can count meaningfully to 10. It is also assumed that the numeration instruction summarized beginning on page 57 has been carried out.) Show the color-coded counting chart of Figure 2-36 (tens digits green). This chart is sequenced vertically rather than horizontally as is commonly the case. Experience has shown that the vertical presentation makes it easier for children to see the patterning of the number sequence.

0	10	20	30	40	50	60	70	80	90	100
1	11	21	31	41	51	61	71	81	91	
2	12	22	32	42	52	62	72	82		
3	13	23	33	43	53	63				
4	14	24	34	44						
5	15	25	35							
6	16									
7	17									
8	18									
9	19									

Figure 2-36

Have the child count by 10s *across* the columns. Now mask out all but the first column (0-9), and have the child read it aloud. Then slide the mask so the first two columns show. Discuss how the second column is like the first. (The ones column in both is the standard counting sequence. This can be related to the idea of "one more" as described earlier.) Have the child note the pattern that all numbers in the second column begin with 1. "This is the teen column." Count from 1 with the child, emphasizing the teen endings of the last numbers read. Slide the mask again to reveal the third column. "This is the 20s column." Have the child read the numbers in the column. "What numbers come next?" Write as the child orally continues the counting sequence to 29, prompting as necessary. For this, as for other columns on the chart, the child can be shown how the standard counting sequence of the ones digits will help.

Later retrace the tens digits with green, recounting aloud with the child to emphasize the "20" part of each number named. Have the child finger trace the first digits during an independent recount, if helpful. Let the child, eyes closed, count the 20s aloud. Then choose a number in a preceding column and count on from there—first using the chart, then looking away. Stress the 19–20 column shift. Repeat for other columns during this or any follow-up sessions. Make the chart available for reference. Use it as long as needed during review sessions in which the child either orally counts or writes the numbers in sequence.

- *Follow-Up Activity 1:* Reinforce the tens transition with repeated oral work. First the teacher says a few patterns emphasizing the switch. Then the student completes patterns started by the teacher.

    Example:
    A. Teacher

    "nineteen—twenty"

    "thirty-nine—forty"

    "eighty-nine—ninety"

    B. Teacher   Student

    "twenty-nine"—"thirty"

    "sixty-nine"—"seventy"

- *Follow-Up Activity 2:* When the auditory pattern for sequential counting is established, use objects (tens and ones) to dramatize and reinforce the meaning of the oral count.

- *Example:* Lay out 2 tens and one (to represent 21). "I will add sticks, one at a time. Count aloud so we can keep track of the number of sticks that are on the table each time" (see Figure 2-37). Repeat, varying the number of tens and ones initially placed on the table.

It may now also be necessary to redevelop concepts and skills for comparing and ordering two-digit numbers. Suggestions from the following section, *Comparing Numbers*, can be adapted to this purpose.

Figure 2-37

7. **By 5s.** Use a worksheet similar to that of Figure 2-38 to lay the groundwork for the patterning involved in skip counting by 5s. Following the sequence of patterns on the worksheet, first review the easier patterns with shapes, then turn to numbers used when counting by 5s.

Figure 2-38

Next show Figure 2-39 (tens digits coded green). Ask the child to read the column, then to describe any patterns seen (numbers end in 5 or 0; in the tens place there are two 1s, then two 2s). In order for some children to see these patterns, they may need to cover first the ones column and then the tens column with a card.

"What two numbers would come next?" Write as the child says them: "30, 35." Prompt if necessary. Discuss why these two numbers were chosen. Then have

Figure 2-39

the child say all the numbers aloud, continuing the count as far as possible (to 100). Write as the child gives the extended count. Underscore the tens digits green if this helps cue additional entries in the sequence. See if the child can repeat the counting pattern without looking at the chart. Make the chart available for future reference, and continue to use it, as needed, during review sessions.

8. **Nickel countdown.** Adapt the *Count On* (Activity 5) to counting by 5s with nickels. The idea of counting by 5s and 10s can be extended to include (a) counting on from clock times or (b) using nickels and dimes first to count by 5s, then switching to counting by 10s (and vice versa). The latter skill is often needed for counting money amounts or checking change received.

   Note: Follow-up Activity 1 for *Turn Over* in Section 1 (*Counting in Early Number Work*), as well as dot-to-dot patterns, can be used to reinforce most of the activities of this section.

COMPARING NUMBERS

Problem area: Difficulty recognizing the greater of two numbers or correctly using greater than (>) and less than (<) symbols. The use of these symbols is not recommended for all children and certainly not in lower grades.

Typical disabilities affecting progress: Difficulties with abstract reasoning, visual discrimination, visual association, spatial organization, and visual memory.

Background: When comparing numbers less than 10, a standard approach is to examine the linear sequence of digits and note that: "When you count, the numbers that mean *more* come after others in the count." The first set of activities that follow suggests ways of prefacing this instruction to build a better concept of *more* (or less) for numbers up to 10.

When comparing numbers greater than 10, children typically are asked to represent the numbers with grouping aids and to match one-to-one as in Figure 2-40. The focus is on starting big, with the tens (hundreds) to compare. Many children with the disabilities identified in this section can understand comparison when illustrated in this manner. Difficulties arise when materials are no longer used or when children are expected to use the "less than" and "greater than" symbols, without being able to associate any meaning with them. Some reverse the symbols when writing them, others forget "which means which." Number line models (e.g., Figure 2-41) sometimes help.

If students study algebra in high school, an attempt must be made to help them correctly use the symbols for number comparison. Otherwise, they may forget the symbols and focus only on the basic idea: "Which means more?" As a daily living skill, this concept is a critical one. It enters into comparison shopping—determining whether one has enough money to buy what is needed—and a myriad of other everyday situations. The important point of the second set of activities in the following sequence is to help students compare larger numbers even when concrete materials are no longer used. The use of symbols is secondary and, in some cases, omitted.

Suggested Sequence of Activities and Exercises

Comparing Numbers to 10

Prerequisite Skill: Understanding the concepts "before" and "after" both orally and visually.

1. **Match up.** A first basic activity is to have children take two handfuls of objects or cubes (up to 10 in each hand) and lay them out or stack them so visual comparison is easy. Matching one to one, children can be led to observe: "The side or stack with extras has more" (Figure 2-42). Consistently and repeatedly, this verbal observation should be stated—both by the teacher and by the child: "The side with extras has more." The child can write or circle the greater number each time.

2. **"Comes after" in the count.** After repeatedly matching and writing to record the comparison of two numbers as before, the link to the counting sequence can be made. Simply ask children to write the numbers 1 to 10 at the top of a sheet of paper, or to use their ruler or a number line. Call out two 1-digit numbers and ask, " Which is greater?" If the child does not know,

a)

b)

Figure 2-40

Figure 2-41

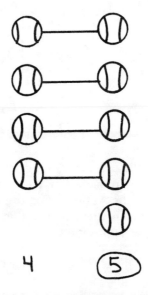

4   ⑤

Figure 2-42

small counters can be used as in the Figure 2-42 "match up" to answer the question. If the child *does* respond correctly, it still is useful occasionally to "match up," as shown, to reinforce correct thinking. Commentary to be repeated in this activity is: "Yes, and did you notice that the greater number comes *after* the other in the count and on your number line?" Relate this idea to the pages in a book, as suggested in Note to Activity 1, which follows, for larger numbers. *When children can comfortably identify the greater of two numbers, the number meaning "more," then parallel activities focusing on "less/fewer than" can be presented.*

Comparing Larger Numbers

Prerequisite Skills:

a. Strong place-value understanding for the numbers involved, as suggested in the teacher *Background* of *Reversals: 2-Digit Numbers* on page 57.

b. Prior work with grouping aids, as in Figure 2-43, for comparing multidigit numbers.

c. Ability to use more/less to compare one-digit numbers.

d. Understanding of the concepts "before" and "after."

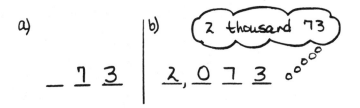

Figure 2-43

Basic Sequence

1. **See it.** Orally present 2- or 3-digit numbers with different first digits. Provide students with number line paper as in Figure 2-44. Have students write the numbers in the section using the correct section of the number line. They can then fill in the sentence (Figure 2-44a) or use symbols (Figure 2-44b), whichever is appropriate.

   Note: This activity is a good starting point for students with spatial problems as it allows them to see that the greater number always comes after the other one in the count. When the numbers are "far apart" in the counting sequence, it is not practical to rely on counting alone to determine a comparison. Instead, the more general tactic of comparing the greater valued digits in the numbers (e.g., tens to tens, or hundreds to hundreds) is far more useful because: "The numbers compare the way the digits compare." Aligning numbers under each other, color cueing, or finger tracing lead digits *in like positions* is used throughout these activities to emphasize this approach. The link to the counting sequence is then made, often with the help of a library book or textbook.

2. **More tens.** Present two 2- or 3-digit numbers with different first digits as in Figure 2-45. Have the children use materials (tens/ones) to represent each

a.

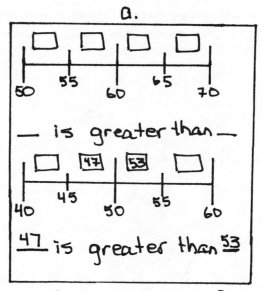

"Which is greater?
47 or 53

b.

"Which is greater?
42 or 37

Figure 2-44

number (Figure 2-45b). Underscore the first digit of each number in green and discuss how you always "start big" to compare. Be sure children recognize that 32 has more tens than 24. "Yes, 3 tens is more than 2 tens, so 32 is more (greater) than 24. And, when you count, the number that is "more" always comes after the other." Repeat with other numbers.

Figure 2-45

3. **Feel it.** To reinforce the "more than" idea and to review the vocabulary "less than."

- Pose the situation where _____ and _____ (use names of people the children know) are reading the same book. Write two 2- or 3-digit numbers on the board and ask students to compare their location in a book (Figure 2-46). "Who has read more pages?" As in Activity 2 (*More Tens*), underscore the first digit of the numbers and have students note their location in the book. Place markers at each page, close the book, and have students feel that 215 pages is less. Repeat with other page numbers.

Figure 2-46

4. **Match and check.** Choose the approach from Activities 2 and 3 which seems to be the most effective. Use 2- or 3-digit numbers as in Activity 1.

- Write two numbers. Have the children copy them onto a worksheet illustration where they "belong." For example, the child is given 118 and 231. The child writes the numbers into a book to show which means more and which means less, as in Figure 2-47. Discuss how 231 means more pages.

Figure 2-47

- Cut out the worksheet illustrations and glue them on cards (Figure 2-48). Write just the two numbers (in random order) on the front of the cards. Underscore the first digits if necessary. The children should then use the deck in the following manner: (a) study the numbers on the front; (b) close their eyes to imagine what the numbers would look like if pictured; (c) write the number that means more and the number that means less; and (d) turn the card over to check their answer.

Figure 2-48

5. **Alligator Al.** Use auditory and tactile cues to help students attach meaning to the comparison symbols. For example, make an alligator hand puppet with its mouth clearly outlined. Use two different colors and textures, as illustrated in Figure 2-49a. Carry through the story line that Alligator Al is always hungry and always reaches for the greatest number. Make a poster or file card miniature of Al's two views for students. Provide sandpaper and felt symbols to be placed between numbers as you show students how to position and read the symbols (Figure 2-49b).

   Use two 2- or 3-digit numbers with different first digits. Invite the children to finger trace the symbol while reading the comparison. For some number pairs, ask the children to retell Alligator Al's story (he always reaches for the greatest number). It is sometimes necessary to have children verbalize an association to ensure they grasp and retain it.

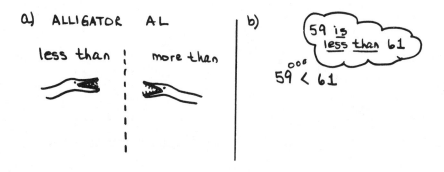

Figure 2-49

- *Follow-Up:* Prepare cards like those of Figure 2-50. Underscore the first digits of each number, if necessary. Have the children copy the numbers and place or write the symbol that indicates the comparison. They can then turn the card over to check the answer. For students with visual-perception, association, or memory difficulties, it may be necessary to provide a pre-recorded tape, keyed alphabetically to the card labels. After they quietly read each comparison, children can use the tape along with the back side of the card to check. In all cases, the hand puppet or poster/file card replication should be available for reference.

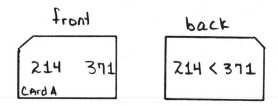

Figure 2-50

6. More comparisons.

- Dictate two numbers, a 2- and a 3-digit number, for children to write on the dotted lines (Figure 2-51). Discuss why the 2-digit number is placed on the last two lines (no hundreds). Write a dotted 0 in the hundreds place, if necessary, to help students with the comparison. Referring to Figure 2-51, you might note: "You always start big to compare. Here, 'big' means hundreds. One hundred is more than no hundreds, so 132 is more than 53." Repeat with other numbers. Use worksheet exercises to reinforce. At this point, the children could simply circle to indicate which number means more (less).

Justifying digit placement and aligning digits one on top of the other, as in Figure 2-51, emphasizes the "greater than/less than" comparison.

$$\underline{\dot{\mathbf{=}}\ \underline{5}\ \underline{3}}$$
$$\underline{\mathbf{1}\ \underline{3}\ \underline{4}}$$

━ = green

Figure 2-51

- Adapt the above activity to focus on two 2- or 3-digit numbers having first digits *alike* (e.g., 46, 49; 258, 262). "You always start big to compare. If the digits are alike, you compare the next two" (Figure 2-52).

- Provide mixed-review exercises that require students to use symbols for comparing all types of 2- and 3-digit numbers.

Figure 2-52

ROUNDING NUMBERS

Problem area: Difficulty rounding 2- and higher digit numbers to the nearest 10 or 100.

Typical disabilities affecting progress: Difficulties with visual perception (figure-ground, visual discrimination), visual or sequential memory, abstract reasoning, or auditory processing.

Background: Most day-to-day work with numbers involves some sort of estimation which, in turn, generally involves rounding numbers to make a statement or decision. Clearly, the ability to round numbers is a functional skill, often underestimated in importance. Since it is a difficult skill to teach, it is frequently avoided, especially with students who already have trouble learning.

Mathematicians use one rounding "rule": look to the digit after. If it is 5 or more, round up; otherwise, round down. Social scientists sometimes use a different rule, one that is based on whether the number after is odd or even. In school, the mathematician guideline typically is adopted. Nonetheless, it is worthwhile discussing with students that the rule or procedure for rounding is man-made and, therefore, may differ across teachers.

Suggested Sequence of Activities and Exercises

Round 2-Digit Numbers

1. **Feel the line.** Have students position the number to be rounded on the number line. At first, do not use a number ending in 5. As in Figure 2-53a, 53 would be placed on the line as shown. Have students visually inspect the distance from the number to either end and then slide a finger along the line to each end.

   Note: If students are strong tactual learners, make the number line longer to involve more gross motor skill, or texturize the line. Also, have them close their eyes as they slide to either end of the line.

   As students inspect/feel the line, relate the idea of nearest endpoint to the concept and vocabulary of rounding numbers. "Sometimes exact numbers are not needed. A close estimate will do. So we often round numbers when we talk. If 28 people come to a party, we might say: 'About 30 people were there'."

   Relate looking/sliding backwards on the number line to rounding *down;* and looking/sliding forward to rounding *up.* In the party example, we rounded *up.* Later extend to other number lines which involve more choices, as in Figure 2-53b.

   Gradually include numbers ending in 5 and introduce the convention of rounding used in mathematics: "To round, examine the digit *after.* If less than 5, round *down* (backward); if 5 or greater, round *up* (forward)."

   Note: Initially the use of *backward* and *forward* may help students more readily visualize the procedure. Later they can be taught the more commonly used synonyms.

Figure 2-53

2. **A fast dime** (rounding to the nearest tenth. Small-group, teacher-led activity appropriate for students who cannot effectively use a number line). Provide two decks of cards: a "banker's deck" and a "fast dime" deck (see Figure 2-54). Place the banker's deck in a bank box along with extra dimes and pennies. This deck contains one card for each multiple of 10¢ (to 90¢). The fast dime deck contains cards that list amounts between 11¢ and 89¢ (no multiples of 10¢ included). Until the students understand the activity, remove all money amounts ending in 5 from the fast dime deck.

Shuffle the fast dime deck and place it face down between the players. Students take turns drawing the top card from the deck and placing it face

Figure 2-54

up in the playing area. They then use dimes (as many as possible) and extra pennies to show the amount on the card.

The banker selects the two cards from the banker's deck that are closest in value to that displayed (see Figure 2-55). The child in this example must decide how a "fast dime" can be made. Is 34¢ closer to 30¢ or to 40¢? The child must either add extra pennies to the 34¢ pile or take some away to indicate the choice made. Thus, either six pennies are added (to make 40¢) or four pennies are taken away (leaving 30¢). The latter decision earns the child one point, since it involves the least number of coin moves. When the students are comfortable handling these tasks, return the money amounts ending in 5 to the deck. Introduce the "banker's rule" that for these cards the "fast dime" is always the greater 10¢ value.

- *Follow-Up 1*: Lay out cards from the fast dime deck, one at a time, and get the students to verbalize the fact that, for example, 34¢ is closer to 30¢ than to 40¢. Allow the students to use dimes and pennies to verify this if necessary.

- *Follow-Up 2*: As in Follow-up 1, but use a new deck in which all cents signs have been eliminated. If the students hesitate, have them find the matching fast dime card. Seeing the card usually triggers the correct idea. If necessary, allow the students to use dimes and pennies to determine "closeness to." "Yes, 34 hundred is closer to 30 hundred than to 40 hundred."

- *Follow-Up 3*: Use worksheets like that of Figure 2-56. Allow students to use fast dime cards as well as dimes and pennies, if these help. When checking the worksheet, refer to the conventional rules for rounding. Post these rules or provide individual index card copies that can be kept in a file box at each student's desk. Be sure the students understand, procedurally, what rounding up (down) means. When rounding to the nearest ten, for example, all digits beyond 10 will be zeroes (and can be dropped). One uses the number *after* to determine whether the 10 digit itself is changed to a digit one higher (rounding up) or kept the same (rounding down).

Figure 2-55

Round to the nearest ten, then match.
(Some may not have a match.)

Figure 2-56

3. **Color cue.** Help students focus attention on the "thinking digit" (the number after) by color highlighting, as in Figure 2-57, the "thinking digit" (4) in green and the "changing digit" (6) in red.

Round to the nearest ten

6 4

— = green   .... = red

Figure 2-57

4. **Numbered chips can help.** Use number lines the length of a standard sheet of paper (Figure 2-58a). Premade worksheets which can be filled in (Figure 2-58b) and numbered chips help students visualize the location of the nearest whole number as they place the chips on the number line and then fill in blanks.

   Note: Students with spatial problems especially seem to benefit from this method as the use of nearest, rather than rounding up, makes more sense to them. It is a more concrete, recognizable approach.

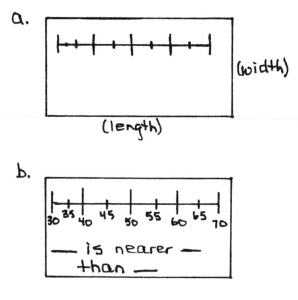

a.

(width)

(length)

b.

30 35 40 45 50 55 60 65 70

___ is nearer ___ than ___

Figure 2-58

5. **Focus here.** The preceding sequence may be adapted to rounding larger numbers and to rounding within numbers. The following idea may help students who understand the concept but have figure-ground difficulties. Using worksheets as in Figure 2-59 help children focus on the correct digit by highlighting the "thinking digit" (8) in green and the "changing digit" (5) *and the corresponding word* (ten) in red.

Round 6 5 8 to the nearest ten.

■ = green   ⋯ = red

Figure 2-59

EXTENDING COUNTING SKILLS: PREREQUISITES FOR MENTAL MATH

Problem area: Difficulty adding or subtracting 2-digit numbers mentally.

Typical disabilities affecting progress: Difficulties with abstract reasoning, visual discrimination, visual association, visual or sequential memory, short-term memory, or expressive language.

Background: As highlighted earlier, children have three choices for computing: paper-pencil, estimation, or mental computation. We live in a society in which calculators are readily available, in which estimates often are good enough, and in which there is great practical value in being able to compute simpler calculations mentally. The ideas which follow can help children with specific reasoning or visual deficits develop counting skills which may be used to add or subtract 2-digit numbers mentally. The focus is on mentally *adding* or *subtracting* multiples of 10.

Children who are accustomed to the right-left, paper-pencil procedure of computing first with ones and then with tens may find it difficult to completely reverse their thinking and compute tens first, then ones. This latter approach generally is faster for mental calculation, however. Color coding, as suggested in Activity 1 (*Cue In*), may help some students make this shift. Alternate approaches that allow children to think more holistically and *count on or back by tens* also are presented. A child might compute 24 + 38 mentally, for example, by first adding 24 and 40, then counting back two numbers to compensate for the extra added. Modeling this count on a hundreds chart (and aided by a "peep hole" card), as suggested in other activities, simplifies an otherwise difficult or almost impossible task. If children have used the vertical hundreds chart of Figure 2-36, adapt the hundreds chart ideas that follow for vertical application.

Suggested Sequence of Activities and Exercises

Prerequisite Skills:

    a. Ability to visualize 2-digit numbers in sequence.

    b. Firm sense of place value for 2-digit numbers.

    c. Auditory-spatial sense of "first," "next," and "last."

    d. Ability to retain information while simultaneously processing other information.

1. **Cue in.** First present problems in which a 2-digit number is added to a multiple of 10 (Figure 2-60a). Color code green the tens digits of the numbers. "Cue in on the tens digits of each number first: '35 + 40: that's 3 tens and 4 tens, which is 7 tens. (If needed, children can write down the 7.) Now think about the ones digits: 5 ones and 0 ones is 5 ones. The answer is 75'." (It helps to verbalize the pattern for students as they learn.)

   At a later time, problems requiring no regrouping can be paired as shown in Figure 2-60b. Children first complete the problem in the cue bubble. Point out that this is similar to what they have been practicing previously (Figure 2-60a). Then problems like those shown in Figure 2-60c can be presented. As above, we *add to the nearest multiple of 10* (in this case, 38 + 60, or 98); *then adjust.* In this case we go back one, to 97.

   Note: It may be necessary to practice extensively with mental calculation and counting on before introducing counting back.

   Students with short-term memory or sequential-memory deficits can use mental calculation, but may need to write down what they are thinking as they proceed, especially when regrouping is involved.

Example: "38 + 45 is 3 tens and 4 tens."
                (student writes 7)
         "8 ones and 5 ones is 13."
             (student writes 13)
           "38 + 45 is 83."

A similar procedure can be used to help students mentally subtract 2-digit numbers with no regrouping. Although similar, this becomes a little more complex when regrouping is added. Hence students may need to write down their thought processes—a technique they may have to use throughout life.

Figure 2-60

2. **Look ahead.** To prepare for the alternate *counting* approach outlined in the next activity (*Count on to Add*), familiarize children with the hundreds chart and gradually build up appropriate counting skills. Provide individual hundreds charts and a 3 × 5 "peep hole" card, with a center cut out the size of one square in the chart (see Figure 2-61). The ideas of this activity and those that follow may readily be adapted to other versions of the hundreds chart (see page 69), for example, by teachers who prefer writing the numbers 0 through 9 in the first row, 10 through 19 in the second row, and so on, or teachers who prefer the vertical format of Figure 2-36.

At first, children simply place the card over numbers the teacher calls out or writes on the chalkboard. Later, the card can be used to count short sequences: by ones, by tens; forwards or backwards. The 39-40, 69-70, 89-90 decade shifts can be emphasized.

Hundreds chart   Chart with "peep hole" card

Figure 2-61

The next task consists of counting by tens. First start with 10 or some other number on the top row. A more sophisticated count is that which begins anywhere mid-sequence, and counts on or back by tens from that number. A final task involves counting on or back by tens and then further by ones. *Bring children to the point where they count first without the chart, then recount using the "peep hole" card on the hundreds chart to identify numbers said.*

3. **Count on to add.** An alternate approach consists of using a hundreds chart and a "peep hole" and COUNT to determine a sum. Being able to think more holistically about a problem, as with this counting approach, helps many students. Given a problem like 35 + 40, children place the "peep hole" card over the first addend and move it down the column as they count on by tens: 35 − 45, 55, 65, 75. When children can comfortably add a 2-digit number to a multiple of 10, the idea of "Add to the nearest multiple of 10, then adjust" is introduced. As in Activity 1 (*Cue In*), first present problems that require no regrouping. In these cases, children count on by tens, then count further (forwards or backwards) to adjust.

4. **Count back to subtract.** For 2-digit subtraction, use a parallel sequence that emphasizes subtracting the nearest multiple of ten, then adjusting.

READING AND WRITING LARGER NUMBERS

Problem area: Difficulty reading or writing 3- and higher digit numbers.

Typical disabilities affecting progress: Difficulties with visual perception (figure-ground, visual discrimination), visual association, closure, abstract reasoning, and auditory processing.

Background: Many factors influence a child's success in reading and writing larger numbers. The opportunity to group objects by 10s and to further cluster the groups into 100s or even 1,000s is helpful to all students (Figure 2-62a). Besides establishing place-value understandings for hundreds and thousands, experiences such as these help generate a *feel* for larger numbers. Graph paper pieces (Figure 2-62b) can also be used to illustrate 3- and 4-digit numbers.

Figure 2-62

Early place-value instruction must use materials to illustrate numbers in some physical, hands-on manner to establish a basis for treatment of common problems, such as writing "20038" for "two hundred thirty-eight" or reading "415" as "forty-one, five."

To remedy the first problem a teacher might, for example, ask a child to gather 2 hundreds, 3 tens, and 8 singles from a box of graph paper pieces. After recording the number of each kind of piece (Figure 2-63), the teacher might write the number in standard form and "model" the way it *should* be read. Teacher and child can then switch roles. After taking graph paper pieces and recording the number of each kind, the child could write the number in standard form and read it to the teacher. As follow-up, the teacher and student can take turns drawing a 3-digit number card, reading it, and asking the other to show it using graph paper pieces (Figure 2-64). Stamps for hundreds, tens, and ones, available from many school supply companies, can also be used. These should be among the teaching aids of every classroom in which mathematics is taught.

Figure 2-63

Figure 2-64

These activities provide an effective visual frame of reference that helps children read and write 3-digit numbers when concrete materials are no longer used. Teacher modeling—correctly writing and saying the number represented by the pieces—is a vital part of the sequence. Correct teacher modeling is also necessary to prevent children from reading "238" as "two hundred *and* thirty-eight." The "and" is properly reserved for the decimal point, as in $2.38 (two dollars and 38 cents) or 4.2 (four and two tenths). Only in special cases are children allowed to use "and." Some students may need to use the word as a pause for remembering how to group digits when reading a number. However, using "and" in this manner should be terminated when it is no longer needed. This situation parallels that of using "uh" or pausing to keep from stuttering.

For students who read "415" as "forty-one, five," underlining the hundreds digit sometimes helps.

Examples:

$$\underline{4}15 \rightarrow \text{"4 hundred 15"}$$

$$\underline{2}23 \rightarrow \text{"2 hundred 23"}$$

Teachers might point out that the only new part is the first digit. Students already know how to read the rest. Provide a card for the child to move along, as in syllabicating, while reading the number. Further, illustrating each 3-digit number with graph paper pieces, as before, also helps.

As students begin to work with 4-digit numbers, more specialized techniques are sometimes necessary for those having the learning disabilities identified above. These techniques are outlined in the suggestions that follow.

Suggested Sequence of Activities and Exercises

Reading and Writing 4-Digit Numbers

Prerequisite Skills:

    a. Ability to read and write 3-digit numbers. This includes a firm grasp of place-value ideas for 3-digit numbers, including the understanding that "when you hear hundreds, the number has three digits. Sometimes a zero is needed to show no tens or ones, as in 403 and 620."

    b. Prior work modeling 4-digit numbers with graph paper pieces (refer to Figure 2-62b).

Basic Sequence

1. **Look!** As a first step, present number pairs visually (Figure 2-65). The thousands digit is green; others are red. Explain that one comma in a number is read "thousand." The only new part comes before the comma. "You already know how to read the rest." Have children finger trace the part that is the same within the pair, then read both numbers.

- Use no 0s in the hundreds place at this time.

- Do not use colored digits with children having closure difficulties to avoid activating their tendency to treat multidigit numbers as a series of disjointed, unrelated digits.

Read this ⟶ 4̣2̣3̣ ᵒᵒᵒ (4 hundred 23)

Now read this ⟶ 1, 4̣2̣3̣ ᵒᵒ (1 thousand
4 hundred 23)

━ = green   --- = red

Figure 2-65

- *Alternative 1:* For children who need color coding but who have closure difficulties, underline the digits as in the example below. Generally, this approach can be used any time and, except in severe cases, works as effectively as color-coded digits.

  Example:

  "Read this: 4̲23"

  "Now read this: 1,4̲23"

- *Alternative 2:* Use no colors. Have the child use a card as when learning to syllabicate (Figure 2-66).

Given
number:

1,423 ⟶ 1,☐ ⟶ 1,423

(1 thousand...423)

Figure 2-66

2. **Word match.** If the children can read number words, written practice exercises like those of Figure 2-67 can be given. The skill being reinforced is used in writing checks. In addition, the exercise prepares for the dictation in Activity 4 (*Hear and Find*). The number of thousands is written in green to match the green underlining of the thousands place. The 3-digit part, both underlining and words, is in red. The words *thousand* and the *comma* are the same color, so the children learn to associate the two. Later, when they need to learn to place the comma themselves, the format can be modified as in the second example of Figure 2-67.

Example 1:

Example 2:

Figure 2-67

3. **Find it.** Children match color-coded words (as in Figure 2-67) to noncolor-coded numbers.

   • *Follow-Up:* Same type of match exercises, but without colors.

4. **Hear and find.** Dictate 4-digit numbers and have the children circle each from a group of numbers. Include 3-digit distractors. At first, use color coding as before.

5. **Zero holds the place.** Dictate "seventy-three" and ask children to write the number on the dotted lines (Figure 2-43a). Discuss why the digits are placed in the last two spots. (No hundreds.) Explain that in higher digit numbers, 0 is used to show no number in a given place. For example, 2,073 means "2 thousands, no hundreds, 7 tens, and 3 ones" (Figure 2-43b). Present color-coded number pairs for children to read (the thousands digit green; the hundreds group red). This time focus on 4-digit numbers having a 0 in the hundreds place.

6. **More hear and find.** Adapt Activity 4 to focus on 4-digit numbers having a 0. Include numbers with 0 in the tens place and the hundreds place, as well

as numbers without any zeroes. When the exercise is complete, have the children read aloud the 4-digit numbers they circled.

7. **Tape it to me.** Dictate 4-digit numbers and have the children write them. Alternatively, have the children play a prerecorded tape that dictates the numbers. Responses can be checked against an answer key.

Extending the Basic Sequence

Reading and Writing 5- and Higher Digit Numbers

Ideas from the previous sequence can be adapted to help students read and write larger numbers. A card chart such as that illustrated in Figure 2-68 is also useful. Within each period, the child reads the familiar 1-, 2-, or 3-digit number and adds the "family" name (i.e., the name of the period). Except for students with closure difficulties, a green-black-red color coding of digits within each period can be used to emphasize the idea. The chart can later be extended and used for reading decimals.

A pleated modification of the chart is illustrated in Figure 2-69. Children enjoy "opening" a number at the comma to check that they are reading it correctly. Cover the writing surfaces with clear contact paper and use a wipe-off pen or pencil. This way the digits can easily be changed.

Figure 2-68

a.

373, 501, 218

Pleats folded behind.

b.

373, million 501, thousand 218

Pleats open.

Figure 2-69

DEVELOPING "NUMBER SENSE"

A major goal of school mathematics is to help all children deal effectively in common, numerical situations like the following:

- Terry thought about the answer he had written for 26 + 48. "Can't be right. Both numbers are less than 50, so the total must be less than 100."

- Mary's mother had given her $10 for milk and bread. Mary knew that a gallon of milk was just under $2 and a loaf of bread was a little more than $1. At the store she put three gallons of milk and three loaves of bread in her cart. She was confident, as she stood in line at the checkout counter, that she would have enough money for the milk and bread, even with tax.

When children feel comfortable with numbers, they develop a better sense of control in numeric situations, in and out of school. They approach problems with a more positive attitude and get better results.

Some students reach this "comfort zone" naturally. Most learning disabled children do not, however. The key to success is the teacher in the daily mathematics lesson who:

- Recognizes the importance of developing number sense in students;

- Constructs situations which stimulate and develop number sense;

- Creates a positive climate where students can grow in their understanding and application of number.

The following facts are critical in an examination of how teachers can improve or further develop a positive climate for building number sense among students.

- Children are more willing to explore numeric situations that involve mathematical ideas with which they are familiar.

- Children approach numeric situations in different ways. Accepting and encouraging variety in pupil response results in more flexible thinking and nurtures a greater potential for student success in numeric situations.

- For learning disabled students who are mainstreamed, the use of cooperative learning groups, for example, provides opportunities to listen to each others' ideas about number. Therefore, children learn that more than one way of approaching a problem or a situation can lead to a successful outcome.

- Children will be more likely to take the risk and make decisions about number if they know it is all right not to be "right" or have the best estimate the first time. In a non-threatening atmosphere, and given many opportunities to practice, children have a greater potential to grow in their ability to make appropriate decisions about number.

- Social studies and science are among the content areas which come alive for students when they possess a sense of number. For example, while planning for a social studies field trip a teacher might ask, "Is one dollar per student enough spending money for the class field trip to the history museum? Why or why not?" When children see that number sense is useful throughout their day, they recognize a greater need for making better decisions involving number.

- Children are great imitators. Having a teacher who uses good number sense makes children want to be like the teacher and use good number sense, too.

Developing Number Sense: Today and Every Day

Teachers who are committed to developing number sense in their students are dedicated to instruction that provides ongoing experiences such as:

- Flashing basic fact cards and having students indicate whether the answer is more or less than a given target number. (Then provide the exact answer or ask a child to do so.)

- Providing opportunities for children to think about and discover other relationships:

  For example: "What's 5 + 5?" (10). "So is 5 + 9 more or less?" (More.) Have the child put five counters in each hand, while you or another child takes charge of the extra counters. "Do we have to give you more counters so you have 5 and 9?" (Yes.) Circle the second addend of each equation and note that 9 is more than 5.

- Having children take a few *seconds* before doing a row of problems to identify the one(s) that will have the greatest answer. (Discuss why.)

- Asking children to indicate those numbers that are "close to" another specified number (e.g., "Which fractions are 'closer to' 1 than to 0? Which are 'close to' ½?" Or, "Which numbers are 'closer to' 50 than to 100?").

Note: If children have difficulty sensing "closeness," try a kinesthetic/tactile approach. "What about 86?" Using a meter stick, the child can place a finger on 86 and close eyes while you run the finger from 86 to 100; from 86 to 50. Which "feels" closer?

- Challenging children specifically to think about numbers in different ways.

For example: Frequently play "I'm thinking of a number." (To aid the thinking process, allow children to use number cards to 20. Have them laid out in two *columns*: 0–10 along the left edge of the desk; 11–20 along the right edge.)
—"It's between 9 and 14." (These cards are moved to the center of the desk.)
  "It's a greater number than any you see on the classroom clock." (Child pushes back any cards that are not needed, i.e., 12 or less.)
  "If I switch places with the digits, I will have 31. What's my number?" (13).
—"I *don't* say it when I count by 2s." (Move odd number cards to center of the desk.)
  "It's more than 8." (Child pushes back any cards not needed, those 8 or less.)
  "It's less than 16." (Child pushes back any cards, 16 or more.)
  "I *don't* say it when I count by 5s." (Child pushes back 10 and 15.)
  "When it's two hours before 1:00 o'clock, the hour hands points to it. What's my number?" (11).

This list samples number-related activities which are beginning to permeate the elementary-school mathematics curriculum in an effort to lead children to be friendly with and make better use of number. *The Arithmetic Teacher*, the official journal of the National Council of Teachers of Mathematics, frequently carries practical articles related to the development of number sense. For example, the February 1989 issue was devoted to this topic.

There is a subtle difference between learning about numbers and learning enough about numbers to show good "number sense." The emphasis in working with learning disabled students is on structured, extended learning experiences which gradually will generate those number concepts, number relationships, and numeric skills which enable students eventually to demonstrate good number sense.

USING A HAND CALCULATOR

Exercises using a hand calculator can be designed to serve two purposes:

1. To reinforce basic number and place-value skills; and

2. To build visual and auditory memory skills.

Since some learning disabled students have difficulty merely locating the numbers on a calculator, teachers must check for the following prerequisites before requiring calculator use:

- Prerequisite 1: Students can discriminate among the numerals and locate the number on the calculator.

- Prerequisite 2: Students have sufficient eye-hand coordination to punch the correct key.
    When these prerequisites are established, exercises such as the following can be carried out.

- *Example 1 (visual memory):* Provide a list of numbers for the children to enter. For multidigit numbers, encourage them to look at, then punch, the *entire number* (or at least as many digits as they can) without looking back.

- *Example 2 (visual memory):* Provide a list of number pairs. The children enter the greatest (least) of each pair, then check against a key.

- *Example 3 (auditory memory):* Dictate a number (or use a prerecorded tape). Have the children punch in the number, then compare it with a key. In early phases of the activity children with severe problems may be allowed to write the number before entering it.

- *Example 4 (auditory memory):* Dictate a number (or use a prerecorded tape). Have the children enter the number that comes after the number given, then check with a key.

CHAPTER

Money and Time

Even before they enter school, many children can discriminate among a penny, a nickel, and a dime. They may not always associate the correct coin with the correct name, but they usually use one of the three names when referring to a coin. Most preschoolers also develop some sense of time, and many even learn to tell time by the hour. For example, they know dinner is at 6:00, when the "little hand is on the six." "If it's on the five, it's not dinner time."

Basic concepts and skills related to money and time are formally introduced, reinforced, and expanded during the primary school years. Thus, most mathematics programs gear early number work to the development of money and time skills. Usually by the end of first grade, children can tell time to the half hour, and most can recognize the difference between the five coins by name and value. Many can even find the value of coin groups to 25 cents and make change for amounts up to 10 cents.

As children's experience and training base broadens, most develop a feel for time that helps them know how long they have to complete an activity or wait for another to begin. Most youngsters also develop a general sense of how much money they need for particular items ("lots" or "a little"), what change is, and how long it will take to save enough money for something they want or need.

As children learn to handle larger amounts of money and to tell time more accurately, the vocabulary involved places greater demands on both receptive and expressive language skills. Children must now begin to deal with familiar words in new contexts. Expressions like "ten minutes *ago*," "*in* a half hour," "*later*," and "making *change*" all include words that may be part of their vocabularies, but are now presented in a different way. If children use these expressions, it should entail more than merely parroting what others say. For example, when a child says, "I'll be there in 10 minutes," it should be based on a real understanding of the underlying concepts.

As students progress through school, the demands on using time and money efficiently increase. By the time children reach the middle grades, they are expected to read time to the nearest minute and deal with large money amounts. Older students in middle school or junior high are expected to count out money amounts and make change without relying on paper-and-pencil calculations. They also must learn to write checks and handle bank accounts—daily living skills of practical importance.

Children's success in mastering concepts and skills for money and time can be greatly hindered by learning disabilities. Many of the tasks outlined in the preceding paragraphs require good visual and auditory memory, discrimination, and sequencing skills. To count money, for example, students must be able to discriminate between size differences and accurately retrieve, from memory, the correct name and/or value to match a given size. To tell time from a standard clock, they must discriminate the size of the hands as well as the correct digit and its meaning. Using money and time on a daily basis involves a high degree of visual and auditory memory, as well as visual and spatial discrimination.

This chapter addresses some of the common problems learning disabled students face in trying to master money and time skills. The first part of the chapter focuses on money. An introductory section suggests materials to keep in the classroom for use in teaching money. The remaining sections present ways to approach the following topics with learning disabled students:

1. Coin discrimination;

2. Counting money amounts to $1.00 (using a quarter, rather than coin substitutes for the quarter, for amounts over $.25);

3. Counting money amounts to $1.00 (using coin substitutes for the quarter for amounts over $.25);

4. Paying for items and making change greater than $1.00.

The last part of the chapter deals with teaching time to learning disabled students. After an introductory section on classroom materials helpful for this purpose, ways of handling the following topics are explored:

5. Reading clock times;

6. Reading and writing clock times;

7. Naming the correct hour;

8. Understanding the many ways to tell time; and

9. Understanding and using temporal expressions.

As in previous chapters, for each topic section, a basic sequence of activities and exercises is presented. When necessary, alternate approaches for meeting the needs of particular disabilities are also noted.

CLASSROOM MATERIALS FOR TEACHING MONEY

Concrete teaching aids and real-life applications help children build and develop confidence with new concepts and skills. This principle is particularly important when teaching children how to handle money. The following materials are useful for this purpose.

- Real money

- Coin and paper money stamps

- Ink pads and bottles of colored ink

- Laminated coin lines

- Play money, including color-coded coins

- Dice games and other money activities

- Practice pages (kept in a file, ready for use)

- Empty food cans (labels on, lids cut from the bottom) or other items for a play store

Real money should be used whenever possible, particularly in early activities (keep a bag of change—locked up when not in use). Experience has shown that even very young children can learn to handle money with care and not lose it. After all: "Money has *value*. We use it to buy what we need and want. People work hard to *earn* money. The coins in the bag belong to the teacher who has worked hard to get them, but who is loaning them out so we can learn about money." These are very basic concepts that are part of "money sense" for young learners.

As work progresses, continue to use real money whenever possible. At times, however, this is not practical, and money substitutes must be introduced. In such instances, it is essential that any play money and pictures used resemble real money as closely as possible. Like many of their peers, learning disabled students find it difficult enough to relate money substitutes to real money without the added frustration of poor resemblance.

Coin stamps, both heads and tails, and paper money stamps are useful items, which can be purchased from many school supply companies. Ink pads are needed for money stamps; keep several on hand for use with different colors of ink. Color-coded coins can be useful when teaching and reinforcing coin discrimination and when dealing with children with figure-ground problems. Use of these coins eliminates the interference of any learning deficit while strengthening retention and overlearning. Figure 3-1 is an example of a color-coded coin line that is easy to make, using either stamps and colored inks or colored paper. The sample can be laminated, covered with contact paper, or kept in a plastic holder for durability.

penny	nickel	dime	quarter	half dollar
1¢	5¢	10¢	25¢	50¢

Coin Line

Penny = brown
nickel = black   quarter = blue
dime = yellow   half dollar = red

Figure 3-1

Although it takes time, realistic simulated money can be made using coin stamps and either colored paper or crayons. (Again, make sure the pennies are brown and the silver coins grey so they resemble real coins as much as possible.) Laminate the coins or cover them with clear contact paper to extend their lifetime. Students with severe visual discrimination problems may benefit initially from coins which match the colors used on the coin number line described in the previous paragraph. Once they have a stronger visual image, they can gradually proceed to using more closely color-related paper coins.

The following sections suggest how to use the color-coded coins and coin line. Additionally, other money and many dice games can be played to reinforce money skills. A master copy of several types of coin dice is provided in Figure 3-2. Ideas for using the dice are also included in the sections that follow.

Throughout the chapter, various worksheet ideas will be illustrated. These can be kept on file and be readily available for homework, learning centers, and extra reinforcement of specific skills.

Figure 3-2

COIN DISCRIMINATION

Problem area: Inability to discriminate coins by name and value.

Typical disabilities affecting progress: Difficulty with visual discrimination, receptive and expressive language, figure-ground, and auditory memory.

Background: Very young children, preschool to about age 6, often have difficulty discriminating fine differences in size while readily seeing gross differences such as that between the size of a dinner plate and a quarter. Developmentally, they may not be ready to do much more than order coins by size with the aid of finger tracing or matching one on top of the other.

With continual exposure, most primary-grade children gradually learn to distinguish coins. They begin to look more closely at them, study them, and feel them. Their understanding of "bigger" and "smaller" may be weak and, thus, it often is meaningless or even confusing to say, "The bigger one is a nickel." What does "bigger" mean? How can it be bigger if the dime is worth 10 cents and the nickel is worth 5 cents? Does "bigger" mean size or value? Through repeated experience, careful instruction, and developmental growth, children learn to associate the correct name with a given coin. By the time they are 6 or 7, most children can accurately match the coin with its name, and often with its value.

For children with disabilities like those just listed, the discrete differences and sequencing required in discriminating coins preclude much chance of them automatically making these associations. A detailed analysis highlights the requirements and sequences involved in responding to the following request: "Give me the nickel, Peter."

- Receptively, the child must understand the meaning of the word "nickel."

- The child must be able to see that coins are, in fact, different sizes.

- The child must be able to (a) revisualize a nickel or (b) tactually feel the difference between the nickel and other coins.

- Once the image has been recalled, the child must be able to retain it long enough to associate it with the correct coin.

For most children, these steps probably take about 1 or 2 seconds to complete once the process has been mastered. However, for the learning disabled child, the effort to comply with the request may end in total frustration, wild guesses, or a refusal to answer. More specialized instruction, such as that outlined below, is needed, therefore. The general approach presented can be adapted to the child's current level. When dealing remedially with an older student, for example, all five coins are introduced, one at a time, in the manner suggested. In introducing the coins to younger children, on the other hand, greater care is taken to correlate the work with the early number program. The quarter, for example, would be introduced only after children can meaningfully read and write 2-digit numbers.

Suggested Sequence of Activities and Exercises

1. **Penny first.** The penny should be introduced first because it is more readily distinguished by its color. Show the children all five coins, but focus only on the penny. Let them pick it up and feel it. If they do not already know it, tell them its name (penny). Discuss similarities and differences between the penny and other coins in the pile. Emphasize color, size, images on the coin, and whether its edge is rough or smooth.

2. **Coin line.** Have the children place the penny on top of the penny pictured on a coin line. Show them how the size and color of the two coins are the same. Some children have difficulty relating a real coin to its picture, thus the need in early lessons to carefully relate the two. If possible, allow the children to use a penny coin stamp on brown construction paper to make their own penny pictures.

3. **Penny line-up.** Give each child an envelope of coins (pennies and silver coins). Have them sort out all the pennies and place them under the penny of the coin line. Personal coin lines may be given to each child for this purpose.

4. **Penny match.** Give each child about 15 pennies, using real coins if possible. If the number of students makes this impractical, use a penny stamp on brown construction paper to make play coins. Provide an activity sheet like the one in Figure 3-3 and instruct the children to cover each penny on the page with the ones given to them. "The penny pictures on the activity sheet are not colored, but they have the same picture and are the same size as the pennies you have. Can you find all of them?" If the page is covered correctly, the pennies should form the letter "P." When naming the penny, discuss how one makes the "P" sound.

Figure 3-3

- *Variation:* For those children who learn best kinesthetically, give tracing paper along with the activity sheet of Figure 3-3. Ask them to place (or tape) the tracing paper over the sheet. Then, using a penny or a stencil the shape and size of a penny, show them how to trace over each penny on the sheet. When finished, the shape formed by the tracing should be the letter "P."

5. **One penny is worth 1¢.** Discuss how money has value, since we use it to buy what we need and want. Introduce the cent sign. Explain that a number with a cent sign (¢) next to it means that the number stands for an amount of money. The value of a penny is 1¢. Write on the board: 1 penny = 1¢. (Use "1 penny → 1¢" if children do not understand the equal sign.) Give each student about 10 pennies. Ask questions and carry out activities like the following:

   - Have students put four pennies in a pile in front of them. "How many cents do you have there?" . . . "Put 2¢ in a pile in front of you. How many pennies do you have?"

   - "Suppose I wanted to trade with you. If I gave you three pennies, how many cents would you give me so we'd have a fair trade?"

   - "If you give me 5¢ and I give you four pennies back, is that a fair trade?"

   - "Suppose you are at a store and want to buy some gum. Look at the price tag (5¢). How many pennies do you need to pay the cashier?"

   Continue until students recognize and understand the meaning of cent in relation to pennies.

6. **What coin next?** Use activities similar to those above to introduce other coins. The normal presentation of coins, in order, is: penny, nickel, dime, quarter, and half dollar. If a child has difficulty with visual discrimination or size perception, use the sequence penny, *quarter*, nickel, dime, and half dollar. In our experience, this sequence is easier because of the greater difference in size between the penny and the quarter. Even when size perception is no problem for students, deviation from the standard sequence is often recommended. After the penny and nickel, introduce the quarter. Both its value and its size are big.

7. **Size it up.** As the coins are introduced, provide reinforcement pages, like that of Figure 3-4, which are color coded to match the coin line. The purpose of these pages is to help the children respond to differences in coin size and emphasize the value of each coin. Initially children match the colored paper coins with the circles. Then these coins are replaced with real coins and grad-

ually the color cues are eliminated. Children can be asked to name the coins they have placed on the sheet.

Coin outlines and values match
colors on Coin Line (Figure 3-1)

Figure 3-4

8. **Bingo.** For children with language deficits, a bingo game is a fun way to build up a weakness while using a possible strength—visual perception. The calling cards, the markers, the pictures on the bingo cards, or the space beneath each picture on the cards can be color coded to match the coin line colors. In the space below each coin picture in Figure 3-5, a child would place the correct word or value when it is called. The calling cards (Figure 3-6) list the name

Figure 3-5

Figure 3-6

of the coin on one side and both the coin and the name on the other. The coin picture clue helps the student know what to call the coin. The winner is the child who covers a row in any direction—down, across, or diagonally.

- *Variation:* Instead of writing the names of coins on the calling cards, write coin values. Children then cover the coin that matches the value called. For example, if 10¢ is called, they place a 10¢ marker beneath a picture of a dime.

COUNTING MONEY AMOUNTS TO ONE DOLLAR USING QUARTERS

Problem area: Inability to determine the value of a group of coins in which quarters rather than quarter coin substitutes are used.

Typical disabilities affecting progress: Difficulty with expressive language, sequential memory, visual perception, particularly figure-ground, and closure.

Background: Once coin recognition and basic values of coins have been established, most children learn to find the value of groups of coins. Early work starts with values up to 10 cents and gradually extends to counting money amounts to one dollar. At this point, it is helpful for children to begin to learn automatically to relate two nickels to 10¢. The ability to do so makes handling money and coin group values much easier.

Two prerequisites to successfully finding the value of coin groups are: (a) the ability to count on from midpoint, and (b) a strong understanding that quantity (size) and value do not always match. There may be fewer coins than the actual cent value, and it is generally easier to recognize small, known groups within a larger group and to count on from that value. A child's ability to perform these tasks often depends upon being able to apply skip counting by 2s, 5s, or 10s to a money situation and to *count on* by 2s, 5s, or 10s from various starting points.

Children having the difficulties identified at the beginning of this section may be unable to use their skip counting skills in this way. They may not recognize what pattern to use or when to switch from one pattern to another. The activities below are intended to help children cope with these problems. The following prerequisites are assumed:

- Students can recognize a number pattern as one which involves skip counting by 2s, 5s, or 10s.

- When dealing with numbers alone, apart from money, students can *continue* a skip counting pattern that has been started.

- Students have been introduced to "switch" skip counting (e.g., they start counting by 5s, then continue counting by 10s, or vice versa). An example of a written exercise that reinforces this skill is illustrated in Figure 3-7.

25   30   35   __ __ __ 60   70   __ __

20   30   40   __ __ __ 75   80   85   __ __

Sample number sequence to reinforce switch skip counting

Figure 3-7

- Students can recognize the following substitutions: two nickels for a dime, five pennies for a nickel, two quarters for a half dollar, three quarters for 75 cents, and four quarters for one dollar. Automatic recognition of these coin equivalents is desirable. An example showing how to use tailed coins on a money line to reinforce coin equivalents is shown in Figure 3-8. Placed end to end, it takes *two* nickels to equal (the length of) the dime. Coin "tails" are made from masking tape, attached to the coin, then folded lengthwise in half. Tails can be colored to match the colors of the coins on the coin line.

Figure 3-8

Suggested Sequence of Activities and Exercises

1. **Count it out.** Keep dittos on hand, such as that illustrated in Figure 3-9. Each line should be a different color. Use colored dittos or give the child four crayons, each clearly different in color from the others but including a green and a red. The child underlines each row of words with a different color, beginning with the green and ending with the red. Next, give the children a shape stencil like that shown in Figure 3-10. The four shapes should be outlined to match, respectively, the colors of the four rows in Figure 3-9. Given a group of coins, the children place them inside the shapes in the appropriate sequence—greatest valued coins first, pennies last. This step will initially require teacher assistance. After grouping the coins, the child fills in the blanks on the worksheet. As each blank is filled, the child should be instructed to read the entire sentence aloud before going on to the next blank. For children with closure difficulties who have trouble finding starting points and continuing patterns, the colors provide the needed cues. For those who have trouble expressing thoughts or retaining a sequence, verbalizing the words "I have . . ." helps focus attention and initiate the thought process. The colors will help maintain the sequence.

2. **"Switch" skip counting.** Finding the value of coin groups can be difficult because it requires "switch" skip counting. Due to integrative processing deficits or perseveration, a student may be unable to switch from one counting pattern to another as so often required when using money. Consider the coin group of Figure 3-11. One way to organize the counting is shown in Figure

I have ____.   I have ____.
Now I have ____.   Now I have ____.
Now I have ____.   Now I have ____.
Now I have ____.   Now I have ____.

Figure 3-9

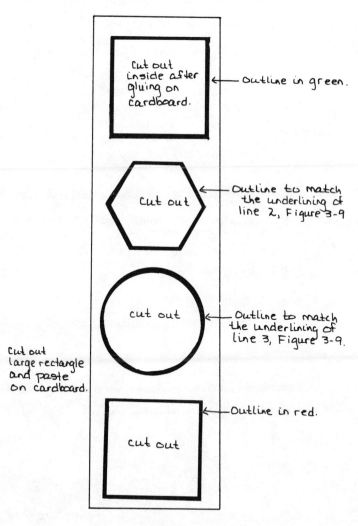

Cut out inside after gluing on cardboard.
← Outline in green.

Cut out
← Outline to match the underlining of line 2, Figure 3-9

cut out
← Outline to match the underlining of line 3, Figure 3-9.

Cut out large rectangle and paste on cardboard.

cut out
← Outline in red.

Figure 3-10

Figure 3-11

3-12. In this grouping, three counting patterns are involved: fives, tens, and ones. To help develop the needed counting skills, keep charts such as that presented in Figure 3-13. Insert the charts into plastic holders and have the children write on the holders with grease pencils. Have them put a large X in any two squares in each row. Instruct them to write into the empty box the money value obtained after they count the coins to the left *and* above the empty space. If fine-motor coordination is a problem, eliminate the writing (the goal is to develop switch counting, not writing). Have the children place chips, with the correct value written on them, in the empty spaces. When the card is filled in, the children can use an answer key to grade it, or the teacher or another student can check it. Children then can read the entire sequence aloud.

Examples (refer to Figure 3-13):

> "Row 1: 25-27¢"
> "Row 2: 10-15-25¢"

- *Follow-Up:* Counting money requires good auditory processing and visual, auditory, and sequential memory. Writing values down while counting aids learning, but eventually one has to be able to add coin values mentally. Consequently, the next step in the preceding activity involves having

Figure 3-12

Figure 3-13

children cover two squares in each row as before. Instead of writing the total value obtained, however, they are to count the entire sequence aloud to the teacher or a friend, or into a tape recorder.

3. **Money line** (alternate approach). Another approach to helping students count to determine the value of a group of coins consists of using tailed coins on a money line. In Figure 3-14a, for example, the child is given one quarter, one nickel, two dimes, and one penny to count. Tailed coins for each of these coins are chosen and placed end to end on the money line, greatest valued coins first (Figure 3-14b). Figure 3-15 illustrates the use of the money line to build or reinforce skills for "switch" skip counting. The children can practice using the tailed coins or refer to them, as necessary, until they master the technique using real coins.

Figure 3-14

Figure 3-15

COUNTING MONEY AMOUNTS TO ONE DOLLAR USING QUARTER COIN SUBSTITUTES

Problem area: Difficulty determining the value of a group of coins which includes a cluster of coins equivalent to the quarter rather than a quarter itself.

Typical disabilities affecting progress: Difficulty with integrative processing and closure.

Background: There are many ways to make amounts like 76¢ or 63¢ using different combinations of coins. Children must learn to recognize various equivalent coin combinations. This is usually most difficult for larger amounts—50¢ to one dollar. The group of coins in Figure 3-16 is representative of a frequently used coin substitution. After a fair amount of experience counting coins, most children automatically recognize two dimes and one nickel as being worth 25 cents. The learning disabled child may recognize this, too. Unfortunately, however, there may not be an automatic transfer in thought to the conclusion "a quarter—therefore, the value of this group is 50 cents, because two quarters make 50 cents."

Figure 3-16

One approach to this problem would be to teach children to group the coins differently and to find another counting pattern. They could, for example, begin with the single coin that is worth the most money. However, for most older children, it is more expedient to recognize the substitution and learn to use it. The following activities help develop this skill.

Suggested Sequences of Activities and Exercises

1. **The odd pieces.** Younger children enjoy puzzles. Those shown in Figure 3-17 can be cut out, pasted on 3 × 5 index cards, and used for individual

activities in a learning center. Note the circling to cue recognition of the three coins as one unit, equivalent in value to a quarter. To encourage thinking, include one or two distractors in the puzzle set, like that shown in Figure 3-18. Children could be challenged to find the odd pieces (the distractors).

2. **Bingo.** Make bingo cards, similar to those in Figure 3-5. The calling cards should have coins pictured on them like those on the right of the Figure 3-17 puzzle pieces. The game is played like regular bingo.

3. **Fill in.** For older children, keep dittos such as those in Figure 3-19. Figure 3-19a is especially helpful for students with expressive language deficits. Gradually the transition can be made to pages like that of Figure 3-19b.

Figure 3-17

Correct amount and correct match

Distractor. Incorrect amount but correct match

Figure 3-18

a)

50¢ = ___ dimes ___ nickels and ___ quarter

75¢ = ___ quarters ___ dimes and ___ nickels

75¢ = ___ half dollar ___ dimes and ___ nickel

Figure 3-19a

b)

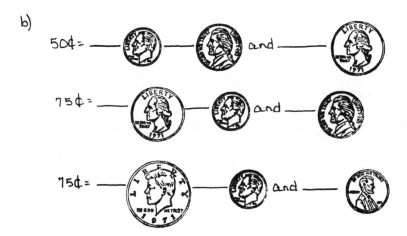

Figure 3-19b

PAYING FOR ITEMS AND MAKING CHANGE FOR AMOUNTS TO ONE DOLLAR

Problem areas: Difficulty selecting, from a larger collection of coins, money needed to pay for an item; difficulty making change for values to one dollar.

Typical disabilities affecting progress: Difficulty with auditory sequencing, integrative processing, closure, sequential memory, visual figure-ground.

Background: Being able to count and tell the value of a group of coins is a prerequisite to a more challenging skill: being able to select, from a larger collection, those coins needed to make a given amount. This latter skill is needed in day-to-day situations as one examines the coins in a purse or pocket to see if there is enough to pay for an item. Some learning disabled students cannot apply the first skill to real-life situations. Children with figure-ground difficulties often have problems finding the coins they want because they cannot sort them out from the group. Other children may become frustrated because the simplest (most familiar) way of making up a given amount is not possible with the coins they have. The first set of activities below suggests ways of handling these problems. The other activities in this section focus on another important skill—checking change received. Modern cash registers subtract the cost from the amount given to a clerk, telling how much change should be given in return. The most efficient way to check in this situation is to *count up* from the cost until the amount paid is reached. This, of course, is the common procedure used by cashiers for giving change if their registers do not internally subtract and display the amount to be given back.

Learning to count out one's change in this way is perhaps the most difficult money skill to master. Children must realize that the *exact* amount of money needed to pay for an item is not always available. Sometimes one has to pay *more* than an item is worth, and then receive change in return. To determine the amount of money to be given (or received) as change, a new counting process is required. When counting to find the value of a group of coins, children often start with the single coin of *greatest* value. It is now necessary to retain the purchase price in memory and count on from this cost using *smaller* valued coins first. Other coins are added until the amount paid is reached. Children with sequential-memory problems usually find this very difficult. Other children having the disabilities identified above may fail to recognize the different skip counting patterns involved or be unable to produce them automatically. The second set of activities that follows has proven helpful in dealing with these problems.

Suggested Sequence of Activities and Exercises

Paying for an Item

1. **You find.** Some students with figure-ground difficulties find it hard to locate, from a larger collection, the coins they need to pay for an item. For them, laminated cards and priced items such as those of Figure 3-20 are helpful. The cards show the coins available to pay for an item. The child draws a card and takes (from a bank of extra coins) all the coins pictured on the card. If necessary, allow the student to place coins on top of those pictured until the card is full. These coins are then placed in a separate pile. Next show the child a picture of an item to be purchased, such as the bat in the first example of Figure 3-20. With a grease pencil draw a circle around the coins on the child's card that are needed to pay for that item. "You need a dime and a nickel" (Figure 3-20a). Instruct the child to select coins from the pile to cover those circled on the card. Repeat, using different cards or different items to be purchased. Children gradually learn to circle and tell the needed coins independently. As they become more proficient, the circling can be eliminated and they can merely cover the correct cards. In our experience, this approach leads to independent recognition of needed coins.

2. **Pay.** Set up a "store" in the classroom and give each child a purse or envelope of coins. (Alternatively, a container of coins could be placed on the cashier's counter for all the children to use.) At first, as students pay for items, accept any coins they give to pay for an item (as long as the amount given is correct). For example, a child may choose to use two nickels rather than a dime. By

a) Example 1

15¢

b) Example 2

20¢

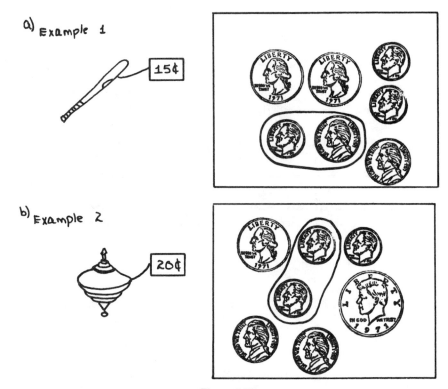

Figure 3-20

observing a child's pattern of coin selection, the teacher can gradually suggest better choices, in a manner that is logical to that student. One might provide enough coins so that a child can pay for a given item at least two different ways. If the child uses the *fewest possible coins* to pay for an item, a compliment is in order. If, on the other hand, the child gives a combination that involves more coins than required, point out that there is a better way. "Yes, a dime and five pennies equals 15¢. That is good, but did you notice that you can use one nickel in place of these five pennies?" Or, "You used six coins. Can you pay using only two coins?"

> *Follow-Up:* Use worksheets such as that illustrated in Figure 3-21. If necessary, use the coin line color to outline the circles on the page. Gradually, eliminate this prompt.

3. **Use what you have.** Point out that sometimes we do not have the proper coins to pay the way we would like. For example, we might want to buy ice cream that costs 25¢. If we do not have a quarter, then two dimes and a nickel, or five nickels, or even 25 pennies will do. Give the student several coins and

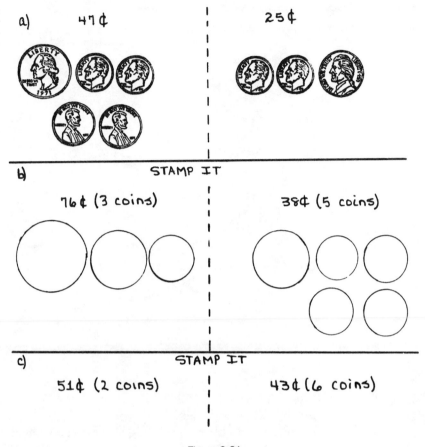

a)   47¢   25¢

STAMP IT

b)

76¢ (3 coins)   38¢ (5 coins)

STAMP IT

c)
51¢ (2 coins)   43¢ (6 coins)

Figure 3-21

ask for an amount of money that cannot be made in the "usual way" with the available coins. For example, give five nickels and ask for 20¢. As children become more proficient, give a quarter, five nickels, and four pennies for this task to force selection from a larger group of coins.

- *Follow-Up:* Use worksheets like that of Figure 3-22. For the example shown, the children can circle or place real coins on those pictured to show 20¢. If necessary, use coin line colors to outline the coins needed in the first few exercises.

Making Change for Amounts Paid up to One Dollar

1. **Count up.** Use tailed coins on a money line, as in Figure 3-23, to introduce the idea of counting up to get from one number (the cost) to another (the

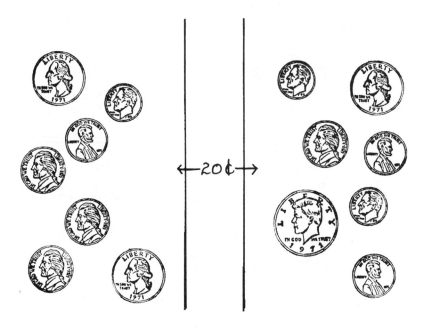

Figure 3-22

amount paid). This approach concretizes the process of counting up and aids visual memory. A set of price tag cards, like that shown, is also needed. Children draw a card and place it on the line as illustrated to indicate where one starts the count. Tailed coins are then used to dramatize the counting on to 25¢. Children should be encouraged to use as *few coins as possible*—four pennies and one nickel rather than nine pennies in this example (Figure 3-23).

Figure 3-23

2. **Go and stop.** At this point, students with auditory-sequencing or memory deficits usually find it easier to turn to worksheets such as that illustrated in Figure 3-24. The first example is for younger children with low reading vocabulary, the second its parallel for older students. Students fill in the first four blanks. Then, as they count up from the cost, they check each coin as if they were actually picking it up. Next they count and record the change—in this example, 9¢.

Figure 3-24

To cue meaning, the words "go on" ("begin at") could be written in green and "stop at" in red. For those in need of extra cueing, the word "cost" ("price") could also be coded in green and the words "you give" ("amount given") in red. Answer lines would be colored to match the words. Gradually, all colors would be eliminated as the vocabulary meanings and the counting process itself become internalized. The amount of information to be personally recorded by students is also gradually reduced as they become more proficient at counting. Recording the numbers to "go on" and "stop at" is dropped first. As short-term memory or counting skills improve, the price and the amount given may be eliminated (Figure 3-24).

3. **Real coins now.** As before, but provide real coins rather than stamped pictures of coins. At first, it may be helpful to keep a worksheet showing the coin stamp as reference. If children tend to perseverate, do not be too quick to eliminate the writing while using real coins. It serves to break the counting and hence decreases perseveration.

Note: Children with integrative processing deficits may have difficulty recognizing whether or not they have the correct coins to pay exactly or to make the needed change. They may try to ignore the problem, as in Figure 3-25. In this example, the value of the dimes became meaningless and they were treated as pennies. To help, have the children first fill in the charts of Activity 2. Then have them compare the coins they checked with the coins they have. In the example of Figure 3-25, the first coin needed is a penny so the child cannot give the needed change.

Figure 3-25

WRITING MONEY AMOUNTS
GREATER THAN ONE DOLLAR

Problem area: Reversal tendencies or other difficulties in writing money amounts using the dollar sign and decimal point.

Typical disabilities affecting progress: Difficulty with spatial organization; visual perception.

Background: Children who are unable to organize their space due to visual or perceptual deficits or spatial disorganization may have considerable difficulty writing down money values. For example, since we say, "Three dollars and 16 cents," children often reverse the position of the dollar value and the dollar sign (see Figure 3-26). Or they may not associate all the words with symbols. Specifically, they may not "see" the dollar sign and decimal point when reading or writing the numbers. The activities outlined below are directed toward helping students with these problems.

Three dollars and sixteen cents = 3$.16

Figure 3-26

Suggested Sequence of Activities and Exercises

1. **Dollar sign.** For those who have reversal tendencies, it often helps to approach the problem in small steps. If children learn well through kinesthetic involvement, have them finger trace felt numerals and symbols, *dollar value first, then the sign.* Then have them rewrite the pattern traced—*dollar value first, then the sign.* Although this is an unusual order, it provides a more immediate association between words and symbols. Each time a word is said, something is written. The more traditional way requires the student to write one symbol ($) while saying or thinking an unrelated symbol (e.g., 4). Figure 3-27 shows a sample page that might be used as a follow-up to this exercise. First, in Step 1, the children finger trace examples and write four dollars ($4) as just described.

In Step 2 the decimal point is introduced and associated with the word "and." In the last step the number of cents is included. All three steps provide space (after the "equals" sign on the worksheet) for children to write the money amount independently.

Step 1 *

$4 = __ __ $8 = __ __
$3 - __ __ $7 = __ __

Step 2
$4. = ____ $8. = ____
$3. = ____ $7. = ____

Step 3
$4. 5 2 = ____ $8. 9 1 = ____
$3. 6 7 = ____ $7. 2 3 = ____

* Bold marks are green; dotted lines are red; the decimal point and dollar sign are black.

Figure 3-27

2. **Greatest value.** This is a practice activity for two or three players. Provide the following five dice:

- Die 1: "$" written on each of the six sides

- Die 2: "." written on each of the six sides

- Die 3: 0,1,2,3,4,5

- Die 4: 0,5,6,7,8,9

- Die 5: 3,4,5,6,7,8

Also provide a five-space chart for the dice (Figure 3-28a) and a "greatest-value" record sheet for each player (Figure 3-28b). Children take turns throwing the dice and arranging them in the five spaces on the chart to show the

Figure 3-28a

Figure 3-28b

greatest dollar value possible. If the amount is written and read (aloud) correctly, it is entered on the player's record sheet for that round. The player with the greatest total after four rounds wins.

Note 1: Using grease pencils or washable markers on the laminated record sheet makes for easy reuse.

Note 2: If the column addition is too difficult for the students, use a tally system: one tally for dollar values $3.00 or less; two tallies for dollar values between $3.00 and $6.00; and three tallies for dollar values of $6.00 or greater.

3. **Follow-up.** For additional drill, keep pages on file like that of Figure 3-29. Children read, then write the given dollar value. If reading is a problem, a cassette tape for the left part of the page can be prepared for the children to use while completing the page. The color coding, important in early work, can gradually be eliminated.

Figure 3-29

Note 1: It may be preferable to have some students write the dollar value first, then the sign, as explained in Activity 1.

Note 2: Being able to read and write number words is important for checkwriting, thus worth the practice focused on in this exercise.

CLASSROOM MATERIALS FOR TEACHING TIME

Most classrooms have a wall clock and perhaps a toy clock for students to use. However, except for workbook pages, there may be little else in the room that is realistically related to teaching time. Several items can greatly aid students in acquiring time concepts and skills:

- Small clock, about four inches in diameter

- Geared clock with a knob on the back to move the hands (the hands should be clearly different in size)

- Clock stamps and ink pads (one red, one green)

The small clock is useful for children with visual discrimination or other perceptual problems. These students may have difficulty with the wall clock because it is too far away for them to make any clear discriminations. Figure 3-30 gives an example of the size and face of the smaller clock. The size of the hands is clearly different, and the minute intervals are spaced far enough apart for the

Figure 3-30

child to point with a finger or a pencil. This type of clock can be used to "feel" the time. This kinesthetic approach is often necessary for children with visual-perceptual or spatial difficulties.

Since it is impractical to teach time only on a real clock, a geared clock provides the next best aid. Children can see how the hands move at different rates. They can actually "feel" the slowness of the hour hand movement in contrast to that of the minute hand.

As digital clocks are so common, children must learn to read them. Most mathematics curricula now include a discussion of them within their chapters on time. Once children can read the numbers on a digital clock, they can be helped to make associations with the standard clock as an aid for "reading" its time.

At this point, it may be appropriate to give a word of caution regarding digital clocks. As convenient and useful as they are for teaching children to tell time, they do not help develop a *sense of time*. It is questionable, at best, whether this sense can be taught at all. The movement of time is mysterious enough, and digital clocks only reinforce the magic. A standard clock, however, at least allows some concrete way for children to develop a feel for how long an activity will last. One can, for example, use the overlay and shading technique of Figure 3-31 to illustrate the time allotted to an activity. On a digital clock this is impossible.

Plastic overlay put over clock with the amount of twelfths colored in to show time.

Figure 3-31

Clock stamps are available commercially, and they should be standard materials for every classroom. They can easily be used by both teacher and student. When drawing in the hands, be careful to distinguish clearly between the lengths of the minute and the hour hands. Figure 3-32 illustrates the type of clock stamp we have found most useful.

The sections that follow suggest ways of using these materials to help learning disabled students develop important time concepts and skills. In addition, several workpages are illustrated that can be kept on file and used for reinforcement, homework, and other independent work.

Figure 3-32

READING CLOCK TIMES

Problem area: Difficulty associating the correct hand on a standard clock with the spoken or written word.

Typical disabilities affecting progress: Difficulty with visual discrimination, visual-sequential memory, short-term memory, visual memory, expressive language.

Background: As mentioned earlier, many children develop some comprehension of time before they enter school. It is not uncommon for young children to be up earlier on school days than on weekends. Once the routine of going to school has been established, their internal clock begins to plan accordingly. They do not automatically begin dressing for school on Saturday. They may not know why they do not have to, but they have a sense that something is different.

Gradually parents' words begin to have meaning, and on school days children understand that at 8:00 it is time to leave. They may not actually tell time, but if a parent says, "In five minutes it will be eight o'clock," the child understands. Later the clock becomes more meaningful and the child thinks, "The little hand is on the 8. It must be time to go to school."

In the primary grades, intuitive understandings such as these are formally developed. While several sequences can be used to teach a child to read time from a standard clock, one of the more common is the following:

- time by the hour (e.g., 2:00)

- time by the half hour (e.g., 2:30)

- time by the quarter hour (e.g., 2:15 or 2:45)

- time by 5-minute intervals (e.g., 2:25 or 2:40)

- time by minute intervals (e.g., 2:26 or 2:41)

For most children this sequence works well. When teaching time on the hour, many teachers simplify the clock as in Figure 3-33a. Using a clock with only an hour hand makes it possible for most children to "tell time" as soon as they can read the numerals 1 to 12. Then the child can relate this one-handed clock to a spinner and "read time" by telling the number the hand is closest to. When children can tell time to the nearest hour in this way, the teacher can point out the hour hand on a *two-handed clock*. The next step is to practice telling time on this type of clock by focusing on the hour hand as in Figure 3-33b. If necessary in early work with the two-handed clock, children may be instructed to cover the minute hand.

When children can read and write 2-digit numbers, the spinner idea can be introduced for reading minutes (Figure 3-33c). Now the child tells time more precisely by reading the "hour" then the "minute" spinner. Gradually, the association can be made between the minutes and the 12 clock digits. Additional experiences with a geared clock can help children see that as the hour hand moves from one hour to the next, the minute hand travels all the way around the clock. Children with good visual perception and long-term memory quickly learn to associate what one says for given configurations of the hands. For example, "The little hand moves from one hour to the next, the minute hand travels all the way around the clock."

a)

b)

c)

Figure 3-33

The above approach often does not work with students who have memory difficulties as there is too much to recall and the sequence is not consistent. Instead, these students often benefit more from learning first to tell time by the hour and then by 5-minute increments. Emphasis is still on the meaning of the clock hands, but visual memory and sequencing are reinforced because the student gradually moves around the clock in a consistent manner. Additionally, students with memory problems, who may not automatically remember to say 6:45, for example, have a way of helping themselves by counting by fives. Later, after the student has learned to tell time in this manner, emphasis can be put on recognizing fractional segments of half hour and quarter hour.

Students using the "5-minute" approach especially benefit from using the spinner described in Figure 3-33. The spinner provides a visual, logical framework for reading minutes and aids in recall when memory fails. In addition, as fractional segments are emphasized, most children can more easily learn to count on from these points.

Learning handicapped children, particularly those with the disabilities described at the beginning of this section, may find even these simple approaches to telling time difficult. One common problem relates to correctly locating where the hands are pointing. Another involves being able correctly to associate each hand with what one should say in order to read the time indicated by the hand. For example, some learning disabled students who can skip count by fives, fail, even after repeated use of the skip counting technique, to make the necessary association. The following activities have proven successful in handling these difficulties. Since the goal is for children to read the hour first, followed by minutes, green color coding is used for hour times, red for minutes.

Suggested Sequence of Activities and Exercises

1. **Hour hand first.** On a large tagboard circle, glue or draw small circles at each of the 12 clock positions, as in Figure 3-34a. Make a deck of 52 cards, all circles, similar to those shown in Figure 3-34b. The circles should be the same size as those drawn in the clock positions of the larger circle. Place the numerals 1 through 12 (four of each numeral) in the same relative position on the smaller circles as they would appear on a standard clock. Write the numeral 13 on the remaining four circles. The numerals and the small arrow that simulates the hour hand should be green. The child "deals," placing one card from the deck face down on each of the 12 clock positions of the large circle. A 13th card is placed in the center. This procedure continues until all 52 cards have been placed on the board (Figure 3-35). The child turns over the first card of the center pile and places it, face up, under the pile on the board that corresponds to the clock position shown (see Figure 3-36). The

top card of that pile is then turned over and play continues as before. Every time "13" is turned over, it is placed face up under the four cards in the center. The child wins the game if all the cards are placed face up in the proper position on the board before the four cards with "13" are uncovered.

- *Variation:* As before, but the child says the hour time whenever a card is properly placed.

2. **Now minutes.** A game similar to that of Activity 1 can be played to reinforce the skip counting pattern of the minute hand. This time, make 52 cards beginning with 00 and stopping at 60 (the 60 is for the center pile). The hand pointing to the minutes numeral must be noticeably longer than the hour hand in Activity 1, and red, as shown in Figure 3-37. Use the large circle of

Figure 3-34

Figure 3-35

Figure 3-36

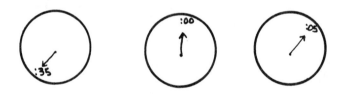

Figure 3-37

Activity 1, but place a rim around the outside containing 12 circles for the 5-minute times (see Figure 3-38).

3. **Both hands.** Play the following bingo-type game. Make a set of calling cards picturing times on standard clocks. Use green for the hour hand and red for the minute hand. Provide 4 × 4 inch gameboards for students with times written at the bottom of each square, as shown in Figure 3-39. Give each child 16 "clock" chips that fit into the space above each time written on the gameboard (see Figure 3-40). These can be made by placing gummed labels on ordinary gameboard chips and drawing a clock face on the label. Do not color code the hands on the clock chips. To play, a caller (child or teacher) holds up a color-coded clock. Players decide whether the time shown by that clock is on their gameboard. If so, they place a clock chip showing the same

Circle from
Activity 1

Surrounded
by "minute rim."

Figure 3-38

4:30	3:10	6:55	8:40
9:20	2:15	7:30	10:50
5:40	6:05	12:45	9:10
8:00	2:30	1:25	4:35

Figure 3-39

Figure 3-40

time on the gameboard just above the written time. The winner is the first person to complete a row in any direction.

Note: If the gameboards are covered with acetate or clear contact paper, color coding can be used, when needed, and wiped off. Hour digit(s) would be green, minute digits red.

- *Variation 1:* Alter the activity by placing clock faces on the gameboard and color-coded numbers on the calling cards. Game chips would also contain the written clock times. If necessary, these can also be color coded.

- *Variation 2:* Place clock chips upside down on the board to match the clock times shown. As a card is held up, the players decide whether they have that time on their individual board. If so, the chip is turned over. The first player to complete correctly a row in any direction wins.

READING AND WRITING CLOCK TIMES

Problem area: Difficulty telling time on a real clock.

Typical disabilities affecting progress: Difficulty with spatial organization, visual perception, visual-sequential memory, short-term memory, and expressive language.

Background: Many learning disabled children need a considerable amount of paper-and-pencil practice before they can use a real clock to tell time. The paper-and-pencil activities provide:

- Overlearning;

- Less interference from visual-perception deficits because of the proximity of the paper;

- Kinesthetic involvement for children who need it (They can run their fingers or pencils along the paper and feel where the hand is); and

- Sequencing cues.

The following ideas can be used to accomplish these goals.

Suggested Sequence of Activities and Exercises

1. **Color-coded dittos.** Several types of dittos can be filed for ready use. In Figure 3-41 the numerals 1 through 12 are green while 00 through 55 are red. The boxes below the clock are also coded, the first green, the second red. The use of boxes rather than lines during early practice strengthens the relationship between digital and standard clocks, a relationship that must be directly reinforced for some children. One approach consists of having the students themselves draw a simple version of a digital clock and then use that picture as a model for the worksheet boxes.

2. **Fade the cue.** Figure 3-42 illustrates one way of gradually fading the color cue. First the red numbers are replaced with red dots. The next step eliminates the colors on the clock hands. For some children, especially those with severe visual-perception difficulties, the colors in the boxes may be eliminated first, followed by the colors on the hands. An alternative would be to keep pages on file, such as those shown in Figure 3-43, with a color-coded example at the top. In Figure 3-43a, the remainder of the clocks have only green and red lines for answers. Make the green line noticeably shorter than the red line. Provide auditory cueing by asking the child which hand on the clock looks most like the short green line. "Which hand do you 'go' on?"

3. **Card to help.** For students needing color reinforcement, especially as they make the transition to the real clock, keep a tagboard clock in the room. Cover

Figure 3-41

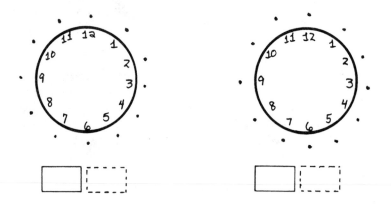

Figure 3-42

it with acetate or contact paper so it can be color coded when needed. If color cueing is necessary, the child can use a green and red marker or grease pencil to write over the numbers. (If this proves too difficult, motorically, the teacher should do it.) The child can use this card to help associate the clock hands and the sequence for reading clock times.

4. **Strips.** As children make the transition to a real clock, they may still need to write down what they see before they are able to express it. This is especially true for:

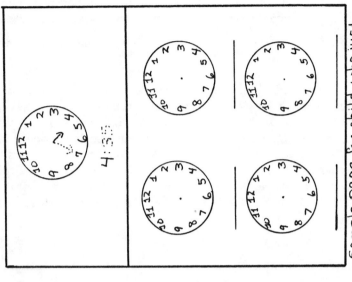

b)

4:35

Sample page for child who just needs a reminder, but is strong in skip counting by 5's. Nothing is color coded except example at the top. (Hour hand and "4" are green; dotted figures are red.)

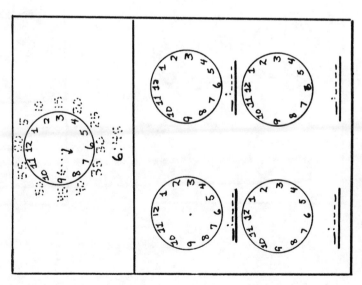

a)

6:43

Sample page for child who still needs colors but is beginning to make a transition. Bold hands and hour digits are green; dotted figures are red.

Figure 3-43

- Students with memory problems that prevent them from retaining an entire sequence; and

- Students with expressive difficulties who have trouble learning if their flow of thought is interrupted.

The writing process is an intermediate step that allows students to focus on one part of the sequence at a time until overlearning has occurred. Keep strips available such as those shown in Figure 3-44. The children can work in pairs to complete the strips. Using the geared clock, one child sets the time shown on one of the clocks in Figure 3-44a. The other writes the time down on paper, as in Figure 3-44b. If necessary, clocks on the strips can be color coded to aid students in expressing times correctly—hour first, *then* minutes. Make the hour hand green and the minute hand red, as suggested earlier.

Figure 3-44

Note: The worksheets illustrated in this section, especially those with color coding and numbers around the outside rim, make it possible to teach time even to children who are weak on skip counting by fives. For many, this approach provides the way to overlearning.

NAMING THE CORRECT HOUR

Problem area: Difficulty knowing which direction to look when the hour hand is between two numbers.

Typical disabilities affecting progress: Difficulty with spatial orientation, visual perception, and memory.

Background: Some children may know what words and numbers to associate with each hand. They may have learned which hand to look at first. Yet, they may still be uncertain about which number to use when the hour hand is between two numbers. If their spatial abilities are weak, telling them to look at the number "in front of" or "before" may be meaningless. Likewise, asking them to look at the lower number is also confusing. What is the "lower number"? There is no numeral underneath the 1. What happens when the hour hand is between the 12 and the 1? The following ideas should prove helpful in handling this problem.

Suggested Sequence of Activities and Exercises

1. **Point the way.** Make a small green arrow, as in Figure 3-45 , which fits around the small desk clock. When the children are working with the clock, have them place the arrow at the top of the hour hand so it curves around and points to the correct number. A small hook could also be used on the clock pages.

a)

b)

Figure 3-45

- *Variation:* If children have trouble manipulating the arrow, keep a clear plastic overlay that covers the clock face. Using a marker or grease pencil, draw an arrow on the face. The child can then place the plastic face over the real clock and rotate it until the arrow is in place.

2. **Reinforce.** When providing children with clock pages for practice, include the arrows on the page. Have the children run a pencil, or preferably a finger, over the line and say the number pointed to. In our experience, with continued kinesthetic reinforcement of this type, even young children are soon able to draw their own lines well enough to determine which number to look to for the hour.

UNDERSTANDING THE MANY WAYS TO TELL TIME

Problem area: Understanding temporal expressions including "past," "after," "before," and "until."

Typical disabilities affecting progress: Difficulty with spatial organization, receptive language, and abstract reasoning.

Background: Time can be expressed in many different ways. For the child with abstract reasoning or receptive language deficits, this can prove very frustrating. When looking at the clock in Figure 3-46, for example, this child is likely to hear it described in any of the following ways:

- six forty

- twenty minutes until seven

- forty minutes after six

- twenty minutes before seven

- forty minutes past six

The child is expected to associate the correct time with all the possible descriptions. For the very young child or for the student with learning disabilities, it is often impossible to make these transfers. Even though the various ways of naming a certain time may not be formally taught, most young children gradually catch on to these expressions as they mature and repeatedly hear them in daily situations. However, because of the deficits just identified, many learning disabled students may be unable to relate to all these expressions without special help.

Children who have trouble with multiple meanings or synonyms need to learn the different expressions one at a time. Initially, tell the time by using only the numbers themselves: "It is now 1:20 and it's time for math." Do not confuse

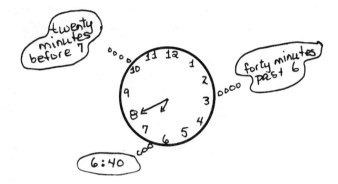

Figure 3-46

the child by saying, "It's twenty past one," until you are sure the child understands the meaning of "past." It may be difficult to use only one format consistently, but it is essential for these children to have a carefully structured program. The various terms can be incorporated into the time unit by using the circular number line described in the following paragraph. After children clearly understand the similarity between 5:20 and 20 minutes after 5, the term "past" can be introduced. Similarly, when children can relate time expressions like 5:40 and 20 minutes before 6, then "until" may be introduced. The sequence outlined here can be adapted for this purpose.

Suggested Sequence of Activities and Exercises

Minutes "After" and Minutes "Before"

1. **Circular number line.** Once children are able to tell time using numbers only, review the concepts "before" and "after" using a circular number line (spinner, with the numbers written in sequence rather than in random order). Establish the idea that, on the circle (spinner), "after" still means that the numbers get larger, only now the direction changes. Instead of going forwards and backwards, we are going around. To help establish eye movement on the clock, present pages such as those shown in Figure 3-47.

2. **Geared clock.** Once the ideas of "before" and "after" are clear to students, begin relating these concepts to a clock. Use the geared clock and ask the

Figure 3-47

children to turn the hands according to your instructions (see Figure 3-48). At his point, the single goal is to get the children to "feel" how clock hands move in different directions.

Teacher: It is 8:10.
Set a new time
that is after
8:10.

Figure 3-48

3. **Worksheets.** Practice pages of color-coded clocks, such as that in Figure 3-49, are often helpful. On these clocks, the numerals 1 through 5 are green and 7 through 11 are red. The child writes the time shown and then fills in the second blank below the clock.

Figure 3-49

Note: A prerequisite at this point is knowing which hand represents minutes and which represents hours. The children will then know what hand to look to when deciding the number of minutes "before" or "after" an hour. Children should also know, for any given hour, what the *next* hour will be. This skill is necessary to help them determine the time before and after an hour. For example, 6:40 means 20 minutes before (the next hour) 7.

4. **Toward "overlearning."** For students requiring overlearning, provide several practice pages using only one concept ("after" *or* "before"). Very shortly, however, the pages should be mixed, using both before and after. Mixing the concepts will avoid perseveration while providing opportunities for reasoning and problem solving.

5. **One step only.** Figure 3-50 shows a useful sequence for students who need help developing a one-step procedure for telling time. As shown in Figure 3-50a, students first write the time and then the equivalent expression using "minutes before" or "minutes after." Initially, decision making is aided by color coding the words "before" and "after." Students who do not have fine-motor problems should be encouraged to write over the phrase as they say it. As students become more secure with this two-step process, begin to eliminate the first

step, that of writing down the digital time, and extend the decision-making process as in Figure 3-50b.

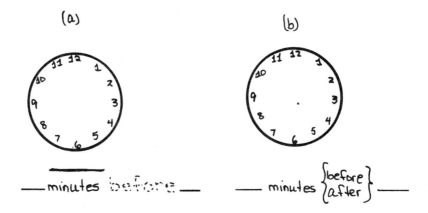

Figure 3-50

Note: An intermediate step might include highlighting each side of the clock in Figure 3-50b as in Figure 3-49.

6. **Puzzle match.** For an independent activity, make puzzle cards like those shown in Figure 3-51. Whenever the word "before" is used, the clock is on the right. For the word "after," the clock is on the left.

7. **Special help.** For children with receptive language deficits, pages like that in Figure 3-52 present a helpful way to build up comprehension. Initially, allow the children to keep a standard clock in front of them. Gradually eliminate the clock, since the use of the words "before" and "after" in time expressions requires comprehension even though no clock may be visible. If the student has reading problems, provide a tape for use in conjunction with the page.

Figure 3-51

$$3:15 \;=\; \underline{15}\;\text{minutes}\;\begin{Bmatrix}\text{before}\\\text{after}\end{Bmatrix}\;\underline{3}$$

$$\underline{\hphantom{3:15}} \;=\; \underline{\hphantom{15}}\;\text{minutes}\;\begin{Bmatrix}\text{before}\\\text{after}\end{Bmatrix}\;\underline{\hphantom{3}}$$

$$\underline{\hphantom{3:15}} \;=\; \underline{\hphantom{15}}\;\text{minutes}\;\begin{Bmatrix}\text{before}\\\text{after}\end{Bmatrix}\;\underline{\hphantom{3}}$$

$$\underline{\hphantom{3:15}} \;=\; \underline{\hphantom{15}}\;\text{minutes}\;\begin{Bmatrix}\text{before}\\\text{after}\end{Bmatrix}\;\underline{\hphantom{3}}$$

$$\underline{\hphantom{3:15}} \;=\; \underline{\hphantom{15}}\;\text{minutes}\;\begin{Bmatrix}\text{before}\\\text{after}\end{Bmatrix}\;\underline{\hphantom{3}}$$

Figure 3-52

UNDERSTANDING AND USING TEMPORAL EXPRESSIONS

Problem area: Difficulty understanding and correctly using temporal expressions like "in ____ minutes," "____ minutes ago," "earlier" and "later," and so on.

Typical disabilities affecting progress: Difficulty with spatial organization, receptive or expressive language, and closure.

Background: For some learning disabled children, the process of telling time signifies nothing more than looking at the clock and saying some numbers. While this helps them get where they have to be on time and know what time an activity is to begin, this skill alone does not enable them to predict or plan their time. Some children, particularly those with language or spatial deficits, do not understand temporal expressions like "in 10 minutes" or "15 minutes ago," "earlier" or "later." They hear a familiar word, such as "in," but because it is used in an unfamiliar context they cannot meaningfully relate to it. Being able to read time from a clock and being able to interpret, predict, and plan, based on one's ability to tell time, are two distinct abilities. It is important that children develop both these skills. The activities that follow address one aspect of developing *a sense of time* or an *awareness of time* beyond merely reading clock numbers. The goal is to help students learn and meaningfully use expressions such as "in _____ minutes," "_____ minutes ago"; "earlier," and "later." The basic ideas presented can be adapted for helping learning disabled children understand and use other temporal expressions as well.

Suggested Sequence of Activities and Exercises

Prerequisite Skills:

Children should be able to handle the following successfully:

- Skip counting by 5s to 55;

- Counting on from within this counting sequence, with visual reinforcement;

- Understanding the meanings of "before" and "after" for clock times;

- Understanding which hand moves most rapidly and, ideally, associate it with minutes;

- Identifying the minute hand on the clock and realizing that one counts on from this hand (the minute hand, not the hour hand) to determine "in _____ minutes" or "_____ ago."

Basic Sequence

1. **Move forward to see.** Set a time on a geared or a real clock. At first, use only "5-minute" times like 2:15, 2:25, or 2:40. Have the children tell or write the time. Then, while moving the hands of the clock, ask the question, "What time will it be in 5 minutes?" As you say ". . . *in* 5 minutes," emphasize the word "in" and move the hands of the clock. The children then say or write the new time. Continue this procedure until the concept of "in" is firmly established. Do not change the hour during the activity.

2. **Move back.** Use the same procedure to answer the question, "What time was it 5 minutes ago?" Initially, it is important to keep the two questions separate. Once the child readily recognizes the difference between the two words, mix

the questions. Children should practice moving the clock hands according to the teacher's instructions. At this point, the teacher may not even require children to tell the time—the major goal is for students to develop, kinesthetically, the feeling of the two expressions. Later, when they cannot move the hands of a clock, the feeling will still be there. Many children actually move their fingers as if turning the clock. This helps them determine, visually, in which direction to go on the clock when counting.

3. **Minute-hand card.** Give the child a clear plastic minute-hand card with a hole in the center and a long minute hand line (Figure 3-53a). Also provide a page of clocks showing various times. The hole in the card should match the dot where the two clock hands meet in the center. First, the child writes the time shown on a clock. Then the card is placed over the clock face so the minute hand points to the next number, as in Figure 3-53b. The child says, "In 5 minutes it will be 6:45." As the child gains proficiency, use intervals other than 5 minutes. Use the minute-hand card as long as it is needed. Direct the child to point it to the next numeral—that which indicates the next time for minutes. This will ensure counting on from the proper place.

Figure 3-53

• *Variation:* For those with good visual imagery, an alternative is to have the child use a finger and point to the next number.

4. **Follow-Up.** Sample pages to reinforce this skill are shown in Figure 3-54a. As noted in the previous section, it is often necessary for the children to go through the two-step process at first. Initially, the pages deal with only one concept. As students are ready, move to pages that mix the ideas, as in Figure 3-54b.

(a)

Time shown: 8:35
In 10 minutes: 8:45

Time shown: ____
In 5 minutes: ____

Time shown: ____
In 5 minutes: ____

Time Shown: ____
In 15 minutes: ____

(b)

Time Shown: ____
20 minutes ago: ____

Time shown: ____
In 15 minutes: ____

Time shown: ____
In 5 minutes: ____

Time shown: ____
25 minutes ago: ____

Figure 3-54

Note: Some children may need help associating "in" and "ago" with "after" and "before." If so, write "in" using green and "ago" using red (refer back to Figure 3-47).

5. **One step only.** When the child no longer needs to write down the time, eliminate this step. Show the child how to use a finger or the minute card to determine the stated time. For auditory cueing, remind the student to "Think: It is now ____, so in 10 minutes it will be ____."

6. **Card game** (for two or three players). A variation of the card game "Go Fish" can now be played. Make a deck of 20 cards with a clock face on each card (Deck A) (see Figure 3-55a). Make a second set of 20 cards with a temporal expression on each (Deck B), as in Figure 3-55b. Each child is dealt five cards from Deck A. The remainder of the cards are placed face down in the center. Deck B is placed face down next to it. Children take turns drawing a card from Deck B and thinking of a card in their hand. Suppose the child has the clock 6:20 from Deck A and draws the expression "in 15 minutes" from Deck B. The person on the left is asked for a clock showing the time 6:35. If that student has the card, it is given to the caller who lays down the pair. The child places the expression card in a discard pile and the game moves on. If the child makes a mistake or if the child to the left does not have the requested clock, the caller draws from the fish pile until the correct clock is drawn or until five cards have been drawn, whichever occurs first. The winner is the one with the most pairs at the end. If necessary, the discard pile is shuffled and reused.

(a)

Deck A

(b)

In 20 minutes

minutes ago

Deck B

Figure 3-55

7. **Compare.** For those children who need concrete associations for particular temporal expressions, keep a gameboard such as that shown in Figure 3-56. Also provide a deck of cards with clock faces. Each space on the board counts for 5 minutes. In turn, children draw two cards and place them, in the order drawn, at the bottom of the gameboard. Children verbally fill in the blank and choose the correct word (e.g., "earlier" or "later"). They move by fives to dramatize the difference between the two clock times. Since the cards drawn

in Figure 3-56 have a difference of 15 minutes, the child moves backwards three spaces, counting by fives. The move is backwards because the second clock shows an earlier time.

Note: It is best to keep all the clocks within a two-hour time span.

Figure 3-56

CHAPTER

The Four Operations: Basic Concepts, Basic Facts

It is essential for all students, including those with learning disabilities, to understand *what it means* to add, subtract, multiply and divide—and to develop a good sense of *when* to use each of these basic operations in day-to-day settings. Confidence in performing these tasks equips children with a certain power in mathematics. It provides them (a) with a strong conceptual base which enables them to reason in problem situations, and (b) with a basis for developing successful computation skills involving mental and paper-and-pencil computation, estimation, or calculator use.

Much of children's success with these tasks depends on adequate mastery of the basic number facts. This chapter addresses the question of how to help learning disabled students develop a conceptual understanding of the basic operations and how to master the basic addition, subtraction, multiplication, and division facts. Specifically, the focus is on the following topics related to basic concepts or facts for each operation:

Section 1. Building Concepts for the Four Operations

Section 2. Interpreting the Printed Word or Sign for an Operation

Section 3. Comparison Subtraction

Section 4. Tracking and Strategy Learning for Basic Facts

Section 5. Addition Facts: Models and Strategies

Section 6. Hiding Activities for Subtraction

Section 7. Subtraction Facts: Models and Strategies

Section 8. Multiplication Facts: Models, Patterns, and Tactile Cues

Section 9. Division Facts: Strategies for Learning

Section 10. Zero

Section 11. Using a Hand Calculator

Like their peers, learning disabled students typically need much oral and manipulative work to build a strong conceptual background for each mathematical operation. Suggestions for using and extending textbook treatments in this regard are discussed in Sections 1, 2, and 3. The other sections of the chapter focus primarily on ideas for helping learning disabled students memorize the basic facts. The suggestions in Section 4 may be applied to facts for all four operations. Sections 5 through 9 look separately at facts for each operation. Handling common difficulties with zero is discussed in Section 10. A final section outlines ideas for helping learning disabled students master basic concepts or facts for the four operations using a hand calculator.

Sometimes students get bogged down in higher level computation because they do not know the basic facts or because they do not recognize simple, *known* facts in multidigit problems. Specific ideas for how to handle these difficulties are outlined in the first sections of Chapter 5. It may be useful to consider those suggestions along with others which follow as background for planning a basic program of fact study for learning disabled students.

A general note regarding the importance of relating basic understandings and skills to common daily settings is in order at this point. Many learning disabled students need a structured program that emphasizes practical applications of the mathematics they are learning. Otherwise, they will not make the transfer and hence will fall short when it comes to using math where it counts—in day-to-day living. With respect to the four operations, activities like the following are helpful.

- *Activity 1:* Pose a situation, such as that involving money to purchase needed items, and ask the children to tell which of two given operations is appropriate.

  Example: "Buy a pencil for 5 cents and a small eraser for 8 cents. What is the cost?" Select situations very familiar to the children. If possible, involve them in dramatizing the situations.

- *Activity 2:* Have the children circle *one* problem on a practice sheet of number facts. Ask them to describe a situation outside the classroom that might involve that number fact.

  Example: 2 + 5 = ___ is circled. The child might suggest: "Two red flowers, five yellow outside our front door; seven in all."

Other applications in the mathematics textbook might be highlighted and more carefully interwoven with the topics of this chapter. Selected story problems and measurement applications, such as finding perimeter and area, also fit this category.

BUILDING CONCEPTS FOR THE FOUR OPERATIONS

Problem area: Inability to associate real meaning with written number sentences for addition, subtraction, multiplication, or division.

Typical disabilities affecting progress: Difficulty with abstract reasoning, visual or auditory association, and receptive language.

Background: Diane looked at the problem "4 × 2" and quickly wrote 8. The teacher asked Diane to make a picture for "4 × 2." Diane did not hesitate at all. She drew four dots beside the 4 and two dots beside the 2. It did not bother Diane that she had drawn six dots but had written 8 to indicate the total number. Conceptually, Diane is in trouble. Unless cued, she will not know when to multiply rather than add in a simple problem situation.

Diane's response is not atypical of other learning disabled students with reasoning or association problems. Children with expressive language difficulties may correctly select the one drawing from several that illustrates a basic fact, but, like Diane, they may be unable to represent it correctly. It is important that children have a good visual image of what it means to "add," "subtract," "multiply," or "divide." Then they will be more likely to use the appropriate operation to solve problems in day-to-day settings. In many situations, it also is necessary that they be able to assign meaning to the written sign for each operation.

"Big ideas" must be understood. Addition means "put together." Subtraction has several interpretations (see Section 3, page 172). The simplest, and the most commonly used in beginning instruction, is "take away." (Some children, for emotional reasons, have difficulty with subtraction because of the idea of *take away*. Being sensitive to this possibility is important.)

Multiplication and division have to do with groups equal in number. To multiply we join or put together equal-sized groups, then tell how many in all. To divide we *share*. This is the simplest approach, now used with increasing frequency in beginning instruction. We start with a larger number of objects and give the same number to each of several persons. Children later learn both to tell the *number in each group* and the *number of groups* as the result of division for particular situations (see Figure 4-1).

Most mathematics textbooks contain excellent suggestions for how to develop these "big ideas" with regular class students. The following activities highlight or supplement these recommendations specifically for learning disabled students having reasoning or association difficulties.

Figure 4-1

Suggested Sequence of Activities and Exercises

1. **Act it out.** Physically dramatize the "big idea" of an operation. Get children to show objects or act out what is meant (see Figure 4-2). This is the basis for what we say and later write with symbols in early addition, subtraction, multiplication, or division work.

   - *Example* (addition): "When we *add* we *put things together.* There are three pieces of chalk on the tray. Take these two pieces and add them to those on the chalk tray." (The child walks to the tray to do so.)
   - *Example* (division): "Eight cookies to share with two boys. *Divide.* Give *the same number* to each." (Physically act out this division.)

Emphasize oral-manipulative work to help children understand other vocabulary related to an operation.

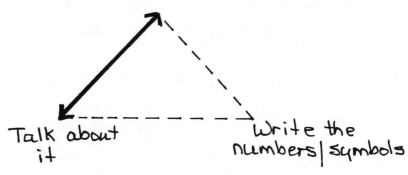

Figure 4-2

- *Example* (multiplication): Give the children a box of chips and request them to lay out rows of four. Comment about the groupings made. "How many fours? (Figure 4-3). . . . One four, two fours, three fours—*three times* you laid out a row of four."

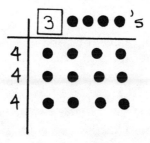

Figure 4-3

2. **Talk it out.** Get the children themselves to use the new vocabulary for an operation. Hearing themselves often triggers the intended meaning or association

3. **Tap it out.** If the children are strong auditorially, have them close their eyes and use sound or kinesthetic cues in association with new vocabulary.

- *Example 1* (subtraction): The children look at five felt hearts (velcro stapled to the backs and attached to a velcro strip as in Figure 4-4). They then close their eyes. "Feel the hearts now. How many? (5). Open your eyes so we can subtract. *Take away 2.* Now how many?"

Figure 4-4

- *Example 2* (multiplication): The children close their eyes. Take one child's finger and tap it on the desk. "Let's tap out groups of four:

(tap-tap-tap-tap) . . . . that's four—one four:

(tap-tap-tap-tap) . . . . that's four again—two fours;

(tap-tap-tap-tap) . . . . that's four again—three fours.

Three *times* we tapped out a group of four." (Later we *will write 3 times 4,* or 3 × 4.)

As follow-up, have the child independently identify the number of times a group of four (or three, or two . . .) is tapped.

4. **Small steps.** Building concepts with learning disabled students, particularly those having the difficulties identified at the beginning of this section, is often a *slow* process. Keep each instructional step size *small.* The following multiplication exercises illustrate the point:

- *Activity 1:* Use colored loops and chips as in Figure 4-5. Reinforcing follow-up worksheets should use the same color coding. Key questions to ask are: "How many groups?" "How many chips in each group?" "How many chips in all?"

- *Activity 2:* As before, with the modification suggested by Figure 4-6. (Note that the color coding is consistent with that used previously.) The children

Figure 4-5

Figure 4-6

complete the example shown by filling in "3 5s = 15." Some children spontaneously draw five dots on the line instead of writing the digit 5. They say it makes more sense. (It does.)

- *Activity 3:* Introduce the "times" sign (×). Use chips to form equal-sized groups as before. Have the children describe the grouping. In Figure 4-7

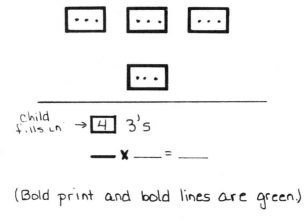

Figure 4-7

there are 4 threes. "Yes, four *times* we have a group of three. This '×' (point) is the multiplication sign. When we see it, we *say* 'times' and *think* 4 threes. 4 × 3, that's 12 in all." (The sign could be texturized or color coded. See Activities 5 and 6, pages 165 and 166.) Follow-up worksheets using the format of Figure 4-7 are then assigned with color coding as illustrated.

Note 1: Discussion at this point should emphasize that multiplication deals with equal-sized groups. "When we have equal-sized groups like this, and we need to know how many in all, we can multiply." Follow-up activities should present some situations in which equal-sized groups are *not* involved. This requires that students decide whether multiplication is indeed appropriate in a given situation. The ability to make this decision affects success with word problems.

Note 2: New vocabulary must be carefully presented. The sequence of examples just illustrated how one might informally use the term *times* in a multiplication context both before and during presentation of the written multiplication sign. An activity sequence similar to that outlined, used remedially for Mark, led him to comment: "So that's what *times* is all about. I could get the multiply part, but I could never figure out that times."

• *Activity 4:* Additional reinforcement is usually necessary. Use colored chips and frames as in Figure 4-7. Provide more chips than needed to force thinking. Have the children fill loops to picture 5 twos, 3 fours (or other groupings). For each, the corresponding multiplication sentence should be written. Next, follow-up worksheets using the format of Figure 4-8 are assigned, with color coding as illustrated.

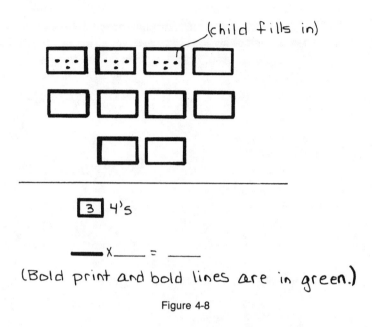

(child fills in)

3 | 4's

___ x ___ = ___

(Bold print and bold lines are in green.)

Figure 4-8

- *Activity 5:* Have the children complete worksheets like that of Figure 4-9. Color code the sign to match the box as in previous activities. This helps establish the relationship between "Four 3s" and "4 × 3." For selected problems, the children may be asked to draw dots or use chips to show the number of *times* a group of a given size appears.

4 | 3's = 4 x 3 = ___

2 | 5's = ___ x ___ = ___

(Bold print and bold lines are green.)

Figure 4-9

5. **Symbol feel.** Texturize the symbol for a new operation. Have children finger trace as they read an expression containing the symbol. Guide the hand, if necessary, so the writing movement is correct from the start. Next ask children to *close their eyes*, finger trace, and say the name for the symbol. As a follow-up, have children trace out the symbol on their desk or in midair.

6. **Symbol look.** Color code each operation a distinctly different color and place it on a wall chart for ready reference. In the chart of Figure 4-10, for example, all terms and symbols relating to subtraction are green. (Note that a diagram appears on the chart which illustrates the meaning of the symbol.) Use the color coding for the operation symbol during board work and on worksheets as long as it appears helpful.

Figure 4-10

7. **Act it out.** Provide experiences where the children themselves use manipulatives to illustrate *written* work (Figure 4-11). For example, for a written fact like 3 + 2 = __, a child might count out three objects, then two more; then recount to find the number in all. Later, as they become more familiar with addition, encourage the children to *count on* from the number in a small sight group rather than count from one each time.

8. **Across and up and down.** Because it follows the left-right reading motion, many teachers introduce the horizontal before the vertical format for simple number combinations. Eventually, the vertical format must be introduced as a prelude to computation. To help the children associate the two forms, it may be helpful to use the technique of Figure 4-12 where the double bar simulates the equal sign.

9. **Turnarounds** (commutative property). Many learning disabled children need special help to recognize that 2 + 4 and 4 + 2 give the same answer, that "When you know one you know the other, too." Glue chips to strips as in Figure 4-13.

   • Have the children write the expression illustrated by the strip (2 + 4).

   • Use chips and a felt addition sign to lay out 4 + 2, as illustrated in Figure 4-13b. Have the children write the number sentence represented by this second configuration.

Figure 4-11

$$3 + 2 = 5 \qquad \begin{array}{r} 3 \\ + 2 \\ \hline \hline 5 \end{array}$$

Figure 4-12

Figure 4-13

- "Are there as many chips in the first row as in the second?" Have the children match the loose chips and sign one-to-one with those on the strip. "Yes, there are just as many." The children should complete the number sentences to tell the number in all (4 + 2 and 2 + 4 = 6). Provide auditory reinforcement: "When you know one, you know the other, too."

- *Adaptation* (for multiplication): Use a similar approach. Provide cards such as that of Figure 4-14.

Figure 4-14

INTERPRETING THE PRINTED
WORD OR SIGN FOR AN OPERATION

Problem area: Failure to associate the correct process with the operation sign or with the written direction to add, subtract, multiply, or divide.

Typical disabilities affecting progress: Difficulty with closure, expressive or receptive language, visual discrimination.

Background: This section deals with two related difficulties. The first, discussed in the introduction to this chapter, involves the printed symbol for each operation. For example, despite solid conceptual understandings, some learning disabled students either misperceive or misinterpret the written operation signs. A second difficulty involves not knowing what to do when presented with written directions to add, subtract, multiply, or divide. Without the sign as a guide, some children are at a loss as to how to proceed. Many mathematics textbooks present skill pages of the type shown in Figure 4-15. Within a structured program, this type of page is useful for building skills due to language deficits. Initially, however, children with receptive language difficulties may not be able to succeed independently with exercises of this type. A chart, such as that of Figure 1-19, can be especially helpful to these students.

The following activities and exercises include techniques for dealing with each of the difficulties summarized in the preceding paragraph. The suggestions assume that students possess a well-established conceptual understanding of each operation. If this is not the case, return to work with physical materials, as outlined in Section 1 (page 157) of this chapter, before proceeding.

Add

48	76	48	795
53	29	73	36

Multiply

37	42	62	82
29	27	45	24

Figure 4-15

Suggested Sequence of Activities and Exercises

Interpreting the Operation Sign

1. **Circle.** Visual discrimination deficits may make it difficult to associate ideas properly. Use textbooks in which the operation signs have been circled, or ask the child to circle each sign on the page before solving the problem. In this way, attention is drawn more directly to the operation sign.

2. **What is the sign?** Use texture cues or color coding, or allow the students to finger trace before solving, as suggested in Activities 5 and 6 of Section 1, page 165. Finger tracing a sign before solving is particularly useful on pages with mixed problem types (e.g., pages of addition and subtraction problems). Sometimes, a verbal reminder or visual cue to "Stop! Look at the sign" (see Figure 4-16) is helpful. In severe cases, require a student to circle all addition problems and work these before turning to the subtraction examples.

Interpreting the Sign or Word for Each Operation

1. **Chart it**

   • Figure 4-17 shows one type of supplemental page that can be prepared at the beginning of the school year and kept on file for future use. Each sym-

Figure 4-16

	Add	Subtract	Multiply	Divide
48 x 6			48 x 6	
54 −19		54 −19		
36 + 8				

Figure 4-17

bol on the page should be the same color as the word that denotes the operation. If the chart shown in Figure 1-19 is present in the room, the colors on the exercise pages should match those of the chart. The teacher writes problems in the left column. The child recopies and solves them in the appropriate box as shown. For some, this might be a two-day assignment. On the first day, students might merely copy each problem into the appropriate spaces. After the teacher has checked the paper, the student solves the problems.

• If a child has difficulty interpreting the operation sign, focus on internalizing its meaning. Eventually, these students learn to copy problems from their textbook into the proper space of the supplemental page.

• If a child has difficulty interpreting the written direction ("add," "subtract," "multiply," "divide"), focus on building vocabulary by association with numeric examples that use the operation sign. Similar sheets can be used to help children build associations for "sum," "difference," "product," or "quotient."

Note: For many students, an operation sign is readily associated with the correct word and process when the numbers used are basic facts. However, when multidigit numbers are used in computation, these same children may experience difficulty with the association. For this reason, it is important that 2- or higher digit numbers be used in the problems of the left-hand column.

2. **Page assignment sheets.** Many children perseverate and need continued help to associate the correct process with given words or symbols. Assign textbook pages or problems on a given page in random order as described in Chapter 1. Figure 4-18a shows an example of a page that can be kept on file and used as an assignment sheet for such children. The child first writes the symbol beside the word and then writes the appropriate problem numbers in the right-hand column of the sheet (Figure 4-18b). If necessary, the operation word can be underlined to match the color used for the word on the wall chart.

Figure 4-18

Interpreting Vocabulary for Each Operation

1. **Circle to match.** At the beginning of the school year, go through the text and find pages such as those illustrated in Figure 4-15. Circle direction words

in the appropriate color to match the wall chart. Instruct the student to place the correct sign beside the word before solving the problems.

2. **Look to the chart.** When the words "sum," "product," "quotient," and "difference" are introduced, use a chart such as the one shown in Figure 4-19. Color the chart to match the coding scheme of Figure 1-19. A small copy of the chart can be pasted to the top of a child's worksheet. If the student needs more specific practice, use pages like that of Figure 4-20. The children can "X" (cross out) inappropriate problems, then work the correct one. The color scheme adopted for the charts of Figures 1-19 and 4-19 should be carried through on pages of this type. In the example of Figure 4-20, if "sum" and "+" are green, then "−" could be black, "×" red, and ")‾‾" blue.

Sum ⟶ + answer
Difference ⟶ − answer
Product ⟶ × answer
Quotient ⟶ ÷ answer

Figure 4-19

Find the **sum** of 29 and 19.

$$\begin{array}{r} 29 \\ + 19 \\ \hline \end{array} \qquad \begin{array}{r} 29 \\ - 19 \\ \hline \end{array} \qquad \begin{array}{r} 29 \\ \times 19 \\ \hline \end{array} \qquad 19\overline{)29} \quad \text{blue}$$

━ = green
···· = red

Figure 4-20

COMPARISON SUBTRACTION

Problem area: Adding instead of subtracting for word problems like: "Dick has 7 marbles. Jack has 4. How many more does Dick have than Jack?"

Typical disabilities affecting progress: Difficulty with abstract reasoning, visual discrimination, and receptive or expressive language.

Background: Most young children, including the learning disabled, have difficulty with comparison word problems such as the given example. The situation of Dick and Jack represents one general type of comparison problem that can be solved by subtracting. It is a situation in which one determines *how much more one has than another.* A second type of comparison is that *which asks how much more is needed.* For example: "Jan has 7¢. An apple costs 12¢. How much more money is needed?" The comparison is between what Jan has and what she needs. Given a comparison situation, children are typically miscued by the word "more" and tend to add rather than subtract.

One root of the difficulty may be that a higher level of reasoning is required to handle problems like these successfully. A second reason is that teachers often do not give adequate attention to problems of this type. Most students need help setting up comparison situations as subtraction problems.

When children are confident with the basic subtraction idea modeled by "take away" situations and have learned at least a small number of subtraction facts, comparison subtraction problems should be introduced. Too often children are left, independently, to discover techniques for how to solve subtraction problems of this type. A worthy goal is to provide many informal opportunities for students to model comparison situations before these occur in word problems. Rather than simply assigning comparison word problems, specifically intervene using suggestions like the following to develop the idea of comparison subtraction. (Note that the step size of the instruction is kept very small.)

Suggested Sequence of Activities and Exercises

1. **Picture it.** Orally pose a situation such as: "Dick has 7 marbles. Jack has 4." Or "Jan has 7¢. An apple she wants to buy costs 12¢." Tape a large sheet to the board and have the children help draw a picture to illustrate each situation (e.g., Figure 4-21). Repeat until the children are comfortable with this task. Save the sheets for use in Activities 2 and 3 below.

   • *Follow-Up:* Have children read situations from teacher-made cards. Help them picture each situation. For students with limited vocabulary, use pictograms as necessary (substitute pictures for words).

Figure 4-21

2. **Match.** Use the sheets from Activity 1. Review the sheets one at a time. For each, pose the problem to be solved: "How many more does one have than the other?" or "How much more is needed?" Help children match one-to-one to compare the two groups pictured.

- When using the pages for the first time, allow the children to count the number remaining after the match (Figure 4-21).

- In subsequent sessions, help children recognize that they can simply subtract to find this number. Ask them to complete the subtraction sentence you have written on the sheet (Figure 4- 22). They should then compare their answer with the number left over in the picture after the comparison.

- Eventually, the children themselves should write the subtraction sentences that solve situations pictured on the sheets. At this point, comment to the children that "It's good to know how to subtract. You can use it to solve so many different kinds of problems."

3. **Sort out.** Review the sheets from Activity 1. As a type of tracking exercise, have the children place in a special pile all the sheets that compare *how much more one has than another.* When the sorting is complete, have the children read (finger trace, if they are strong tactual learners) the subtraction fact that solves each situation. Orally emphasize the relationship between subtraction and this type of problem. "To find how much more one has than another, you subtract. Read the subtraction fact that solves this problem." Underline the question, "How much more does one have than another?" and the sub-

Figure 4-22

traction sign of the fact problem written to answer the question with the same color.

Note 1: At another time, have the students sort out sheets for situations asking *how much more is needed.*

Note 2: Technically, the "How much more is needed?" type of question is a missing-addend problem. However, we do not emphasize it as such. Rather, we prefer to focus on the simple subtraction fact that will solve the problem.

4. **Search.** As a follow-up tracking exercise, have the children search for comparison subtraction problems on worksheets or textbook pages that contain a mix of take-away and comparison types (Figure 4-23). For each comparison problem identified, ask them to draw a picture and write the subtraction sentence that solves the problem.

5. **Make up.** Help the children make up their own word problems for the two types of comparison subtraction. If they demonstrate expressive language difficulties, provide a sheet of sentences they can draw from while creating their problems. Children could trade, picture, and solve each other's problems.

Do those that COMPARE.
Draw a picture to help.
"X" all that don't compare.

1. Mary had 15¢ and spent 7¢. How
   much money does she have now?

2. Ted has 8¢ and Jan has   How
   much more does Ted have than Jan?

$$\begin{array}{r} 8¢ \\ -\ 6¢ \\ \hline 2¢ \end{array}$$

3) Sharon had 7 cookies. She ate 4 of
   them. How many cookies does she
   still have?

Figure 4-23

TRACKING AND STRATEGY LEARNING FOR BASIC FACTS

Problem area: Difficulty memorizing the basic facts.

Typical disabilities affecting progress: Difficulties with visual, auditory, or long-term memory; visual or auditory discrimination, expressive language.

Background: Even for regular class students, school mathematics textbooks rarely include enough work on basic facts to promote real mastery. This problem is aggravated for learning disabled children. Memory, discrimination, or expressive language deficits may interfere to make learning the facts very difficult. Many teachers find that children can succeed when they specifically intervene to teach recall *strategies* such as those suggested in the remaining sections of this chapter. For learning disabled students a critical part of this process is promoting the desired mastery by tracking as described and illustrated in the following sequence.

Tracking basically involves presenting only a few carefully chosen facts at a time. Much as a hunter would track a deer in the woods, children track or look for a small set of facts that are mixed in with others. Figure 4-24 shows a sample page with selected doubles at the top of the page. The technique (a) forces children to focus on given facts; (b) builds visual memory; and (c) assists with expressive language difficulties. The student follows the directions below the line. Short, frequent practice of this type helps students learn the facts faster and retain them longer.

Tracking is not a cure-all. Rather, it is a general approach that has proven especially useful in early fact work where the goal is to help children memorize the facts. Tracking can be applied to fact learning for all four operations as part of or as an alternative to a *strategy approach* for teaching basic facts (endorsed by the National Council of Teachers of Mathematics, 1989). Thornton (1989) suggested the following general 6-phase teaching framework:

1. *Look ahead* (to review or teach prerequisite concepts, counting and other skills which make it easier for children to learn helpful recall strategies).

2. *Teach* Retrieval *Strategies* (such as "Start with the greater number and count on"; or "Think of the picture to help with the double"; or "See × 5?"— "Think of the clock to help." These and other strategies are presented below or in the remaining sections of this chapter).

3. Help children *use* the strategy (with emphasis on accuracy, not speed of response).

4. Help children *choose* when the strategy "fits." (This is an aspect of *tracking*.)

5. Provide practice to *speed up* response (so facts are answered *quickly* as well as *accurately*. Carry through to the point of overlearning, so *consistency* and *retention over time* also are promoted).

6. *Check up* (Activity 10, page 182).

Easy Doubles

$$
\begin{array}{cccccc}
4 & 6 & 5 & 8 & 9 & 7 \\
+\,4 & +\,6 & +\,5 & +\,8 & +\,9 & +\,7 \\
\hline
8 & 12 & 10 & 16 & 18 & 14
\end{array}
$$

Add the DOUBLES.
"X" all the others.

$$
\begin{array}{ccccc}
5 & 8 & 6 & 4 & 7 \\
+\,5 & +\,8 & +\,5 & +\,4 & +\,2 \\
\hline
10 & 16 & \times & 8 & \times
\end{array}
$$

$$
\begin{array}{ccccc}
3 & 9 & 4 & 7 & 6 \\
+\,5 & +\,9 & +\,5 & +\,7 & +\,8 \\
\hline
\times & 18 & \times & 14 & \times
\end{array}
$$

Figure 4-24

Elements of this framework, highlighting the *tracking* technique, are emphasized in the following sequence. Since fact mastery implies giving *accurate* answers *quickly*, and being *consistent in performance* over time, follow-up exercises are necessary. Activities such as those described near the end of the following sequence are useful for this purpose.

Suggested Sequence of Activities and Exercises

1. **Preassessment.** Determine each child's fact mastery level. Timed written tests of themselves do not tell which specific facts are indeed mastered. Instead, individual testing, either written or oral, is preferable. One can then circle on a matching sheet those facts for which correct answers are given without hesitation. Or, if flash cards are used, two piles can be formed: "mastered" and "not mastered."

2. **Cluster.** Group facts into clusters for easier learning. Count on facts, +2s and their turnarounds (commutatives), for example, might be grouped. That is: 2 + 1, 2 + 2, 2 + 3, 2 + 4, 2 + 5, 2 + 6, 2 + 7, 2 + 8, 2 + 9. 1 + 2, 3 + 2, 4 + 2, 5 + 2, 6 + 2, 7 + 2, 8 + 2 and 9 + 2. Later, other easy facts such as 10 sums or doubles might be tracked. (Refer to the following sections for grouping facts, easy to hard.)

3. **Model it.** If possible, use manipulatives to dramatize finding answers for facts within a cluster.

   • *Example 1* (10 sums): Use chips (two colors) and a 10-frame made by stapling half-pint milk cartons together (Figure 4-25). Have the children: (a) Count the cartons in the frame (10).

Figure 4-25

(b) Place a chip (all one color) in each of eight cartons. "How many chips are needed to *fill* the 10-frame?" (two). (c) Place two chips (second color) in the 10-frame to fill it up." (d) Pick out the flash card that describes this situation and tape it to the board or chart (Figure 4-26a). Picture the 10-frame as a visual cue with the chart. Repeat, using different combinations for 10.

Figure 4-26a

   • *Example 2* (addition doubles): Use the suggestions of Activity 5. Picture the cues on a chart (Figure 4-26b).

(b)   DOUBLES

5 + 5 = 10   6 + 6 = 12   8 + 8 = 16

Figure 4-26b

4. **Circle it.** Provide tracking pages on which the children find and circle, from among distractors, facts in a given cluster. Children can refer to the board or wall chart, or even use the model(s) if necessary.

5. **See and write.** Plan short sessions during which flash cards for selected facts in a cluster are presented one at a time. As the cards are flashed, the child says the problem, gives the answer, and writes it on the line of a worksheet such as that of Figure 4-27a or 4-27b. At first, present only a small number of facts, those easiest or already known by the child. Then gradually, one at a time, introduce harder facts in the cluster.

(a)

10 = ___ + ___ ,   ___ + ___
     ___ + ___ ,   ___ + ___

(b) Doubles:

___ + ___ = ___
___ + ___ = ___
___ + ___ = ___
___ + ___ = ___

Figure 4-27

6. **Match.** Provide worksheets such as those shown in Figure 4-28. As a form of visual training, the children study the top part of each page before completing the tracking exercise at the bottom.

(a)   10 Sums

8+2   6+4   3+7

Add all 10 sums. "X" all others.

3×6=_____   3+7=_____

8+2= 10   2×7=_____

5×6=_____   6+4=_____

(b)   x9

4×9=36   7×9=63
6×9=54   8×9=72

Multiply all 9's. "X" all others.

3×7=_____   7×9= 63

4×9= 36   8×9= 72

2×6= _____   3×5=_____

Figure 4-28

7. **Find it.** Provide tracking pages such as that illustrated in Figure 4-29. Have the children find and write answers *only to those facts in a given cluster.* Include about 20 problems from the cluster.

• *Variation:* Have the children give answers orally to facts in the given cluster.

What's 10?

6+4= 10   3+8 = _____

8×9=_____   7+3= 10

2+8= 10   6×5= _____

8×6= _____   5+5= 10

Figure 4-29

8. **Hear and write.** For each cluster, have the children read facts—problem and answer—into a tape recorder. Later they can listen to the playback for extra reinforcement.

9. **Trace and write.** Use the answer side of flash cards. Have children finger trace facts within a cluster, problem and answer, as they read it aloud. Then have them close their eyes as they say the problem and answer quietly to themselves. Finally, ask the children to turn the flash card over, read the

problem, and give the answer. If they forget, finger tracing the problem may trigger the response. Some teachers have found it helpful to trace over flash card answers with glue. When dry, the raised surface adds an extra stimulus to the finger tracing.

10. **Quiz.** Regular quizzes to test both short- and long-term retention of facts are necessary. Short quizzes of six or eight facts can serve to spotcheck facts mastery within one or more clusters. Longer quizzes can also be used from time to time. Keeping simple (personal) bar graphs of the number correct on each quiz is usually very motivating to students. Oral timed quizzes would not be required of students with auditory discrimination problems since, auditorially, they cannot process rapidly enough to succeed. For similar reasons, timed written tests would not be used with children having visual memory difficulties. Students with expressive language disabilities will also have difficulty with traditional timed tests. For these students one option is to place answers randomly in front of them. They can then find and point to the correct answer for a given fact problem. Progress may be tracked by noting the time it takes to find answers to a given number of problems and comparing it over several days.

11. **Review.** Systematically review facts from a cluster as new facts are studied. Games and traditional drill-and-practice activities and worksheets are appropriate at this stage.

ADDITION FACTS: MODELS AND STRATEGIES

Problem area: Difficulty mastering the basic addition facts.

Typical disabilities affecting progress: Difficulties with visual, auditory, or long-term memory; visual or auditory discrimination; expressive language.

Background: The activities of this section focus on strategies and models for learning the basic addition facts. Children who are good at memorizing do not need to rely on these approaches. Learning disabled students, however, who have memory or other difficulties such as those previously identified, can profit from ideas like those outlined in the following activities. The basic approach is to help students master easy facts first. Models are used to help the children "picture" the facts in their minds. Then more difficult facts are mastered by relating them to the easier, known facts. Typically, this involves deviating from traditional textbook treatments of the facts. What helps one child may not prove effective with another. The teacher's role becomes one of suggesting relationships, models, or strategies while remaining open to children's ideas and being sensitive to individual learning styles.

One word of caution: Keep instruction for learning disabled children *very simple.* If presented too many "tricks" for remembering facts, some cannot sort out one from another. Others, however, can handle a variety of strategies during fact learning. Teachers may draw on the following suggestions, as needed, to plan a tracking sequence for individual or small groups of students. Ideas for adapting the basic sequence to meet remedial needs are included.

Suggested Sequence of Activities and Exercises

Basic Sequence

Easy Facts First

1. **Count ons.** Review, if necessary, the extended counting activities of Chapter 2. For sums less than 10 and for other facts having 1, 2, or 3 as the addend, encourage the children to *count on* from the greater addend rather than starting from 1 each time.

   - *Example:* 6 + 3 = ___. "That's 6—7, 8, 9." Experience shows that learning disabled children as well as trainable mentally handicapped students *can* perform this type of problem. Children do not need to count from 1 for addition facts.

   Note 1: The relationship of a fact to its commutative should be stressed from the beginning. Use simple models like a card with dots or clothespins (Figure 4-30) to help children recognize that, for any given fact, its "turn-around" (commutative) has the same answer. "When you know one, you know the other, too."

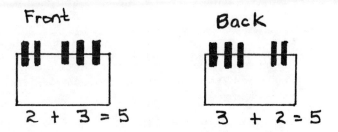

Figure 4-30

Note 2: Teachers may want to take time out at this point to help children note the "+ 0" pattern. $0 + 3 = 3$; $7 + 0 = 7$, and so on. Add 0, and the answer is what you started with.

2. **10 sums.** Refer to Example 1 in *Model It*, page 179. Use chips and the 10-frame as a model or simply draw a 10-frame on cardboard or paper (Figure 4-31) to help the children learn sums of 10. Have the students themselves write the number sentences to describe each situation dramatized. Get children to the point where they track for 10 sums, using techniques from Section 4 (page 177), then use the 10-frame to check.

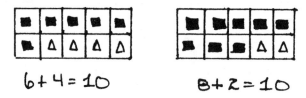

Figure 4-31

3. **Doubles.** Use models such as those of Figure 4-32 to help children memorize addition doubles. Among other activities, involve the children in:

   • Writing number sentences to match cue cards;

   • Reading cue and associated number sentences into a tape recorder and listening to the playback (e.g., "6 + 6 is the 'dozen eggs' fact; $6 + 6 = 12$." Show students how, if you only want half of a dozen eggs, you would split as pictured);

   • Finger tracing over the cue card and then *writing* the double that is illustrated;

   • Tracking exercises, as in the section beginning on page 177;

   • Practice activities where children match number sentences with associated cue cards. A variation on the card game Old Maid is good for this purpose (see Figure 4-33);

   • Crossing off these and other facts as they are mastered. A chart such as that described in Activity 7, page 190, might be useful.

4. **Pattern 9s.** Use a 10-frame (see Activity 2 above) to illustrate that 9+ (any number) is just 1 less than 10+ (that number). This is a helpful *number pat-*

Double	Visual Cue	Auditory Cue
2+2		The car fact (2 front tires, 2 back tires)
3+3		The grasshopper fact (3 legs on each side)
4+4		The spider fact (4 legs on each side)
5+5		The fingers fact. (10 fingers)
6+6		The egg carton fact -- (6 in each half.)
7+7		The 2 week fact. (14 days)
8+8		The crayon fact (8 in each row)
9+9		The double 9 domino fact

Figure 4-32

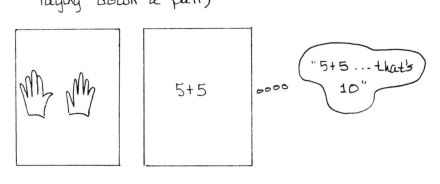

(child says fact answer when laying down a pair)

"5+5 ... that's 10"

Figure 4-33

tern. +9 facts are just "one step away" from easier +10 facts. Track +9 facts, as suggested in Section 4.

Other favorite patterns include:

- *Strategy 1:* "Make it a '10' problem." Use the "−1, +1" idea: "9 + 6 is the same as 10 + 5 (15)."

- *Strategy 2:* "Note the pattern." The ones digit of the answer is always 1 less than the digit added to 1 (see Figure 4-34).

(Bold digits are green.)

$$\begin{array}{r} 9 \\ +\mathbf{6} \\ \hline \mathbf{1}\mathbf{5} \end{array} \qquad \begin{array}{r} \mathbf{4} \\ + 9 \\ \hline \mathbf{1}3 \end{array} \qquad \begin{array}{r} \mathbf{7} \\ + 9 \\ \hline \mathbf{1}6 \end{array}$$

Figure 4-34

Note: When *Pattern 9s* have been mastered, allow students to mark them off a master list, such as that described in Activity 7.

Now Harder Facts

5. **One more than.** Help the students master harder facts by relating them to easier, known facts. The "one-more-than" strategy is a powerful help in this regard. Mastering a difficult fact is just "one step away." The strategy has a mushroom effect. As facts are mastered, they can be used to help learn others. Follow-up tracking (in the section on page 177) is usually necessary.

- *Example 1* (based on a double): 5 + 5 = 10, so 5 + 6 is 1 more (11). 5 + 6 = 11, so 5 + 7 is 1 more (12).

- *Example 2* (based on a 10-sum): 7 + 3 = 10, so 7 + 4 is 1 more (11). 7 + 4 = 11, so 7 + 5 is 1 more (12).

- *Assist 1:* When presenting examples like these, orally emphasize the underlined numerals.

- *Assist 2:* It sometimes helps to color code as in Figure 4-35 to emphasize the "one-more-than" relationship. The coding helps children focus on the intended relationship. This approach is particularly helpful for children who are working independently or who, for auditory-discrimination reasons, may not hear the oral emphasis placed by the teacher when reading the pair of number sentences. Color coding may be necessary as well for students who are weak in making associations. These students may not relate the 5 and 6 without cueing.

(Dotted line digits are red.)

$$5 \qquad\qquad 5$$
$$+\ 5 \qquad so \qquad +\ 6$$

Figure 4-35

- *Assist 3:* It is often necessary to dramatize a relationship for children. It is not enough simply to discuss it.

- *For example:* (a) Use rocks. Have the children make a picture of 5 + 5 and then write the number sentence to describe the picture (Figure 4-36a). (b) Give a child *one more* rock. "Place the rock with the others. It doesn't matter which side." Have the child write a second number sentence to describe the picture now. (c) Even as the child writes, emphasize the idea that you now have *1 more than 10* (11), as illustrated in Figure 4-36b.

Note: For *Doubles*, children just add one more finger, egg, crayon, . . . to the picture.

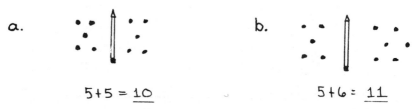

$$5 + 5 = \underline{10} \qquad\qquad 5 + 6 = \underline{11}$$

Figure 4-36

- *Assist 4:* Many children, especially those with expressive language deficits, have trouble thinking of an easy, known fact to help them with a fact they do not know. These same children may be able to use a "helping fact" (the easier, known fact) once it is located. For these students, plan activities like the following with flash cards. (a) Present a fact the student has not yet memorized (4 + 7 in the example of Figure 4-37a). (b) Ask the students to select the easy "helping fact" from two other flash cards you place along the chalk tray. (c) Have the children turn over the card that does not help and give answers to the two related facts. ("3 + 7 = 10, so 4 + 7 is 11.") Follow-up worksheets, which direct children to select the helper from two given facts, may also be used. The fact that does not help should be crossed out, as in Figure 4-37b.

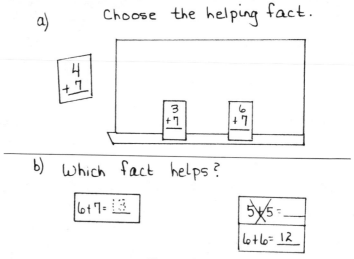

Figure 4-37

- *Assist 5:* Another alternative for helping children use an appropriate helping fact is illustrated in Figure 4-38. Although the exercise is related to missing addends, do not emphasize it as such. The focus should be on building new facts from easy, known facts (e.g., "3 + 7 = 10, so 4 + 7 is one more." [11]).

$$\begin{array}{r} \vdots \\ + \ 7 \\ \hline \end{array} \quad so \quad \begin{array}{r} \square \\ + \ 7 \\ \hline \end{array}$$

(Dotted digits and lines are red)

Figure 4-38

Note: Although children typically find "one more" easier than the following strategies these are viable alternatives for some students:

- *Strategy 1:* "Two more." 6 + 6 = 12, so 6 + 8 is 2 more (14).

- *Strategy 2:* "−1, +1." 6 + 8 is the same as 7 + 7 or 14.
  (Some children refer to this as the Robin Hood idea of sharing: Take 1 from the rich and give it to the poor.)

Allow students to use any strategy which seems helpful to them, as long as it shows correct thinking. Figure 4-39 illustrates two different approaches for figuring out 5 + 7. Since the addends are large, both illustrate a thinking process that is faster than counting on.

Approach 1: 5 + 7 = ____   I know 5 + 6 = 11 So 5 + 7 is one more (12).

Approach 2: 5 + 7 = ____   I know 5 + 5 = 10 So 5 + 7 is 2 more (12).

Figure 4-39

Although learning disabled students may not independently discover these strategies, many are able to use at least one of them if cued as previously suggested. Choose one strategy that you think will be easiest. Even if the child has difficulty, give it a good try (including tracking as in the section on page 177) before turning to a different approach. Too much change too fast is confusing.

6. **Other "1 less" facts.** Like the "1 more" relationship, the "1 less" idea is powerful. Many children use easier, known +9s to help with harder +8 facts like 8 + 4, 8 + 5, and 8 + 6. "I know 9 + 4 = 13, so 8 + 4 = 1 less." (12). Use a 10-frame to illustrate this. Reinforce with the tracking suggestions of Section 4 as follow-up.

7. **Cross off known facts as these are learned.** Children who know the 45 "count ons," 19 zero facts, 10 sums, doubles, and 9s already have learned over 80 of the 100 basic addition facts. Consequently, these and other "one more than a double" and "10 sum" have been marked off the Figure 4-40 master list. Some children may also have mastered one or more of the remaining facts, perhaps by using strategies discussed in Activities 5 or 6.

   As children progress, let them cross off facts they learn from a master list like that shown in Figure 4-40 or the one presented on page 222 in Chapter 5. Besides typically being very motivating by showing children how much they know, the list also provides a mind set for what should still be studied.

8. **Make 10, add extra.**
   Prerequisite skills: Ability to add 10 to a 1-digit number.

   • Visual color cueing, as in Figure 4-41, or auditory cueing through sound emphasis should be used if this seems helpful. The ones digit of the sum and of the digit added to 10 could also be texturized to allow for finger tracing.

   • *Example:* (Use the answer side of a flash card [10 + 4 = 14], with both 4s texturized. Retrace each 4 with Elmer's glue. When the glue dries, it leaves a raised imprint of the digits.) "Read the number sentence." (The child reads 10 + 4 = 14.) "Now close your eyes and trace over the 4s as I read the number sentence . . . Now put your hands in your lap . . . Say the answer to this problem: 10 + 4 = __." Next ask the child, with eyes open, to read the front side of the flash card problem and give the correct answer.

     Use a 10-frame and chips to introduce the "make 10, add extra" strategy. The goal is to help children "see" that 8 + 5 is the same as 10 + 3 (13). The value of previous work with the 10-frame now pays off, because many children look at "8 + 5" and see that 8 and 2 more make 10, so it is a matter of adding in the extra 3. Continue until children can write the answer

Figure 4-40

C: 45 Count Ons
O: 19 Zero Facts
D: 6 Other Doubles
10: 2 Other 10 Sums
9: 10 Pattern 9's
D+1: 8 Doubles Plus
              One Facts
10+1: 2 Facts 1 More

(Bold digits are green.)

$$\begin{array}{r} 10 \\ + \ 3 \\ \hline 13 \end{array} \qquad \begin{array}{r} 10 \\ + \ 6 \\ \hline 16 \end{array} \qquad \begin{array}{r} 10 \\ + \ 4 \\ \hline 14 \end{array}$$

Figure 4-41

and use the 10-frame to check, then track on the new facts being learned, as suggested in Section 4.

Remedial Sequence

Many older remedial children know most of the easier addition facts. Their greatest difficulty is often with more difficult teen sums. One approach is to *start* with *Doubles* and *Pattern* 9s (Activity 3 and 4 in the basic sequence). "Big" numbers like these seem sophisticated to students and tend to be more motivating for older learners than facts with smaller numbers. When these are mastered, review the *Count Ons* and *10 Sums* (Activities 1 and 2). Then treat the harder facts (Activities 5 through 8). Integrate tracking, as in the section beginning on page 177.

HIDING ACTIVITIES FOR SUBTRACTION

Problem area: Prolonged reliance on counters or fingers for finding answers to subtraction facts.

Typical disabilities affecting progress: Difficulty with visual, auditory, or long-term memory; visual or auditory discrimination; expressive language; abstract reasoning.

Background: In beginning subtraction instruction, give children situations in which they see and count the number of objects in the remaining set (Figure 4-42). After repeated opportunities to remove objects from intact groups, the children who are good at memorizing will remember this number for solving written or orally presented facts. However, children with these types of learning disabilities can benefit from some of the following "hiding" activities. These activities show objects in the intact group, but hide the number in the remaining subgroup. Hiding activities challenge children to *think about* rather than see or count the number left over each time. For this reason, they are stepping stones to subtraction work without objects, thereby paving the way to memorizing the facts.

Figure 4-42

Suggested Sequence of Activities and Exercises

Prerequisite skills:

The basic concept of subtraction, as modeled in take-away situations, must be well established.

Step 1—How many do you see? Use pennies or other small, familiar objects. Let the children see you put five pennies in a box. "How many pennies did I put in the box?" (5). Write the correct number for all to see.

Step 2—Cover. Put the lid on the box. "How many pennies are hidden in the box?" (5). If the children are unsure, allow them to open the box and check.

Step 3—Take out. Hold the box high so the children cannot see the pennies as you take the lid off. Have a child take two pennies out. "How many pennies did we take out?" (2). Complete the written expression for all to see: "5 − 2."

Step 4—How many left? Ask how many pennies are left hidden in the box. Encourage the children to quickly tell, even guess, the number left hidden in the box. They can then empty the box or peek to see.

> **Note 1:** Children who can recall addition facts related to given subtraction facts have a ready clue to subtraction answers.
>
> *Example:* "13 − 6 = 7. I know this because 7 + 6 = 13." Most learning disabled children need help in recognizing and using this relationship. (Refer to the following section.) Teachers can orally cue children by the type of feedback they give at this point in the hiding activity sequence.
>
> *Example:* "See—you are right. 5 − 2—that's 3, because these three pennies in the box and two more make the five we started with."

> • *Optional Follow-Up:* Have the children select flash cards for 5 − 2 = 3 and 3 + 2 = 5 and place them side by side on a chalk tray or table near the box. Discuss how the cards describe what was done with the pennies.

> **Note 2:** Repeat to illustrate other subtraction combinations. As the children become more familiar with the activity, *they* should be required to write the subtraction sentence that describes each situation.

SUBTRACTION FACTS: MODELS AND STRATEGIES

Problem area: Difficulty remembering subtraction facts, particularly those with teen minuends. Heavy reliance on counting.

Typical disabilities affecting progress: Difficulty with visual, auditory, or long-term memory; visual or auditory discrimination; expressive language.

Background: Virtually without exception, subtraction facts are more difficult than addition for all children to master *including those with learning disabilities.* In early work, very few learning disabled children can think of and use related addition facts to help. Most children will *count.* Unfortunately, many students continue to count even when larger numbers and longer counts are involved.

> • *Example:* "13 − 6 = 7 because 7 + 6 = 13." A large number of learning disabled students do (among other things) the following:

- Count back: "13 − 6—that's 13—12, 11, 10, 9, 8, 7, 6."
- Count up: "13 − 6—that's 6—7, 8, 9, 10, 11, 12, 13." (The children finger count as they say the numbers.) "That's 7."
- Finger count everything: The children raise fingers to represent the minuend, they lower (take away) fingers to represent the subtrahend, and then count and tell the number left. These students face real trouble when having to work with teen minuends.

When fact memorization is the goal in subtraction, the challenge is to lead students to use the *most efficient strategy* they are capable of learning to answer unknown facts. And, just as children grow from year to year, it is hoped that the kind of retrieval strategies they employ also grow. For example, students may at first *always* count back or count up, as previously illustrated, to answer unknown facts. Hopefully, if these same students master awareness of the addition-subtraction relationship, they will later use known addition facts or some other more efficient strategy instead of always counting to derive answers to facts they do not know.

The sequence below emphasizes counting only when *short counts* are involved. Visual cues are introduced to help students with subtraction doubles and 10-minuend facts. Throughout this work with easier facts, adding to check work is recommended. This approach nurtures an understanding of the addition-subtraction relationship and increases the possibility that children will USE addition to help, especially when answering more difficult, teen-minuend facts.

Towards this end, we suggest that subtraction be delayed until students have mastered a modest group of addition facts. It also is better not to teach addition and related subtraction facts in back-to-back units of instruction. Students cannot *use* addition to check or to answer subtraction facts unless they first know related addition facts *well*. Delaying subtraction allows time for the necessary consolidation and the possibility that children will use addition as a retrieval strategy in subtraction number fact work. For students who continue to experience difficulty doing so, a method of using "10 as a bridge" is presented to help with more difficult, teen-minuend facts.

Suggested Sequence of Activities and Exercises

Prerequisite skills:

- Ability to recognize when two or three numbers have been said;
- Ability to count on (from any number, 4 to 9);

- Ability to count back (from any number, 4 to 12);
- Mastery of related addition facts.

   Note: Refer to *Counting in Early Number Work*, page 40 in Chapter 2, for help with the first three prerequisites.

Instructional Overview

- 27 Count backs: (10, 9, 8, 7, 6, 5, 4, 3, 2) −1; (11, 10, 9, 8, 7, 6, 5, 4, 3) −2; (12, 11, 10, 9, 8, 7, 6, 5, 4) −3.
- 19 Zeros: n − 0 and n − n (n = any number, 0 to 9).
- 6 New Doubles: (8 − 4, 10 − 5, 12 − 6, 14 − 7, 16 − 8, 18 − 9).
- 7 Ten-Frame Facts: 10− (9, 8, 7, 6, 4); also 9 − 5, 9 − 4 (see Figure 4-43).
- 15 Count ups: (12, 11) −9; (11, 9) −8; (9, 8) −7; (9, 8, 7) −6; (8, 7, 6) −5; (7, 6, 5) −4.
- 26 Harder Facts: (17, 16, 15, 14, 13) −9; (17, 15, 14, 13, 12) −8; (16, 15, 13, 12, 11) −7; (15, 14, 13, 11) −6; (14, 13, 12, 11) −5; (13, 12, 11) −4.

9: All but one in the 10-frame

9 − 5 ooo Start with 9. Take out top row. 4 are left.

9 − 4 ooooo Start with 9 Take out bottom row. 5 are left.

Figure 4-43

Basic Sequence

1. **Count back.** Let children use interlocking cubes. For each *Count-Back* fact you select, students form a train with the cubes and count back as they break

off cubes to model the subtraction. In this example, students start with a train of 12 cubes and count back as, one by one, they break off three cubes. Initially, using cubes helps avoid counting pitfalls which leave a child one *off* in the backwards count. Get students to the point where they touch or look at the greater number (12 in 12 − 3), count back mentally, and use the cube train to check. Follow with tracking exercises as in the section on page 177. *Language emphasis:* "See −1 (take away 1), −2, −3? Start big and count back."

2. **Add to check.** As soon as students can use a strategy accurately and efficiently to solve a group of unknown subtraction facts, provide *add to check* activities. These are *not* introduced on the same day as a new strategy.

   - *Example 1:* **Break a stick.** For "7 − 2," children make a train of 7 cubes, break off 2, and write or tell (for teacher to write) the subtraction sentence that models what was done (7 − 2 = 5). They then put the parts back together: add to check. "7 − 2 = 5 *because* 2 + 5 = 7." Repeat for other facts.

   - *Example 2:* **My favorites.** On a regular basis, invite students to circle two or three *favorite* problems on a worksheet and write the "add to check fact" beside each. Afterwards select one number fact pair on a page and ask the child to use counters to prove that what is written makes sense.

3. **Show with objects.** Introduce subtraction zero facts. Be sure students can use objects to illustrate number sentences involving zero.

4. **Use a picture to help.** Familiar pictures from addition can be used to help children with subtraction doubles (see Figure 4-32). For example: 10 fingers, remove 5: 10 − 5 = 5 are left. Or 12 eggs, remove 6: 6 are left. Integrate tracking suggestions from the section beginning on page 177, until children can *write* an answer, and then use the picture to check. Later emphasize "Add to check" activities, as in Activity 2.

   Note: As students master each new group of subtraction facts, cross them off a master list.

5. **Use the 10-frame to help.** Provide counters and individual 10-frames. Starting with a full frame, students can take out some to model the subtraction (see Figure 4-44). Integrate tracking suggestions from Section 4 until students can write an answer and then use the 10-frame to check. Later emphasize "Add to check" activities, as in Activity 2.

6. **Model the counting up.** When children do not know a fact and do not recognize it as a *Count Back* (a −1, −2, −3 fact), double, or 10-minuend fact, it often is easiest for them to count up. Start with counters, as suggested in Figure 4-45, use color coding to help students recognize, and start with the

10: A full house

Figure 4-44

Count up from the known part.

Figure 4-45

known part. When using the *Count Up* cards as in Figure 4-45b, alternate with the child as follows.

Teacher (showing the card): "Say the part you know."
Child: "7."
Teacher (continues the count): "8,9. How many numbers did I say?"
Child: "Two."
Teacher: "Yes, so the answer is 2."

Repeat immediately for other *Count Ups*. At a later time, teacher and child can switch roles—the teacher can say the known part, the child can count on and say the answer. Alternating roles helps avoid counting pitfalls which leave students one off in the count. Integrate tracking suggestions from Section 4 until children can *write* an answer and use the *Count Up* card or counters only to check. Later emphasize add to check activities, as in Activity 2.

Note: If "Add to check" work has been carried out consistently in earlier work, some students may be able to use known addition instead of counting out answers.

7. **Help with harder, teen-minuend facts.** Of the 100 basic subtraction facts, those with teen minuends are typically the most difficult to master. Some learning disabled children can learn to think of and use related addition facts as a help. For example: "13 − 6 = 7 *because* 6 + 7 = 13." Others find it easier to build on doubles or 10-minuend facts which they already know. For example: "12 − 6 = 6, so 13 − 6 is one more" (7); "12 − 6 = 6, so 11 − 6 is one less" (5); "10 − 7 = 3, so 11 − 7 is one more" (40); "10 − 7 = 3, so 9 − 7 is one less" (2). To subtract 9, some students notice and use one of the number patterns illustrated in Figure 4-46. In each case, follow-through tracking exercises, as suggested in Section 4 (page 177), typically are useful.

Figure 4-46

8. **Subtract through 10.** When none of the suggestions help students with harder, teen-minuend facts, teachers might:

• Help students recognize how fact pairs like those of Figure 4-47 differ. Color coding, as illustrated, may also help. Children should note that 13 is 3 more than 10. Model, if necessary, using a 10-frame: place 3 counters outside a full frame. Comment that the answer to 13 − 6, then, is just *three* more than that of 10 − 6. Repeat for other number pairs. For the moment, do not focus on answers at all. Continue until children are aware of the pattern. Then tell them that you will show them how to find answers to difficult problems like this (point to 13 − 6) by first thinking of the easy 10 problem (point to 10 − 6).

• Help students identify their "zero" finger. "You'll need a zero finger to help you think of the easy '10' fact." Have children examine the index fingers of their right hands. Get them to note how the fingernail resembles a 0 (zero). Write a "0" on the nail or put a hole reinforcer on it. "This is your zero finger."

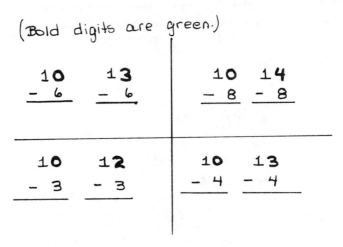

Figure 4-47

- Show students how to use their zero finger. Refer to the sheet of Figure 4-46 again. Have the children use their zero finger to cover the ones digit of a problem like 13 − 6 (the second of a pair). "See how this problem now 'looks like' the easy '10' problem? With your finger in place it reads '10 − 6.' "

- Practice subtracting from 10 and adding the extras. (Refer to Figure 4-48.)

   —Write a teen-minuend problem like 13 − 6 on a sheet of paper.
   —Have children cover the ones digit of the minuend with their zero finger and give the answer to the easy 10 problem.

Figure 4-48

—Children should then remove the zero finger and add in the extra ones.

—Repeat for other teen-minuend facts. Incorporate tracking as in Section 4 and follow through with an "Add to check" activity as in Activity 2.

MULTIPLICATION FACTS: MODELS, PATTERNS, TACTILE CUES

Problem area: Difficulty memorizing the basic multiplication facts. Use of wild guessing or inefficient counting techniques.

Typical disabilities affecting progress: Difficulty with visual, auditory, or long-term memory; visual or auditory discrimination; expressive language.

Background: When planning a program of fact study for learning disabled students teachers must consider the following:

1. The techniques children use to figure out unknown facts.

2. The sequence in which unknown facts are clustered for study.

Children who have not yet mastered the multiplication facts often use wrong or inefficient techniques for arriving at answers to given facts. Sometimes, particularly when their concept of multiplication is weak, children tend to guess at answers and often miss. Or they may resort to some form of counting. Some, given a problem like 7×5, very tediously lay out counters or use tally marks to show seven groups of five, and then count by 5s to determine the total number. Some children do not rely on objects but skip count mentally to find simple products.

Skip counting by 2s and 5s is relatively easy and enables a child to figure out answers to multiplication fact answers. Otherwise, skip counting is difficult for children and, in general, slower than other techniques and models, such as those that follow. If the disability is so severe that children cannot learn to apply the more efficient approaches to memorizing the facts, serious thought should be given to using a hand calculator for multiplication and division.

The extent to which children succeed in fact mastery is tempered by the sequence in which facts are presented for study. Thus, traditional textbook sequences must often be replaced by a program of study that maximizes success and minimizes frustration in early sessions with facts. The following sequence has proven highly effective in this regard.

The basic plan in the suggested sequence is "easy facts first." Motivated by success at learning "so many facts so fast" (relatively speaking), students are encouraged to study hard the few that remain. First 2s and 5s, then 9s—since, with the following approaches, these are the easiest to learn. (It is assumed that the commutatives of facts are studied at each step throughout the sequence.) Thus, if children also know 0s and 1s, there are only 15 other facts to be studied. Ideas for helping children master these last facts are included in the activities which follow.

> *Note:* Sometimes it is preferable that children begin memorizing their multiplication facts after they have learned the addition facts. Traditionally, however, addition and subtraction facts are presented first, then multiplication and, finally, division. For some students, especially those who require overlearning and are weak in abstract reasoning, a more reasonable sequence involves learning the multiplication facts before the subtraction facts. (The assumption is that the concept of multiplication is addressed first, even if only at a very concrete level.)

Suggested Sequence of Activities and Exercises

The following ideas are intended to be used in early sessions with each cluster of facts with tracking pages and reinforcing practice activities carried out systematically during later sessions.

1. **2s and addition doubles.** Children who know addition doubles usually have little difficulty with multiplication 2s. Use the models for doubles in Figure 4-33 to help with multiplication 2s.

   - *Example:* $2 \times 6 = 12$ (egg carton model). "Two rows of six, or *2 times* 6—that's 12." After the $\times 2$ facts are established, children study the commutative facts. Model the commutative idea. For example, use the egg carton model or dots on cards to illustrate that 2 rows of six and 6 rows of two give the same total number: 12. Cueing exercises such as those suggested by Figure 4-49 can be used, if necessary. If additional auditory reinforcement is needed, have the children read matching pairs into a tape recorder and listen to the playback.

   - *Example:* The child reads into a tape recorder: "2×8. That's 16, the crayon fact." "2×6. That's 12, the egg carton fact . . . ." Matching pairs could also be colored or texturized alike on charts or cards for ready reference.

(b) Which has the same answer?

2 X 6

6 X 2
3 X 6

2 X 5

2 X 3
5 X 2

Figure 4-49

Note: Techniques similar to those just presented are used to reinforce the learning of other multiplication facts.

2. **5s and clock times.** If children can tell time on the clock, use this skill to help them memorize multiplication 5s. (For special help in teaching clock times, refer to Chapter 3.) The half-hour time should cue the answer to 6×5 and 5×6 (30). For 9×5 and 5×9, the children should think of a time like 2:**45** (big hand on the 9). For 7×5 and 5×7, children can think of the big hand on the 7 (2:**35**). If they cannot recall the minute time right away, cue them to think of the minute hand moving from the 6 to the 7: 5×6 = 30 (the half-hour fact), so 5×7 is 5 more (35). Similarly, if 3×5 and 9×5, facts associated with the quarter hour times, are learned first, then other more difficult facts can be related to them.

- *Example:* $3 \times 5 = 15$, so $4 \times 5 = 20$ (5 more). $9 \times 5 = 45$, so $5 \times 8 = 40$ (5 less). It usually helps to use a geared clock during instruction to illustrate answers to flash card problems. Visual, auditory, and kinesthetic cueing should also be used, as needed, to teach to the *strengths* of individual students. Ideas suggested in Activity 1 or in Figure 4-50 can be used for this purpose. Follow through with tracking, as suggested on page 177.

3. **9s patterns or finger cues.** Many patterns can be derived from the 9s tables (refer to Figure 4-51). For example, the sum of the answer digits is always 9; the first digit of the product is always one less than the factor being multiplied

Figure 4-50

by 9. Some learning disabled students can learn to recognize and use these patterns as a help in fact recall. Most cannot, however—there are too many separate patterns to be integrated and remembered. But students can use their hands for multiplication 9s. To do so, they first "number" their fingers, left to right, from 1 to 10 as in Figure 4-52a. Then, to multiply 9 × 3 (or 3 × 9), students fold their 3rd finger down (Figure 4-52b) and read the product from their fingers: 2 fingers to the left and 7 to the right of the folded finger: 27. For 7 × 9 or 9 × 7, they fold their fingers: 6 fingers to the left and 3 to the right of the folded finger: 63. Whether 9s are approached through patterns or finger cues, reinforcement, as noted elsewhere in this chapter, should be provided, along with tracking pages (page 180).

4. **Take stock.** If the students do not already know multiplication of 0s and 1s, these strategies could be introduced at this point (see page 211 of this chapter for ideas on "× 0"). It is assumed that the commutatives of facts is studied throughout the sequence. So when students have mastered 0s, 1s, 2s, 5s, and 9s—the "easy" facts—there are only 15 facts (and their commutatives) left for study: 3 × (3, 4, 6, 7, 8); 4 × (4, 6, 7, 8); 6 × (6, 7, 8); 7 × (7, 8); and 8 × 8. Because the sequence to this point has emphasized the easy facts, it helps children learn many facts in a relatively short time. It is important now to determine along with the students what facts they have learned and what remains to be studied. Charts like those of Figures 4-53 or 4-54 can be used for this purpose.

Note: While they are not technically "basic" facts, some students may enjoy studying 10s and 11s before turning to harder facts. Since they probably can already skip count by 10s, the multiplication pattern for 10s is

X	9
1	9
2	18
3	27
4	36
5	45
6	54
7	63
8	72
9	81

Figure 4-51

a)

b)

Figure 4-52

Figure 4-53

Figure 4-54

easy to learn. Permit students to use a hand calculator to discover the patterning for 11s.

5. **15 to go.** Some learning disabled students will need to rely solely on tracking pages and other practice activities to master the 15 remaining facts. Others can handle cues or strategies like the following in the early stages of learning the facts. Several of the following strategies, such as "twice as much" and "add on", require a higher level of reasoning. If used, cueing techniques similar to those presented in Activity 1, are recommended.

- **Twice as much.** The distributive property can be applied to "slicing down" harder facts for easier study. The basic idea is to use two easier facts to figure out a harder one.

- *Example:* 7 × 8. The child can add as in Figure 4-55. Parentheses have purposely been avoided. Still, writing out everything is visually confusing to many children. Keep the presentation oral, perhaps writing just the "16 + 40 = 56." The easiest use of this idea is:

Figure 4-55

"Figure out half, then double it." Approximately half the remaining 15 facts can be learned using this approach.

- *Example:* "4 × 6. Think of half: 2 × 6 = 12. Now double it: 4 × 6 = 24." "Twice as many cards," pictured in Figure 4-56, can be used to illustrate the point.

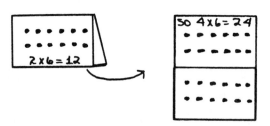

Figure 4-56

- **Add on.** An example of this familiar notion will serve to emphasize the idea: $5 \times 8 = 40$, so $6 \times 8 = 48$ (8 more). Children build from known facts. Encourage them to think: "5 eights. Now we have 6 eights. What do we add?" (8).

- *Variation:* Subtract from (a known fact): $5 \times 4 = 20$, so $4 \times 4 = 16$ (4 less). "5 fours. Now 4 fours. So 4 less."

- **It's a square.** Five of the remaining facts are perfect squares and can be shown as in Figure 4-57. Children with strong visual memories might be cued by thinking of the squares.

Figure 4-57

- **Other cues.** Children themselves have suggested the following cues. (a) 6s rhyme: 6×4, 24; 6×6, 36; 6×8; 48. (b) The "grade school" facts: In order, grades 1, 2, 3, and 4 ($12 = 3 \times 4$); 5, 6, 7, and 8 ($56 = 7 \times 8$). Sharing ideas like these sometimes helps children create their own.

DIVISION FACTS: STRATEGIES FOR LEARNING

Problem area: Difficulty memorizing division facts.

Typical disabilities affecting progress: Difficulty with visual, auditory, or long-term memory; visual or auditory discrimination; expressive language.

Background: Learning disabled students find it difficult to master division facts for two major reasons: (a) They do not know related multiplication facts; hence they cannot use them to derive or check answers to related division facts; and (b) specific disabilities stand in the way. The suggestions which follow are based on the assumption that the first obstacle can largely be removed if division is *delayed* until students have mastered a reasonable number of multiplication facts. The suggestions otherwise are based on cueing and tracking strategies which have proven effective with many students.

Suggested Sequence of Activities and Exercises

Easy Facts: ÷2s, ÷5s, ÷9s

1. **Teach a way to work out answers fast.** If students do not know ÷2s, ÷5s, or ÷9s, they can use retrieval strategies parallel to those for multiplication 2s, 5s, and 9s to help. Language emphasis:

   "See ÷2? What's the picture?" (For 14 ÷ 2, for example: 14 days, divided by 2 weeks—7 days in each week.)

   "See ÷5? Think minutes after. Where's the minute hand?" (For example: 35 ÷ 5: think 35 minutes after—minute hand is on the answer digit, 7.)

   "See ÷9? What's the pattern?" (Refer to the suggestions of Figure 4-58.)

   In addition to the auditory language emphasis, visual cues including color coding, can be used to promote more rapid recall of unknown facts.

Figure 4-58

2. **Multiply to check.** No matter how the subtraction or division answer is obtained, follow through, when possible, with feedback like the following: "Yes, 15 ÷ 5 is 3 because 5 × 3 = 15." Use materials to illustrate the relationship between a pair of facts: 15 objects shared among 3, each gets 5. And (return to the original position) 3 fives = 15.

- *Variation:* Have the children write answers to a small set of division facts and listen to a tape recorder to check. The taped message should give not only the answer but the related fact each time.

3. **Find it.** Provide exercises like that of Figure 4-59 in which children cross out the wrong helping fact and answer the related helping fact along with the division fact given. Follow through with tracking as in Section 4, page 177. Include flash cards where children answer a given division fact, then flip over to the side with the related multiplication fact to check. Use color cueing as in Figure 4-60 if this seems helpful.

4. **Circle favorites.** On a regular basis, invite students to circle two or three favorite division problems on a worksheet and write the "multiply to check" fact beside each. Afterwards select one number fact pair on a page and ask the child to use counters to show that what is written makes sense.

5. **Helpers.** Place multiplication facts that the children *know* at the top of a worksheet. Suggest that they use them to help answer the division fact problems on the page. Students may even write the helper fact beside the fact given.

$$35 \div 5 = \underline{\hspace{1cm}}$$

| 5 × 6 = _____ |
| 5 × 7 = _____ |

Figure 4-59

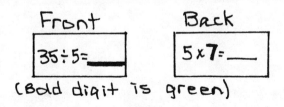

Front

$$35 \div 5 = \underline{\hspace{1cm}}$$

Back

$$5 \times 7 = \underline{\hspace{1cm}}$$

(Bold digit is green)

Figure 4-60

6. **Throughout.** Encourage finger tracing (of textured number sentences) or use color coding throughout the preceding activities as necessary. Such cues are systematically withdrawn until the children can *independently* recall related multiplication facts to help with division problems.

7. **Teach related division facts.** For example, when students know 35 ÷ 5 = 7, they can use this fact to learn 35 ÷ 7 = 5. Or, if they know 36 ÷ 9 = 4, they can use this fact to learn 36 ÷ 4 = 9. Follow the previous suggestions including tracking, as in Section 4.

8. **Consolidate learning by finding fact "families."** Provide an opportunity for students to sort flash cards into families like 35 ÷ 5 = 7, 7 × 5 = 35. Related facts could be color coded alike in early sessions. Alternatively, the backs of cards containing related facts could be keyed alike (e.g., all carry a red dot).

   • *Variation:* Provide puzzles of familiar objects with related facts written on the pieces of each puzzle (Figure 4-61). Encourage thinking by using the same color for pairs of puzzles the children are asked to piece together.

Figure 4-61

Special Facts

Use objects and story lines to help illustrate ideas. For example, 0 ÷ 5 can be interpreted as having nothing to share—so each of the five gets 0 things. Carry out sorts in which students mark only those facts having an answer of 0 (or 1).

Harder Facts

If "multiply to check" work has been carried out systematically as suggested before, many learning disabled students will be able to use this technique to derive answers to the remaining, more difficult division facts. If not, use the tracking suggestions of Section 4, page 177. As each new fact is mastered, help students learn related division facts. Consolidate learning by emphasizing fact families.

ZERO

Problem area: Confusion over answers to facts like $0 + 3$, 0×3, $3 - 0$, and $0 \div 3$. "Is the answer 0 or 3?"

Typical disabilities affecting progress: Difficulty with visual, auditory, or long-term memory; visual or auditory discrimination; expressive language; abstract reasoning.

Background: It is common for students to be confused over fact answers to problems containing 0 (zero). Learning disabled students are no exception. Often the problem does not show itself right away in addition and subtraction. After students have been introduced to multiplication, however, the difficulty quickly emerges. When *multiplying*, the product for facts containing 0 as a factor is always 0. When *adding* 0 to any other addend, the non-zero digit is the sum. Children become confused about when to write 0 (zero) for a fact answer. The following ideas may help when these difficulties appear.

Suggested Sequence of Activities and Exercises

1. **Act it out.** Introduce "0" facts dramatically. For example, have the students act out number facts containing 0.

   - *Example:* "3×0." Use a bag filled with candy. Dramatize reaching into the bag *three times* and, each time, bringing out no candy. "How much candy did I pull out of the bag?" (None.)

2. **Auditory cueing.** In the above activity and on other occasions when a "$\times 0$" fact appears, use an auditory cue to reinforce (prompt) the correct answer.

• *Example:* "× 0 is a wipeout. You get nothing at all."

3. **On the card.** Use number sentence cards for addition and multiplication "0" facts. Color all "+" signs green; all "×" signs brown. Mix the cards. In turn, have the students draw a card, give the answer, and use counters to prove they are right. The students should place counters for addition sentences on a green card, counters for multiplication sentences on a brown card. Emphasize to the students how the operation sign and card color match. Form two lines with the cards: one for addition, another for multiplication. Underscore that the brown cards have nothing on them. "× 0 is a wipeout—you get nothing at all."

> **Note:** Though this example focuses on addition and multiplication, a similar approach may be used for zero facts involving subtraction or division.

4. **Sort.** Have the students sort cards containing "0" facts into two piles: "a zero answer" and "not-a-zero answer" pile.

5. **Move.** Create games in which the children draw a "0" fact card to determine the number of moves made along a path. Carry through the color coding on the cards as before, if this seems helpful. The children drawing a "× 0" number fact would stay where they are. "× 0 is a wipeout. You get nothing at all."

USING A HAND CALCULATOR

Several suggestions for using a calculator to build concepts or basic fact skills for the four operations follow.

• **Punch the sign.** Give the students sheets like the one presented in Figure 4-62. The children fill in the correct operation sign and punch out the problem on their calculators to see if they are correct.

$$\begin{array}{r} 3 \\ 5 \\ \hline 8 \end{array} \qquad \begin{array}{r} 10 \\ 3 \\ \hline 7 \end{array} \qquad \begin{array}{r} 6 \\ 4 \\ \hline 10 \end{array}$$

Figure 4-62

- **Turnarounds.** To review or reinforce the idea of commutatives, give the children sheets like that of Figure 4-63. They can use the calculator to check if both facts of a pair have the same answer.

- **Beat the calculator.** Have students compare times for completing a practice sheet of facts—with and without a calculator. They should find that sometimes they can work faster without a calculator.

- **Pick the helper.** (Subtraction or division facts.) Give the students a sheet like that in Figure 4-64. Have them circle the helper fact, then punch it into the calculator. If they get the green minuend (quotient) number as the answer, they know their response is correct.

$$3+7 = \underline{\hspace{2cm}}$$

$$7+3 = \underline{\hspace{2cm}}$$

$$5+4 = \underline{\hspace{2cm}}$$

$$4+5 = \underline{\hspace{2cm}}$$

Figure 4-63

a)

$$13 - 6 \quad \boxed{\begin{array}{c} 7+6 \\ \hline 7+8 \end{array}}$$

b)

$$56 \div 7 \quad \boxed{\begin{array}{c} 8 \times 7 \\ \hline 6 \times 7 \end{array}}$$

━ = green

Figure 4-64

CHAPTER

Whole Number Computation

In the previous chapter, whole number operations were discussed. Various methods were suggested as being effective ways to help learning disabled students understand and differentiate among the four operations. Ideas also were presented for helping students master the basic facts for each operation.

This chapter has three purposes: (a) to help learning disabled students select and use the appropriate computation method, particularly, estimation or mental calculation—in addition to calculator and standard paper-and-pencil approaches; (b) to help children extend and apply concepts and skills they know to longer, more complicated paper-and-pencil computations; and (c) to provide remedial alternatives for how to cope with some of the difficulties learning disabled students encounter with paper-and-pencil computations at the abstract level.

Computation involves using symbols and operation signs to arrive at numerical answers. Some children, because of abstract-reasoning, integrative, or auditory-processing deficits, lack important conceptual understandings necessary for success at the symbolic level. Other learning disabled students may, in fact, understand the concepts involved but still be unable to succeed with a computation.

Children may lack the memory and association skills that normally allow one to incorporate previously learned skills and to arrive at correct answers. For example, associating the correct operation with a sign or symbol involves two skills:

1. The ability to differentiate among all the different symbols; and
2. The ability to associate the correct symbol with the correct process—addition, subtraction, multiplication, and division.

215

For many children, these steps are extremely difficult. These are the students who often say, "Tell me what to do; then I can solve the problem." That statement does not mean that they do not understand the isolated operations conceptually. They may be capable of showing what to do for each operation. However, at this stage they are not being asked to show what they know. Instead, they are being asked to determine the correct process based on a symbol. Once they identify that process, they are on their way.

Children with visual-perception problems may have trouble with this type of association because they incorrectly discriminate among the signs. Children with receptive language deficits, in turn, may be able to associate the sign with the correct *word*—add, subtract, multiply, or divide; but the word may carry no meaning for them! Another group of students, those with expressive language deficits, may not be able to elicit—either verbally or to themselves—the correct process without being cued visually or auditorially.

Once children have associated the correct symbol with the correct process, they must determine the sequence that applies. Since most estimation and computational procedures involve more than one step, confusion often arises. To further complicate the situation, many computations involve two or more operations, even though only one sign is used.

Consider the problem of Figure 5-1a. One common approach to the mental calculation is shown. Even though the operation sign is subtraction, the first step is addition: adding **1** to **19**. Then, after the simple subtraction, $48 - 20$, is carried out, it is necessary to subtract 1 to adjust the result back to the original problem. To carry out the paper-and-pencil computation of Figure 5-1b in sequence it is necessary to subtract, add, subtract, and subtract; yet, the process is called subtraction.

Correct sequencing of steps is an especially difficult task for many students. Children with additional impairments to learning find it even more difficult, especially those with a memory-sequencing deficit, whether visual or auditory.

Further, the child with a discrimination difficulty, who confuses the "+" and "×" signs, may perceive the operation differently each time it is seen. Figure 5-2 illustrates how this disability can affect paper-and-pencil computation. At first glance, it would appear that this student needs more work, conceptually, on the process of multiplying a 2-digit number by a 1-digit number. However, listening to the student verbalize the procedure revealed that after carrying the 7, the student misperceived the sign and completed the computation using addition.

Alignment poses another difficulty. Consider multiplication of two 2-digit factors. Even with a good understanding of place value, basic facts, and multiplication by ones and tens, the ability to align numbers accurately can be tedious for some children. Figure 5-3 shows a step-by-step breakdown of the mental process involved.

For the child with poor motor coordination or impaired spatial organization, the process of solving the problem becomes twice as long. Every time it

$$\begin{array}{r} 48 \\ -19 \\ \hline \end{array}$$

a) Mental Calculation.

$$\begin{array}{r} 48 \\ -19 \\ \hline \end{array} \quad \text{ooo}$$

48-20
   that's 28.
Then subtract 1.

b) Paper and Pencil Calculation.

$$\begin{array}{r} 3 \\ 4\!\!\!/8 \\ -19 \\ \hline \end{array} \qquad \begin{array}{r} 3\;\;18 \\ 4\!\!\!/\,8\!\!\!/ \\ -19 \\ \hline \end{array} \qquad \begin{array}{r} 3\;\;18 \\ 4\!\!\!/\,8\!\!\!/ \\ -19 \\ \hline 9 \end{array} \qquad \begin{array}{r} 3\;\;18 \\ 4\!\!\!/\,8\!\!\!/ \\ -19 \\ \hline 29 \end{array}$$

Figure 5-1

$$\begin{array}{r} 1\!\!\!/ \\ 48 \\ \times\;\;9 \\ \hline 112 \end{array}$$

Figure 5-2

is necessary to write a digit, this student must stop and look at the problem. The digits already present must be sorted out, and it is necessary to coordinate what is seen with what the hand does. Although this child may possess a solid understanding of place value and the steps involved, the sequence is interrupted, considerably and consistently, whenever it becomes necessary to write a number.

Visual figure-ground deficits and reversal tendencies also impede accuracy of paper-and-pencil computation. Consider Figure 5-4 in which a child is asked

$$
\begin{array}{r}
46 \\
\times\,34 \\
\hline
\end{array}
$$

Figure 5-3

$$
\begin{array}{r}
{}^{8}{\not9}\,{}^{11}{\not{16}} \\
-\,2\,4\,5 \\
\hline
6\,2\,1
\end{array}
$$

Figure 5-4

to perform a common subtraction problem. At first sight, it would appear that the difficulty might be inadequate mastery of facts (and, in many instances, it may well be). However, upon questioning the child, it became apparent that the difficulty lay in having to visually align the numbers in order to compute accurately. The first step was correct; the student thought "6 take away 5" and wrote

1. Next, the numbers were correctly regrouped. But then the student lost the place and saw "6 subtract 4." The last step, "8 subtract 2," is accurate.

For students with reversal and visual memory deficits, regrouping causes special problems. So does long division. Figure 5-5a shows how a child who tends to reverse might solve a division problem. In the first example, the 6 was perceived as a 2, but otherwise the computation and the procedure are correct. Obviously, this student understands the steps for long division and knows the required facts for the problem.

Figure 5-5b shows the same division problem, but this time the way it would challenge somebody with reversal and discrimination difficulties. The student initially perceived the 6 as a "6" and wrote 1 in the quotient. However, at the multiplication step, the divisor was seen as a 2, thus, the product 2. In the subtraction step, the 2 was perceived as a "6," resulting in a difference of 2.

At first glance, this student appears to be careless and unsure of the basic facts involved. However, in examples like this, questioning or looking at a computation in light of a child's previous work may reveal that the child does know the needed facts and is familiar with the correct process. Specific learning disabilities may be at the root of the problem.

Figure 5-5

Computational accuracy often involves estimating to check whether an answer is reasonable. This is difficult for most students and especially for many children with learning disabilities. Although an essential part of learning how to estimate involves concrete presentations, actual application of the skill is abstract and requires a considerable amount of reasoning and retention. Therefore, children who have any kind of processing deficit must learn to estimate through a highly structured approach. Many will not intuitively recognize when an answer is incorrect. Others may sense that something is wrong, but be unable to figure out or express exactly what it is.

In the following pages we recommend sequences and techniques for helping students who have difficulties like those previously described. Suggestions are clustered under five major headings. The first, general difficulties with whole number computation, examines special problems that children may experience with basic facts in computation or in associating operation sign and process. Thereafter, ideas are presented for how to handle computational difficulties for whole number addition, subtraction, multiplication, and division. Ideas for using the hand calculator to help learning disabled students master whole number computation are interwoven throughout the chapter.

GENERAL DIFFICULTIES

Controlling for Unknown Facts

Problem area: Failure to succeed in estimation, mental or paper-and-pencil computation because of inadequate fact mastery.

Typical disabilities affecting progress: Difficulty with visual, auditory, or long-term memory; visual or auditory discrimination; expressive language.

Background: Computing involves using the basic facts. Learning disabled students, like their peers, become frustrated and often fail on computation involving facts they have not yet mastered. Many students are ready, developmentally, to learn the more complicated computational procedures but have not yet committed the basic facts to memory. *To require them to learn the facts first may hold them back unnecessarily.* With these students, it is important to keep in mind, as noted in Chapter 1, the goal of a particular assignment. If the goal is to learn and use the various computational procedures, then memorizing the facts is a secondary and separate topic. The following are two approaches for dealing with this issue.

Suggested Sequence of Activities and Exercises

1. **Controlled facts program.** One approach consists of controlling the entire math program around known facts. This very specialized approach involves considerable preparation and care. Specifically, it requires that one select or create computational exercises so that only *known* facts are required for deriving answers. This approach is obviously not a practical one in mainstreamed or other instructional situations where teachers work with larger groups of students. However, it may be necessary in special cases.

Note: Most children know at least some of the easier facts, such as doubles in addition or twos and fives in multiplication. Easy facts like these can be used to present or review computational procedures. In this way, learning disabled children can still be a successful part of the class even though they may still be working on isolated facts.

2. **Only known facts.** Many children benefit from controlled fact pages as shown in Figure 5-6. Place two basic facts that are being worked on at the top of the page. The computation problems on the page involve only these and any other known facts, in this case twos and fives.

Figure 5-6

3. **Cross out.** Give each child a sheet of facts such as that shown in Figure 5-7. Help students cross out (blacken *completely*) all the facts they have already mastered. Then allow them to refer to the sheet whenever necessary. In the meantime, challenge them to learn several unknown facts each week. Choose the facts carefully, following the suggestions from Chapter 4.

   • *Example:* Select facts that are *one more than* some fact a child already knows. If a child knows $10 - 7 = 3$, select $9 - 7$ (1 less than $10 - 7$). Make sure the children are aware of any relationships between new and known facts; suggest that they use those relationships to figure out answers if they become confused. Each day, provide tracking pages on the three or four facts being studied. Then, at the end of the week, test the new facts in a mixed review quiz that also includes other known facts. These facts should be blackened as they are mastered.

   To check for consistency over time, some teachers circle or yellow highlight a fact the first time the student answers it correctly (and quickly) in an assessment setting. If the fact is also answered correctly (and quickly) in a second assessment setting, it is blackened *completely* as shown in Figure 5-7.

Glue to 4x6 index card.

Figure 5-7

Basic Facts: Transfer to Larger Problems

Problem area: Failure to answer correctly KNOWN facts embedded within larger computational problems.

Typical disabilities affecting progress: Difficulty with visual discrimination or visual association; abstract reasoning; expressive language, memory.

Background: Many learning disabled students are unable, independently, to use basic facts within a computation until they have learned the procedure and feel comfortable with it. These are students who do reasonably well on fact tests. But they are unable to incorporate the facts into the computation until over-learning has occurred. It requires too much retention and sequencing for them to learn a new skill while trying to recall other isolated pieces of information. Hence they fail to transfer fact learning to computational situations. The suggestions that follow may help deal with this problem.

Suggested Sequence of Activities and Exercises

1. **Write it out.** If children get stuck within a larger computation because they cannot recall a known fact, suggest that they write the problem fact to one side. Seeing the fact in isolation often triggers recognition and allows children to proceed.

2. **Finger trace.** If students are strong tactual learners, suggest that they finger trace over the problem fact, quietly saying it to themselves. If they are strong auditory learners, on the other hand, simply saying the fact to themselves may do.

3. **Circle.** Have students circle the problem fact within a problem or write over it as a means of better focusing on it.

4. **Side by side.** Help train for the desired transfer by providing practice sheets that place a basic fact beside a larger computational problem using this fact (Figure 5-8).

(Bold digits are green.)

a) 7   47   b) **7**   47
   +8   +68   **+8**   +**6**8

Figure 5-8

5. **Color code.** Provide extra visual reinforcement, if this is helpful, on the Activity 4 sheets, by color cueing as suggested by Figure 5-8b.

6. **Track.** Provide tracking pages containing larger computational problems. Have the students look for and circle a given fact any time it appears on the page.

7. **Look to the chart.** Allow children to use a multiplication chart, their *Cross Out* sheet (modification of the Figure 5-7 chart, with all facts visible), or a fact box. Experience has shown that as children feel comfortable with a computational procedure, the need for these aids disappears.

SELECTING THE COMPUTATION METHOD

Problem area: Difficulty recognizing that a computation can be carried out best by estimating or making a quick mental calculation, rather than computing by hand.

Typical disabilities affecting progress: Difficulty with abstract reasoning; short-term and sequential memory; integrative processing.

Background: Because of changes in technology, it is no longer necessary or useful for students to spend large amounts of time learning to perform routine computations by hand. This was recently emphasized by the National Council of Teachers of Mathematics in its *Curriculum and Evaluation Standards for School Mathematics* (1989), and already is having impact on school mathematics textbooks. Perhaps the greatest implication for the teaching of computation involves:

- Restricting paper-and-pencil computations to simpler numbers. Certainly, additions and subtractions beyond 3 or 4 digits and divisors or factors beyond 2 digits are "out."

- Fostering an emphasis on *selecting the most appropriate method* for performing a given computation.

As the National Council of Teachers of Mathematics noted, one might "estimate the amount of a tip in a restaurant, use a calculator to fill out a tax form, or use a computer to determine how long it will take to pay off a credit-card balance" (1987, p. 69). On the other hand, particularly if a calculator is not readily available, one might compute by hand the total cost of an order placed by mail, figure out the amount of cloth needed for a costume, or even balance a checkbook!

Using Calculators

Most learning disabled students will readily turn to calculators as an alternative to paper-and-pencil computation because they can be used to get answers quickly. And, when the calculators are in good working condition and properly used, they are accurate.

Since there are many different models from which to select, students typically can find one that works well for them. For example, calculators which have a print out are helpful for students with motor or memory difficulties. The tape can be used for reference when input cannot be remembered. The tape also can be used to check whether digits were entered accurately. Calculators with larger numbers on the print out, or ones which print out in different colors accommodate students with visual deficits. Talking calculators, if the auditory output is very clear and consistent with what is displayed, are useful or even necessary for others.

> **Note:** Many calculators display outputs in the thousands or greater with commas at the top of the number (e.g., 3'765). This type of display can not only be confusing, but also requires that students must learn and then ignore (unlearn) a procedure.

In general, a calculator should be selected that carries out simple arithmetic functions like 3 + 4 = _____ in the typical linear sequence:

- Enter first addend;

- Enter "+";

- Enter second addend;

- Enter "=."

Some calculators would have the user enter the two addends, then push the operation symbol, "+". This style, of course, is more difficult. Some calculators display the entire input, such as 6 + 4 = 10. Although difficult to find, the latter models are not expensive and for students with memory and sequencing problems might be the best choice.

Whatever the calculator model, instructional emphasis in mathematics should include helping children use calculators accurately, with all the power they possess. Some children work with calculators *inefficiently* because they do not know how to use the memory key. Ideas for how to integrate calculator use in instruction on the paper-and-pencil algorithms are included in other sections of this chapter. The suggestions below focus on helping students determine *when* to select the calculator as an alternative to other computational approaches.

Making Mental Calculations

Learning to compute mentally, that is, to calculate exact numerical answers without the aid of calculators or paper-and-pencil algorithms, is a useful skill. Many everyday problems can be solved mentally. For example, it is now 2:30. I should bake the brownies for 35 minutes. When do I take them out? Or, I want to buy a tape that costs $9.95. I have $7.15. If I make $2.50 cutting grass for the neighbor, will that be enough?

The ability to compute mentally requires integrative and simultaneous processing, short-term and visual memory, and reasoning skills—areas which some students find extremely difficult or lack entirely. In spite of their disabilities, other students can learn modified mental algorithms which make it possible for them to carry out mentally at least the most simple additions and subtractions.

The premise pertinent to the focus of this section is that if students are to select appropriately among computational alternatives, an effort must first be made to develop each individual's potential for computing mentally. Specific, systematic instruction designed to develop mental computation skills is necessary. One might, for example, consider the following instructional sequence:

- Introduce a new mental technique or focus on a mental skill;

- Reinforce the new technique or mental skill;

- Review the new technique or mental skill in the same lesson during which a previously learned technique or skill is reviewed; compare and contrast the two; and

- Provide review sessions on a regular basis which alternate among techniques or mental skills previously taught.

One important aspect of teaching mental math is developing mental imagery to help students perform a computation "in their heads." Visual, auditory, kinesthetic/tactile approaches may be used. For example, students might use their fingers to "write" a problem in the air or on the desk. For some mental algorithms, using teaching aids such as hundreds charts, money, base-ten blocks or number lines during initial instruction may provide a frame of reference for later recall. Perhaps the key with learning disabled students is to help them explore what they are able to do, and then help them develop "modified mental algorithms." These are algorithms which also include *writing* some numbers as an aid to the mental thinking process.

"One step at a time" is also necessary for instructional planning and student success. For example, building student skill in the following areas leads to success with simple mental computation tasks.

Developing basic skills (extensions of basic facts; counting)

Look Ahead to Addition and Subtraction

- Add multiples of 10 and 100 (3 + 4 = 7, so 30 + 40 = 70, and 300 + 400 = 700). If students experience difficulty with basic facts, use ideas from General Sections 1 and 2 (this chapter).

- Count on and back by 10s on the hundreds chart (e.g., Chapter 2, Figure 2-35); start with 34; with 62; . . .

Look Ahead to Multiplication and Division

- Skip count by 10s, 20s, 30s . . . .

- Skip count by 25s, 50s . . . .

- Multiply multiples of 10 and 100 (3 × 2 = 6, so 3 × 20 and 30 × 2 = 60; 30 × 20 = 600; 3 × 200 and 300 × 2 = 600).

Applying to mental addition

- Apply basic skills to mentally adding problems like 34 + 10; 34 + 40. Students may continue to count on by 10s from 34, as on the hundreds chart (Figure 2-35). Students may, in fact, be helped if they can refer to a hundreds chart. For 34 + 40, some students may focus on the tens digits, use known facts, and immediately say "74."

- Apply previous skill to mentally adding problems like 34 + 42, as in Figure 5-9.

   Note: Some students will need specific practice on visualizing and retaining the relevant part of the addition problem. Have short practice sessions where addition problems, with the important digits highlighted, are flashed. Ask the student to state and solve the highlighted part, as in Figure 5-9a. Later, practice without highlighting, as in Figure 5-9b.

- Next consider 34 + 49 types. As in Figure 5-10, some students may find it easier to add 34 + 50, then subtract 1 to compensate. Others may prefer to add 34 to 40, and count on 9! While the second approach clearly is less efficient, it may be more straightforward for some and could be allowed. On the other hand, some students might initially prefer the second approach only because they do not understand any other. Most teachers at least introduce the first (more efficient) method to see whether it is within a student's range of thinking.

a) 34
  +4 2...   Student says: "34 plus 40 is 74 and then 2 more"

b) 43
  +25   43
         +20 ...then +5

━━ = green
···· = red

Figure 5-9

First:

34
+49   34
       +50 ···· then − 1

Figure 5-10

Applying to mental subtraction

- Apply basic skills to mentally subtracting problems like $65-10$; $65-40$. Students may continue to count back by 10s from 65, as on the hundreds chart. Students may be helped if they can refer to a hundreds chart. For $65-40$, some students may focus on the tens digits, use known facts, and immediately say "25."

- Apply previous skill to mentally subtracting problems like $65-42$, as in Figure 5-11.

- Next consider $65-49$ types. As in Figure 5-12 , some students may find it easier to subtract $65-50$, then add 1 because they subtracted 1 too many. Others may find it easier to use the tens digits that are visible, think "$65-40$, then count back 9"; or "$65-45$, then count back 4" to complete the subtraction. In the latter case, problems in which the ones digits are "1 or 2 different"—as in **$65-46$** or **$65-47$** might be used initially.

First

$$
\begin{array}{r} 65 \\ -42 \\ \hline \end{array} \,\,\circ\!\circ\!\circ
\left(
\begin{array}{r} 65 \\ -40 \\ \hline \end{array}
\right) \cdots \text{ then } -2
$$

Figure 5-11

First:

$$
\begin{array}{r} 65 \\ -49 \\ \hline \end{array} \,\,\circ\!\circ\!\circ
\left(
\begin{array}{r} 65 \\ -50 \\ \hline \end{array}
\right) \cdots \text{ then } +1
$$

Figure 5-12

Although these latter approaches clearly are less efficient, they may be more straightforward for some students and could be allowed. On the other hand, as commented for addition, some students might initially prefer these methods only because they do not understand any other. Most teachers typically introduce the more efficient method to see whether it is within a student's range of thinking.

Applying to multiplication and division

The major use of the basic skills involves multiplying multiples of 10 or 100 to check whether a given product or quotient is reasonable, as in Figure 5-13. Some students can learn to carry out simple 1-digit multiplications like 12 × 3, 31 × 4, or $2.50 × 2 mentally. Unless the student is interested in doing so, further mental calculation of products may not be useful. The value of mentally computing simple quotients beyond division basic facts is limited.

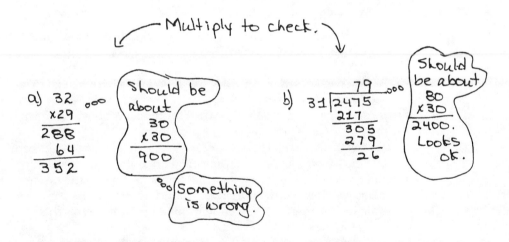

Figure 5-13

Assessment

Alternative ways of assessing progress must also be devised. Controlling time on each problem is critical. This can be accomplished by displaying each problem on an overhead transparency for only a brief time (10 seconds or 15 seconds or . . .) and then removing it. Students are to try to solve the problem mentally and may record only the answer in the the time allotted.

Using Computational Estimation

Estimation involves giving an answer that is "close to" the actual one. As such, it involves the ability to carry out some calculations mentally and assumes skills related to place value, rounding, and basic facts. Everyone estimates every day in one form or another. "I think I can eat that much bread." "I think I have enough time to get to school." "I think this is enough to pay for what I'm taking to the check out counter." Every day, newspaper headlines are full of estimates, and referring to them is a good way to acquaint students with the fact that in *most* everyday situations involving number, an estimate is "good enough."

When discussing estimation, instructional emphasis on the following steps is useful:

- Developing an awareness of what estimation is about (an approximate rather than an exact answer, as one is used to giving in math).

- Developing an awareness of how frequently an estimate is used in everyday numeric situations.

- Developing an awareness of when an estimate is "good enough" and when one is not "good enough."

At times, exact answers are needed. If your neighbor agreed to pay you $2.10 an hour for a job, and you worked 2 hours, then "about $4 is *not* good enough." If there are 23 people at a party and the host thought "about 20" when she brought out the party treats, that is *not* good enough.

On the other hand, there are times when an estimate might actually be the better choice. Consider the following. You are going to meet some friends at 8:00. It usually takes about two and one half hours to drive to the meeting place. You may want to allow a little more time than that just in case something happens. An estimate is certainly "good enough" and probably better than relying on the exact time it took on previous trips.

- Focus on front-end addition (Figure 5-14a). As a first approach, this method typically is easier for children than rounding.

- Focus on "getting closer." In the example of Figure 5-14a, since there are 8 ones, it means that 70 is an underestimate. There is almost enough to make another 10. Therefore, a closer estimate is 80.

- Focus on front-end subtraction (Figure 5-14b). Later, include refining of initial estimates.

- Focus on rounding to the lead digit. In Figure 5-14a, one would think: "About 40 + 40, or 80." This is the estimation method typically emphasized in school textbooks.

- Introduce the idea of looking for "nice" numbers. In Figure 5-15a, there clearly is enough to pay for one tape, but not enough for two. In Figure 5-15b, if only one can is needed, it is easier to overestimate as shown.

- Introduce the ideas of averaging in order to arrive at an estimate. When all numbers are "about the same"—as they may be in rainfall patterns in some areas, or in the individual meal costs of people sitting together in a restaurant—use the number that seems to be central. This number is sometimes called a "cluster point" or "average"—though an average is not actually calculated.

Figure 5-14

Figure 5-15

Making Paper-and-Pencil Calculations

Other sections of this chapter treat ways to help learning disabled students succeed with paper-and-pencil calculations. To be consistent with modern thinking, these calculations should be (a) those for which an estimate is "not good enough"; (b) restricted to smaller numbers; and (c) those which cannot be computed mentally.

The following suggestions emphasize ways to help students decide when one computation method may be "better" than others.

Suggested Sequence of Activities and Exercises

1. **Look for very big numbers.** As computation for each operation is treated, provide exercises which present a mix of problems, including smaller and larger numbers of digits. Have students just look for problems with larger digits and use a calculator to solve them.

   Note: To assess students' progress in estimation skills, consider a two-part assignment. Provide an assignment of mixed problems in a multiple-choice format. In the first part of the assignment the student merely decides which method of calculation is most appropriate and circles the choice. After the answers are checked, the student proceeds to solve the problems using the different methods.

2. **Look for quick ones.** Similarly, provide a mix of problems which include some that can be computed very quickly using mental calculation techniques students have mastered. Students who mentally can add problems like 34 + 40, but not 34 + 42 (see Figure 5-9) might be given just the first type of problem along with others which they would normally hand compute. More capable students might be given both types mixed with others. Directions for this exercise would be to "Look for and write down quickly the answer to just those problems you can work out in your head." When this step is checked, the remaining problems can be computed using the standard paper-and-pencil algorithm.

3. **Just do those with answers more than 40 (or any other target number).** Students must first develop estimation skills as previously suggested. Then ask them to apply that skill in an interesting way. For example, ask them to estimate and then hand compute just those problems for which they think the answers are above the target number.

It may be necessary to ask some students first to estimate and circle problems with answers over the target number. *When this step is checked*, students could be directed to hand solve the circled problems. Students working out of hardback books could place an acetate sheet over a page before circling. After this part of the assignment is checked, they could solve the circled problems on paper.

Each of the above activities required students to decide between hand computation and some other calculation method. It also would be useful to systematically ask students to decide between estimation and mental calculation, estimation and using a calculator, and mental calculation and using a calculator. These types of activities involve viable alternatives and provide students with a background for deciding which computation method is "best" in a given situation in light of their abilities.

WHOLE NUMBER COMPUTATION: IS MY ANSWER REASONABLE?

Problem area: Difficulty recognizing or failing to check whether a given computational answer "makes sense."

Typical disabilities affecting progress: Abstract reasoning; short-term or sequential memory; integrative processing problems; distractibility.

Background: Even when some students take the time to check over computation, they do not always recognize whether a given answer "makes sense." The previous section outlined estimation activities which are prerequisite to success in judging whether given answers are "reasonable." In addition, a good sense of number relationships—lacking or undeveloped in many learning disabled students—is an important part of the process.

The suggestions for how to develop number and operation sense provided in Chapters 2 and 4 bear directly on the prerequisites needed for the following activity suggestions, designed to lead to distinguishing whether given answers are "reasonable." When implementing suggestions like those which follow, one also must recognize that there is a difference between estimating to see whether an answer is unreasonable and checking to see if it is correct. Unless directions are explicit, students tend to redo the computation rather than simply estimating—the desired response in this case.

Activities like those which follow should take place *before* any related paper-and-pencil computational procedure is introduced or reviewed within a school year. This is necessary in order to increase the likelihood that students recognize when derived answers are "unreasonable."

As emphasized in several sections of this book, being "good" at estimating and detecting unreasonable answers is difficult. Some learning disabled students will acquire this skill after many structured experiences. Others may be able to make accurate decisions only when answers are "way off." We consider this last achievement major and worth working toward.

To help achieve this goal, a positive, supportive environment and role modeling are essential. Toward this latter end, some teachers consciously "think aloud," or call on students to do so, as they discuss how they determine whether an answer in a given situation "makes sense."

Suggested Sequence of Activities and Exercises

1. **Select the most reasonable.** Students need opportunities to react to what is reasonable in a variety of contexts and situations. Noncomputational examples like those of Figure 5-16 may be used.

   Note: In order to estimate, some students (not just small children) will need visual reminders. It may be helpful to provide real objects, have students weigh them, and then decide. Alternatively, use pictures of common objects accompanied by approximate weights. In this way, especially students with expressive-language or memory problems will have something upon which to draw to help them estimate.

1) The telephone weighs about _____ pounds.

     3   30   300

2) The number of books Tom carried in his bag to school was about _____.

     4   40   400

Figure 5-16

2. **Predict the number of answer digits.** Having students identify the number of answer digits for specific computational examples helps them focus on the size of the answer. Later they can examine the "size" of an answer to judge, rather quickly, whether it is unreasonable. One would expect the Figure 5-17 problem, for instance, to contain three digits. So "something" is wrong.

3. **One right on, one way off.** To start, it is easier for students to detect unreasonable answers when the *same problem* is presented twice: once with a correct answer; once with an answer which is "way off" as in Figure 5-18. Many students find it easier to detect wrong answers when they are paired with correct ones or when they know that one of the pair is wrong. Each time, talk through the estimate(s) used to make the decision. This type of activity prepares for the recommendation in Activity 4.

4. **Does my answer "make sense"?** Give students calculations as in Activity 3, but mix the problems in with others. Gradually present random problems of the same general type:

$$\begin{array}{r} \cancel{2} \\ 34 \\ \times\ 5 \\ \hline 50 \end{array}$$

Figure 5-17

Which makes sense?

$$\text{a)}\ \begin{array}{r} 34 \\ \times\ 5 \\ \hline 50 \end{array} \qquad \text{b)}\ \begin{array}{r} 34 \\ \times\ 5 \\ \hline 170 \end{array}$$

Figure 5-18

- Some which have correct answers;

- Others with answers that are "way off target";

Ask students to identify those that "make no sense." Talk through the estimate(s) used to make the decision.

ADDITION OF WHOLE NUMBERS

Multiples of Ten

Problem area: Difficulty adding 10 or a multiple of 10 to other 1- or 2-digit numbers.

Typical disabilities affecting progress: Difficulty with auditory association, auditory memory, auditory figure-ground, and visual figure-ground.

Background: The ability to add multiples of 10 to other numbers is especially helpful for regrouping in subtraction or performing other mental calculations. Many children who have difficulty recognizing relationships or patterns have difficulty with these additions. For example, they may not recognize—visually or auditorially—the relationship between "30 + 40" and "3 + 4." Some students even have difficulty with the simpler additions, such as adding 10 to a single-digit number. For these students, it is essential to work on the underlying pattern of "adding 10" before introducing regrouping. Once regrouping has been introduced, frequent review may still be necessary to ensure that the students incorporate the skill.

The suggestions that follow have proven helpful in our work with learning disabled students who have difficulty "adding tens." The ideas assume that the children have already worked extensively with materials—tens and ones—as the basis for understanding the computational procedure required to add 2-digit numbers: Add like units; if there are 10 or more singles, trade for 1 ten. As the children turn to work at the symbolic level, activities and exercises such as those that follow frequently are necessary.

Suggested Sequence of Activities and Exercises

Adding 10 to a Single-Digit Number
(Helpful for regrouping in subtraction)

1. **A bundle plus.** Provide numeral cards (one each for 1, 2, 3, ... 9), a bundle of 10 popsicle sticks, and 9 extra single sticks. Lay out the 10-bundle, making

sure the children realize that there are 10 sticks banded together in the bundle. Mix the cards and place them face down in a pile. The children, in turn, draw a number card and place the corresponding number of single sticks beside the 10-bundle (Figure 5-19a). They then tell the number of sticks in all (16 in this example). If a child does not know, ask for a guess before a count is made to check. Encourage the students to count on from 10 rather than count from 1 each time. Make a chart showing the result of each draw (Figure 5-19b). Color emphasize the like digits.

Figure 5-19

- *Follow-up 1*: Assign exercises like that of Figure 5-19c. Allow the students to use a 10-bundle and extra sticks if needed.

- *Follow-up 2*: To encourage mental calculation, use a mask like that of Figure 5-20 on the chart of Figure 5-19b. Ask the children to give answers orally. Allow them to use a 10-bundle and extra sticks if they get stuck.

2. **Slide and see.** Use a ruler and a " + 10" card like that shown in Figure 5-21a. (A laminated worksheet of Figure 5-21b should also be provided.) The teacher writes a single-digit number on a green line of the worksheet to indicate where the student should place the green circle on the ruler (in this example, on the "6"). The child slides a finger along the arrow to get the "feel" of "adding 10." Then the ruler number sentence is read aloud: "6 + 10 is 16." The child

writes the result of the addition on the red worksheet line. A 10-bundle and extra sticks could be used to verify the result. Repeat with the other numbers, until four or five examples are written on the sheet. Help the children analyze their written work. Model the auditory emphasis of the two like digits in each example: "*Six* plus *ten* is *sixteen*." If the children benefit from kinesthetic involvement, have them finger trace the like digits in each example they read.

3. **Slide and check.** Tape a flap over the red hole of the "+ 10" card (Figure 5-22). Repeat Activity 2, but this time have the child tell the sum, then lift the flap to check the answer.

Figure 5-20

Figure 5-21

Figure 5-22

4. **On their backs.** Copy incomplete "+10" problems like those of Figure 5-23 on the board, and provide the numeral card deck of Activity 1. Mix the cards and place them face down in a pile. In turn, the children draw a card, look at it, show it to the teacher, and place it upside down on the table or desk. After the teacher traces the numeral on each child's back, the child walks to the chalkboard and completes one of the "+10" problems. (The walk provides a medium for forcing the child to think about the numeral that recurs twice in the completed problem.) When the "+10" problem is complete, ask the student to read it aloud. Encourage auditory emphasis of the repeated digit. Then hold up the card the child left behind. Check that the numeral on the card does appear twice in the completed problem. If necessary, the child can use the "+10" card and ruler of Activity 1 to correct any error.

10+	10+
10+	10+
10+	10+

Figure 5-23

Adding 10 to 2-Digit Numbers

1. **Calculator help.** If children possess the necessary skills, allow them to use a hand calculator to complete exercises such as that shown in Figure 5-24a. When a page is complete, have the student read across each row as follows: "26 plus 10 is 36; 48 plus 10 is 58." It often helps to give the child a card to uncover the numerals while reading (Figure 5-24b). Toward the end of the page, cover up the answer and have the child say the sentences, giving answers without the visual reinforcement.

a) 26 + 10 = 36
   48 + 10 = 58
   37 + 10 = 47

b) 26 ☐
   26 + ☐
   26 + 10 ☐

Figure 5-24

2. **Highlight the pattern.** In exercises of this type some children are helped when a vertical format and colors are used, as in Figure 5-25. Highlighting the digits helps emphasize the pattern of change in the tens digits. The children could be instructed to complete the first part of a page with problems like those shown, leaving the last six or seven problems unsolved. When they have completed the first part, have the children analyze their work. Help them notice the pattern by pointing (a) first to the green tens digit in the problem and (b) then to the tens digit in the sum. While pointing, say each numeral: "two . . . three," "four . . . five," "six . . . seven." Continue this verbal patterning as the children fill in the green blanks of the unsolved problems. A similar procedure is used with the ones digits. When the page is complete, have them read the problems as in Activity 1. Model the auditory emphasis of the tens digit pattern. For example, "*Twenty*—six plus ten is *thirty*—six."

$$
\begin{array}{r}
2\,6 \\
+1\,0 \\
\hline
\end{array}
\qquad
\begin{array}{r}
4\,8 \\
+\,1\,0 \\
\hline
\end{array}
$$

— = green   - - - = red

Figure 5-25

- *Follow-Up*: To encourage mental calculation, follow up with similar worksheets in which children give answers orally (or dictate them into a tape recorder) before writing.

3. **Practice.** To build up automatic addition of tens, present pages with color-coded horizontal problems, as in Figure 5-26. The colors are used for focusing and visual association with the vertical problems previously completed. The students read the problems as in Activity 1 and fill in the blanks.

56 + 10 = ____

— = green   - - - = red

Figure 5-26

4. **Toss up** (a practice activity for two players). Prepare a gameboard as in Figure 5-27 and laminate the center strip. Using a grease pencil, write fifteen 2-digit numbers in the center strip. Provide about 10 markers for each player and two dice:

Die 1: Marked 4, 5, 6, 7, 8, 9.
Die 2: Marked 1, 2, 3, 4, 5, 6.

In turn, the players roll the dice and place them in the squares to the left of the center strip to form a 2-digit numeral. This number is added to 10. If the sum is on the board, a marker is placed beside it as shown. If players give an incorrect answer, they must remove one marker from their side of the board. If the sum is correctly stated but not on the board, the dice go to the next player. The winner is the first player to place five markers in a row.

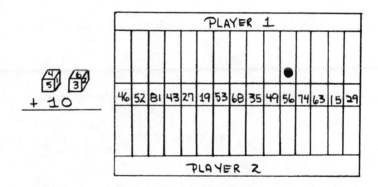

Figure 5-27

- *Variation:* To encourage mental calculation, give each player markers of two different colors (e.g., orange, worth 2 points; blue, worth 1 point). The game proceeds as in Activity 4, but use an orange marker if answers are given after mental calculation; blue otherwise. The winner is the first to accumulate 6 points.

Adding Other Multiples of 10 to a 2-Digit Number

1. **Calculator help.** As in Activity 1, page 239, (*Calculator Help*), but introduce multiples of 10 (20, 30, . . . 90) as the second addend.

2. **Relate to the basic fact.** To help develop the visual/auditory pattern and relate the addition to basic facts, exercises such as that shown in Figure 5-28

Figure 5-28

are helpful. Colors or bold print and underline could be used to focus attention on the related basic facts. In Figure 5-28a, the child begins on the left and reads across the line, filling in the answer on the line. Encourage auditory emphasis to highlight the relationship: "*Six* plus *two* is eight, so *sixty* plus *twenty* is *eighty.*" Examples of this type may later be extended to include adding a multiple of 10 to any 2-digit number, as in Figure 5-28b. The vertical format of the second set of problems is more effective for some students. Whatever the format, finger tracing like parts of related problems might be encouraged for a student who requires a high degree of kinesthetic involvement.

- *Follow-Up:* Encourage mental calculation. Use the exercises described above, but ask the students to give the answers orally before writing. Provide answer keys so that students who work independently can check their own work.

3. **Pick up** (for two or three players). This game reviews adding 10 or other multiples of 10 to a 2-digit number. Provide a laminated gameboard such as that illustrated in Figure 5-29, 25 chips, and two dice:

> Die 1: green numerals, 1-6.
> Die 2: red numerals, 1-6.

The numerals in the left column of the gameboard are green; those in the top row are red. To begin, the students cover the entire board with chips. In turn, they roll the dice to see which numbers should be added. In the example of Figure 5-29, the green "3" refers to the 3rd green number (left column); the red "4" refers to the 4th red number (top row). These two numbers, 36 and 10, are to be added. The student locates the numbers and says, "36 plus 10 is 46." To check, the player removes the chip corresponding to the addends.

Figure 5-29

If the answer is correct, the child keeps the chip. Otherwise it is replaced. The player who has the most chips when the board is uncovered (or at the end of a given number of rounds) wins.

One- and Two-Digit Addends

Problem area: Difficulty adding a single-digit and a 2-digit number.

Typical disabilities affecting progress: Difficulty with visual memory, visual discrimination, auditory figure-ground or sequencing, abstract reasoning, and closure.

Background: Study the problems of Figure 5-30. In early developmental work, as background to paper-and-pencil computations like these, children typically use 10-stacks and 1s or other physical materials to dramatize the combination of two 2-digits or a 1- and a 2-digit addend. At this stage, children learn to combine like units—all the ones, all the tens—and to trade 10 singles for 1 "ten" whenever possible (Figure 5-31a).

Figure 5-30

The result of combining ones and tens is written (Figure 5-31b), so the children have a record of what they did. Gradually, because the children "see" what the computational procedure is all about, the materials are dropped, and they learn to compute independently of manipulative aids. They now enter a practice phase that emphasizes obtaining the correct answers more rapidly.

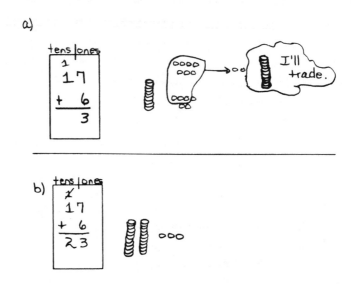

Figure 5-31

At this skill level, addition involving a 1- and a 2-digit addend can be approached in two ways:

1. As a paper-and-pencil computation, with or without regrouping; or

2. As a mental computation—an extension of the basic facts.

By the time a child is doing fourth- or fifth-grade work, problems such as those of Figure 5-30 can be treated as an extension of the basic facts. Since the problems can be computed mentally, it is unnecessary to use regrouping marks. There are payoffs to handling problems of this type mentally.

• The mental calculation approach may help children "add by endings" in column addition (Figure 5-32a).

• The mental calculation approach prepares children for multiplication with regrouping (Figure 5-32b).

Figure 5-32

Many children who *do* know their basic facts are unable to recognize them in the context of a bigger problem (e.g., 32 + 5, not just 2 + 5). The single-digit addend causes confusion that may be linked to a visual-perception or memory difficulty, or to an inability to reason abstractly. Alternately, it may be that, auditorially, the children do not hear the basic fact within the problem. Although they say the problem to themselves (silently or aloud), they may not recognize the particular fact. This latter difficulty may be due to auditory figure-ground or closure deficits. (See Chapter 1 for definitions of terms.) If the problem is presented visually, the empty space in the tens place can be confusing, even for students who demonstrate solid place value comprehension. For many, adding a "concrete" symbol to an empty space is more difficult than adding two 2-digit numerals.

The following exercises are intended to build or reinforce skill in adding a 1- and a 2-digit number. The emphasis is on developing confidence with mental calculation. A suggestion for paper-and-pencil computation of these problem types is included at the end of the section. It is assumed that extensive work with materials, such as those previously outlined, has already been carried out. This is a necessary prerequisite to ensure that the children possess an intuitive basis for work at the symbolic level like that described.

Suggested Sequence of Activities and Exercises

1. **How does it end?** Figure 5-33 shows an exercise that has proven helpful for relating problems involving a 1- and a 2-digit addend to basic facts. At

first, only problems that require no regrouping are presented. Blank file pages, using the format of Figure 5-33b, can be kept on hand and filled in as needed by the teacher. The colors will:

• Focus attention on the basic fact;

• Develop reasoning skills;

• Give visual reinforcement to students with auditory deficits; and

• Give auditory reinforcement to children with poor visual memory.

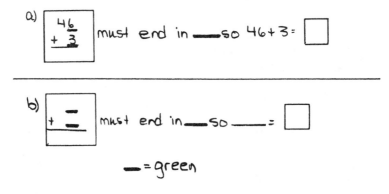

Figure 5-33

As pointed out, it is necessary to check for intact color vision. In serious cases of color blindness, bold print and underscoring can be substituted to highlight and cue responses. In the example of Figure 5-33a, the student begins on the left, reading silently or aloud, depending on preferred learning style. The horizontal part of the exercise follows the left-right reading sequence and reflects what a child should *think* while computing a problem of this type. The blanks are filled in as the student approaches them verbally. Figure 5-34 suggests a sequence that may be used to help build the needed skill. By the time a child is working exercises like that in Figure 5-34c, colors may no longer be needed. If they are still necessary, however, the student could underline with a green pen before solving.

2. **Help for book problems.** These same pages can be used, if necessary, for textbook problems. Have the student copy out the problem, place it in the left-hand box, and then compute.

3. **Listen and read.** For students who need the verbalization illustrated in Figures 5-33 and 5-34 but cannot read or express themselves well, prepare cassette

a) $\boxed{\begin{array}{r} 54 \\ + \;\underline{4} \end{array}}$ must end in _____ so $54 + 4 =$ _____

b) $\boxed{\begin{array}{r} 54 \\ + \;\underline{4} \end{array}}$ must end in _____ so _____ = _____

c) $\boxed{\begin{array}{r} 54 \\ + \;\underline{4} \end{array}}$ must end in _____ so _____ = _____

Figure 5-34

tapes that match pages you keep on file. Have the child read along with the tape, problem by problem, until the process is internalized and the student feels comfortable. Experience has shown that use of the tape or other external verbalization can be eliminated within a relatively short time.

4. **Flash! How does it end?** Once the student has internalized the thought process, flash a color-coded card like that of Figure 5-35. With the card as a cue, the child states the problem and completes the sentence, as in the exercises of Figures 5-33 and 5-34.

Figure 5-35

5. **Side by side.** For children who have either internalized the preceding pattern or who can readily recognize visual patterns, present practice pages containing exercises like that of Figure 5-36. (Though similar to many now

Figure 5-36

presented in texts, the exercise uses a discontinuous pattern.) The child is forced to focus on the pattern in each problem, thus eliminating the tendency to perseverate. By encouraging children to recognize and use a pattern, the approach fosters reasoning skills.

> *Note:* If color coding is necessary, the original basic fact—in this case 4 + 5—should be written or outlined in green. In the remaining problems, the fact is underlined in green by the teacher or the student before the problem is solved. Figure 5-37 shows a sample format for sheets that can be prepared in advance and kept on file. These pages can also be used with the controlled fact program described in Activity 1 of the section on general difficulties earlier in this chapter. The specific facts being worked on are immediately incorporated into actual problem situations.

Figure 5-37

6. **Three by three.** Keep blank gameboards like that shown in Figure 5-38 on hand. Put the boards in plastic holders and give one to each child. Use a grease pencil to fill the boxes along the left side and top with numbers appropriate to the child's level. (Figure 5-38 uses numbers that require regrouping only sometimes.) Use a standard deck of cards, with picture cards and 10s removed. Each child is given a set of chips. The child draws two cards (e.g., 5 and 3) and tells the sum.

   If possible, the fact is related to the numbers on the gameboard, and the child finishes by saying, "So 85 + 3 must be 88." If the answer is correct, the child places a chip in the appropriate square. Answers can be checked

Figure 5-38

on a calculator or against an answer sheet. The first person to cover a 3 × 3 square wins.

7. **Paper-and-pencil work.** When paper-and-pencil computation is to be carried out, allow the children who need the help to place a zero in the empty 10s space before computing.

Note: Do not place the zero in the space for the child. Force the child to deal with the problem. Most children place the zero in the space when it is time to add the 10s digits.

Regrouping for Addition

Problem area: Difficulty regrouping when adding 2-digit numbers.

Typical disabilities affecting progress: Difficulty with abstract reasoning, perseveration, figure-ground, and reversals.

Background: Many students are unable to retain a lot of information at one time. The many discrete steps involved in adding 2-digit numbers are difficult enough for them, and they may not readily recognize when or know how to regroup. Automatic recognition becomes even more difficult as regrouping is extended to the 100s place. The student must continually make decisions while trying to recall correctly the sequence for carrying out the computation. In many cases, regrouping difficulty is a result of poor conceptual understanding of place value. For the learning disabled child, however, all too often it is simply due to an inability to think without obvious, visual cues.

The following suggestions are helpful for children who have difficulty knowing when or how to regroup when adding two 2-digit numbers. The suggestions assume that the children

- Possess adequate numeration understanding for 2- and 3-digit numbers (see Chapter 2); and

• Understand, at least informally, that when adding two 2-digit numbers you add like units and trade 10 ones for 1 ten whenever you have 10 or more ones.

The latter prerequisite assumes that the students have used grouping aids such as popsicle sticks (10-bundles and extra sticks), chips (10-stacks and extra chips), or graph paper 10s and 1s to dramatize these ideas. Once this foundation is established and the child is ready to begin regrouping with symbols only, perceptual or other deficits may make it necessary to use activities like those that follow to aid in the transition. These same activities can, of course, be used in remedial situations as well.

Suggested Sequence of Activities and Exercises

Chips, 10-stacks, and ones are used. In implementing the sequence, use any grouping aid with which the children are familiar.

1. **Picture it: 10 ones for 1 ten.** Review the idea of exchanging 10 ones for 1 ten, using color-coded tens-ones frames as in Figure 5-39a. The child fills in the spaces to describe the picture on the left and is then reminded that "Something is not right. There are two digits in one of the spaces." The student crosses out 10 red chips and replaces them with a green 10-stack on the right-hand frame, again filling in the blanks (Figure 5-39b). Auditorially reinforce what is being done: "Yes, if there are 10 or more ones, trade 10 ones for a 10-stack."

   Note: For students needing concrete aids to review, use 10-stacks and extra single chips together with laminated tens-ones frames as illustrated in Figure 5-40. Design the frame so that no more than nine chips can be placed in the ones column. (The inside of a file folder can be used to draw the frames. Simply use a felt-tipped pen to outline the slots in which you wish children to place their 10-stacks and single chips.) Problems may be set up as in Activity 1, but students can trade 10 single chips for one 10-stack. Using grease pencils or wipe-off markers, they can fill the spaces to describe the pictures both before and after the trade. The limited frame-space idea can also be carried out in follow-up paper-and-pencil work.

Figure 5-39

Figure 5-40

2. **Picture the picture.** Once a student masters the work presented in Activity 1, introduce exercises like that illustrated in Figure 5-41. Fill in the left-hand boxes with numbers previously used with the tens-ones frames. The basic teaching sequence is illustrated in the following narration:

> Teacher (pointing to the left-hand box of Figure 5-41a): "Something is not right. There are two digits in one of the spaces. What did we do with the chips whenever there were 10 or more ones?"

Figure 5-41

> Student: "Traded 10 loose chips for a 10-stack."
> Teacher: "Yes, and what did we do every time we put another 10-stack in the frame?"
> Student: "We wrote a different number on the green line, because now there's one more." (At this point, the teacher writes + 1 on the green arrow and instructs the students to do the same on their sheets.)
> Teacher: "That's right, and 4 + 1 is 5" (writing "5" on the right-hand green line). "Whenever we put another 10-stack in the frame, what did we do with the red chips?"
> Student: "Took off 10." (At this point, the teacher writes "– 10" on the red arrow, instructing the children to do the same.)
> Teacher: "That's right, and 12 – 10 is 2" (writing "2" on the right-hand red line).

Note: For the first few examples, particularly for students with visual-memory or sequencing deficits, it may be necessary to use 10-stacks and single chips with the tens-ones frames to dramatize each step.

3. **Need to trade?** An important question should now be asked in conjunction with exercises like those illustrated in Figure 5-42: "Are there two digits in one space?" Children may be asked to examine the right-hand boxes to answer this question for each example. They may then be instructed to circle those boxes that "are not right"—those in which the ones place is overloaded.

Figure 5-42

4. **If yes, then trade.** Children who have mastered the previous step have an edge in recognizing *when* to regroup. The issue now is knowing *how* to regroup at the symbolic level. The answer to the question in Activity 3 is now given direct attention (Figure 5-43). A procedure similar to that outlined in Activity 2 (*Picture the Picture*) is carried out. At this stage, however, most students do not need to relate vocally each step of a problem to the movement of chips. They already have internalized the concept and need to practice to build skill in regrouping whenever there are two digits in the ones column. Previous work is extended as the children fill in the right-hand box in exercises (see Figure 5-44).

Figure 5-43

To encourage the child to consider when regrouping is necessary, some of the problems do not require regrouping (Figure 5-44b). A wall chart similar to Figure 5-43 or a mini-pasteup on the child's page is helpful during early stages of independent work with exercises of this type.

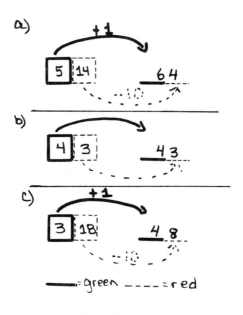

Figure 5-44

5. **Now add.** The previous exercises required that students, working with numerals alone, recognize when the ones place was overloaded. When this skill is mastered, apply it to 2-digit addition problems. Figure 5-45 shows one type of page that can be used. *Part of the page is visually similar to previous work. This may take some pressure off the student.* Each problem is first solved without regrouping. The answer is then examined, and the student decides whether or not to regroup. If it is necessary to point out the similarity to previous work, provide the child with a card to cover up the actual problem. The extra step of seeing two digits in the ones place often provides the necessary reinforcement to remember to think about regrouping.

> **Note:** The discrete steps of the preceding sequence are essential for many learning disabled students, particularly for overlearners or those with sequencing or abstract-reasoning difficulties. Using colors (or other visual

Figure 5-45

highlighting techniques) and repeated drills helps the child more readily learn *when* and *how* to regroup.

6. **A box cue.** Color-coded reminder boxes, such as that pictured in Figure 5-46a, serve two needs by providing:

   • Help in the transition to the standard computational format for addition with regrouping; and

   • Help for students with reversal tendencies.

   In the example of Figure 5-46a, the children first add to obtain 13 ones. The normal pattern for writing 13 is "1" then "3"; so urge the children to follow this sequence when recording their answer. The color scheme of Figure 5-46 encourages this: 1 first (in the *green* box), then *3* on the *red* "stop" line. Figure 5-46b suggests how to format pages in advance. Pages can be filed and pulled later as needed. When preparing the pages, include the boxes on all problems, even when regrouping is not needed. This forces the students to determine whether regrouping is needed.

7. **Doctor the text.** When using a text or workbook page, allow the students to draw dashes under each problem to match the columns (e.g., two columns, two dashes). This often serves as a reminder that only one digit is allowed per space. (If the textbook problems are too small for the students to mark, ask adult volunteers to help prepare texts in advance.)

Figure 5-46

Column Addition

Problem area: Inability to complete the sequence in column addition.

Typical disabilities affecting progress: Difficulty with short-term or sequential memory and visual figure-ground.

Background: Although a student may, conceptually, understand column addition, perceptually, this can be extremely difficult, especially when "ragged columns" or regrouping are involved as in Figure 5-47. Children with figure-ground difficulties find it especially hard to "keep the place" while copying or computing problems of this type. To complicate matters, the three-addend problem is really a four-addend problem because of the regrouping. The child who worked the example of Figure 5-47 handled the ones column addition correctly, even the regrouping, but forgot the "1" while adding the tens column.

$$
\begin{array}{r}
\not{1} \\
35 \\
4 \\
+\ 27 \\
\hline
56
\end{array}
$$

A mix of 1- and 2-digit addends.

Figure 5-47

For some students, using a hand calculator for column addition is a viable alternative to paper-and-pencil computation. Indeed, sometimes calculator use or estimation should take precedence over hand calculations. Yet, most learning disabled students can learn to add a sequence of three or four numbers. Compensatory techniques such as the following have proven effective in helping students acquire this skill.

Suggested Sequence of Activities and Exercises

1. **One step at a time.** Approach column addition one step at a time. Prepare practice pages containing problems like that shown in Figure 5-48a. Use green for the first two addends and the answer line, red for the arrow and the last addend. Before writing the final sum, the student fills in the blank line with the sum of the first two addends.

Figure 5-48

Note: Pages using the problem format of Figure 5-48b can be kept on file and used as needed. The teacher fills in specific numbers if a controlled-fact program is used. Students can also copy problems from the text onto these pages. Alternatively, if textbook space is not too confining, the students can color code text problems before solving. If difficulty with column addition is anticipated, textbooks could be coded in advance (perhaps at the beginning of the school year) by adult volunteers.

2. **Cross out means 10.** For children with good visual but poor sequential memory, the approach of Figure 5-49 has proven helpful. The child adds down the column until a 2-digit answer ($8 + 9 = 17$) is reached. The last digit added, in this case 9, is crossed out to represent the 10 in the sum. The student retains the 7 mentally and combines it with the 6. The 6 is crossed out to indicate

the one 10 in 13, and the child writes down the 3. The number carried is the same as the number of digits crossed out, in this case 2. The same approach is used for remaining columns.

3. **Write the ones.** If visual memory or reversal deficits require that a child write subsums, the procedure suggested in Figure 5-50 can be used. The student adds the first two addends. Since the sum (16) is a 2-digit number, the second 8 is crossed out and the 6 is written down, in that order. 6 + 9 is 15, so the 9 is crossed out and the 5 is written below the line. As before, the number of crossed digits represents what should be carried.

$$
\begin{array}{r}
2 \\
6\!8 \\
\not{4}\not{9} \\
3\not{6} \\
\hline
1\,5\,3
\end{array}
$$

Figure 5-49

$$
\begin{array}{r}
2 \\
5\,\not{8} \\
\not{7}_0\not{8}\,_6 \\
+\,4\,\not{9}\,_5 \\
\hline
1\,4\ 5
\end{array}
$$

Figure 5-50

4. **Visual helps.** For students having visual figure-ground or other perceptual deficits, any of the following techniques may be used.

- Teach the children to color highlight a column before adding it (Figure 5-51a).

- Provide square centimeter paper and instruct the students to write one digit per square (Figure 5-51b).

- Provide vertically lined paper and instruct the students to write every digit on a line (Figure 5-51c).

- Provide a tachistoscopic card for covering columns not being added. The card should only cover the problem, with room to write the carried number at the top and the answer in the proper place. As the student works, the card is moved along so that only the numbers being added show through

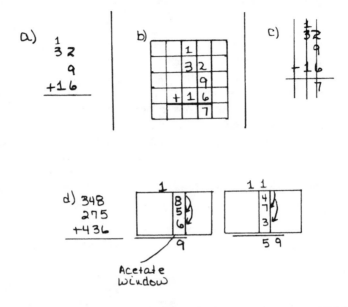

Figure 5-51

the slot. Figure 5-51d shows a step-by-step approach for using the card to solve an addition problem with three 3-digit addends.

Note: The entire card may be covered with acetate and children be allowed to use a grease pencil to write the ones digit of sub-sums directly on it (see Activity 3). The acetate is wiped clean before another column is added.

SUBTRACTION OF WHOLE NUMBERS

When children turn to subtraction, they meet difficulties similar to those encountered in whole number addition. It is not uncommon for students to have problems subtracting a single-digit from a 2-digit number; some find it hard to subtract multiples of 10. Knowing *when* and *how* to regroup is a major challenge in subtraction, as in addition, especially for children with learning difficulties. Many of the activities described in the previous sections can be adjusted and used to aid in handling parallel difficulties in subtraction. Since some problems with regrouping require slightly different techniques than those previously discussed, the following two sections will present additional suggestions for this topic.

Two- and Three-Digit Subtraction with Regrouping

Problem area: Difficulty knowing when and how to regroup in subtraction of 2- and 3-digit numbers.

Typical disabilities affecting progress: Difficulty with abstract reasoning, perseveration, visual figure-ground, reversals, and sequencing.

Background: As with addition, knowing when to regroup in subtraction is difficult for many students. Many tend to subtract the smaller from the larger number, regardless of position within the problem. Figure 5-52 illustrates this error, typical also of children who do not exhibit specific disabilities. Often this error stems from poor conceptual understanding of the process of subtracting with regrouping. Some learning disabled children have strong concepts, but visually reverse the numbers.

$$\begin{array}{r} 64 \\ -35 \\ \hline 31 \end{array}$$

Figure 5-52

Other factors contribute to the widespread difficulty in this area. Figure 5-1 illustrated, step by step, how subtraction with regrouping is really a combination of subtraction and addition. The process requires a tremendous amount of mental computation and constant switching from one operation to the next and then back again. Thus, children are continually having to make decisions—they must not only know when to regroup, but also how. That involves realizing what operation to use and then applying it at each discrete step.

Several approaches may be used to develop the proper procedure for 2-digit and 3-digit subtraction with regrouping. Generally, it is most helpful to use the simplest model, that of "take away," as the basis for subtraction computation. In the problem 68 − 49, for example, students can be cued to think: "8 take away 9. Since there are not enough ones, a trade must be made (1 ten for 10 ones)." The "take away" approach aptly dramatizes the "big ideas" underlying subtraction computation: subtract like units; if there are not enough, make a trade. This approach constitutes the basis for the suggestions that follow.

Suggested Sequence of Activities and Exercises

1. **Fair trade** (to prepare for a natural, meaningful transition to 2-digit subtraction with regrouping). Provide a deck of laminated cards like that pictured in Figure 5-53a and a "band" of 10-stacks and loose chips. In turn, the children draw a card and use the chips to picture the problem on the card. The teacher leads the following discussion:

   "The bank needs another 10-stack. Will you trade one of yours for loose chips? How many loose chips would make a fair trade? (10 loose chips for the 10-stack.) Write what you have now" (see Figure 5-53b).

   Repeat with other cards, making a record of the trade each time.

Figure 5-53

2. **Take away.** Relate the trade idea of Activity 1 to 2-digit subtraction with regrouping. In the example of Figure 5-54a, the children use 10-stacks and loose chips to show what you start with (42). Now subtract: "2 take away 8." There are not enough loose chips to take 8, so trade a 10-stack for 10 chips and write to tell the number of remaining 10s and 1s (Figure 5-54b). Now the

children can "take away" 8 loose chips and one 10-stack, leaving two 10-stacks and four loose chips (Figure 5-54c).

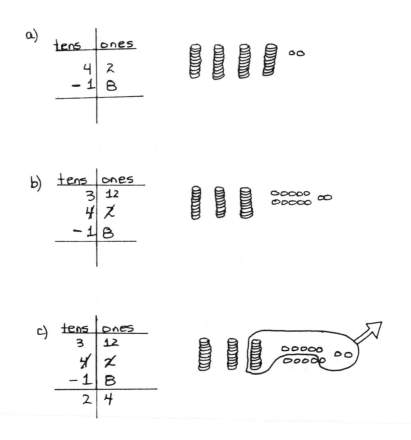

Figure 5-54

3. **Are there enough?** Some children—particularly the careless, the impulsive, and those who perseverate—may fall into the pattern: regroup, subtract, regroup, subtract. This pattern is continued whether regrouping is required or not. Force children to decide about regrouping. One suggestion is to present mixed problem types like those of Figure 5-55. Note that the ones digit of the minuend has been visually highlighted to focus attention on it. The children start with this digit each time and decide whether there are enough, so they can "take away" the number represented by the digit directly beneath it. (Use chips as in Activity 2, if necessary, to dramatize the first few problems.)

Are there enough?
Circle if you must make a trade.

$$\begin{array}{ccccc} 43 & 26 & 52 & 35 & 97 \\ -18 & -14 & -26 & -22 & -59 \end{array}$$

―― = green

Figure 5-55

Ask the children to circle the problem if there are not enough. Do not require that they complete the problems at this time.

4. **Help them decide.** Some students need more structured assistance before they can succeed with the task presented in Activity 3. Figure 5-56 shows one type of exercise that can be used. The underlining helps the children focus on the correct starting point in each problem. To force them to think more clearly about the relationship between the numbers, ask them to read across the line and fill in while doing so. Eventually, they internalize the sentence. As they do other problems, they are more likely to think about the way the exercise has prompted them.

   Note: The phrase "make a trade," used during work with 10-stacks and loose chips in previous activities, is used throughout the rest of this sequence. Some teachers may prefer to use the term "regroup." Whatever the students understand best should be adopted.

$$\begin{array}{c} 43 \\ -2\,7 \end{array} \underline{\quad} \text{ is } \left\{ \begin{array}{c} \text{more} \\ \text{less} \end{array} \right\} \text{than} \underline{\ \ \ } \text{so you} \left\{ \begin{array}{c} \text{trade} \\ \text{do not trade} \end{array} \right\} \begin{array}{c} 3\ 13 \\ \cancel{4}\ \cancel{3} \\ -27 \end{array}$$

―― = green   - - - - = red

Figure 5-56

5. **Cue box.** For children who have trouble sequencing or who do not automatically associate written words with numbers, the cueing technique in Figure 5-57 has proven helpful. Problems of this type can be used to reinforce the last step of the sequence discussed in Activity 4. Even with the cueing, the students must decide whether it is necessary to make a trade. If so, the teacher can help by discussing the number available and the number to be "taken away;" 10-stacks and chips could then be used to verify thinking. If a trade must be made, then there is "1 less ten, 10 more ones."

$$-1 \left(\begin{array}{cc} \square & \\ 4 & 5 \end{array} \right) \rightarrow + 10$$
$$-36$$

▬ = green   .... = red

Figure 5-57

6. **Block out.** As regrouping is extended to the tens and hundreds places, it is often necessary to remind students to continue thinking in the correct way. The "block out" card shown in Figure 5-58 is helpful in this regard. Used by the child as a marker while solving subtraction problems, the card serves to block out extraneous numbers, thereby allowing the child to focus on the pertinent numbers.

▬ = green ---- = red

Figure 5-58

7. **Different strokes.** Subtract like units . . . If there are not enough, make a trade. These are the "big ideas" behind subtraction. Some students apply these ideas, step by step, when computing: first ones, then tens, and so on. Others benefit by first going through an entire problem, noting all places where regrouping is necessary. Once this is done, they can backtrack and perform the computation. Children who benefit most from this latter method are those who have trouble sequencing or making switches in their thought process, and those who have difficulty with number alignment. Rather than forcing one procedural pattern on all students, note which method is easiest for an individual.

8. **Do it backwards!** Children with severe reversal problems often benefit from working problems left to right (see *Note*). In the example shown in Figure 5-59 the child begins with $9 - 2 = 7$. Next, the student thinks, "5 take away 9." Recognizing the need to make a trade, the child crosses out the 7 and writes 6 beneath it. The 5 is crossed out and 15 is written above. The explanation is that, after the first subtraction, we still have 7 hundreds left, enough to trade, when necessary, for the 5. A similar procedure is used to complete the problem. (The approach is similar to the equal-additions methods illustrated in Figure 5-60, but it is easier for children with reversal tendencies to understand and follow.) For those who need help with number alignment, use graph paper or pages containing examples like that of Figure 5-61.

> *Note:* This method looks longer and more cumbersome to many of us, yet for the learning disabled child with visual-perceptual problems, it eliminates one obstacle to learning—the tendency to reverse.

Figure 5-59

Figure 5-60

Figure 5-61

9. **Into the maze** (for two or three players). To reinforce the correct sequence, the need to regroup, and the skill of adding 10 to a number, prepare a game-board as in Figure 5-62a. Also provide a grease pencil and wipe-off rag, a deck of laminated cards with subtraction problems like those of Figure 5-62b, an envelope for the cards, and a game marker for each player. To begin, cards are mixed and placed in the envelope. In turn, the players draw a card, state the problem, and decide whether or not a trade is necessary. If so, a grease pencil is used to show the trade. After the players add 10 to the green number, they move that many spaces. If no trade is needed, the players simply subtract the two numbers. The result is the number of spaces they may move. Answers can be checked by flipping to the back sides of cards. The first student to reach the garden in the rear of the maze wins.

> *Note:* If the deck is used up before the winner is found, the cards are wiped off and reused.

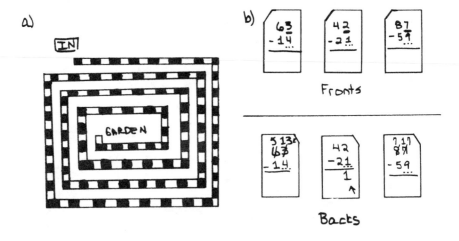

Figure 5-62

Zero in Subtraction

Problem area: Difficulty regrouping when zero appears in the minuend.

   Typical disabilities affecting progress: Difficulty with sequencing, spatial organization, and memory.

   Background: Zero difficulties are more prominent in subtraction than in addition. In subtraction of 2-digit numbers with zero minuend digits, for example, the tendency to reverse is more dominant than when only nonzero digits appear (see Figure 5-63). Some children simply ignore the zero (Figure 5-64). Because of these and other erratic errors children often make, it is generally more beneficial to teach the concept and process of subtraction with regrouping before introducing zero in the problem. The specific lessons, incorporating ideas such as those that follow, could be carried out to help the children deal with zero in subtraction computations.

$$
\begin{array}{r}
50 \\
-36 \\
\hline
26
\end{array}
$$

Figure 5-63

$$
\begin{array}{r}
4\;\;15 \\
\cancel{5}0\cancel{5} \\
-196 \\
\hline
3\;9
\end{array}
$$

Figure 5-64

Suggested Sequence of Activities and Exercises

1. **Act it out.** Use the *Fair Trade* and *Take Away* activities of the previous section to provide a physical frame of reference for 2-digit subtraction with 0

in the minuend. Use multiples of 10 (20, 30, . . . 90) for the "fair trade" activity and include these same numbers in the minuend for the "take away" activity. (A sample problem for this latter activity is 60 −13.)

2. **Think about it.** Prepare pages using the format of Figure 5-56, placing zero on the green line. If the child does not respond to the verbal association, adapt the *Cue Box* activity of the previous section to work with zero.

3. **Circle.** Follow up with pages that mix zero and nonzero digits in the minuend for 2-digit subtractions. Include both regrouping and nonregrouping. At first, just ask students to circle problems where a trade must be made. At a later time, they can complete the subtractions.

4. **One step.** Show the children how to make a trade (regroup) in one step, as in Figure 5-65. Initially, underline the 60 to focus attention. "We can think of this as 6 one-hundreds and no tens. We can also think of it as 60 tens. That's easier. When we borrow 1 ten we have 59 tens left. Now we give that 1 ten to the 2."

5. **Hidden zero.** The method of Activity 4 can also be used with a hidden 0, as shown in Figure 5-66. The student still views 71 as 71 tens, thus eliminating one regrouping step.

6. **Do it backwards.** An alternative to the "one step" is the method of subtraction explained in Activity 8 of the previous section (*Do It Backwards!*). This approach has proven helpful to some students when a zero is in the tens place, as in Figure 5-67. Often children become confused when they reach

Figure 5-65

Figure 5-66

$$
\begin{array}{r}
\cancel{6}\cancel{0}\cancel{4} \\
-\ 196 \\
\hline
\end{array}
$$

Figure 5-67

the step shown in Figure 5-68. Continuity has been broken, and many, particularly those with short-term memory deficits, forget why they were doing what they did. The "backwards" left-right approach may help eliminate this problem.

Figure 5-68

MULTIPLICATION OF WHOLE NUMBERS

Multiples of Ten

Problem areas: Difficulty knowing how many to record when one or both of the factors is a multiple of 10; inability to get started when faced with factors that are multiples of 10.

Typical disabilities affecting progress: Difficulty with abstract reasoning.

Background: An essential part of multiplication involving a 2-digit multiplier is the ability to multiply by a multiple of 10. Often, however, unless it is specifically taught, children do not see the relationship between the number of 0s in the factors and product. For this reason, it is important that, in introducing 2-digit multipliers, the children work on the patterning involving 0s. The ideas that follow may be used for this purpose. As a prerequisite, it is assumed that the children's numeration understandings are strong enough so they can relate 8 tens to 80, 14 tens to 140, and so on.

Suggested Sequence of Activities and Exercises

1. **Side by side.** Present multiplication problems like those shown in Figure 5-69. Children solve the first problem in each pair. Then, using a calculator, they arrive at the product for the second problem of the pair. (If there are not enough calculators for each student to have one, the children take turns.) When the product is read to the class, it can be written on the board or an overhead. Use the colors as indicated to help the students notice the pattern. Gradually, extend the process to higher multiples of 10 and color code in the same manner.

$$
\begin{array}{cc}
48 & 48 \\
\times\ 2 & \times\ 20
\end{array}
$$

$$
\begin{array}{cc}
63 & 63 \\
\times\ 3 & \times\ 30
\end{array}
$$

Figure 5-69

2. **Relate.** A problem sequence like that of Figure 5-70 can be used effectively with students who, perceptually, cannot work the calculator. Remind the students of the relationship between multiplication and addition by initially setting up the problems as in Figure 5-70a. Most children who know their facts and are strong conceptually will use multiplication to solve the problem, even in this form. Students who do not know the facts, but understand the relationship between addition and multiplication can use a multiplication chart to solve the problems and cue them to the general pattern. The following narration, based on the problem of Figure 5-70a, suggests the type of discussion that might take place.

> Teacher: "Did you add the zeros each time?"
> Student: "No, they sort of tagged along each time."
> Teacher: "Right. What about the 4s? Did you add them?"
> Student: "No. 6 × 4 is 24, and that's easier."

a) 6 40's = ___
40
40
40
40
40
40
___

b) 3 50's = ___

2 30's = ___

c) 2 90's = ___
×

16 80's = ___
×

d) 90   50
×2   ×3
___   ___

Figure 5-70

By the time the students are working problems like those of Figure 5-70d, they generally note how "It's like multiplying by 2; since 90 ends in 0, so does the answer." A similar rationale can be used to support the multiplication of Figure 5-69. For 48 × 20, you write a 0 in the product to show you are multiplying by a multiple of ten. Otherwise, it is just like multiplying 2. Placing related pairs side by side on worksheets, as shown, reinforces this idea.

3. **Call it** (a practice activity for two players). Prepare a laminated gameboard like that of Figure 5-71. Write the numerals 1 – 6 (in green) along the bottom row and 1 to 6 (in red) up the left-hand column. All other gameboard spaces should show a product, with one factor being a multiple of 10. For students who are just beginning, it is best to make one of the factors 10. As the students gain experience in the game and confidence in themselves this can be changed. Provide an answer sheet of possible factors for each product and two dice:

   Die 1 (green): Marked 1, 2, 3, 4, 5, 6;
   Die 2 (red): Marked 1, 2, 3, 4, 5, 6.

   Also provide three sets of markers, each a different color: one set for each player, and one set to cover the entire board at the beginning of play. In turn, the players throw the dice and read them as points on a graph. For example, a green 2 and a red 5 correspond to (2, 5) or 720 on the gameboard of Figure 5-71. If the player can correctly name two factors forming the product (one must be a multiple of 10), the black chip is replaced with the child's colored one. If necessary, the student can consult the answer sheet to check. The winning pattern should be determined before the start of the game.

Figure 5-71

Beyond One-Digit Multipliers

Problem area: Difficulty multiplying two multidigit numbers.

Typical disabilities affecting progress: Difficulty with spatial organization, integrative processing, sequencing, abstract reasoning, visual memory, and reversal.

Background: Many children have trouble multiplying two numbers when both factors contain two or more digits: The sequence is long and continually broken up by addition; a considerable amount of spatial organization is required, not only to place the numbers on the correct line, but also to align the digits properly; and visual memory is needed to retrieve the basic fact and to regroup the correct number.

For many students, it is necessary to provide visual or auditory cues in early work involving 2- or higher digit multipliers although they have a strong place value comprehension and understand the use of the distributive idea for multiplication computation. The following activities suggest ways in which this can be done once the children are ready to begin this work at the symbolic level. It is assumed that the students can multiply 2-digit numbers by 1-digit factors and by multiples of 100.

Suggested Sequence of Activities and Exercises

1. **Color cue.** Color-coded grid boxes, as in Figure 1-16, have been most effective in helping student organize the multiplication process, both spatially and sequentially. Figure 5-72 shows a sample problem completed by a child using

Figure 5-72

the grid boxes. The student first multiplied by the green number (3). The digit to be carried was recorded in the green circle, and the units digit was placed in the appropriate green box. Next, the child multiplied 3 × 4, and added the 2 in the green circle. After crossing out the 2, the answer (4) was recorded in the two green boxes. The student proceeded similarly with the multiplication by 20, this time using the red carrying circle and red boxes.

> *Note:* Students must be taught to write the carried digit first at all times and thereby avoid any tendency to reverse. Crossing out the carried digit should be a carryover of work with 1-digit multipliers. When the colored circles are no longer used, the crossing-out technique will eliminate confusion over which digit to add whenever two or more carry digits appear.

2. **Fade out.** As the students begin to feel comfortable with the process, the colors can gradually be eliminated, depending on the student's progress. Two suggestions follow.

   - Children whose major difficulty appears to be spatial organization may be able to do without all the colors almost immediately. They will continue to need grid paper for a while, however, until they have overlearned the kinesthetic feeling and sequence. Gradually, the grid paper sheets can be replaced with pages using the format illustrated in Figure 5-73.

   - Students having primarily sequencing difficulties may need to retain the color cue for the factor digits and carrying circles for quite some time.

3. **A special case.** Using the same color-coded grids as described previously, the presentation can be varied for children with more severe reversal difficulties. For these students, the 10s digit of the multiplier is green and the 1s digit is red. The child "goes on green" (Figure 5-74) and multiplies 2(0) × 7. As the product is said, the student writes 1 in the green circle and 40 in the appropriate

Figure 5-73

Figure 5-74

green boxes. The procedure continues in a similar manner for the remaining digits.

4. **A zero card.** Children with figure-ground or abstract-reasoning deficits often benefit from being allowed to use a zero card or factor slide. Figure 5-75 shows, step by step, how a child uses a zero card. The student first uses the blank side of a card and covers the 6 (to block out extraneous numbers). After completing this multiplication, the card is flipped over and the 0 is placed over the 4. The idea being reinforced is that, to multiply by 64, you multiply first by 4 then by 60. Finally, you add the result. Figure 5-76 shows how a factor slide can be used in a similar way.

Figure 5-75

Figure 5-76

Regrouping in Multiplication

Problem area: Difficulty adding the carried digit.

Typical disabilities affecting progress: Problems related to short-term memory, visual memory, reversals, and sequential memory.

Background: Many students have trouble adding the carried digit because they cannot perform the required mental computation. They may know the basic facts, but, if they cannot retrieve an accurate image of the 2-digit number, they are bound to have trouble computing with it. Consider Figure 5-77. This student had no trouble with multiplication. Numbers were carried properly and aligned properly, and the operations were sequenced correctly. What happened then? Notice the 85 in the product. After correctly recording first the 10s and then the 1s digit of 48, the student mentally reversed the digits for 18 (6 × 3). The child thought "81," and for that number the sum 85 (81 + 4) is correct. The digits of the product 48 were probably not reversed because they were recorded as said. There was no need to sort out a confused visual image.

$$
\begin{array}{r}
38 \\
6 \\
\hline
85\,8
\end{array}
$$

Figure 5-77

We have noted how, as computational skills are expanded, the number of steps increases and accurate sequencing becomes essential. Unless children have a clear conceptual understanding of the process and have overlearned each discrete procedure involved, it is often difficult for them to maintain the correct sequence and compute successfully at the symbolic level.

The activities that follow address one small step of the computational process for multiplication: adding the carried digit. The suggested exercises have proven effective in dealing with the problem highlighted in the example of Figure 5-77 as well as other related difficulties.

Suggested Sequence of Activities and Exercises

1. **Relate.** If students have difficulty regrouping in multiplication, exercises like those of Figure 5-78 often prove helpful. These are an extension of the work begun in Section 2 of the addition part of this chapter, illustrated in Figures 5-33 and 5-34. Now an effort is made to relate the addition to its role in multiplication computation. In Figure 5-78 the student first solves an embedded addition problem and then a related multiplication problem. In example 1, students first find the sum of 24 and 4, filling in the spaces as they approach them verbally. The related multiplication is then carried out. When they reach the addition part of the problem, the children can look back at the answer. This eliminates the need to retain a reversed digit mentally.

   In the second example, the students complete the first addition and multiply 68 by 9. Then they do the second addition before finishing the multiplication. The speed with which the children can independently incorporate the addition procedure into multiplication will depend on how comfortable they are with the entire multiplication process. Allow them to use pages of this type so they can multiply with a minimum of interference from their learning deficits.

2. **Color cue.** Figure 5-79 shows how to use color coding to help students who have trouble sequencing even though visual discrimination presents little difficulty. The children are reminded to use the colors as a stoplight—multiplying first and then adding.

3. **Different strokes.** The previous example can be adjusted as in Figure 5-80 for students who have trouble revisualizing the product in order to be able to combine it with the carried number. After multiplying the 10s digit, the product (45) is written on the green line and added to the number carried.

Example 1:

$\begin{array}{r} 24 \\ + \ 4 \\ \hline \end{array}$ must end in _____ so 24+4= _____

$\begin{array}{r} 36 \\ \times \ 8 \\ \hline \end{array}$

Example 2

$\begin{array}{r} 54 \\ + \ 7 \\ \hline \end{array}$ must end in _____ so 54+7= _____

$\begin{array}{r} 68 \\ \times 49 \\ \hline \end{array}$

$\begin{array}{r} 24 \\ + \ 3 \\ \hline \end{array}$ must end in _____ so 24+3= _____

Figure 5-78

— = green   ... = red

$\begin{array}{r} 57 \\ \times \ 9 \\ \hline \end{array}$

Figure 5-79

— = green   ... = red

$\begin{array}{r} 45 \quad 57 \\ \times \ 9 \\ \hline 3 \end{array}$

Figure 5-80

4. **Another alternative.** Students whose major difficulty is digit reversal when having to retain a number mentally should be encouraged to write the number down. Providing a box to the side of the problem, as in Figure 5-81, often is sufficient to avoid digit reversal. For left-handed students, place the box to the left of the problem.

Figure 5-81

5. **In and out.** A board game that provides practice in adding the carried number is shown in Figure 5-82. Each child needs a marker and, if necessary, an answer key. Provide a maze board and a set of cards containing partially completed multiplication problems. Each child, in turn, draws a card and states the remaining partial product. In this case, 44. If correct, the child advances a marker as many steps into the maze as indicated by the carry number. In case of a wrong answer, the marker is moved back an equivalent number of spaces. The winner is the first to get out of the maze.

Figure 5-82

DIVISION OF WHOLE NUMBERS

The increased availability and lower cost of hand calculators, together with the infrequent need to use long division in day-to-day situations, has caused mathematics educators to question whether we should continue to teach the long-division algorithm. Until this issue has been generally resolved, however, we must continue to find effective ways of presenting long division. The purpose of this part of the chapter is to provide suggestions to help regular classroom and special education teachers of learning disabled students to accomplish this goal.

> **Note:** We hope that the presentation of long division is limited to a dividend of 3 or 4 digits and a divisor of 2 digits, as recommended in the *Standards* (NCTM, 1989).

Beginning Long Division

Problem area: Difficulty transferring from the concrete to the symbolic level for long division; inability to interpret meaningfully written long division problems.

Typical disabilities affecting progress: Difficulty with visual memory, sequencing, abstract reasoning, and retrieval.

Background: For many children, the concept of division—using blocks, chips, money, and other concrete aids—is relatively easy to grasp. Thus, they soon learn to divide (separate) things into groups with the same number in each group. The difficulty arises when only symbols are used in the written problem. The functional division sign ($\overline{)}$) tends to confuse students with reversal tendencies, whether visual or auditory. Yet, the other division sign ($\div$) is not particularly useful, at this point. Generally, rather than confronting children with both symbols simultaneously, it is better to teach them to use the more functional one first, relating it as much as possible to concrete aids.

Because of the inherent reversal tendencies and involved sequencing in division, the process lends itself well to color coding. The colors provide the student with a starting point as well as a way of determining and maintaining the sequence. Suggestions along this line follow.

Suggested Sequence of Activities and Exercises

1. **Say it with chips.** As children make the transition to symbolic work for long division, it is often helpful to relate the work with materials directly to the written computational problems. Make puzzles available like those shown in Figure 5-83. Have the children cut the puzzles apart before beginning, then place the two pieces of each together, upside down, at the side of the desk. Using an overhead projector or felt board, the teacher places chips under the division sign ($\overline{)}$) and goes through the sequence described below. The chips should be colored green, black, and red to match the colors on the puzzles.

Fronts

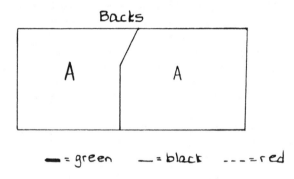

Backs

— = green   —— = black   ---- = red

Figure 5-83

For each puzzle, the presentation is similar to that indicated below. The children work with real chips and the *left* side of each puzzle.

Teacher: "Start with seven green chips." (After the seven green chips are taken, the teacher tells the students to find the left piece of the puzzle A.) "Write 7 on the green line to stand for the seven chips."
Teacher: "Use your chips again. Let's put two chips in each group." (In conjunction with this activity, the children write a 2 on the black line of the puzzle piece.)
Teacher: (Using the chips under the $\overline{)}$ forms groups of two.) "How many groups did I make? Right. I made three and had one chip left over." (The children are instructed to put numbers in the appropriate places of their puzzle pieces to indicate this.)

This procedure continues until all left-hand puzzle pieces have been filled in. The children then put the puzzles back together to check their work.

2. **Puzzles alone.** Once students understand the previous work at the concrete level, show them the picture part of the puzzles and ask them to rewrite each problem on their own paper, using *numbers* rather than dots. To check, the children again match the puzzle pieces.

> **Note:** This method of presentation and reinforcement is effective even with upper-primary grade children. First it offers the concrete aspect so essential to comprehension. In addition, the direct teaching of the transition and the overlearning help build a strong base. Visual memory, sequencing, auditory memory, and abstract reasoning are all reinforced.

3. **Follow-up.** After work with chips and puzzles, exercises like those of Figure 5-84 can be used by students with adequate reading skills. These pages are especially good for children who need to verbalize while learning, but have trouble retrieving the words. Before solving the problem using numbers, the left-hand section is completed. The teacher fills in divisor dots at the presentation. Then the children fill in the numbers at the right and solve the problems.

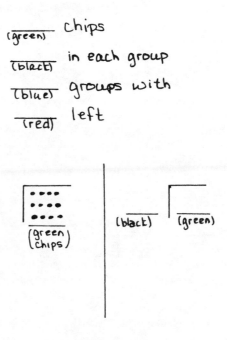

Figure 5-84

4. **Transition.** Figures 5-85 and 5-86 show transitional pages that can be used as the children develop better conceptual understandings and become able to sequence using symbols only. In Figures 5-85b and 5-85c the student can fill in numbers from textbook problems or the teacher can fill in numbers which are appropriate to the student's level. Figure 5-86a acts as an example which the teacher can fill in before the student begins copying textbook problems in the rest of the page.

Beginning Long Division: Special Help

Problem area: Using only symbols to solve division problems.

Typical disabilities affecting progress: Difficulty with auditory processing, perseveration, sequencing, visual memory, and closure.

Background: Even when the concept of division is established and the students can interpret the written long division problem, many children are still unable to proceed independently. For many, it is due to an inability to retrieve the needed

Figure 5-85

Figure 5-86

facts. For others, the required sequencing and constant operation switch make it difficult to complete a problem accurately. Memory deficits may have prevented them from learning the basic facts and perseveration makes skip counting or the use of charts too difficult.

The following activities contain suggestions for how to help children deal with these problems. The assumption is that students' concept base is strong and that the division problem difficulty is primarily due to individual learning difficulties.

Suggested Sequence of Activities and Exercises

1. **In the squares.** Many children need to see and feel what they are saying. Figure 5-87a illustrates a format idea for pages that can be kept in the file

Figure 5-87

and used, as needed, to provide such reinforcement. The children place dots, lines, or chips (if necessary) in each square as they skip count (Figure 5-87b). For those who need assistance with stopping, provide a stoplight above the last box needed or outline this box in red. Encourage the students to keep one finger on the dividend number and to compare it with the number of chips placed.

Note: As overlearning occurs, the children independently place numbers rather than pictures or objects in the squares to show the skip count (Figure 5-87c).

2. **Transition.** As a transition to the long division procedure, Figure 5-88 illustrates a format for pages that can be filed and used. The teacher fills in dividend and divisor numbers at the time of presentation (Figure 5-89a). The student fills in the squares and determines the number of groups that have been made. Then a count is made to see how many things have been "used up" (15 in this example). The child now subtracts to find the number left over.

Note: For right-handed children the boxes should be to the left of the computation. For left-handed children they should be on the right.

3. **Help for sequencing.** As students need the squares less, but still require visual cues for sequencing, use pages containing problems like that of Figure 5-90. After filling in the quotient, the student is reminded to multiply by the box at the left. Figure 5-91 shows an alternative format designed to help with sequencing. Pages of this type are especially useful for students who have receptive language deficits. The pages can be color coded if necessary. Assuming

left

Figure 5-88

a)

5$\overline{)17}$

b)   3R2

5$\overline{)17}$

−15

2

Figure 5-89

2$\overline{)17}$

☐ 2's =

Figure 5-90

___ groups of ___ each = ___ × ___ =

used up

with ___ left

Figure 5-91

there is no perceptual or spatial organizational difficulty to bar copying, the student can fill in the blanks with problems from the text. Ideally, the problems should be copied as one assignment and solved as a second.

4. **Relate.** The sequence suggested by Figure 5-92 can be used to help students more readily determine the correct quotient digit. An effort is made to relate division with remainders directly to basic facts. In the first set of problems, the basic fact answer is given. The child is cued to use this to help solve the given division with remainder. In Figure 5-92b, the students must answer the basic fact problem themselves before computing the long division example. The last problem set (c) requires that students write in the dividend closest to, but less than that of the given long division problem. The idea of a left-hand basic fact problem can also be used in conjunction with the exercises suggested by Figures 5-90 and 5-91.

Figure 5-92

Note: Throughout these explanations, the divisor has been used to describe the number of objects in each group. This interpretation has proven successful, given our approach, with the learning disabled students with whom we have worked. Obviously, the divisor can also mean the number of needed groups, with the quotient describing the number of objects in each group. This latter interpretation describes situations in which the children divide or share a given number of objects (see Figure 5-93). Because of research documenting the ease with which regular class children relate to the idea of sharing, the concept is becoming increasingly popular in mathematics textbooks that present long division. Whatever the approach, it is important to be consistent until the process is learned. Once understanding and

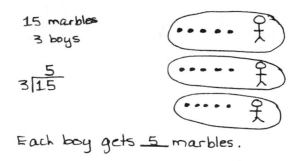

15 marbles
3 boys

$3\overline{)15}$ $\dfrac{5}{}$

Each boy gets __5__ marbles.

Figure 5-93

retention have been achieved, it is essential to introduce also the other interpretation. A suggestion for how to introduce the "sharing" idea is outlined in the story line that follows.

5. **Story line for sharing money.** A money story line can be used to provide auditory reinforcement for and give meaning to the procedure for long division. The problem of Figure 5-94a can be related to four students who find a bag of money containing 2 one-hundred dollar bills, 3 ten-dollar bills, and 5 one-dollar bills. They cannot locate the owner. After turning the bag in to the police, the boys are allowed to keep the money and split it among themselves. How do they go about sharing the money? They are most excited about splitting the one-hundred dollar bills first. (This fact reinforces the left-to-right procedure for computing long division problems.) With only 2 one-hundred dollar bills and four people, what should they do? Tear the bills? No! They trade the 2 one-hundred dollar bills in for 20 ten-dollar bills. Now with 23 ten-dollar bills, what's the *greatest number* of ten-dollar bills each can receive? (Refer to Figure 5-94b.)

The story continues along these lines as the children divide what is left, thereby computing the long division problem. With 1-digit divisors, play money can be used to dramatize the story. Eventually, the students should be asked to analyze the sequence suggested by the story line, noting that there are *five basic steps* (Figure 5-95). Further ideas for focusing on the five basic steps of the long division process are contained in the following section.

Five Basic Steps

Problem area: Difficulty retaining and sequencing steps in long division.

Typical disabilities affecting progress: Difficulty with memory, sequencing, figure-ground, integrative processing, and spatial organization.

Figure 5-94

1) ÷
2) X
3) —
4) compare
5) bring down

Figure 5-95

Background: The long division process is cumbersome and often unnecessary, particularly for children with the learning deficits just noted. Although their conceptual understanding is adequate, these children may not be able to sequence the steps and place the numbers correctly to arrive at an answer. Sometimes the use of a calculator for long sequences is a viable and preferable alternative. However, if students are not able to use the calculator at this level (i.e., for division which involves remainders) or if their visual perceptual difficulties make the calculator more complicated than paper-and-pencil exercises, then repeated drill, with the goal of overlearning the sequence, is recommended.

Suggested Sequence of Activities and Exercises

1. **Fill in.** Figure 5-96 shows a way of helping students organize their thoughts and build up a mental image of the sequence for long division. Before com-

_____ chips
_____ chips in each group

$$9\overline{)58}\ \ ^{\text{___ groups}}$$

−_____ used up

_____ left

Figure 5-96

puting, the student fills in the blanks of the rectangle as a reminder of what the numbers represent. The student then continues, reading the words as they are approached to help with the sequencing and to give meaning to the numbers. If necessary, chips may be used to dramatize problems. Eventually, the procedure should be related to the basic steps of Figure 5-95. It is often helpful to display these steps on a wall chart or write them on cards the children can keep at their desks for ready reference.

>   **Note:** If color coding is necessary during early work with exercises of this type, colors would match those of Figure 5-84.

2. **Longer problems.** As problems become longer and more involved, students typically encounter even greater difficulty in correctly placing digits. Figure 5-97 suggests one way of handling this situation. The words in the center column aid sequencing and eventually lead to overlearning. Encourage students to memorize them. The color coding within the problem helps students organize the sequence and properly place the numbers while computing. When dividing by the green 3, for example, the student writes the quotient on the green line. When multiplying by the green numbers, the product is recorded on the green line.

Figure 5-97

Note: Examples of pages similar to that of Figure 5-97 are shown in Figures 1-14 and 1-15. These can be prepared in advance, filed, and used as needed. Problems from the text can be copied directly into the boxes by students. If students need help with spatial organization, draw lines on some of the pages. This also helps those who have difficulty copying.

3. **Card slide.** For children who tend to reverse or for those with figure-ground deficits, provide a sliding card as in Figure 5-98. Instruct the children to cover up the digits not being used, as in the sequence shown.

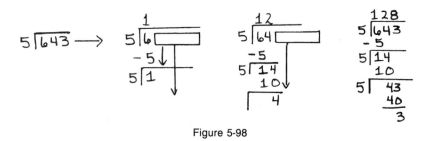

Figure 5-98

4. **"Problem" problems.** In early work with both 1- and 2-digit divisors, avoid giving students problem types on which you anticipate a high percentage of errors. One such class of problems is that which contains a middle zero in the quotient (Figure 5-99a). Another is that which involves expected rounding errors, as in Figure 5-99b. Give students a chance to feel comfortable with the computational process for long division before introducing more difficult problems.

Figure 5-99

5. **Two-digit divisors.** Many of the previous suggestions can be modified for work with 2-digit divisors. (Even the money story line in Activity 5 of the previous section can be adapted.) The problem of Figure 5-100, for example, might be viewed as sharing $2,176 with 31 people. Using the card slide of Figure 5-98, we realize that there are not enough thousand-dollar or one-hundred-dollar bills to share among so many people. However, bank trades would give us enough ten-dollar bills: a total of 217. The rest of the story is adapted accordingly.

Figure 5-100

6. **Minimize frustrations.** Figure 5-101 illustrates an idea for how to maximize drill while minimizing student frustration. Since the dividend in each example is the same and the divisors similar, only the first problem is "hard." The remaining two problems provide the necessary practice, but should be relatively easy.

Figure 5-101

7. **Round down.** A mixture of rounding-up and rounding-down procedures can be efficient for arriving at correct quotient digits. Some learning disabled students, however, become confused by the many decisions they have to make using this approach. Therefore, it may be simpler to require them only to round down (never up) for all examples. If the correct quotient digit is not found right away, as in Figure 5-102a, the direction of the error will always be the same: "Too big, so I'll need to make it one less" (Figure 5-102b).

a)

$$74\overline{)5073}$$
518

I rounded the divisor down and got "7." But it's too big.

b)

$$74\overline{)5073}$$
444
60

1 less is just right

Figure 5-102

Longer Computations: Special Help

Problem area: Difficulty aligning digits or otherwise placing them correctly within the problem.

Typical disabilities affecting progress: Difficulty with visual perception, spatial organization, eye-hand coordination, reasoning, and figure-ground.

Background: The division algorithm, aside from being sequentially difficult, also requires good visual perception. Even with strong place value comprehension, many students have difficulty aligning the digits in the quotient. Others, like the child who worked the problem in Figure 5-103a, are miscued perceptually by the problem itself. In this case, the child understood the long division

a)

$$4\overline{)926}$$ 23 R 6
8
12
12
6

b)

$$4\overline{)9\square}$$ 23 R 6
8
12
12
6

Figure 5-103

process. He knew the remainder was too large, but was confused because he saw nothing more to bring down! When questioned about digit placement in the quotient, he could only correct his error when a card was placed over the 26 (Figure 5-103b) to make the placement more obvious. This technique and others that follow make it possible for most learning disabled students to succeed with long division.

Suggested Sequence of Activities and Exercises

1. **Think ahead.** The formatted pages of Figures 1-14, 1-15, and 5-97 can be prepared in advance, filed, and used to help students, as needed, with digit placement in long division.

2. **Show where.** Many children find it necessary to determine the number of digits in the quotient before solving. To help, they can use a finger or a card and uncover the digits in the dividend one at a time, as in Figure 5-104. As the student determines where quotient digits should be placed, short lines are drawn to indicate the placement over the appropriate dividend figures.

Figure 5-104

3. **Practice.** Some children have trouble reasoning and, therefore, do not automatically notice if an answer does not make sense. (They will only notice if there is not enough room or if there is too much room for the digits.) For them it often helps merely to practice determining where quotient digits should be placed. Have the students place lines above the dividend numbers to show the correct placement, as in Figure 5-104. Do not require that they complete problems at this time. Gradually, through discussion and repetition, the student should begin to notice that when the divisor is larger than the first digit of the dividend that space must be empty.

4. **Graph paper.** As with multiplication, graph paper is helpful for aligning digits in long division. Keep some pages set up as in Figure 5-105. Many children,

Figure 5-105

especially those with severe figure-ground problems, cannot copy numbers on to the graph paper unless it is spatially organized as shown. However, once the initial organization is provided, the graph paper boxes help with alignment. Gradually, as the child feels comfortable determining the number of digits in a quotient, it also becomes easier to set up and compute the problem independently.

Problems within Problems

Problem area: Difficulty recognizing and solving the subtraction part of a long division problem.

Typical disabilities affecting progress: Difficulty with figure-ground, closure, and integrative processing.

Background: Once the sequence of steps for long division has been established, students must sort out the subtraction problem within the division. Figure 1-2 illustrates how degree of difficulty can affect computation. Locating and accurately solving the subtraction part of the problem seems to be the hardest in the first subtraction. At that point, there are many numbers to deal with and, especially if regrouping is involved, it becomes difficult to sort out properly. The suggestions that follow help overcome this problem.

Suggested Sequence of Activities and Exercises

1. **Block out.** Keep tachistoscopes, as in Figure 5-106, that can be used to block all but the relevant part of a long division problem.

$$7\overline{)463}$$

$$7\overline{)463} \quad 7\overline{)} \quad 7\overline{)463}$$

Figure 5-106

2. **Transition.** As a transition to working the problems independently, have the child use the tachistoscope before solving. Figure 5-107a shows the original problem. The student decides where the first digit of the quotient will be, in this case over 6, and places a line to mark that position. The tachistoscope is then placed as shown, and the student traces around the rectangle before removing the stencil (Figure 5-107b). The problem of Figure 5-107c is now "ready" for the child to compute.

Figure 5-107

3. **Outline the sign.** Sometimes it is helpful to outline the division sign in a bright color. This helps the student distinguish the isolated parts of the problem.

4. **Circle.** Provide practice pages of *completed* problems, as in Figure 5-108. Have the student circle each subtraction (or just the first) within the division. This could be part of a 2-day assignment. On the first day, the student circles the subtraction problems. The next day, after the page is checked, the student receives a second sheet containing the same problems (*not* worked) to solve independently.

$$
\begin{array}{r}
5\ 1 \\
9\overline{)46\ 7} \\
-45 \\
\hline
9\overline{)\quad 17} \\
9 \\
\hline
8
\end{array}
\qquad
\begin{array}{r}
1\ 19 \\
7\overline{)835} \\
-7 \\
\hline
7\overline{)13} \\
7 \\
\hline
7\overline{)65} \\
-63 \\
\hline
2
\end{array}
$$

Figure 5-108

CHAPTER

6

Fractions and Decimals: Early Concept Work

Children's early ideas about number pertain only to whole numbers. When they extend these whole number ideas, first intuitions stem from day-to-day settings: half a glass of milk; part of a cracker. As children turn symbolically to fractions and then to decimals, their mathematical power grows. Now they are in a position to represent and solve a new variety of problems involving measurement geometry, probability, graphing, and other topics. They are learning ideas and skills which later can be applied to proportion, algebra, and other advanced topics.

The emphasis in early concept work for learning disabled students should be on appropriate use of physical models and on appropriate language, visual, auditory, or kinesthetic/tactile cueing techniques which link manipulation in meaningful ways to written symbols. These students frequently need specific help if they are to read, write, and interpret fractions and decimals accurately. Most of them need ongoing, structured experiences which nurture development of number sense for fractions and decimals.

Acquiring a good sense for fractions and decimals involves first developing a solid understanding of and good intuitions about the relative size of given numbers. It also requires the ability to relate fractions and decimals in accurate, meaningful ways. Number sense for fractions and decimals extends to students' abilities to use and apply these numbers in appropriate day-to-day settings. Further, as will be discussed in the next two chapters, "number sense" leads to a more solid "operation sense," which enables students to judge whether the results of their computation are reasonable.

This chapter presents an instructional sequence for learning disabled students which integrates early work with fractions and decimals. The focus is on developing a basic understanding of rational number and on nurturing students' abilities to *read*, *write*, and *interpret* fractions and decimals in meaningful ways. The overriding goal is to enable students to demonstrate a good sense for these numbers in a variety of settings. Eight major sections provide a framework for discussion:

1. Fractions: General Areas of Difficulty

2. Writing Fractions

3. Improper Fractions and Mixed Numbers

4. Decimals: General Areas of Difficulty

5. Understanding, Reading, and Writing Decimals

6. Using an Inch Ruler

7. Using a Centimeter Ruler

8. Number Sense for Fractions and Decimals

The rationale for the suggested sequence is to first build strong concepts and related skills with fractions, and then proceed to use the more concrete path of fractions to develop related concepts and skills in early work with decimals. Finally, with a strong base of each type of number students can more easily begin to apply these skills in daily activities such as measurement and problem solving.

To prepare for this, early fraction experiences should include some work with tenths, along with fractions having denominators of 2, 3, 4, 5, 6, 8, 16 (for inch rulers). The National Council of Teachers of Mathematics (1987) recommends that only these more familiar fractions be emphasized and, when possible, in applied settings.

FRACTIONS: GENERAL AREAS OF DIFFICULTY

Perceptual Skills

Perceptually, fractions can be difficult. The mere act of correctly writing a fraction requires *spatial* organization that many learning disabled children lack. It is not unusual to see children writing fractions or mixed numbers as in Figure 6-1. This type of copying may appear careless when, in fact, children may be perceiving the positions exactly as written.

Figure 6-1

Figure-ground deficits can also make it difficult for some children to sort out the relevant parts of a picture. Textbook illustrations, like that shown in Figure 6-2, can be visually confusing, making it impossible for students to use them effectively. These same children may have trouble computing because all the isolated digits of the fraction "run together."

Figure 6-2

Abstract Reasoning

As concrete as the idea of fractions can be, much of what we teach children about fractions relies on a high degree of abstract reasoning. Using objects and pictures, we show them that $\frac{1}{3}$ means one out of three equal parts. The idea is fairly simple; after repeated presentations with whatever aids are needed, most children learn to label fractional parts of geometric regions and, eventually, of groups of objects. However, consider Figure 6-3 in which both pictures represent the fraction for $\frac{2}{5}$. Children who have trouble with multiple meanings find this extremely complex. While the concept "two out of five equal parts" may be clear, the difficulty arises because the equal parts of the two shapes are different sizes. The unit, the "one whole," in each case is different.

Language and Vocabulary

Expressive and *receptive language* problems also commonly interfere with the ability to understand and use fractions. Since students are used to "hearing horizontally" they often have trouble associating the vertical fraction with the words.

Figure 6-3

As teachers we need to remain sensitive to the problems these students experience and attempt to find simple ways to help them.

The language of fractions involves many familiar words used in a new context. Most children have heard the words "third," "fourth," "fifth," and so on. By about second grade, it is generally expected that they can readily relate numeric symbols to them. However, now they must also begin to apply new meanings to these words and make immediate decisions about how they are being used.

Suppose a teacher writes "$\frac{3}{4}$" on the board and (a) instructs the student to shade three fourths of a rectangle or (b) asks how many people are in a third of the class. The child hears the fraction and may even be able to relate the words to the correct written form. However, when asked to apply the fraction in this new context, which is no longer horizontal (linear) in nature, confusion sets in. When the language of fractions is used to describe a group of things, such as "a third of a class," the relationship becomes even more abstract. The child hears the fraction, but finds it meaningless in this context. How much is a "third of a class?" A number may not be readily associated with the words "of a class." Although most children can readily switch their thought processes back and forth, learning disabled students often need considerably more time in order to do so.

These same children frequently experience difficulty when other fraction terms are introduced: "equivalent," "common," "simplest," "reduced," "improper." They have to relate fractions to each other using any of these or other words. The task is overwhelming for many children. The words are used over and over again—not necessarily in the same contexts—and many find it difficult to retrieve and associate the proper meanings at the proper time. For example, each of the fractions in Figure 6-4 can be referred to using a different word, yet they can all be considered equivalent.

$$\frac{8}{6} = 1\frac{2}{6} = 1\frac{1}{3}$$

Figure 6-4

Since most fraction terms can easily be associated with numbers or concrete objects, it helps to make a "dictionary" available to students (see Figure 6-5). Store it in a place to which children have easy access—at the teacher's desk or on a nearby shelf. Alternatively, make it into a wall chart to which students can readily refer when they are faced with a troublesome word during class or independent study.

$$\text{Improper Fraction} \rightarrow \frac{4}{3}, \frac{7}{2}$$

$$\text{Mixed Number} \rightarrow 1\frac{1}{3}, 2\frac{3}{4}$$

$$\text{Proper Fraction} \rightarrow \frac{2}{5}, \frac{5}{8}$$

$$\text{Equivalent Fractions} \rightarrow \frac{4}{6} = \frac{2}{3} = \frac{10}{15}$$

$$1\frac{7}{8} = 1\frac{28}{32} = 1\frac{14}{16}$$

Figure 6-5

WRITING FRACTIONS

Problem area: Difficulty writing fractions and mixed numbers.

Typical disabilities affecting progress: Difficulty with spatial organization, eye-hand coordination, and receptive language.

Background: Once fraction concepts have been established using physical materials, it generally is assumed that children will have little difficulty reading and writing the numbers. This is not always the case, however. Sequentially, students may know the order in which fraction digits should be read or written, but, spatially, they may be unable to place the digits properly (see Figure 6-6). Similarly, they may hear the correct sounds, auditorially, and associate them with the symbols, but retrieving and writing them properly may be an entirely different matter.

For younger students or for those who have learning difficulties, it often is necessary to provide specific practice in writing and reading fractions, much like

$$3\text{--}4 \quad \text{instead of} \quad \frac{3}{4}$$

Figure 6-6

what is done with handwriting. As these students make the transition from concrete or pictorial representations to symbolic representations, it may be especially necessary for the teacher to review the goal of individual lessons. Is the goal to *associate* the correct fraction with its concrete or pictorial representation? Is it to *write* the correct fraction for a given model? Is it to *write* a fraction which is heard? Is it to *read* a fraction which is written?

Too often we think of these steps as one and the same, but for many learning disabled children they are not. Thus, students with the learning deficits noted above must internalize, for example, what it *feels like* to write the digits of a fraction in the proper spaces. Only then will they be able to concentrate on what the numbers mean. Until they begin to feel more comfortable with the spatial orientation needed to write fractions, most of their energy will be expended on number placement rather than on understanding.

The following activities suggest ways to help children write fractions correctly. The major assumption is that the children's difficulties are not due to conceptual misunderstanding.

Suggested Sequence of Activities and Exercises

1. **Trace.** Felt numbers or a sand or salt tray often are helpful for students who need kinesthetic involvement and gross-motor activity while learning to write fractions. Children trace over a given fraction and then immediately write it, perhaps with chalk or a large crayon. The gross-motor activity helps build the more difficult, fine-motor control needed for standard paper-and-pencil writing of fraction digits.

2. **Color cue.** When students are ready for paper-and-pencil work, start by using exercises such as those in Figure 6-7. The goal is to help students develop the spatial organization, *visually* and *kinesthetically*, required to write fractions correctly. As previously, colors are used to help with sequence and number placement: "When you write, green goes first—on top." Coat the green shading and box outline of several examples with glue. When the glue is dry, the children

Figure 6-7

can finger trace over the raised surfaces. Eventually, they will write the number independently (at the end of the line following the equals sign).

3. **Choose.** If the goal of the assignment is to write fractions to describe a shaded region, the example in Figure 6-8 shows how to avoid difficulties due to spatial deficits. The children cross out the wrong answer and write over the correct one. The fraction is then written independently, immediately after tracing.

Figure 6-8

4. **Mixed numbers.** Writing mixed numbers presents even greater problems for children with spatial difficulties. Now a sense of midpoint is added, in addition to up-and-down movement. Figure 6-9 shows one type of exercise that can be prepared in advance and kept on file. The colors are used to help students:

- Develop the correct sequence for writing numbers;

- Locate the correct position for each digit; and

- Associate the parts of the number with the related parts of the picture.

The goal of the assignment is to help students spatially organize their writing of mixed numbers.

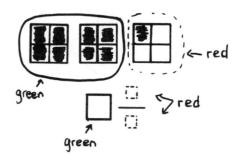

Figure 6-9

5. **Stencil first.** For students with more severe deficits, keep stencils on hand as in Figure 6-10a. Instruct students first to use a stencil to write a fraction, and then to write it again without the stencil. The two fractions—the stencil and the nonstencil copy—should be written side by side. In this way, the first serves as a pattern for writing the second.

6. **Tape it.** The stencils shown in Figure 6-10a also can be used for students who have trouble writing fractions without a visual cue. Provide boxed paper as described in Chapter 1. Have students listen to a tape recorder and write the fractions dictated. If color coding is needed, put tape around the sides of the stencil as in Figure 6-10b. Students "go" on green and write the *first* digit of each proper fraction dictated on top (in the numerator).

7. **Words to numerals.** Many students have trouble associating number words with the correct position of the digits in a fraction. Color-coded exercises, as in Figure 6-11, often help both with spatial organization and language association. Note that the students rewrite the fraction independently as a last step of the exercise.

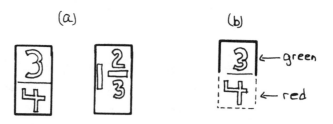

Figure 6-10

$$\text{three} = \frac{3}{5} =$$

■ = green
···· = red

Figure 6-11

- *Extension:* To develop the idea further, the colors can be used as in Figure 6-12. In the first two examples, children read the words, fill in the blanks, then write the fraction independently. The variation in the last example requires that students describe the picture verbally before proceeding.

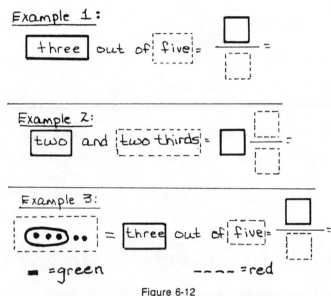

Figure 6-12

Note: Throughout these exercises, bold, dotted, or regular line drawings can be used instead of color cueing for color-blind students.

8. **Fringo.** A variation of bingo can be used to reinforce basic fraction concepts and provide practice writing fractions. Make a set of calling cards representing fractions, as in Figure 6-13a. Also make a set of gameboards with fractions in each square (Figure 6-13b). Instead of chips, provide the players with plastic overlays and grease pencils. Players take turns pulling a card and stating the fraction name. If the symbol is on the gameboard, the student writes over it with the pencil. The winning pattern should be determined before the game.

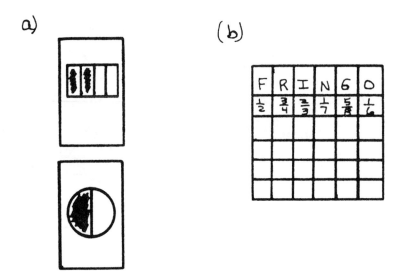

Figure 6-13

Note: For students with auditory-sequencing or memory problems, the calling cards can be color coded, if necessary. Use the suggestions from the exercises in this section for the coloring scheme.

IMPROPER FRACTIONS AND MIXED NUMBERS

Problem area: Difficulty writing a quotient as a mixed number; difficulty changing an improper fraction to a mixed number.

Typical disabilities affecting progress: Difficulty with spatial organization, visual figure-ground, abstract reasoning, sequencing, and auditory processing.

Background: Many learning disabled students need specific, structured help if they are to learn how to write a quotient or change an improper fraction into a mixed number. Spatially, writing and aligning numbers is demanding. Additionally, at the symbolic level, because there are often many numbers to sort out, children may forget what the numbers mean. As a consequence, they lose track of the correct sequence for writing the digits. Certain techniques may be used to deal with these types of problems. The exercises that follow have proven effective in our own work with learning disabled students.

Suggested Sequence of Activities and Exercises

1. **Color code.** Color-coded pages for simple division problems with remainders, as in Figure 6-14, constitute the initial practice needed to help students spatially organize their work. The children follow the color cueing and merely copy the numbers in the correct boxes. Then the mixed number is rewritten, independently, to provide extra reinforcement. The *completed* division example is given at this stage. The goal is to help students learn the correct placement of digits for the mixed-number equivalent of the given quotient. The color scheme controls for extraneous interferences by drawing students' attention only to relevant digits and their placement.

Figure 6-14

2. **Divide, too.** Once students feel more comfortable about transferring the quotient to a mixed number, have them do the division as well (see Figure 6-15). Generally, it is a good idea to encourage the children first to write the final answer in the form _____R_____. This method tends to prevent them from losing the remainder in the mass of other numbers. Then the transfer to the mixed number form can be made. As in previous exercises, the example in Figure 6-15 requires that students rewrite the mixed number independently as a final step.

3. **Sample problems.** Pages with color-coded examples at the top can be used to help students make the transition from colors to no colors. Colors are not used for the other problems on the page. If the children get stuck, they can refer to the coded example at the top of the sheet.

$$\overset{=R-}{\sqrt{49}} \quad = \quad \square \overset{=}{{}_{---}} \quad = $$

— = green

--- = red

Figure 6-15

• *Variation:* Keep a poster on the wall with the color-coded example or provide a card the children can keep at their desks.

4. **Relate.** Figure 6-16a shows a way to help students discover the relationship between a fraction and the division process. This exercise also paves the way for changing improper fractions to mixed numbers (Activity 5). The students solve the division and fill in the blanks. Have them read aloud and, for selected examples, partition the objects into groups to dramatize what is said. As a follow-up, present exercises like those of Figure 6-16b.

The children could copy mixed numbers from previously worked division problems into the boxes and rewrite each in the form ____R____ (Figure

a)

$\overset{R-}{7\sqrt{64}}$ = ___whole groups with ___ out of ___ left.

$\overset{R-}{8\sqrt{59}}$ = ___whole groups with ___ out of ___left.

$9\frac{1}{7}$ = ___whole groups with ___out of ___left.

$7\frac{3}{8}$ = ___whole groups with ___out of ___left.

b) $\boxed{9}\frac{1}{7}$ = ___R___

$\boxed{7}\frac{3}{8}$ = ___R___

c) $\boxed{}$ ___ = ___R___

$\boxed{}$ ___ = ___R___

Figure 6-16

6-16b). Ask them to verbalize how the quotient (____R____) and the mixed number expressions mean the same thing. Tie this in with the work of Figure 6-16a by allowing students to place small objects in groups to prove the equivalence. Sample file pages are shown in Figure 6-16c.

5. **Improper fractions to mixed numbers.** Figure 6-17a suggests a preformatted page that can be kept on file and used with teacher-made problems or with problems students copy from the text. As suggested by the example, colors are often essential at this point. Specifically, they reduce difficulties due to deficits in visual perception and spatial organization; they emphasize associations that help students understand the process for changing from an improper fraction to a mixed number. As before, the objects can be divided into groups to dramatize what is said. A completed example is presented in Figure 6-17b.

Figure 6-17

6. **Tic-tac-toe.** Make a set of cards with division problems, like those shown in Figure 6-18a. Until the children are more advanced, do not include problems whose quotients require reducing when written as a mixed number. Have the children fill in tic-tac-toe boards with the mixed number for each quo-

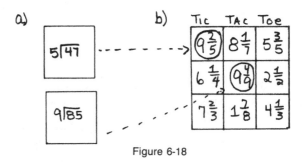

Figure 6-18

tient (see Figure 6-18b). After checking the boards, laminate them or cover with contact paper. For practice, the students play tic-tac-toe, alone or with a partner, by drawing a card and circling the correct mixed number if it is represented on the board. The first person to circle three in a row wins.

DECIMALS: GENERAL AREAS OF DIFFICULTY

Today's school mathematics curriculum focuses on decimals much earlier than in the past. For many learning disabled students, this hastens the emergence of two major obstacles to early success in decimal work.

The first obstacle involves orally interpreting and reading decimals. Because of *auditory-discrimination deficits*, many learning disabled students find it difficult to distinguish ten*ths* and hundred*ths* from the more familiar tens and hundreds.

The second obstacle relates to writing decimals accurately, and interpreting or reading decimals in written form. The written fraction form for three-ten*ths*, for example, is much more "concrete" than its decimal counterpart. The fraction form has two digits: "three" and "ten," whereas the decimal form only shows ".3." For students with *abstract-reasoning* and *memory* deficits, this incongruity can cause great difficulties. The only way for these students to clearly understand decimals is through the more concrete approach of fractions. The following sections present ideas for modifying standard approaches to introducing decimals so the concept is made accessible to learning disabled students.

In particular, early fraction experiences with tenths and hundredths provide the link to decimal interpretation and meaning. Through experiences such as those outlined, the relationship between fractions and decimals is established and strengthened. Students need to understand this relationship and be able to convert between fractions and decimals in order to use most calculators efficiently.

UNDERSTANDING, READING, AND WRITING DECIMALS

Problem areas: Difficulty interpreting written decimals in a meaningful way; difficulty appropriately attaching "tenth," "hundredth," and other decimal names to decimals.

Typical disabilities affecting progress: Difficulty with abstract reasoning, auditory or visual memory, auditory discrimination, and expressive language.

Background: Decimals are typically introduced using models like that of Figure 6-19a. As long as the models are present, students may be able to write and read the decimals associated with them, as in Figure 6-19b. These same students, particularly those with the deficits just identified, may be unable to read written decimals without visual aids, however. A meaningful and effective way to help students become functionally independent with written decimals is to relate them to the familiar fractional notation. Even in the symbolic form, fractions are more "concrete" than decimals. The 10 in the denominator of $\frac{1}{10}$, for example, cues a child to say "one tenth." No similar cue for saying "tenth" is given by ".1." Thus, students must simply remember what to say, and this can be difficult.

Figure 6-19

The following sequence outlines steps for helping learning disabled students read and write decimals by relating them to fractions. It is assumed that the students have a firm understanding of the fraction concept as equal parts of a whole. It also is necessary that they have worked with the blocks (or graph-paper substitutes) to illustrate decimal numbers.

1. **Review.** Present the three blocks shown in Figure 6-20 and help students write the fraction for each. Discuss the name of each, orally emphasizing the "th."

   Note: Sometimes it is necessary to color emphasize the "th" in words for students with auditory-discrimination deficits. Doing so focuses attention on the endings, which differ from those used for whole numbers.

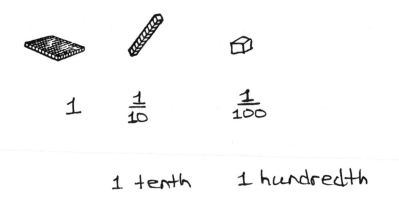

Figure 6-20

2. **Tell it to me.** Present pages like that in Figure 6-21. At first, cover the bottom of the page and have the children match real blocks to those appearing in the top row. Discuss the fraction written beneath each. Have the students read the fraction and note the color cueing: "$\frac{1}{10}$ has one zero, .1 has one decimal place," and so on.

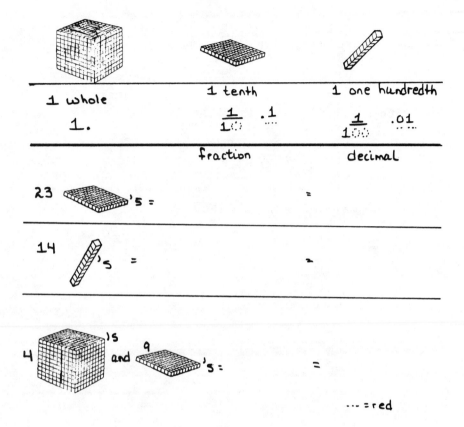

Figure 6-21

3. **Write it out.** Help the students complete the bottom part of the page. Here an effort is made to relate the visual model (the blocks) and the familiar fraction notation to the decimal form. Cue students to look at the number of zeros in the fraction, which tells the number of decimal places needed. "One zero (one decimal place) for tenths; two for hundredths."

   Note: Omit decimal examples like .03, which require a zero in the tenths place, until the children are more at ease writing other numbers with two decimal places.

4. **Reinforce with money.** Once the concepts of decimal place value and writing decimals are established to hundredths, decimals can be related to money as

in Figure 6-22. Review how to write money (Figure 6-22a), but focus on the decimal part. Eventually, eliminate the dollars and just use pennies (Figure 6-22b). Now is a good time to introduce zeros in the tenths place: "$.06—that's 6 out of 100 possible pennies." Continue color coding, if needed.

Figure 6-22

Note: When money concepts and skills are strong, students with expressive-language or visual-memory deficits may benefit from introductions of decimals by using money as a base.

5. **Relate.** To make use of students' strong visual association skills, pages like that of Figure 6-23 can be provided as follow-up to the work in Activity 4. Pages with mixed fraction and decimal problems also can be presented.

6. **Phase out.** Eliminate picture cues except at the top of the page, and require students to complete exercises like that shown in Figure 6-24.

7. **Decimal number words.** If the students have auditory weaknesses but can read, have them complete exercises like that of Figure 6-25. Initially, they must write the fraction form first, then the decimal. This sequence helps internalize the association between the decimal number names and the numerals themselves. Throughout decimal work, if the students get stuck when reading or writing a decimal, encourage them to think of or write the related fraction. The denominator of the fraction should help cue them to say "tenths" or "hundredths" and also indicate the appropriate number of decimal digits.

8. **Punch it in** (a practice activity for two players). As follow-up to Activity 7, provide a hand calculator for each student and a deck of cards, such as those in Figure 6-26. The children mix the cards and spread them, face up, between them. Then, in turn, each draws a card. After both players punch the number into their calculator, they compare the visual displays. Then they turn the card over to check. Players earn one tally point for each correct entry.

   • *Variation* (as an independent activity): The child draws cards, one at a time, and punches each number into the calculator. The child turns over the problem card to check the answer and gets a tally point for each correct response. Encourage the child to keep a log of the number correct for a given time period and work to improve the record.

   • *Variation* (to build auditory-memory and association skills): Ahead of time, "read" (or have the child read) the numbers on the cards into a cassette tape recorder. The child listens to the tape, punches the number heard, and uses the card deck to check the answer. If the tape does not allow sufficient pause between entries, instruct the child to push the stop button after each number is given.

USING AN INCH RULER

Problem area: Difficulty reading fractional parts of an inch on a ruler.

   Typical disabilities affecting progress: Difficulty with abstract reasoning, visual perception, and eye-hand coordination.

Figure 6-23

1 whole = 1. $\frac{1}{10}$ = .1 $\frac{1}{100}$ = .01

Write the decimal form for each fraction.

$\frac{4}{10}$: ____ $\frac{7}{100}$: _____

$\frac{32}{100}$: ____ $\frac{3}{10}$: _____

Write the fraction form for each decimal.

.9 =   .47 =

.06 =   .2 =

Figure 6-24

$\frac{6}{100}$ = six one hundredths = .06

$\frac{9}{10}$ = nine tenths = .9

Write the fraction and decimal for each.

	fraction	decimal
four tenths =	=	
eighteen one hundredths=	=	
seven one hundredths =	=	

Write the decimal for each.

decimal

nine one hundredths   =

sixteen one hundredths   =

five tenths   =

... = red

Figure 6-25

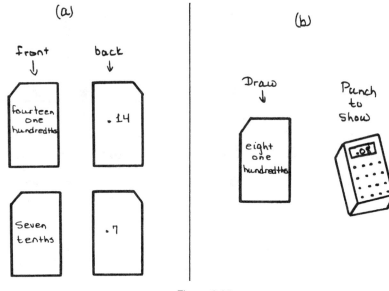

Figure 6-26

Background: To date, the United States has not made giant strides toward "going metric." As a result, students must continue to use inch rulers even as they learn to use centimeter rulers (see page 323 for further discussion of centimeter rulers). Visually the inch ruler causes more problems than the centimeter ruler. Thus, rather than just being able to associate a specific number with a specific line, the student must be able to:

- Differentiate visually among four different lengths;

- Associate the length of the line segment with the preceding ideas; and

- Read or write a symbol that is visually, spatially, and auditorially difficult to sequence.

When using an inch ruler to draw a line, students must know where to place the ruler in relation to the object to be measured. Eye-hand coordination problems often interfere. This section will not deal with this problem except to say that, if the goal is accurate measuring, give the students guide lines to follow, as in Figure 6-27, or allow them to use lined paper. For children with figure-ground deficits, however, the latter alternative can be more difficult than using guide lines.

Figure 6-27

The basic approach to teaching students how to use a ruler involves measuring many objects. In addition, some children may require more specialized instruction, such as that outlined below.

Suggested Sequence of Activities and Exercises

1. **Simplified rulers.** Younger children and children with learning disabilities usually start out with simplified rulers, which show only quarter, half, and whole inches. Even then, they may have trouble perceiving size differences for the various parts of an inch. Colors are often helpful. Properly used, colors can focus student attention and make size differences more obvious. Figure 6-28a shows an example of a homemade ruler that can be run on ditto paper and kept on file. As children become ready, the paper can be cut, glued to cardboard, and marked as in Figure 6-28b. Covering rulers with contact paper makes them more durable.

Figure 6-28

- *Variation 1:* For color-blind students, use bold, dotted, and regular line markings.

- *Variation 2:* For very young or developmentally immature children, prepare rulers with only inch markings or with only inch and half-inch markings.

2. **Measure.** To help children use the ruler in Activity 1, provide opportunities for them to measure many objects. Structure these experiences as follows: Attach masking tape strips to several items, as shown in Figure 6-29a. At first, make sure the measurement is an exact number of inches. Later, the tape mark can be slightly longer or slightly shorter so the children can learn how to measure to the nearest inch.

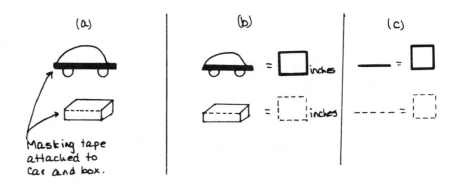

Figure 6-29

Gradually introduce half- and quarter-inch lengths. If the measurement is to be made to the nearest inch, the colored line segment on the tape should be blue to match the inch marks on the ruler. Similarly, the tape markers should be red (green) when half-inch (quarter-inch) measurements are to be made.

This color-cueing technique draws the child's attention to the appropriate ruler mark needed for a given measurement. Having the numbers on the ruler is especially important for students who require overlearning or have difficulty with retrieval. After an object is measured, the measurement is recorded on the worksheets that picture the object (see Figure 6-29b).

• *Extension:* As a follow-up to work with objects, have the children find and record the measurements of line segments drawn on paper. Figure 6-29c shows a sample exercise. Figure 6-30 shows another type of page that is helpful for students who have spatial deficits which make it difficult to write proper fractions and mixed numbers, or for children who have retrieval or expressive-language deficits and, therefore, need visual cues. The color-coding scheme, introduced earlier, is used as long as it seems helpful.

Figure 6-30

3. **Draw a line.** The color coding of Activity 2 can also be used to help students draw a line of a specific length. A sample exercise is presented in Figure 6-31a. The children use their rulers to draw over the given line, then draw another line of the same length under it. Gradually, still using color to specify the length (Figure 6-31b), instruct the students to draw the segment indicated. This latter exercise still provides some guidance because the color used for the written direction draws attention to the appropriate marks on the ruler. Even non-readers quickly pick up on the cueing and learn to perform the measurements accurately.

   Note: Some students may require the additional guidance of "start" and "stop" marks (see Figure 6-31c) as a transition between exercises like those shown in Figures 6-31a and 6-31b.

a) $2\frac{1}{2}$ inches = ---------------------

   (Written in red to match $\frac{1}{2}$ inch markings on ruler)

b) $2\frac{1}{2}$ inches =

c) $2\frac{1}{2}$ inches = x   x

Figure 6-31

USING A CENTIMETER RULER

Problem area: Difficulty interpreting or writing centimeter measures.

Typical disabilities affecting progress: Difficulty with abstract reasoning, visual perception, and eye-hand coordination.

Background: Centimeter rulers are considerably easier for children to use than inch rulers, which are based on fractions. Visually, centimeter rulers are less confusing. Thus, each line on the ruler can be more readily associated with a verbal expression. Even if the students have difficulty retrieving the correct decimal number name, there is still the readily available "one point three centimeters"—an important point for these children in terms of being able to interact with their peers.

The following activities can be used to help children interpret and read centimeter measurements. If eye-hand coordination problems interfere when students attempt to measure objects, provide guide lines (Figure 6-27) or masking tape strips (Figure 6-29).

Suggested Sequence of Activities and Exercises

1. **Simplified ruler.** Younger children with learning disabilities should use rulers marked in centimeters with a midline between each centimeter. As with inch rulers (page 319), different colors can be used for the centimeter versus the midline.

2. **Overhead rulers.** Enlarge the ruler and create a transparency (Figure 6-32) so students can more easily examine the subdivisions. Project the picture onto a wall and let children run a finger from the left ("start") edge to the first midline.

   A fraction bar as in Figure 6-32 can be used to illustrate that the distance from the end covers 5 out of 10, or $\frac{5}{10}$ (.5) of the total distance to the centimeter mark. Continue to "read" other measures as children, each time, run a finger from the left edge of the ruler: 1 cm, 1.5 cm, 2 cm, 2.5 cm, and so on. Later have students write what is read. Because the United States has not adopted the metric system, many teachers accept $1\frac{1}{2}$ cm, $2\frac{1}{2}$ cm, . . . , even though technically it may not be appropriate to use the fraction instead of the decimal notation.

3. **Overhead ruler showing millimeters.** For use with older students who have no severe visual deficits, the sample ruler with millimeter markings in Figure 6-33 can be kept on file. Create an overhead transparency of the ruler and project it onto the wall.

Figure 6-32

1 cm.   1.3 cm

Figure 6-33

Extend Activity 2 to millimeters. Each line on the ruler is associated with a specific decimal numeral. Follow with ample opportunities for students to measure, using rulers marked in millimeters.

NUMBER SENSE FOR FRACTIONS AND DECIMALS

Problem area: Poor intuition regarding the relative size of and relationship between fractions and decimals; difficulty making an appropriate estimate using fractions or decimals in practical settings.

Typical disabilities affecting progress: Difficulty with abstract reasoning, receptive and expressive language, short-term and sequential memory, visual perception.

Background: Number sense develops slowly, even with the best role modeling and structured, ongoing experiences. Consistent efforts along the lines suggested in the following activities and exercises are critical. If we are to nurture a student's potential to develop good number sense for fractions and decimals, structured activities related to this goal belong as an ongoing, important thrust of both the fraction and the decimal program.

Suggested Sequence of Activities and Exercises

1. **Sort fractions.** Use fraction cubes, fraction bars, and numerical representations to conclude that a fraction is "close to":

   - 0—when the numerator is very small in comparison to the denominator;
   - $\frac{1}{2}$—when the numerator is about half the size of the denominator;
   - 1—when the numerator is very close in size to the denominator.

   Ask students to sort fractions, as suggested by Figure 6-34.

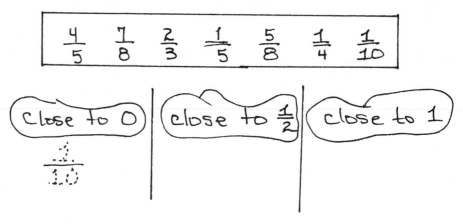

Figure 6-34

2. **Sort decimals.** Similar activities can be carried out with decimals to determine whether a given decimal is closer to 0, .5, or 1 (see Figure 6-35).

To estimate the size of a decimal less than 1...
   Look at the digit <u>just</u> <u>after</u> the decimal point.
   Ignore the rest.

   .03 _ _ _ _ _ is near **0**
   .47 _ _ _ _ _ _ is near **.5** (one half)
   .91 _ _ _ _ _ is near **1**

Figure 6-35

Note: Providing a number line and allowing students to finger trace the distance from a given fraction/decimal to each of the target numbers (0, half, 1) may help them make the correct decision.

CHAPTER

7

Extending Decimal Understandings and Skills

In the typical school curriculum early work with fractions precedes work with decimal numbers. Generally, however, beyond that introduction, the emerging trend is to treat the decimal topics of this chapter before parallel fraction topics. The rationale for this change is:

- Computation with decimals is generally easier and more closely related to whole number computation than is computation with fractions.

- Calculators and microcomputers use decimal notation.

As pointed out in the following pages, however, for some learning disabled students and for some topics, the use of fractions in basic developmental work is more effective than other techniques. The fractional approach and other techniques for handling decimal problem areas that typically are troublesome for learning disabled students are discussed in the seven sections of this chapter:

1. Comparing Decimals

2. Rounding Decimals

3. Computation: Choosing the Calculation Method

4. Checking: Is the Answer Reasonable?

5. Adding and Subtracting Decimals

6. Multiplying Decimals

7. Dividing Decimals

Calculator work is integrated throughout this chapter. At times, because alternate sequences are suggested, teachers must ensure that *prerequisite fraction concepts and skills* are intact if needed in the decimal program selected for an individual child.

Before turning to the recommended sequences, one final note relative to decimal computation is in order. The authors agree with the view expressed by the National Council of Teachers of Mathematics (NCTM) in its *Curriculum and Evaluation Standards for School Mathematics*: "Valuable instructional time should not be devoted to learning to compute 0.31×0.588 using paper and pencil, since this is done more appropriately on a calculator" (1987, p. 68). NCTM stresses the importance of keeping paper-and-pencil calculations simple (e.g., 0.3×0.6), and otherwise choosing between using a calculator or estimating for calculations involving larger numbers.

The time saved by incorporating either of these alternatives in computation can be devoted to problem solving and important new content, such as probability. Specific examples are provided to emphasize this point: "The ability to correctly compute 0.17×45 is not so interesting for its own sake as it is, perhaps, for estimating the number of times a certain result will occur on a spinner in a game or in determining a discount when buying a new tennis racquet" (National Council of Teachers of Mathematics, 1987, p. 68).

In problem-solving settings like these, instruction should focus on helping children (a) select the correct operation; (b) decide on the most efficient method of arriving at a workable answer (e.g., mental calculation, calculator, paper, and pencil); and (c) use a calculator efficiently and accurately. Instruction should also strive to develop children's ability to estimate so they can check whether answers are reasonable.

Certainly, it is important that students' *concepts* for decimals be strong. In addition, it is reasonable to require that the student be able to order decimals and carry out simple computations involving decimals. In some cases, because of state or regional minimal-competency examination requirements for receipt of graduation diplomas, more complicated computational skills related to multiplication or division of decimals must also be mastered.

Whatever the case, a student's understanding of decimals and of their use in applied settings should be developed in ways that lead to meaningful intuitions about decimal numbers. The general perspective taken in the following sections is that, throughout the decimal number program, care should be taken to develop concepts and skills in a way that builds number sense and stresses the practical usefulness of decimal numbers.

COMPARING DECIMALS

Problem area: Tendency to focus on the numerals rather than on the place value represented; that is, in examples like .48 and .6, calling .48 the greater. (Here there is a basic confusion between whole and decimal number meanings.)

Typical disabilities affecting progress: Difficulty with abstract reasoning, spatial organization, and auditory memory.

Background: Even students with no disabilities tend to have trouble comparing decimals. For students with abstract-reasoning deficits, the difficulty is compounded. Therefore, it often is necessary to teach these students a *procedure* for comparing. Then, when they feel comfortable with that procedure, use visuals to demonstrate that it is reasonable. For students with spatial-organization difficulties, the standard sequence of using objects/pictures first in developmental work is appropriate, so long as number lines or other aids that rely on accurate size perception are avoided.

A sample sequence that has been used effectively with the first group of students is based on Activities 4 (saving the "prove" step until later), 5, 6, and then 1, *in that order*. The sequence of the activities that follow, with the exception of Activity 3, can be carried out with students having spatial-organization deficits. Other children with learning disabilities, including those with visual-perception and visual- or auditory-memory difficulties, have been helped as well by these suggestions.

Suggested Sequence of Activities and Exercises

---

1. **Shade in.** Given a pair of decimals, have the students shade hundreds squares as in Figure 7-1 to see which is greater.

2. **Use money** (if money concepts and skills are strong). Figure 7-2 suggests how dimes and pennies can be used to compare decimals to hundredths.

3. **On the line.** Many school textbooks suggest that students position decimals on a number line as an aid to comparing and ordering decimals (Figure 7-3). (This approach is inappropriate for students with spatial-organization deficits.) "Walk-on" number line segments where students walk from the lesser to the greater number helps children who benefit from kinesthetic/motor involvement.

.48   .3

___.48___ is greater

Figure 7-1

4 dimes
8 pennies

.48

6 dimes

.60

6 dimes
is more.

Figure 7-2

Arrange in order from greatest to least.
.6   1.3   .4   .06

.06   .4   .6   1.3
         1.

Figure 7-3

4. **Line them up.** Typically, it is effective to have students align decimal points to compare decimals, as in Figure 7-4. Then, digit by digit, they can "read" left to right to compare the numbers. (This procedure is similar to placing words in alphabetical order.) As soon as the child finds a difference in a column, the number with the greater digit has the greater value. If students require kinesthetic involvement, have them finger trace digit pairs, stopping when they find a difference. Using ideas from Activities 1, 2, or 3, help students "prove" that this procedure always "works."

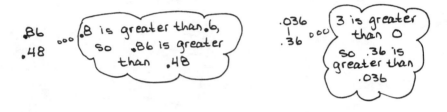

Figure 7-4

5. **Color cue.** Figure 7-5 illustrates how color coding can be used to draw attention to critical digits in the comparison. This technique is especially helpful during early developmental work for students with figure-ground or other perceptual deficits. Eventually, students themselves can learn to color highlight critical digits as a way of internalizing the comparison.

6. **Add zeros.** Whenever the number of decimal places in two given numbers differs, many students find it easier to compare when extra zeros are added, as in Figure 7-6a. "Evening out" the number of decimal digits as shown makes the comparison more obvious, particularly when decimal points are aligned as previously suggested. In this case, 360 thousandths, which is greater than 36 thousandths, is illustrated: "We have 360 of the thousand it takes to make one whole, which is much more than having just 36 of the thousand needed."

   Note: Adding zeros frequently is helpful when interpreting calculator displays as money, as in Figure 7-6b. Shading as in Figure 7-1 can be used to illustrate that the two decimals, .7 and .70, are equivalent.

8 6
4 8

.036
.36

■ = green

Figure 7-5

(a)

.036
.360

(b)

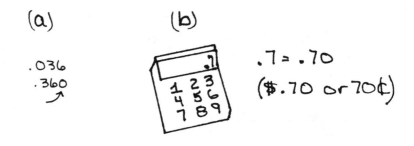

.7 = .70

($.70 or 70¢)

Figure 7-6

ROUNDING DECIMALS

Problem areas: Difficulty remembering what to do in order to round; difficulty sorting one number from another in the rounding process.

Typical disabilities affecting progress. Difficulty with abstract-reasoning, visual figure-ground, closure, and memory sequencing.

Background: By the time students work with decimals, they should have also studied rounding of whole numbers. Applying rounding skills to decimals is not difficult for most students who have mastered this skill for whole numbers. However, some learning disabled students, particularly those with abstract reasoning deficits, can be misled by the decimal point. They recognize that "something is different," but they do not intuitively make the transfer from whole number to decimal use of the rounding rule.

Other students, such as those with figure-ground difficulties or other perceptual deficits, become confused when three or more digits appear in a problem. These students may also have had difficulty rounding multidigit whole numbers and the decimal point now causes particular difficulties. Students may automatically round by leaving only one or even no digits to the right of the decimal point, regardless of directions given.

Students with memory deficits may have had difficulty rounding whole numbers and now carry this difficulty with them to decimals. A mistake typically made by these students, and also by those with abstract reasoning deficits, is shown in Figure 7-7. In this example, the students rounded by dropping all digits beyond tenths. If they had been instructed to round to the nearest hundredth, they would automatically have dropped all digits beyond hundredths.

The following are several suggestions for helping students with these kinds of difficulties. The section concludes with ideas for how to adapt the rounding of decimals to a common use in decimal division.

Figure 7-7

Suggested Sequence of Activities and Exercises

1. **Review.** Be sure the students know and can apply the convention of rounding used in mathematics: To round, examine the digit *after*. If less than 5, round *down* (backward); if 5 or greater, round *up* (forward). (See Figure 7-8a.)

   Note: Initially, the use of *backward* and *forward* may help students more readily visualize the procedure. Later, they can be taught the more commonly used synonyms.

2. **Feel the line.** Have students position the number to be rounded on the number line. In Figure 7-8a, .53 would be placed on the number line as shown. Have students visually inspect the distance from the number to either end and then slide a finger along the line to each end.

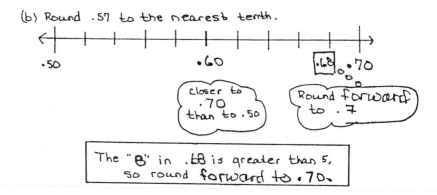

Figure 7-8

Note: If students are strong tactual learners, make the number line longer to involve more gross-motor skill or texturize it. Have students close their eyes as they finger slide to either end of the line. Later extend to other number lines which involve more choices, as in Figure 7-8b.

3. **A fast dime** (rounding to the nearest tenth, informal introduction: a small-group, teacher-led activity appropriate for students who cannot effectively use a number hill). Provide two decks of cards: a "banker's deck" and a "fast dime" deck (see Figure 7-9). Place the banker's deck in a bank box along with extra

Figure 7-9

dimes and pennies. This deck contains one card for each multiple of $.10 (to $.90), whereas, the fast dime deck contains cards that list amounts between $.11 and $.89 (no multiples of $.10 included). Until the students understand the activity, remove all money amounts ending in 5 from the fast dime deck.

Shuffle the fast dime deck and place the cards face down between the players. Students take turns drawing the top card from the deck placing it face up in the playing area. They then use dimes (as many as possible) and extra pennies to show the amount on the card.

The banker selects the two cards from the banker's deck that are closest in value to that displayed (see Figure 7-10). The child in this example must decide how a "fast dime" can be made. Is $.34 closer to $.30 or to $.40? The child must either add extra pennies to the $.34 pile or take some away to indicate the choice made. Thus, either six pennies are added (to make $.40) or four pennies are taken away (leaving $.30). The latter decision earns the child 1 point, since it involves the least number of coin moves. When the students are comfortable with this activity, return the money amounts ending in 5 to the deck. Introduce the "banker's rule" that for these cards the "fast dime" is always the greater $.10 value.

- *Follow-Up 1:* Lay out cards from the fast dime deck, one at a time, and have students verbalize that, for example, $.34 is closer to $.30 than to $.40. Allow the students to use dimes and pennies to verify this statement if necessary.

- *Follow-Up 2:* As in *Follow-Up 1,* but use a new deck, one in which *all* dollar signs have been eliminated. If the students hesitate, ask them to find the matching fast dime card. Seeing the card usually triggers the correct idea. If necessary, allow the students to use dimes and pennies to determine "closeness to." "Yes, 34 hundredths is closer to 30 hundredths than to 40 hundredths."

- *Follow-Up 3:* Use worksheets like that of Figure 7-11. Allow students to use fast dime cards as well as dimes and pennies, if these help. When checking

Figure 7-10

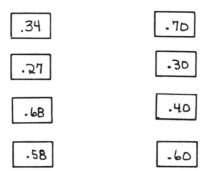

Figure 7-11

the worksheet, refer to the conventional rules for rounding. Post these rules or provide individual index card copies that students can keep in a file box at their desks. Be sure the students understand, procedurally, what rounding up (down) means. When rounding to the nearest tenth, for example, all digits beyond tenths will be zeros (and can be dropped). One uses the *number after* to determine whether the tenths digit itself is changed to a digit one higher (rounding up) or kept the same (rounding down).

4. **Color cue.** Help the students focus attention on the "thinking" digit to use (the number after) by color highlighting that digit as in Figure 7-12a.

- *Extension 1*: For students who are strong in money concepts and skills, Figure 7-12b suggests one way to use money to build or reinforce rounding skills for decimals. In the example illustrated, green represents the "thinking number," while red indicates the number of digits in the final answer.

Figure 7-12

- *Extension 2*: A natural progression from the example in Figure 7-12b consists of introducing students to rounding off, using a calculator. Provide a calculator and worksheets or index cards as in Figure 7-13. Highlight as needed. (Prerequisites: (a) determine the child's visual-perceptual skills; and (b) provide appropriate practice and/or calculator.)

Round to the nearest tenth

CHILD COMPLETES INDEPENDENTLY

Interpret as money and round to the nearest cent.

CHILD COMPLETES INDEPENDENTLY

Figure 7-13

- *Follow-Up Practice Game: Rounding War* (for two players): The students mix and deal out all cards of a 2-digit decimal deck. Each child turns over the top card and rounds it to the nearest tenth. The player with the greatest tenth captures both cards. Ties are resolved in traditional "war" fashion. The winner is the first to capture all cards.

5. **In decimal division.** Although the usefulness of paper and pencil for division of decimals may be limited, there are times when it becomes necessary or when it is the most expedient procedure to use. At such times, students must often round when the actual division is complete. At first, give problems for which the division is complete, but underscore or box (as in Figure 7-14a) the digit after. This technique helps students focus on the digit to be used in rounding. Gradually, introduce exercises like that in Figure 7-14b. The division is not given, but the cue box remains to remind students which digit they should use when rounding. Eventually, the cue box would also be eliminated.

   Note: At first, avoid presenting division problems like 24 ÷ .3, where zeros must be introduced in the dividend to carry the rounding out as far as

Decimal division:

a. Round the answer to the nearest tenth.

$$.2 \overline{) .364} \longrightarrow \underline{\qquad}$$

CHILD FILLS IN HERE

b. Round the answer to the nearest hundredth.

$$.2 \overline{) .364} \longrightarrow \underline{\qquad}$$

CHILD FILLS IN HERE

Figure 7-14

is requested. Techniques similar to those illustrated above can be used to help students when the need for extra zeros is introduced.

- *Follow-Up Practice Game: Take one* (an independent or small-group activity): Provide a deck of cards showing decimal division problems, already computed, with at least two decimal digits in each quotient (Figure 7-15a). Also provide a second deck of arrow cards as in Figure 7-15b. Note the green top stripe and the bottom red stripe on the arrow cards. The stripes help the children determine whether the card is a "round up" or a "round down" arrow card.

   To begin, the arrow deck is shuffled and cards are placed face down between students. Cards from the problem deck are spread face up in the playing area. In turn, students draw an arrow card. If it is a round-up arrow, they select one problem card which requires rounding up to obtain the

Sample Problem card

$$2 \overline{) 6.94}$$
round to nearest tenth

Sample arrow cards

━ = green
---- = red

Figure 7-15

nearest tenth. Similarly, if a round-down arrow card is drawn, the student must select one problem card requiring rounding down to arrive at the nearest tenth. Students keep any matches they make. When all cards are used up the player with the most pairs wins the round.

Note: It is helpful to provide an answer key for students to use when they are in doubt.

COMPUTATION: CHOOSING THE CALCULATION METHOD

Computation must be taught meaningfully. This means careful attention to underlying concepts and relationships. A conceptual approach to computation often precludes many of the problems children otherwise would experience in learning to compute, and also minimizes the amount of instructional time.

One also must be mindful that technology has drastically changed the methods by which we compute and that a meaningful approach also includes making good choices. To function in today's world, therefore, it is necessary to be able to compute and estimate in a variety of settings. Inexpensive calculators are readily available to perform routine computations accurately and quickly. The National Council of Teachers of Mathematics (1987) recommends that students be encouraged to choose and use the method that is most appropriate in a given situation: estimation, a quick mental calculation, computing with paper and pencil, or using a calculator.

Learning disabled students often encounter trouble using a calculator for *perceptual* reasons, but by choosing a calculator with a large display window and large numbers on the keys this problem can often be overcome. Students with *abstract-reasoning* or *short-term memory* problems may encounter difficulty keying in numbers and operations. Additionally, ongoing decision making related to the choice of calculation is often hampered by a lack of flexibility in thinking that is required to make good judgments.

- *Provide good role modeling.* For example, given a multiplication problem in problem-solving situations beyond two-digits: "Let's use a calculator. It's not worth the time to crank that one out." Do a quick estimate to check whether the answer obtained "makes sense."

- *First do the "good" mental calculation problems;* then do the rest using paper and pencil. Provide specific exercises using a mix of problems—some that lend themselves to quick, mental calculation. Challenge students to find and do the "quick math" problems in their heads. For example: 30.15 + 26.14. Children can think 30 + 26, about 56 plus some.

- *Build estimation skills.* Modify the ideas presented in Chapter 5 for whole numbers to decimal computation. Frequently ask students to take a minute before doing an exercise and identify sums (differences, products, or quotients) which are "close to" $10.00 (or to some other target number you identify). To carry out this direction, students will need to estimate. Afterwards, allow them to use a calculator to check their thinking.

- *Emphasize situations where an estimate is "good enough."* Many daily situations require only an estimate. Newspaper headlines and articles daily carry examples of estimates. As situations present themselves, help students sort out when an estimate is "good enough" and when it is not. For example, if there will be 11 of us at a party, is it "good enough" to say, "That's close to ten, so I'll ask for 10 party treats?" (Of course not!) On the other hand, when figuring whether $5 is enough to pay for two gallons of milk and a loaf of bread, an estimate will do. Use real-world applications like this extensively in mathematics. Real-world settings communicate the message that estimation is a useful and important skill.

- *Foster a positive attitude.* Children take a risk when they follow your direction to "choose a calculation method" or "estimate." Decision making is required, and more than one response may be correct. (This situation, of course, parallels real-world use of number in daily problem settings.) Students are stimulated and encouraged by a nonthreatening, supportive environment. Hold back from labeling a response "right" or "wrong." Accept a broad range of answers and alternative solutions. When comparing calculator answers to estimates, explore with students ways to "get closer."

CHECKING: IS THE ANSWER REASONABLE?

Asking students to check work they have computed is not a new requirement in classroom teaching. What is new is the introduction of a sequence, similar to the following, which allows students to recognize errors and, consequently, become more accurate in their calculations.

Prior to Introducing Any New Computational Procedure:

1. Develop estimation mental math skills which allow children quickly to check completed problems. (Ideas from Chapter 5 may be adapted to decimals for this purpose.)

2. Present calculations which already are complete: some that are correct; others with answers which are "way off target."

3. Ask students to find and circle answers which do not "make sense."

This simple sequence helps sensitize students and has proven to increase the possibility of them recognizing their own computational errors.

As suggested in Chapter 1, many teachers find that children are more successful if they can carry out some mental math daily (or at least, frequently). Toward this end, 5- to 10-minute mini-math sessions which focus on topics like estimation, quick (mental) math, and checking whether given answers "make sense," carried out throughout the school year, reap big rewards.

Students with learning disabilities can also extend their mental computation skills, but they need a more directed approach. For example, *expressive-language* deficits may make it difficult, initially, for students to elicit the numbers, especially if they are calculating silently. Teachers may need to assist them in their practice by providing a lot of frequent, structured, oral mental calculation where the students' thoughts and words are guided. In this way, a language base is being established for future use. In general, be aware of (or, better yet, try to anticipate) what may be interfering with these skills.

Without calculator assistance, students must be able to estimate and do simple calculations in their heads. The ability to do so helps them outside the classroom in many daily situations. Both within and apart from problem-solving settings, this ability also helps in day-to-day checking of written, mental, and calculator-derived computations.

ADDING AND SUBTRACTING DECIMALS

Problem area: Difficulty visually aligning digits within a column in order to compute; tendency to be misled by the decimal point or by decimal problems that are not right justified.

Typical disabilities affecting progress: Difficulty with visual figure-ground, spatial organization, abstract reasoning, and auditory memory.

Background: It is common for learning disabled students to make mistakes like those illustrated in Figure 7-16a. In Joey's work, digits rather than decimal points were aligned. Ann mistakenly added the 4 to the 5 as the first step of her computation. In the last step, she skipped columns and added the whole number 8 to 2 before completing the addition.

In Figure 7-16b the child started by bringing down the 3, then continued the subtraction. In Figure 7-16c, the decimal part, then the whole number part was added. Both subsums were recorded independently. Although mistakes like these are sometimes careless ones, they can stem from specific disabilities, particularly those identified at the beginning of this chapter. Children forget what to do, find it difficult to relate meaningfully to numbers (and then make all kinds of errors), or have problems sorting out all the numbers within the computation. Ideas for how to deal with problems such as these, in relation to decimal addition and subtraction, are outlined on the following pages.

(a)

Add: 3.5 + .24 + 8.3

Joey's work

$$\overset{1}{3.5}$$
$$.24$$
$$\underline{8.3}$$
$$1.42$$

Ann's work

$$\overset{1}{3.5}$$
$$.24$$
$$\underline{8.3}$$
$$14.09$$

(b)

$$\overset{6}{\cancel{7}}.\overset{12}{\cancel{2}}$$
$$\underline{-\ .63}$$
$$6.63$$

(c)

$$6.3$$
$$\underline{+3.8}$$
$$9.11$$

Figure 7-16

Suggested Sequence of Activities and Exercises

1. **Use base-10 blocks** (or graph-paper pieces) to help children understand when decimals need to be aligned. Have students use blocks to picture written problems, then physically move the materials to carry out the indicated operation. At each step, student or teacher should record what is being done in the problem itself. This step is often essential for learning disabled students who do not readily transfer concepts based on concrete aids to the written task. Doing this now will make it easier, at a later stage, for students to check their work with or without blocks.

2. **Use auditory cueing.** Encourage the students themselves to verbalize what they are doing. If necessary, review the first "big idea" of addition (subtraction) of decimals: add (subtract) like units (Figure 7-17). Help the students recognize that doing so helps align decimal points.

> **Note:** If the students have abstract reasoning difficulties, use the idea of auditory cueing *first* until they feel comfortable with a procedure they can follow. Then help them recognize that the procedure makes sense by using the idea in Activity 1.

Figure 7-17

3. **Line them up.** If the students have visual-perception difficulties, encourage them to do the following:

- Add extra zeros to right justified problems like that of Figure 7-16a (Ann's) and Figure 7-16b. Use shading as in Figure 7-1 to illustrate, for example, that 3.5 = 3.50 (i.e., adding the 0 does not change the value of the decimal).

- Use a highlighter, pen, or pencil to mark vertically all digits in a column before adding or subtracting.

- Use square cm paper and write one digit per space. Show the students how to place decimal points on a line.

- Turn lined paper 90° and use the lines as a vertical guide to column alignment.

- Make the decimal point a bright color, as in Figure 7-18a. This helps the students notice it when they recopy the problems to compute. *For special cases, color highlight the decimal point* for the students and, during early work, also align the points in vertical form as shown in Figure 7-18b. Children with spatial or figure-ground deficits may require such additional assistance until they have learned to deal with the decimal point.

(a)

$$4.6 + .83 + 7.45$$

• = bright color

(b)

$$4.6 + .83 + 7.45$$

Figure 7-18

Note: If children are strong tactual learners, it helps if they are allowed to finger trace all numbers in a column (all like units) before adding or subtracting.

MULTIPLYING DECIMALS

Problem area: Misplacing the decimal point in decimal products.

Typical disabilities affecting progress: Difficulty with abstract reasoning, sequencing, auditory memory, visual figure-ground, and spatial organization.

Background: Students who have mastered whole number multiplication have a good start toward learning to multiply with decimals. The focus now is on learning to place the decimal point in the product. For many learning disabled students this can be difficult. One of the most common errors made by students, including those with specific disabilities, is illustrated in Figure 7-19. Although the problem may stem from confusion over the familiar procedure for addition and subtraction, other reasons, including those linked to the preceding disabilities, also may contribute to mistakes in this area. Assuming that skills for multiplying whole numbers are strong, the following suggestions have proven effective for helping students avoid decimal multiplication errors. They also have been useful for correcting erroneous practices.

$$\begin{array}{r} 1.2 \\ \times\ .4 \\ \hline 4.8 \end{array}$$

Figure 7-19

Suggested Sequence of Activities and Exercises

Prerequisite Skills:

The most critical prerequisite for decimal multiplication is the student's ability to handle whole number multiplication. Another prerequisite—one that is often overlooked—is the ability to locate and count the digits of a given number. Students may have trouble interpreting and following instructions because of difficulty related to understanding and applying the meaning of "number" and "digit." Keep pages like that in Figure 7-20 on hand and fill in the first blank before giving it to students. The color cueing and verbal patterning help focus students properly so they can differentiate between the meaning of "number" and "digit."

Later, when the students recognize the distinction, they can independently copy given numbers into the circles before rewriting the digits. In exercises patterned after Figure 7-20b, numbers are given for which students indicate the number of digits involved before writing them in the spaces provided.

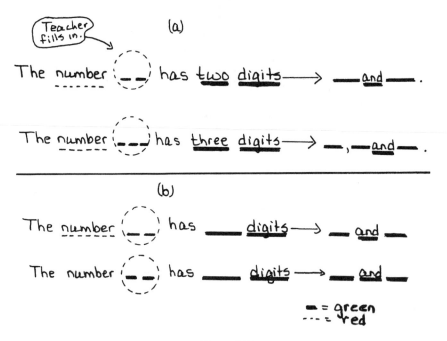

Figure 7-20

1. **Find and chart.** Students with sequencing or memory problems, and/or abstract-reasoning deficits may benefit from the approaches that follow. Make a chart of all completed problems. (See Activity 2, *Study the Chart.*)

   • *Use fractions.* If students can multiply fractions well and have no difficulty changing from decimal to fraction form (and vice versa), have them solve decimal multiplications as illustrated in Figure 7-21. Choose problems that can be readily calculated mentally (though the student is required to change to fractions, compute, and rewrite as directed).

   Note: Encourage students to "think ahead" about the answer. "Where will the decimal point go?" Some children may be helped if asked to write down their "think ahead" answer.

1) Change each decimal to a fraction.
2) Multiply.
3) Write the answer as a decimal.

	Steps 1 and 2	Step 3
a)	$.4 \times .03 = \frac{4}{10} \times \frac{3}{100} = \frac{12}{1000}$	.012
b)	Steps 1 and 2 $\quad .8 \times .6$	Step 3

Figure 7-21

   • *Use area.* If students have studied area, this topic can be used to help with decimal products. Figure 7-22 illustrates, for example, how $.1 \times .1 = .01$ (1 of the 100 squares) and $.6 \times .2 = .12$ (12 of the 100 squares).

   • *Estimate.* (Prerequisite: Understanding the language involved: ".5 times [a number]" means the same thing as "$\frac{1}{2}$ of [a number].") Present problems like those of Figure 7-23a, where .5 (one-half) and .9 (almost 1) are used as factors. (Notice that the product is complete except for placing the decimal point.) Help students estimate to be able to place the point correctly in the product. Suggestions for how to do so are illustrated in Figure 7-23b.

Figure 7-22

Figure 7-23

- *Use a calculator.* A final alternative for students who can read a calculator accurately is to allow them to use a calculator to obtain decimal products for given problems.

2. **Study the chart.** (Prerequisite: Ability to readily associate numbers [number parts] with the words "problem," "digit," and "product.") When decimal products are determined and charted using one of the approaches outlined in Activity 1, help students study the chart and note the recurring pattern (see Figure 7-24a). Color coding as in Figure 7-24b (same colors as in Activity 1a) helps the students with self-discovery, a skill which frequently is difficult to

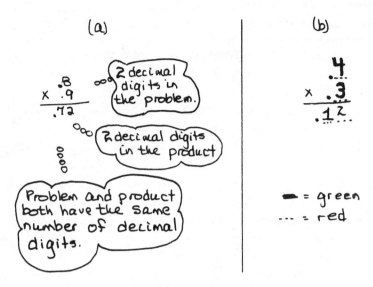

Figure 7-24

develop. Leading questions also help: "Two decimal digits in the problem (circle the problem part). How many are in the product?"

3. **Carry through.** Assign problems like that of Figure 7-25, using either a horizontal or a vertical format. The color scheme, the same as that used earlier, outlines the sequence to be followed. The green box and digits cue the first step: "Multiply given digits." Red indicates the last step. "Count digits and place the decimal point."

$$.\mathbf{2} \times .\mathbf{3} = \boxed{.\_\_}$$
red

━ = green
--- = red

Figure 7-25

Note 1: The red digits are purposely placed in the center of the green box to force thinking when placing extra zeros.

Note 2: Keep the products simple so they can be computed mentally.

4. **The one-step.** To reinforce the pattern for decimal point placement in products, gradually eliminate colors and present problems like those of Figure 7-26. The students complete just the one last step of each problem: that of placing the decimal point in the product.

$$
\begin{array}{r}
7.2 \\
\times\ .6 \\
\hline
432
\end{array}
\qquad
\begin{array}{r}
9.6 \\
\times\ 3 \\
\hline
288
\end{array}
\qquad
\begin{array}{r}
5.41 \\
\times\ \ 4 \\
\hline
2164
\end{array}
$$

Figure 7-26

5. **Different from +, −:** To reinforce the decimal multiplication procedure, present exercises like those of Figure 7-27. Pages like that shown can be prepared

	To add or subtract decimal numbers line up decimal points first.	To multiply decimal numbers, multiply first and then count the decimal places.
+	═	═
×	═	═
1.2 − .3	$\begin{array}{r} 1.2 \\ -\ .3 \\ \hline .9 \end{array}$	
×		

━ = green   ···· = red

Figure 7-27

in advance and kept on file. The teacher (and later the students themselves) fills in addition, subtraction, and multiplication problems involving decimals down the left edge of the sheet. The children recopy in the appropriate column. The two-column arrangement highlights, procedurally, the basic distinction between addition/subtraction and multiplication. The column headings serve as backup in case the students forget or confuse the sequence for adding, subtracting, and multiplying. When the work is checked, get the students themselves to read or verbalize independently the procedures summarized in the column headings.

Note: Problems along the left edge of the paper are purposely written in horizontal form. This forces the students, when recopying into vertical form, to think whether it is necessary to align decimal points to carry out the computation. For students who have visual-motor or other perceptual deficits that make the transfer from horizontal to vertical form difficult, provide lines as in the first two problems to help with alignment.

DIVIDING DECIMALS

Problem area: Difficulty knowing where to place the decimal point in decimal quotients.

   Typical disabilities affecting progress: Difficulty with abstract reasoning, sequencing, auditory memory, visual figure-ground, and spatial organization.

   Background: Even learning disabled students who are confident with the long division process may have special problems with division involving decimals. Figure 7-28 illustrates a typical error. This student automatically placed the decimal point in the quotient above that in the dividend, just as is done when dividing money amounts by whole number divisors. If decimal division is included as a mathematics learning goal for a learning disabled child, the suggestions that follow may be helpful.

$$.3\overline{)15.9} \quad \frac{5.3}{} \qquad .04\overline{)4.84} \quad \frac{1.21}{}$$

Figure 7-28

Suggested Sequence of Activities and Exercises

1. **Color highlight.** School textbooks typically begin decimal division with easy problems first: those with counting numbers as divisors. Since the need to divide money amounts is a common occurrence in daily life, problems like that illustrated in Figure 7-29 often are posed. Some textbooks may include problems like that of Figure 7-30. In either case, cueing can be used as illustrated in Figure 7-31 to help students focus on the decimal placement in the quotient of an "easy" problem: right above that of the dividend.

2. **"Hard" problems: decimal divisors.** Rather than including these types of problems in a child's instructional program, allow students to estimate or to use a calculator. If paper-pencil calculation with decimal divisors is included as a learning objective, the child's interests and learning strengths will dictate which of the following approaches might be used to introduce problems with decimal divisors.

   • *Use fractions.* If the students are skillful with fractions, they can find answers to given decimal division problems by (a) rewriting as a fraction and dividing; (b) writing the answer as a mixed number; and (c) rewriting, finally, as a decimal. Figure 7-32 illustrates the format of a color-coded worksheet that can be used to help students with memory, sequencing, and perceptual or spatial-organization deficits.

Figure 7-29

Use graph paper hundred squares.
Divide 3.27 into 3 piles.

$$3 \overline{)3.27} \quad \frac{1.09}{}$$

1 and 9 one hundredths in each pile.

Figure 7-30

$$5 \overline{)2.35}$$

Figure 7-31

1) Rewrite as a fraction and divide.

2) Write the answer as a mixed number.

3) Rewrite as a decimal.

Step 1   Step 2   Step 3

━ = green   --- = red

Figure 7-32

• *Use a calculator.* (Prerequisites: The students can carry out decimal divisions for problems having whole number divisors, and they can use a calculator accurately.) Allow students to use a calculator to find answers to problem sets like that of Figure 7-33. They will find that each pair of problems has the same answer. "To divide hard problems with decimal divisors, change them to easy problems like those shown."

$$\overset{20.2}{.4\overline{\smash{)}8.08}} \qquad \overset{12.3}{.24\overline{\smash{)}2.952}}$$

Figure 7-33

• *Follow-Up 1: Should I move it?* To change a "hard" problem into an "easy" one, the student must move the decimal point in the divisor to make it a counting number. Of course, the decimal point in the dividend must be shifted similarly, as illustrated in Figure 7-34a.

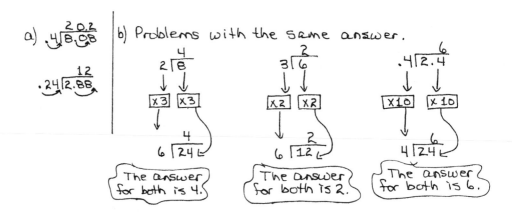

Figure 7-34

What "shifting" the decimal point really means is illustrated in Figure 7-34b. Review whole number operations to help students understand that "multiplying both divisor and dividend by the same number does not change the answer." Similarly, a quick calculator check may be a simpler way of verifying that multiplying both divisor and dividend by the same decimal number yields a problem with the same answer.

An important first step when dividing with decimals is to recognize whether a decimal shift is needed. To focus on this, present a mixture of problems—some with decimal divisors, others with counting numbers as divisors. Have students circle any problem for which the decimal point *should be moved* to turn it into an "easy" problem. Save student papers for use in the following activity, to be carried out during a subsequent session.

- *Follow-Up 2: Then do it.* (Use papers from the preceding activity.) Re-examine the above problem set. Many students can be helped using ideas from Figure 7-34 to realize that, in moving the decimal point to get a counting number as divisor, one really multiplies *both* divisor and dividend by 10 or by 100 or . . . (by some power of 10). Procedurally, one must orally emphasize:

"What you do to the divisor,
you do to the dividend, too."

Color-coded exercises using the format of Figure 7-35a or 7-35b emphasize the movement of the decimal point within given problems. In Figure 7-35a, color highlighting is used to help the student focus on the number of digits involved in the decimal point shift. In Figure 7-35b, the green coding emphasizes the need to move the decimal point first. Last of all, students divide.

Note: Omit decimal division problems like $24 \div .3$, where extra zeros must be added in the dividend, until students are comfortable carrying out other decimal divisions.

Figure 7-35

CHAPTER 8

Extending Fraction Understandings and Skills

Current Emphasis

There is ongoing discussion within the mathematics education community concerning how much emphasis to place on fraction computation in the elementary-school mathematics curriculum. The position of the National Council of Teachers of Mathematics (1987) is that fraction computation and *estimation* should be integrated with the study of underlying fraction number concepts as a tool for problem solving. The rationale for this position is the goal that students need to develop "number sense" for fractions and be able to demonstrate their good sense for fractional numbers in a variety of settings.

Because technology has changed the methods by which we compute, there is a greater demand today on our abilities to make appropriate decisions about available data, including our ability to estimate, judge the reasonableness of results, and decide on the best tool to use for calculation.

The need for involved computation and work with any but the more commonly used fractions is obsolete. The National Council of Teachers of Mathematics is specific on this point:

Students should [also] learn to perform simple mental or paper-and-pencil calculations with fractions, such as $\frac{1}{2} + \frac{1}{4}$. Simple problems like this one can be readily represented using concrete or pictorial models, promoting conceptual understanding of the operations. However, valuable instruction time should not be devoted to exercises like $\frac{17}{24}$ + $\frac{5}{18}$, which are much harder to visualize and unlikely to occur in real-life situations. Specifically, it is recommended that addition, subtraction, and multiplication of fractions and mixed numbers be limited to fractions with denominators chosen from the numbers 2, 3, 4, 5, 6, 8, 10, [12], 16, and 100, which can be easily visualized concretely or pictorially and which are apt to occur in real-world settings. Division of fractions should be approached conceptually (through examples like $\frac{3}{4}$ ÷ $\frac{1}{4}$, with none more difficult than $1\frac{1}{4}$ ÷ $\frac{1}{2}$) and without concern for computational proficiency. (1987, pp. 67–69)

Perspectives on the Learning Disabled

Even with a strong conceptual understanding of fractions many learning disabled students still have trouble with fractions, especially at the beginning. The following section first addresses some of the areas which may prevent learning disabled children from succeeding with fractions. Following that, some especially difficult areas are discussed.

1. General Areas of Difficulty

2. Equivalent Fractions

3. Simplifying Fractions

4. Developing Number Sense for Fractions

5. Finding Common Denominators: Comparing, Adding, and Subtracting Fractions

6. Regrouping in Subtraction

7. Multiplying Fractions

8. Dividing Fractions

GENERAL AREAS OF DIFFICULTY

The use of concrete aids is essential during early developmental work with fractions as manipulative experiences help give meaning to the written work. Eventually, however, the use of physical objects becomes cumbersome and it is necessary to rely on pictures. Most children make the transition from object to pictures easily. However, some learning disabled students encounter trouble with textbook illustrations.

Figure-Ground

As pointed out earlier, children may be unable, visually, to interpret the pictures as intended. Suppose the task requires adding fractions with unlike denominators, such as $\frac{3}{4} + \frac{1}{3}$. The children may understand and enjoy representing each fraction with its fraction strip, then trading the $\frac{3}{4}$ for a $\frac{9}{12}$ strip, the $\frac{1}{3}$ for a $\frac{4}{12}$ strip, and adding the twelfths. However, these same children may have difficulty sorting out the necessary steps from textbook pictures that accompany the explanation of how to find common denominators. They may even have difficulty interpreting pictures for simpler problems, such as the addition in Figure 8-1a.

Figure 8-1

For textbook illustrations like this, it is sometimes necessary to provide children with unshaded pictures, but otherwise similar to those of the textbook, as in Figure 8-1b. Placing a card over all but the first addend in the equation, as in Figure 8-1c, the student colors $\frac{1}{6}$ of the figure. By moving the card, the next addend is exposed (Figure 8-1d), and the child proceeds to color in an additional $\frac{2}{6}$ of the rectangle. The card is then removed and the answer written down. Finally, a comparison is made between the worksheet and the textbook page.

Patterning

Patterning requires that students be able to draw conclusions, a skill specifically taught in reading but not always in mathematics. Making the transition from concrete aids to symbolic understanding requires a strong ability to recognize number patterns. Generally, specific work on recognizing patterns is limited to kindergarten and first grade. At about fourth or fifth grade a high degree of abstraction is required as explanations begin to deal more with numbers than with either concrete aids or pictures. As the children begin to use symbols, their ability to recognize patterns, both obvious and implied, is important.

The fractions in Figure 8-2a illustrate an often unnoticed need for pattern recognition. The primary goal in changing mixed numbers to improper numbers is to understand, conceptually, what is happening. Ultimately, however, students remember what to do because they know they must "multiply the 4 and 3 and then add 2." In order to determine and retain the pattern, it helps students to see what the numbers do.

Figure 8-2

To help students see and "hear" what the numbers do as they conceptualize what is actually happening (see Figure 8-2b), "think" bubbles, tape recordings to match problems, and teacher verbalization are effective.

Spatial Organization

Generally, we write letters or numbers in one direction—horizontally and left to right. With fractions, however, the standard organization is different. Students are now required to switch between horizontal and vertical alignment, and many of them, especially younger ones, cannot clearly discriminate the differences. Therefore, it is not unusual to see children writing fractions or mixed numbers as in Figure 8-3. As they mature, children usually develop an ability to handle

Figure 8-3

these distinctions unless specific learning disabilities interfere. Many learning disabled students, for example, need visual cues to guide correct writing and placement of the fractions as they learn the various computational processes.

Figure 8-4 presents ideas for types of preformatted pages that can be kept on file and used to help students with fractions. Example 1 in the figure is useful when teaching children to add or subtract mixed numbers. With the boxes already there, students need not be as concerned about number placement. Instead, they can focus on the major goal: deciding whether to find a common denominator. To help them make this decision, the page is set up in two columns: The child writes in the first column when it is necessary to find a common denominator, in the second when this is not necessary. (Examples 2 and 3 of Figure 8-4 illustrate similar page ideas for multiplication and division.)

These pages also reinforce reasoning by presenting the *maximum* number of spaces and requiring the student to decide whether it is necessary to use all the spaces. Figure 8-5, for example, shows a sample problem that does *not* require use of all the spaces provided.

Another simple, yet important practice that helps spatially organize the writing of fractions involves the fraction bar that separates numerator and denominator. Encourage children to draw this line *horizontally* ($\frac{3}{5}$), not diagonally (3/5). With the horizontal bar, there is less tendency to read a fraction as a whole number (35 or 315 for $\frac{3}{5}$) or to confuse mixed numbers (42/7 for $4\frac{2}{7}$).

A final suggestion has been found helpful for children who must copy fraction problems from a textbook (see Figure 8-6). Use of a stencil helps the students focus on just one fraction at a time. As a result they tend to make fewer errors in copying. The stencil should be made of clear plastic so that the entire problem can be viewed.

Sequencing

Next to spatial organization, sequencing is probably the greatest problem involved in computing successfully with fractions. As computational processes become more involved, what appears to be a single step may actually be two or three steps. Consider the problem of Figure 8-5, which requires addition of two proper frac-

Example 1:

Without a Common Denominator

$$\square\ {-} \ = \ \square\ {-}$$

$$\square\ {-} \ = \ \square\ {-}$$

$$\square\ {-} \ = \ \square\ {-}$$

With a Common Denominator

$$\square\ {-}$$

$$\square\ {-}$$

$$\square\ {-} \ = \ \square\ {-}$$

Example 2:

Multiplying Mixed Numbers

$$\square\ {-} \ \times \ \square\ {-} \ =$$

$$-\ \times\ - \ =$$

$$-\ =\ \square\ {-}$$

Example 3:

Division of Fractions

$$-\ \div\ - \ =$$

$$-\ \times\ - \ =$$

$$-\ =\ \square\ {-}$$

Figure 8-4

$$\frac{2}{3} = \frac{16}{24}$$

$$+\ \frac{1}{8} = \frac{3}{24}$$

$$\frac{17}{24}$$

Figure 8-5

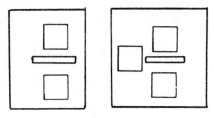

Figure 8-6

tions with unlike denominators. What generally is considered the first step—
that of finding the common denominator—actually involves three steps:

1. Deciding whether or not a common denominator is required;

2. Deciding what the common denominator should be; and

3. Deciding what each numerator should be.

Children who have trouble retaining the isolated steps of a sequence often
benefit from doing *one step at a time* until they can perform the sequence
automatically. For example, if students fail to check whether a common
denominator is needed, have them focus on this one step before introducing
additional steps. (The practice page ideas presented in Figure 8-7a may help.)
Instruct the students to copy problems from the book onto the pages, as in Figure
8-7b. The green circles in the denominators will help draw attention to what
the first step should be: check for *common* denominators. For children with difficulty copying problems from a text, use workbooks or textbooks in which the
denominators have already been circled green. This preparatory work could be
done in advance, even at the beginning of the school year.

After children have mastered individual steps and must put them all together,
pages with the format of Figure 8-8 are helpful. This example is set up to show

Figure 8-7

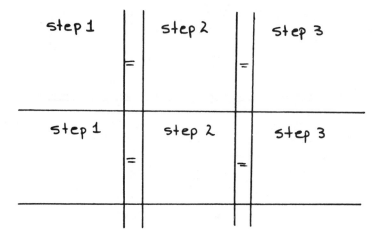

Figure 8-8

the maximum number of steps needed to add or subtract fractions. Encourage decision making. Remind the students that not *all* problems require *all* steps. If necessary, a sample problem can be placed at the top of the page or on a 5 × 8 index card.

EQUIVALENT FRACTIONS

Problem area: Difficulty identifying equivalent fractions.

Typical disabilities affecting progress: Difficulty with closure, visual memory, integrative processing, abstract reasoning, retrieval, and visual figure-ground.

Background: Equivalence, an essential part of computation with fractions, is one of the most difficult skill areas for many children. The concept itself, although readily illustrated with physical models, requires a considerable amount of abstract reasoning. In addition, work with equivalent fractions requires several discrete subskills:

- Knowing *when* to find an equivalent fraction is appropriate;

- Knowing *how* to find an equivalent fraction;

- Knowing *how* to determine the greatest common factor or the lowest common multiple; and

- Recognizing *when* a fraction is in simple form (lowest terms).

Problems associated with the latter two skill areas will be discussed on pages 374 and 380 of this chapter. The present section will focus principally on developing the concept of equivalence and fostering the ability to find equivalent fractions.

During early developmental work with equivalent fractions, when the emphasis is on *understanding the concept*, physical and pictorial models must be used to dramatize the concept of equivalence. Typically, students are asked to compare shaded parts of regions, as in Figure 8-9. Children with abstract-reasoning, figure-ground, or spatial deficits may not readily recognize that an equal amount of space is colored in both drawings. The added lines in Figure 8-9b can be very confusing and prevent children from making the comparison visually. Children with this problem need more careful instruction if they are to form correct mental images for equations like $\frac{1}{4} = \frac{2}{8}$.

Figure 8-9

Though specialized techniques like those that follow can help establish a conceptual basis for equivalence, other difficulties related to finding equivalent fractions must also be resolved. Some children can write a "family" of equivalent fractions by multiplying a given fraction first by $\frac{2}{2}$, then by $\frac{3}{3}$, $\frac{4}{4}$, and so on (see Figure 8-10). But these same children may have difficulty finding the numerator for a given denominator as in Figure 8-11. Consider what is involved in locating a fraction equivalent to $\frac{3}{4}$ with a denominator of 24. The student must:

• Find the missing factor for the equation $4 \times$ ____ $= 24$;

• Switch the thought process to a more standard form of an equation;

• Find the product of 3×6; and

• Fill in the numerator.

$$\frac{1}{3} = \frac{2}{6} = \frac{3}{9} = \frac{4}{12} = \frac{5}{15} = \cdots$$

Figure 8-10

$$\frac{3}{4} = \frac{\square}{24}$$

Figure 8-11

Children with *memory, sequencing, or closure difficulties* often find this procedure especially difficult.

Students *can* learn to deal with these problems. To this end, they must be actively involved in a learning program that is carefully tailored to meet their special learning needs. Suggestions for how to plan such a program for early work with equivalence are outlined below. The emphasis is on developing strong visual images with language and kinesthetic reinforcement, keeping the step size small and, equally important, making provision for overlearning.

Suggested Sequence of Activities and Exercises

1. **Match ups.** Give the students a construction paper rectangle like that of Figure 8-12a. Have them verbally name the fractional part that is colored. If the children are strong tactual learners, texturize the shaded part. Glue pieces of felt, or spread glue and sprinkle salt or sand, over the region; then glue string or straws over the lines that partition the shape. Have the students close their eyes, feel, and then name the fraction represented by the texturized area.

    Repeat the procedure with the rectangle of Figure 8-12b. Help students notice that the second rectangle is the same shape and size as the first. To check, they can place the two shapes on top of each other.

    As a final step, have the students cut out the shaded part of the second shape and place it on top of the shaded part of the first. Have students them-

a)   b)

Figure 8-12

selves verbalize how the two shaded regions match up: "$\frac{2}{3}$ of the first rectangle is just as much as $\frac{4}{9}$ of the second." Repeat with other examples.

> *Note:* Visual perceptual problems may interfere with some students' ability to "see equivalence." They need to feel it by finger tracing; they need to manipulate it by seeing that one shape, although divided differently, actually fits over another. The preceding activity provides for these needs. For students with more severe Figure-ground problems, see Activity 4.

2. **Write it out.** As before, but this time ask students to write the fractions they name. In the final step, the children would write $\frac{2}{3} = \frac{6}{9}$. Remind them that we use the equals sign to signify that the shaded parts match up (are equal).

3. **Pictures now.** Because many children cannot readily recognize equivalence when comparing two pictures they cannot move (see Figure 8-9), it is often helpful for them to use only one picture. In Figure 8-13, the students are presented first with the rectangle divided into thirds. Have them tell you, then *write*, that two-thirds of it is colored. Next, direct them to connect the hatchmarks with a ruler and write the fraction that describes the colored part. Several problems of this sort, in which the student actually uses the same space, help build up the equivalence idea without relying totally on visual perception.

4. **Plastic overlays.** Using permanent marker and clear plastic overlays, draw rectangular shapes as shown in Figure 8-14a. Provide predrawn worksheets (Figure 8-14b) that contain shapes congruent to those on the overlays, as

Figure 8-13

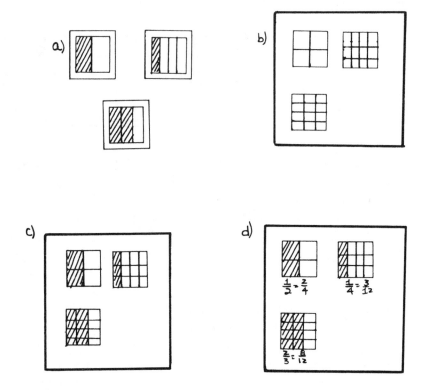

Figure 8-14

shown. In the first part of the assignment, the children color in a designated fractional part of each shape on the worksheet (see Figure 8-14c). To determine equivalence, they then match the plastic overlays with the rectangles they colored. When they think they have a matching shape, a grease pencil is used to outline the shaded area as a means of checking for accuracy. The fractions represented by the colored regions of the two rectangles are written below the worksheet shape, as in Figure 8-14d.

5. **Dot it.** Figure 8-15 illustrates another technique that helps eliminate visual confusion and focus attention correctly. Matching shapes are aligned one above the other on worksheets, and a dotted line is used to help the students recognize the equivalence being demonstrated. It also helps to have the children draw around the colored (uncolored) area of both figures to get a better "feel" for the congruence in size.

Figure 8-15

6. **Help in transition.** To help students make the transition to symbolic representation only, have them write equations (e.g., $\frac{2}{6} = \frac{1}{3}$), or find equation cards that describe the shaded (unshaded) parts of pictures like those of Figure 8-15.

7. **Talk about it.** Set aside time to analyze the equivalence demonstrated by picture pairs. The following dialogue, based on the example of Figure 8-16, suggests how such a discussion might proceed:

Teacher: "You said that $\frac{2}{5}$ of this figure (8-16a) is colored. Into how many equal parts is the rectangle divided?"
Student: "5."
Teacher: "Correct. In this second rectangle (Figure 8-16b), the same amount of space is colored, but we divided it up differently. How many total parts in the second rectangle?"
Student: "10."
Teacher: "Yes, we could also say the second rectangle has *two times as many total parts* as the first. Compared to the first, how many times as many colored pieces are in the second rectangle?"
Student: "Two times as many."
Teacher: "That's right, we colored in four parts of that rectangle, which is *two times as many* as were colored on the first one."

Figure 8-16

Note 1: If the children have trouble with this presentation, make sure they understand the words, "Two times as many as." Sometimes it is necessary to review this idea even though students understand the notion of multiplication. Some students may not readily make the transfer to the multiplication idea in the new context.

Note 2: Tenths were used for this activity. Tenths should be used along with halves, thirds, fourths, and other commonly used fractions during early developmental work to pave the way for an earlier introduction and use of decimals.

8. **The general idea: multiply.** When the children are comfortable with discussions like that in Activity 7, introduce the idea of forming equivalent "families" by multiplying. Have the children use fraction strips for $\frac{1}{3}$ and $\frac{2}{6}$. If necessary, lay them on paper and draw in the dotted line, as in Figure 8-15. Have the children verbalize that, compared to the strips for $\frac{1}{3}$, $\frac{2}{6}$ has *2 times as many colored parts, 2 times as many total parts.* "Yes, and $\frac{2}{2} \times \frac{1}{3} = \frac{2}{6}$." We can multiply and get the same result. Repeat for other fractions equivalent to $\frac{1}{3}$. Lead the children to see how a whole family of equivalent fractions can be formed by multiplying both numerator and denominator times 2, or times 3, and so on. In early work, the children should use the fraction strips to verify the multiplication. Three or four strips can be placed under each other (on paper, using dotted lines, if necessary) to picture families that have been formed.

9. **You multiply by "1."** Gradually, strips or pictures are eliminated, and the children use the multiplication technique to find fractions equivalent to a given fraction. One final point should be made before pictures are entirely laid aside. Use the technique of Figure 8-17 to color-emphasize that you really multiply by $\frac{2}{2}$, $\frac{3}{3}$, $\frac{4}{4}$, and so forth, when you find equivalent fractions. That is the same as *multiplying by 1*, so the area you start with is the same as the area with which you end. All you actually change are the size and number of pieces on the strip. The colored space stays the same size.

10. **Find the numerator.** Difficulty finding a new numerator for a given denominator is often the result of an inability to retrieve the missing factor. Many students need specific training before they can retrieve the factor as well as a controlled fact program like that described in Section 1 of Chapter 5. Initially, the equivalent fractions used on workpages would involve only basic facts the children have worked on, as in the examples of Figure 8-18.

In Example 1, the children use the given multiplication sentences to help them identify the missing factor in the denominator and in the numerator. After they fill in the number, they can use the fraction-strip picture cue to check their work. Example 2 of Figure 8-18 is similar, but here the picture cue is withdrawn. If necessary, the children can use a set of fraction strips to check this answer.

In Example 3, the extra space reminds students of the multiplication to be done. In the extra space, allow them to extend the fraction line and write

2 times as many shaded parts

so

2 times as many total parts

$$\frac{2 \times 1}{2 \times 3} = \frac{2}{6}$$

Same as multiplying by 1

4 times as many shaded parts

so

4 times as many total parts

$$\frac{4 \times 1}{4 \times 3} = \frac{4}{12}$$

━ = green

Figure 8-17

$5 \times \boxed{2} = 10$ $6 \times \boxed{3} = 18$

$6 \times \boxed{4} = 24$ $9 \times \boxed{2} = 18$

Example 1:

$$\frac{2 \times \square}{5 \times \square} = \frac{}{10}$$

Example 2:

$$\frac{2 \times \square}{5 \times \square} = \frac{}{10}$$

Example 3:

$$\frac{2}{5} \quad = \frac{}{10}$$

↑
extra
space

Figure 8-18

"×2" in the numerator and in the denominator if this is helpful. This practice can be continued even when the space to the left of the equals sign is less obvious. Gradually, eliminate the multiplication helps at the top of workpages. If necessary, children can refer to a multiple choice.

Note: It is generally preferable not to encourage dividing the new denominator by the old one in order to determine the missing factor. This practice adds an extra step to the already complicated thought process. Although the student may obtain the correct missing factor using this technique, the division step often interferes with what should be done in the numerator. The visual cueing of Figure 8-18 prompts children to "think multiplication" instead.

11. **Turn over** (a practice activity for two players). Make a gameboard and an answer sheet for missing numerators as shown in Figure 8-19. Also make two sets of 50 circles, each set a different color. Place the numbers 1 through 20 on the circles and give each child a set of circles. To begin, all circles are placed upside down. Children take turns flipping one of their circles to expose a number. The circle is placed on the board so that an *equivalent pair of fractions is formed.* A player can be challenged if it is thought an error has been made. If the person challenged cannot prove, by correctly stating what to multiply the numerator and denominator by, the circle must be removed. The answer sheet can be used to resolve any differences. The winner is the first to form five pairs of equivalent fractions.

Figure 8-19

12. **Divide to find equivalent fractions.** Introduce the following method of forming equivalent fractions: *divide* the numerator and denominator by the same number. Adapt activities of this section to accomplish this goal. This topic is too frequently slighted, leading to difficulties when children are required to simplify fractions (see page 374).

13. **Decimal equivalents.** Finding decimal equivalents of given fractions is an important skill. It generally is necessary to convert fractions to decimals in order to compute with a calculator. Some fractions, like those of Figure 8-20 are equivalent to fractions having 10 or 100 in the denominator. When the exercises of this section are extended to help students deal with these fractions, the changeover to decimals is relatively simple for those who can read and write decimals: Examples: $\frac{5}{10} = .5$; $\frac{75}{100} = .75$.

$$\frac{\boxed{5} \times 1}{\boxed{5} \times 2} = \frac{5}{10}$$

$$\frac{\boxed{2} \times 3}{\boxed{2} \times 5} = \frac{6}{10}$$

Figure 8-20

14. **Divide to find.** Sometimes children find it easier to divide, as in Figure 8-21, to find the decimal equivalent of a fraction. The "divide numerator by denominator" rule is simple enough, and a calculator can be used to carry out the division. Some children can understand why the division works. The focus, of course, is on the denominator, which tells the number of parts into which the one whole is divided. For the fraction of Figure 8-21a, the one whole is divided into fourths (.25), and we have 1 of those parts—.25 of the whole. In Figure 8-21b, the one whole is also divided into fourths (.25), but we have 3 of them, or .75 of the whole. Instead of dividing into fourths and then multiplying by 3, we combine steps when we divide 3 by 4—numerator by denominator.

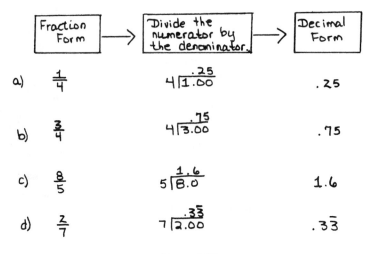

Figure 8-21

SIMPLIFYING FRACTIONS

Problem area: Difficulty writing fractions in simple form.

Typical disabilities affecting progress: Difficulty with visual memory, sequencing, and abstract reasoning.

Background: When children compute, we generally ask that they express all answers in simple form since it makes it easier to construct answer keys and to grade student work.

The ability to simplify fractions, however, involves more than understanding what to do. Actually, the easiest part is dividing the numerator and the denominator by the same number. The difficulty arises because children either:

- Do not know which divisor to use as numerator and denominator in order to simplify a fraction; or

- Fail to recognize the need to simplify further.

Initially, to help students concentrate on each step of the sequence, do not require the final step of simplifying an answer when teaching to add or subtract fractions. This way students are not forced to learn to do two new things simultaneously:

- Add/subtract in the new context of fractions;

- Simplify in the new context of computation.

In early work with equivalent fractions, it also is important to examine equivalences like: $\frac{4}{6} = \frac{2}{3}$ or $\frac{6}{8} = \frac{3}{4}$. This will provide the children with a background for *dividing* numerator and denominator by the same number. All too often this emphasis is slighted, since most examples are those in which one *multiplies* to find an equivalent fraction.

Deal directly with the problems children encounter when reducing fractions to simple form. The following ideas have proven helpful with learning disabled students. The focus is on:

- Knowing when to reduce; and

- Recognizing the correct divisor for numerator and denominator.

Suggested Sequence of Activities and Exercises

1. **Number strip.** Prepare a strip listing the numbers 2 through 9, as in Figure 8-22. Tape the strip along the chalkboard or have students glue strips to individual index cards they can keep for personal reference. As the children begin reducing, they can use the strip to assist thinking as they answer the following questions:

Figure 8-22

- *What's the greatest number or "factor" that will divide both numerator and denominator?* If the given fraction is $\frac{6}{8}$, then the greatest factor is 2 (Figure 8-23a). For $\frac{12}{18}$ (Figure 8-23b), one could divide by 2 and then by 3; but the *greatest* factor, 6, makes it necessary to divide by just *one* number rather than by two.

- *This done, look once more. Can I divide both numerator and denominator by any other number?* Because fraction computation is more limited in focus, size of number used, and quantity of problems listed in exercises, the typical answer to this question will be "no." Using this process, occasionally, as in Figure 8-24, fractions may require two divisions.

a)

$$\boxed{2,3,4,5,6,7,8,9}$$

↑

$$\frac{6 \div 2}{8 \div 2} = \frac{3}{4}$$

b)

$$\boxed{2,3,4,5,6,7,8,9}$$

↑

$$\frac{12 \div 6}{18 \quad 6} = \frac{2}{3}$$

Figure 8-23

Divide once:

$$\boxed{2,3,4,5,6,7,8,9}$$

↑

$$\frac{24 \div 6}{36 \div 6} = \frac{3}{6}$$

Divide again:

$$\boxed{2,3,4,5,6,7,8,9}$$

↑

$$\frac{3 \div 3}{6 \div 3} = \frac{1}{2}$$

Figure 8-24

2. **Divisibility rules.** Even with a list of numbers, many children still have trouble simplifying fractions because they do not know by what number to divide. Divisibility rules often are helpful besides stimulating interest in number patterns. In our experience, children who know the rules find it easier to recognize what to divide by initially.

DEVELOPING NUMBER SENSE FOR FRACTIONS

Problem area: Difficulty noting relationships between fractions; estimating answers to fraction computation; good number sense.

Typical disabilities affecting progress: Difficulty with abstract reasoning, sequential memory, expressive language.

Background: Number sense for fractions involves the ability to (a) demonstrate good conceptual understanding for fractions, (b) use relationships between numbers, and (c) think about and use fractions in meaningful ways. Each of the suggestions listed above also involves *mental* activity and a degree of critical thinking.

Being "good" in any one of these areas requires time and frequent opportunities to carry out activities or exercises related to the areas identified. To facilitate better *thinking*, less computation of exact answers is sometimes preferable. At other times, written work can be reused in different ways, as suggested in the *"Close To"* activity in this section.

Just as important, however, is a positive, supportive environment and good role modeling which emphasizes common-sense estimation with fractions. Hearing teachers think aloud in fraction situations, or hearing other students do so, often provides a new perspective on fractions for individual students.

If common-sense thinking about fractions is an important goal, suggestions like the following may be in order. These experiences should take place *before* any related paper-and-pencil computational procedure is introduced or reviewed within a school year.

Suggested Sequence of Activities and Exercises

1. **"Close to."** Ask students to study a list of fractions or answers to problems they have completed. Ask them to identify fractions that are "close to" 0, $\frac{1}{2}$, 1, $2\frac{1}{2}$, or some other target fraction. (See also Chapter 6, page 323.)

2. **Estimate sums and differences of fractions.** The ability to identify fractions close to 0, $\frac{1}{2}$, and 1 can be used to estimate sums, as suggested by Figure 8-25. Extend to situations that involve finding differences and using mixed fractions.

3. **Adjusting estimates.** In many cases, estimates may be adjusted. In Figure 8-25, for example, each addend is less than the number used in the estimate, so the estimate given is an overestimate. Students should consider whether estimates they have given are *over* or *under* the actual figure. In many practical situations, as when buying material to make a dress or build a fence, it is better to be over than under.

Figure 8-25

4. **Accept a range of estimates.** Knowing that any number of alternate responses can be correct is helpful to timid students. Particularly in early stages, when the goal is to encourage students to take the risk and make an estimate, an accepting, supportive environment is critical. For the problem of Figure 8-25, for example, any one of the following responses might be accepted:

- About $1\frac{1}{2}$;
- A little more than 1;
- About 1;
- $1\frac{1}{2}$ − (The "−" indicates that the estimate is a little less than $1\frac{1}{2}$);
- Less than 2.

In early stages, accept a broader range of estimates and help students explain their thinking rather than concentrating on very close estimates.

5. **Estimate a fractional part of a number.** The idea of finding $\frac{1}{3}$ of 18, for example, is related to splitting 18 into 3 equal parts, or dividing 18 by 3. When

given a practical situation like that of Figure 8-26, students can be cued to use known basic facts to help estimate.

> **Note:** See Activity 4, page 396, for use with students who have trouble with this process either due to *abstract-reasoning or sequencing* problems.

old price

$19

$\frac{1}{3}$ off

$\frac{1}{3}$ of \$18 = \$6

A little more than \$6.00 off

Figure 8-26

6. **Estimate other products.** Students can apply skills developed in the "*Close To*" suggestion to estimating products. Given $1\frac{3}{4} \times 2\frac{1}{8}$, a student might estimate that the product is "close to" 2×2, or 4.

7. **Estimate quotients.** When examining problems like $2\frac{5}{8} \div 3\frac{1}{4}$, it helps to view the problem as asking, "How many three and $\frac{1}{4}$ size pieces can I get (out of $2\frac{5}{8}$)? Since $2\frac{5}{8}$ is less than the divisor, "*less than one*" is a good enough estimate. Similarly, for other problems, responses like the following can be accepted:

   • More than 1 $(3\frac{1}{4} \div 2\frac{1}{2})$;

   • About 2 $(5\frac{1}{4} \div 2\frac{1}{8})$.

In some situations, being able to estimate like this is more useful than being able to give an exact answer. For example, if I see a remnant of cloth marked $5\frac{1}{4}$ yards, is that enough to make two costumes (each requires $2\frac{1}{8}$ yards of material)?

8. **Listen to their thinking.** Encourage students to explain how they "thought out" given estimates. "What did you think of to help you work that out?" In the example of Activity 7, some students may note that $5 \div 2$ is pretty *close to* $5\frac{1}{4}$ yards $\div$ $2\frac{1}{8}$ yards; others may simply add. The goal is to help students feel comfortable enough about fractions to enable them to think through situations like this. An important attitude toward fractions is being formed.

9. **Does my answer "make sense?"** *Prior* to introducing or reviewing a paper-and-pencil computational procedure, give students calculations which already are complete:

- Some which have correct answers;

- Others with answers that are "way off target."

Ask students to identify those that "make no sense." Talk through the estimate(s) used to make the decision. Given a background of experiences like those just mentioned, students typically have a more positive attitude toward fractions and often are more likely to catch errors when they turn to paper-and-pencil computation.

FINDING COMMON DENOMINATORS: COMPARING, ADDING, AND SUBTRACTING FRACTIONS

Problem area: Difficulty finding the least common denominator of two fractions in order to compare and to add or subtract.

Typical disabilities affecting progress: Difficulty with closure, sequential and long-term memory, and visual memory.

Background: Children use the idea of finding common denominators both to compare *and* to add or subtract fractions. This section discusses ways to help learning disabled students master the technique of finding common denominators to make it easier to compare or compute fraction sums and differences.

> **Note:** Although not specifically addressed, increased vocabulary and the need to apply new meanings to old words often interfere with successful use of fraction skills. Teachers need to be aware of this and consider previewing vocabulary when necessary.

Comparing Fractions

Learning disabled students generally have little difficulty using physical models to compare fractions. Using fraction pieces on workmats like those of Figure 8-27 is useful. Loose pieces laid on the workmat can be compared, visually or tactually, to the unit as well as to each other.

Have students themselves discuss, then fold and cut the fraction pieces on premarked division lines. The strips and pieces can be used on the workmat during early work to illustrate specific fractions and to help students "see," for example, that $\frac{4}{4}$ as well as $\frac{2}{2}$ or $\frac{3}{3}$ . . . equals *one* whole unit. To compare fractions,

Figure 8-27

students can again use the workmat as a base and, for example, lay a "$\frac{1}{2}$" piece on top of two "$\frac{1}{3}$" pieces to see that $\frac{2}{3}$ is more. Alternately, using preshaded bars, children might compare shaded parts of fraction strips, as in Figure 8-27a.

Students with perceptual deficits may experience some difficulty when asked to compare preshaded fraction bars or *pictures* of shaded regions on worksheets or textbook pages. (Ideas from the *Plastic Overlay* and *Dot It* activities on pages 367 and 368 can be adapted here.) The real difficulty arises when students are asked to compare fractions using either the common denominator or the cross-products method illustrated in Figures 8-27b and 8-27c. Of these two approaches, the more popular in early work involves changing each fraction *to an equivalent fraction with a common denominator.*

Teachers interested in developing the cross-products approach of Figure 8-28 can use fraction strips as shown to validate results. The upper cross-products are really the *numerators* of fractions equivalent to the original. The common

The fractions compare the way
their upper cross products compare

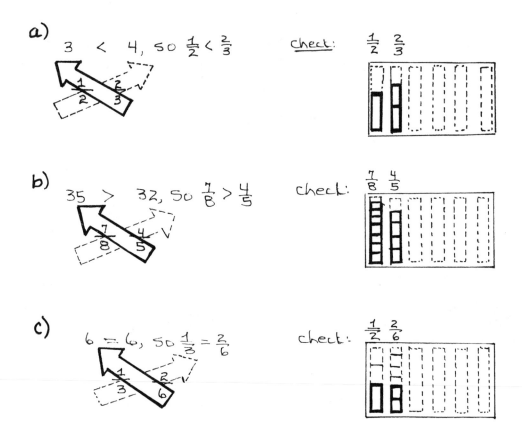

Figure 8-28

denominator is the product of the denominators in the original fraction (6 in Figure 8-28c).

Students can cross-multiply and chart several examples of *each type* of comparison shown to develop or verify the general pattern: *the fractions compare the same way their upper cross-products compare.* The color cueing illustrated in this figure is helpful to many students when finding upper cross-products: green first, then red.

Adding or Subtracting Fractions

Given the current de-emphasis on fraction computation and the rare need to add or subtract fractions in daily living, many teachers seek to balance out the amount of time students spend on involved paper-and-pencil computations in relation to other more important areas of mathematics. As suggested in the previous section, sometimes an estimate is sufficient.

Given that some paper-and-pencil calculation with familiar fractions is needed if: (a) this type of calculation is still part of the curriculum, or (b) a calculator is not available, it typically is helpful to emphasize two *big ideas* which apply to fractions as well as to whole number and decimal computation (Tucker, 1983):

For Addition:

1. Add like units.

2. If there are enough of a kind to trade up (regroup), do so.

For Subtraction:

1. Subtract like units.

2. If there are not enough to take what is needed, trade down.

The first "big idea"—adding or subtracting *like units*—is directly related to finding a like denominator when a computation involves fractions with different denominators. Good number sense for fractions includes the recognition that, when the sum or difference of two *unlike* fractions is needed, as for $\frac{1}{3} + \frac{1}{4}$, a common *label* for both fractions must first be found. Otherwise, how should the sum be labeled? (See Figure 8-29a.) If fractions equivalent to each of those in the original problem are found, as in Figure 8-29b, completing the computation makes sense.

a) 1 third
+ 1 fourth

But →

b) $\frac{1}{3} = \frac{4}{12}$
+ $\frac{1}{4} = \frac{3}{12}$

4 twelfths
+ 3 twelfths
7 twelfths

Figure 8-29

Beyond recognizing *why* and *when* like (common) denominators are needed, perhaps the most difficult aspect of hand calculating the sum or difference of unlike fractions involves finding like denominators.

Locating equivalent fractions when the new denominator is already given and determining the common denominator for two given fractions are two completely different skills. The former requires far less abstract thinking because much of the final answer is already in sight. The latter skill, on the other hand, requires a great deal of visual association, overlearning and quick retrieval. Students must master this latter skill in order to be successful with addition and subtraction of unlike fractions.

Finding the Lowest Common Denominator

In line with the desire to balance out the amount of time spent on fraction computation in relation to other more important mathematical topics, many teachers have adopted the following approach to finding a common denominator:

1. Check: *Is one denominator a multiple of the other? If so, that number is the lowest common multiple.*
   Let students use multiple strips (Figures 8-30 and 8-31) to help determine the answer to the question. In the $\frac{1}{2} + \frac{3}{4}$ example of Figure 8-30a, "4" is on both strips so 4 is the lowest common multiple of both numbers. Used as the *new* denominator for the two fractions, it is called the lowest (least) common denominator.

2. *If one denominator is not a multiple of the other, multiply the two denominator numbers to find a common denominator.*
   This step does *not* always provide the *lowest* common denominator. On the other hand, it very quickly provides a denominator that works and allows students to move on to more important mathematics topics.

Teachers who consider it desirable for students *always* to find the *lowest* common denominator when comparing, adding, or subtracting fractions can select from two alternate approaches:

1. Use individual multiple strips (Figure 8-30b) to locate the least common multiple as the new denominator. (This is the approach typically presented first in school mathematics textbooks.) Help students slide one strip under the other stationary one until the least common multiple is found.

2. Find the prime factors of each denominator number and multiply, being careful to use as factors only the minimum number of primes needed to make the product a multiple of each denominator number.

Multiple Strips

a) $\frac{1}{2}$

| 2 | 4 | 6 | 8 | 10 | 12 | 14 | 16 | 18 | 20 |

+ $\frac{3}{4}$

| 4 | 8 | 12 | 16 | 20 | 24 | 28 | 32 | 36 | 40 |

b) $\frac{1}{4} = \overline{24}$

| 4 | 8 | 12 | 16 | 20 | 24 | 28 | 32 | 36 | 40 |

+ $\frac{1}{6} = \overline{24}$

| 6 | 12 | 18 | 24 | 30 | 36 | 42 | 48 | 54 | 60 |

Figure 8-30

Figure 8-31

Both of these methods can be cumbersome and difficult. In our experience, the first approach has proven easier, given that the goal is *always* to find the *lowest* common denominator. Listing the multiples also reinforces the basic multiplication facts for children who still need practice. If necessary, provide individual *Cross Out* sheets for unknown facts, as suggested in Section 1 of Chapter 5.

When dealing with more frequently used denominators, it is desirable that students automatically recognize the lowest common multiple. Though some children may find it difficult at first, it generally comes with practice for more common pairings. In the interim, ideas for helping students become familiar with the "listing multiples" procedure for determining the lowest common denominator of two fractions follow.

Suggested Sequence of Activities and Exercises

Teachers interested in students *always* using the *lowest* common denominator may use the following activities:

1. **Multiple strips.** Use heavy tagboard to make a personal set of multiple strips for each student (refer to Figure 8-30a). If the children are familiar with multiplication charts, have them cut apart the rows, as in Figure 8-31, and glue then onto tagboard. If possible, laminate the strips or cover them with contact paper. Check that students understand the meaning of "multiples"— "answers you get when you multiply."

2. **Find it** (developmental activity for individuals or small groups). Provide two decks of cards. The first deck should contain a card for each of the commonly used denominator numbers: 2, 3, 4, 5, 6, 8, and 10. Make the second card deck a different color, and have two cards for each number between 2 and 50. Arrange the cards *sequentially* to make it easier to locate specific cards.

   Also make a pocket chart like that of Figure 8-32a, or use masking tape on the floor or desk to partition a space into three columns. The chart should be labeled as shown. The children take turns drawing two cards from the first deck. In the example of Figure 8-32a, the cards 6 and 8 were drawn. After the cards are placed in the chart, the children work together, using multiple strips if needed, to take multiples of 6 and 8 from the second deck. These cards are placed in the appropriate multiple column of the chart. The children then examine the chart and remove any numbers that appear in both multi-

Figure 8-32

ple columns. One card for each of these numbers is moved to the "common multiple" section of the chart (Figure 8-32b). Finally, the lowest or smallest multiple (24) is moved to the "lowest common multiple" section. Replace the cards in the decks and draw again to continue.

3. **Just the denominator.** Give the students a workpage of about 10 addition or subtraction problems with unlike denominators. Allow them to use their multiple strips (to build visual memory) and find just the *lowest common denominator* of the two fractions. Given the problem of Figure 8-33a, for example, the students may find it helpful to circle common multiples on the

Figure 8-33

laminated strips, match up the strips as in Figure 8-33b, and then write the smallest of the common multiples (24) as the new denominator for the problem (Figure 8-33c).

Do not require the children to finish the problems at this time. The sheets can be collected, checked, and redistributed at a later date so that the problems can be completed.

> *Note:* If the multiple strips are not laminated, show the students how to place them under a clear plastic sheet so they can circle common multiples (see Figure 8-34a). Alternatively, for children with severe motor, figure-ground, or discrimination problems, glue the multiple strips to longer pieces of paper for use in a homemade tachistoscope. Children pull the strips through the tachistoscope and stop when one number appears on both strips—this is the lowest common multiple (Figure 8-34b).

4. **Color cue.** Some students need to *write out* the multiples of each denominator to be able to identify the least common multiple. To help students organize their workspace when listing the multiples, set up pages as shown in Figure 8-35. Highlighting the space where the common multiple will fall helps children with perseveration or figure-ground deficits know when to stop.

5. **Say aloud.** Some students need to *hear* themselves count the multiples in order to memorize them. Oral skip counting practice is necessary.

6. **Transition.** As the students become more proficient at finding multiples, a simpler cueing system, as suggested by Figure 8-36, can be used. Instead of listing all the multiples, the child skip counts until the circle is reached and then writes the number in that circle. This method has proven particularly effective with students who need help organizing their work for computation.

Figure 8-34

$$8 = \text{— — —}$$
$$3 = \text{— — — — — — — —}$$

$$1\frac{5}{8}$$
$$+2\frac{2}{3}$$

— = green

Figure 8-35

7. **Concentration** (a practice activity for two players). Students enjoy *Concentration*, a game that helps build retrieval and visual memory. The game requires two sets of cards. The cards of one set each show two numbers from the commonly used denominator numbers : 2, 3, 4, 5, 6, 8, and 10. The cards of the second set should show the least common multiple for each pair in the first deck. Shuffle the decks and lay them out in two separate groups, face down.

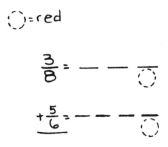

Figure 8-36

Players take turns turning over one card from the first deck and trying to select its match from the other set of cards. *Concentration* game rules are followed. The winner is the one with the most pairs of cards at the end.

- *Variation:* As an independent activity, have the students time how long it takes them to pair cards from the two sets. Encourage them to keep a log of their time and gradually to try to improve their records.

REGROUPING IN SUBTRACTION

Problem area: Confusion over renaming 1 (tendency to think of "borrowing" 1 ten, as in whole number subtraction, rather than 1 in fraction form as cued by the common denominator); difficulty sequencing the steps in the regrouping procedure.

Typical disabilities affecting progress: Difficulty with memory sequencing and abstract reasoning.

Background: Students may realize *when* they must regroup and even *why* they need to do so. However, these same students may not know *how* to regroup. The error in the Figure 8-37 problem is typical. The student confused the regrouping with the familiar whole number procedure: 1 less ten, 10 more ones. Having completed the subtraction, the child reduced to lowest terms, unaware that anything was wrong.

Anticipating difficulties like this during early developmental work, many teachers dramatize the regrouping. Thus, trading activities are often used. In the example of Figure 8-38a, the children use materials to model $3\frac{1}{8}$. They trade 1 whole for 8 eighths and record the total number of eighths (9 eighths). Repeated experiences with fair-trade activities of this type for different fractions help most children "see" what is happening. This enables them to apply correctly the regroup-

$$\begin{array}{r} \overset{2}{\cancel{3}}\overset{11}{\cancel{\frac{4}{8}}} \\ -\ 1\frac{5}{8} \\ \hline 1\frac{6}{8} = 1\frac{3}{4} \end{array}$$

Figure 8-37

Student trades
8 eighths

for

a)

Ones | eighths

3 1/8

Trade 1 whole for 8 eighths

Ones | eighths

2   9
$\cancel{3}$ $\frac{\cancel{1}}{8}$

b)

$$\begin{array}{r} \overset{2}{\cancel{3}}\overset{9}{\cancel{\frac{1}{8}}} \\ -\ 1\frac{5}{8} \\ \hline 1\frac{4}{8} = 1\frac{1}{2} \end{array}$$

Figure 8-38

ing procedure to subtraction problems like that of Figure 8-38b. In this figure, the *similarity* between the recordkeeping format of (a) and the regrouping shown in (b) helps children transfer the regrouping skill to computation with fractions.

Some students do not make the transfer, however. Despite any care taken in early developmental work, specific learning disabilities cause them to fail at the symbolic level. For example, abstract-reasoning difficulties may inhibit the meaningful transition of the procedure to paper-and-pencil computation, or memory-sequencing deficiencies may make it difficult to remember all the isolated steps of the regrouping process.

Given subtraction problems requiring regrouping, these children may refuse even to attempt the work, or they may revert to the more familiar procedure of always adding 10 when regrouping is necessary. For these students, more specialized cueing techniques, such as those illustrated in the following sequence, are necessary.

Suggested Sequence of Activities and Exercises

1. **Regroup.** Before turning to regrouping within subtraction, focus on just renaming numbers that might appear in the minuend of subtraction problems. Figure 8-39a presents the format for a color-coded page that can be kept on file and used as needed. This type of page has proven helpful with children who have visual, sequential, or abstract-reasoning difficulties. Figure 8-39b presents a completed example of the problem. If the children recognize the need for regrouping, the colors remind them what to do—they order the steps and increase reasoning. Experience has shown that, because the students notice the different colors, they tend to recall more readily the reason why the steps are carried out.

2. **Talk about a shorter way.** After practicing the preceding isolated step, most students begin to notice the regrouping pattern. Some, however, will need extra help to eliminate the longer procedure. Make a chart of problems that have previously been solved through the longer procedure (Activity 1), but this time write only the original number and the regrouped one as in Figure 8-40. If the students have figure-ground deficits and cannot readily sort out the numbers, use the colors as shown. The denominator of the second fraction is green to indicate a starting point. Most students will quickly notice that the denominators in both pairs are the same. The discussion can then focus on the pairs of black numbers and finally on the red ones.

Figure 8-39

$$8 \frac{1}{3} = 7 \frac{4}{3}$$

■ = green
— = black
··· = red

Figure 8-40

The basis of discussion for the sample problem of Figure 8-40 is the idea that 1 *whole* or 3 thirds is taken from the 8 and added to the $\frac{1}{3}$, resulting in 7 wholes and 4 *thirds*. Similar discussions would take place for other number pairs. If helpful, materials could be used to show that the regrouping is correct. After analyzing the chart numbers in this manner, the students should be given other problems for which they independently carry out the regrouping.

3. **A middle step.** To help children retain the sequence while going to the standard format for regrouping, the intermediate step shown in Figure 8-41 is often useful.

4. **Now subtract.** Next, present subtraction problems like that of Figure 8-42. Once the children recognize the need to regroup, allow them to use a card, if necessary, to block out all but the minuend number until the regrouping is complete.

> *Note:* If the students have difficulty recognizing whether regrouping is needed, adapt suggestions from Chapter 5 on whole number subtraction to work with fractions; then proceed with the ideas just outlined.

$$\overset{5}{\cancel{6}}1\tfrac{1}{4} \;=\; 5\tfrac{5}{4}$$

Figure 8-41

$$6\tfrac{1}{4}$$
$$-2\tfrac{3}{4}$$

Figure 8-42

MULTIPLYING FRACTIONS

Problem area: Finding common denominators; confusing the process for multiplying with that for adding or subtracting fractions; difficulty changing mixed numbers to improper fractions for multiplying; difficulty remembering the step-by-step procedure for multiplying.

Typical disabilities affecting progress: Difficulty with figure-ground, sequential memory, and abstract reasoning.

Background: In daily situations, we rarely need to carry out paper-and-pencil calculations involving multiplication of fractions. Yet, sometimes the skill is useful for converting recipes, when buying material, or deciding how much carpet is needed to cover a room. If necessary, however, one can convert fractions to decimals and use a hand calculator to derive these answers.

On the other hand, the skill must be taught to those who can learn it because multiplication of fractions (a) is still part of the modern mathematics curriculum, and (b) is sometimes easier if no calculator is available or if a student has trouble retaining the conversions. Finally, it is a prerequisite for students who plan to take algebra in high school since the procedures for handling rational algebraic expressions have their basis in the simpler computations with fractions.

Multiplication of fractions is relatively easy to teach. Some teachers, particularly those planning upper-grade review sessions, prefer to present multiplication as the first area of computation with fractions. Because there are no common denominators to be found, most students have greater success with multiplication than with addition or subtraction. Therefore, the goal is to build in many success experiences by dealing with multiplication early in the computational sequence.

The suggestions that follow have been used successfully with learning disabled students. The format includes a basic sequence as well as alternative techniques that have been helpful in meeting special needs. Regardless of whether the multiplication topic is approached first or introduced after addition and subtraction, the ideas should prove useful.

Suggested Sequence of Activities and Exercises

1. **Shaded discs.** Using discs or construction paper circles, shade $\frac{1}{2}$ of 2, $\frac{1}{3}$ of 6, $\frac{2}{5}$ of 10, $\frac{2}{3}$ of 9, and so on. Help the students write equations to describe the shaded parts. Example: $\frac{1}{2}$ of 2 = 1; $\frac{1}{3}$ of 6 = 2.

2. **Picture it on paper.** Provide worksheets that contain geometric regions like that of Figure 8-43. Have the students use pencil or crayons to color $\frac{1}{2}$ of 2; $\frac{2}{3}$ of 6; $\frac{2}{3}$ of 9, and so on. As in Activity 1, have the students write equations to describe the shaded parts.

Figure 8-43

3. **Look for patterns.** Have the students note that answers could be found simply by multiplying numerators, multiplying denominators (or, alternately,

multiplying numerators, then dividing by the denominators). To reinforce the idea that "of" means "times" or "multiply," rewrite each equation to use the multiplication symbol ($\times$) instead of the word "of." Examples: $\frac{1}{2}$ of $= \frac{1}{2} \times 2 = 1$.

4. **Different strokes.** Some students may suggest the pattern of dividing first, then multiplying. Example: $\frac{2}{3}$ of 63. First, divide 63 into 3 equal groups (21 in each group). Then take 2 of the groups, or 42 things.

- At this stage, this approach may be the best one for students who have trouble sequencing. Figure 8-44 illustrates how color coding can be used to support this thinking. Because the vocabulary is simple, reading generally causes no difficulty.

$$\frac{1}{4} \text{ of } 20$$

Start with ▬ things

divide the ▬ things

into ⋯ equal groups

$\frac{1}{4}$ of 20 things = ___ things

▬ = green

⋯ = red

Figure 8-44

- Figure 8-45a presents a variation of color cueing for factors other than unit fractions. In this example, a child's attention is focused first on the number of equal groups into which 16 is divided (8), and then on the number of groups to be used (5). To help students picture this multiplication, give them a sheet like that of Figure 8-45b and a set of geometric shapes. After the shapes are drawn, the children place chips in the shape to illustrate the problem (Figure 8-45c).

  For this example, the children take 16 chips and place them, *one by one*, into the shapes until all 16 are distributed. They then note that 10 of the 16, or $\frac{5}{8}$ are inside the red frame. When they are ready to eliminate visual/manipulative aids like this, color coding digits as in Figure 8-45a can serve to remind them of what was done previously with shapes and chips.

Figure 8-45

As before, help the students see that there is a pattern in what the numbers do.

Note: Placing chips in the shapes requires one-to-one matching. Some students may need specific help with or review of this skill.

5. **Whole number x fraction.** Use construction-paper fraction strips (all the same size). Subdivide some into halves, thirds, fourths, and so on. Have the students label the pieces and cut them apart on the subdivision lines. (Strips and pieces are illustrated in Figure 8-46). Ask the students to place the pieces into the workmat (Figure 8-46): 2 of the $\frac{1}{2}$ pieces, or 6 of the $\frac{1}{3}$ pieces, or 10 of the $\frac{2}{5}$ pieces, and so on. They should write equations to describe the finished picture each time. Example: $2 \times \frac{1}{2} = 1$; $6 \times \frac{1}{3} = \frac{6}{3}$ or 2; $10 \times \frac{2}{5} = \frac{20}{5}$ or 4.

6. **Both factors a fraction.** Repeat Activities 1 to 3, asking students to show $\frac{1}{2}$ of $\frac{1}{8}$, $\frac{1}{4}$ of $\frac{1}{3}$, $\frac{1}{3}$ of $\frac{1}{2}$, and so on. Have them verbalize the pattern for multiplying fractions: multiply numerators, multiply denominators. Ask students to check each equation to see if it follows the pattern.

7. **Alternative approach.** Some students have difficulty changing a mixed number to an improper fraction in order to carry out the computation. Given a problem like $4 \times 2\frac{3}{5}$, they tend to multiply the whole number 4 by both the numerator *and* the denominator of $\frac{3}{5}$. To eliminate the extra step of changing to an improper fraction, it is helpful at times to teach students to multiply a whole number by a mixed number using the distributive property. (Figure 8-47 presents an example using this approach.)

Figure 8-46

$$4 \times 2\tfrac{3}{5} = 4 \times \left(2 + \tfrac{3}{5}\right)$$
$$= (4 \times 2) + \left(4 \times \tfrac{3}{5}\right)$$
$$= 8 + \tfrac{12}{5}$$
$$= 8 + 2\tfrac{2}{5}$$
$$= 10\tfrac{2}{5}$$

Figure 8-47

DIVIDING FRACTIONS

Problem area: Confusion over which fraction to invert; tendency to invert the dividend rather than the divisor.

Typical disabilities affecting progress: Difficulty with visual memory and abstract reasoning.

Background: Many students, not merely the learning disabled, invert the dividend rather than the divisor when dividing fractions. The activities of the following sequence have proven helpful in dealing with this problem.

> ### Suggested Sequence of Activities and Exercises

1. **Use fraction strips and pieces.** Present problems like those of Figure 8-48 (whole numbers divided by a unit fraction).

   - Students fold and cut unit strips (or trade fraction pieces for unit strips) to find the number of divisor-size pieces that can be had.

   - Show students that the same result can be found by multiplying by the reciprocal of the divisor: "invert and multiply." (Confine numbers to those which can be checked using strips and pieces.)

   Note: NCTM (1987) does not recommend a heavy emphasis on division of fractions beyond what can be modeled. Should district policy or student interest proceed beyond this point, the following suggestions may be helpful.

$$\text{Given} \longrightarrow \quad \frac{6}{1} \div \frac{2}{3} = \underline{\quad}$$

$$\text{Child writes} \longrightarrow \quad \frac{6}{1} \times \frac{3}{2} = \underline{\quad}$$

Figure 8-48

2. **Color highlight.** To divide fractions, invert the divisor and multiply. When students understand this notion, color underscore the divisor in each of several problems to emphasize which fraction should be inverted.

3. **Box it.** As a follow-up, provide a sheet with several fraction division problems. Instruct the students to box or finger trace the divisor—the number to be inverted—for each problem on the sheet.

4. **Do just one step.** Have the students perform just the one step of writing the first equation toward solving each problem on the sheet (see Figure 8-48).

CHAPTER

"Hard-to-Learn," Upper-Grade Topics

This chapter deals with some of the topics generally developed in the upper-elementary and junior-high grades. The following areas are emphasized; other topics are included when relevant:

- Ratio

- Proportions

- Percent

- Integers

- Exponents

Each of these topics involves the transfer of lower level concepts and skills to new contexts. For learning disabled students, this transition is not easily made. Many students can, for example, master simpler concepts or computational skills related to ratio, proportion, and percent; they may be able to solve a proportion problem by filling in a missing numerator or denominator, but be unable to set up the correct proportion in a given situation. Students may be able to describe the shaded part of a 10×10 grid using percents, yet be unable to determine the percent for a base other than 100. They may even be able to carry out some or all of these rubrics, yet have little sense of what they are doing or how to apply that learning in practical situations.

In some instances, students may not have mastered prerequisite concepts and skills, hence they cannot make important associations. At other times, difficulties with *sequencing, abstract reasoning,* or *visual* or *auditory memory* may interfere with retrieval and application of previously learned material.

As integers, exponents, and rules governing the order of operations are introduced, other difficulties emerge. Visual-perception problems, for example, are at the root of many errors in this area. The exponent is easily misperceived; some students even interpret a number written in exponential form as a different whole number (see Figure 9-1). Many students with abstract-reasoning or receptive or expressive language deficits have difficulty with the new language (Figure 9-2). Success with integers requires good visual memory and discrimination as well as memory-sequencing skills. A strong language base also helps. Difficulties like those identified in the preceding paragraph as well as the fact that the context is new leave many learning disabled students unsuccessful with mental or paper-and-pencil computations.

$$5^3 \longrightarrow 53$$

Figure 9-1

$$5^3 \longrightarrow \text{Five to the third power}$$

Figure 9-2

An effort has been made to deal with several of the hard-to-learn, upper-grade topics from the point of view of how learning disabilities affect understanding, retention, and application. In some instances, the suggested sequence differs from that commonly used. Generally, however, the emphasis is on directly relating new material, visually and auditorially, to previously learned concepts and skills. The approaches outlined are among those that have proven effective in our own work with learning disabled students.

RATIO

Problem area: Difficulty with the language and symbolism of ratio.

Typical disabilities affecting progress: Difficulty with receptive and expressive language, abstract reasoning, closure, and visual perception.

Background: Ratio involves *comparing* the number of one group to that of another. Typically, the comparison is between dissimilar units: balls to bats, or cups to spoons, as in Figure 9-3a. However, ratio situations can also involve similar units, like that pictured in Figure 9-3b (balls to balls).

Although a ratio is not a fraction, the fraction form is often used to represent a ratio (Figure 9-4). Conceptually, this can be very confusing to students

a)

2 bats to 1 ball: $\dfrac{2}{1}$

3 cups to 2 spoons: $\dfrac{3}{2}$

b)   (R) (R) (R)

(B) (B) (B) (B)

3 red balls to
4 blue balls
   Ratio is 3 to 4
      $\dfrac{3}{4}$

Figure 9-3

who are used to thinking of $\frac{7}{4}$ in the manner illustrated in Figure 9-5. When introduced to ratios, students, therefore, must learn to relate to a familiar symbol in a new context and give that symbol a different interpretation. What used to be thought of as a fraction is now visually the same but means something different. The language of ratio is abstract and that adds to the difficulty. The ratio $\frac{7}{4}$ is often read "7 to 4." This statement itself is confusing. A much more meaningful, but longer statement would be: "Think: for every 7 (cups of flour) we need 4 (cups of milk)." The second type of expression makes the necessary language association far easier.

We say

The ratio of cups to spoons is 3 to 2.

We write

$\dfrac{3}{2}$

Figure 9-4

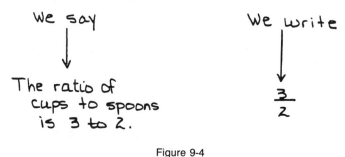

$\frac{7}{4}$ means
seven fourths
one and three fourths
seven divided by four

Figure 9-5

Setting up a ratio from a simple one-step problem like that of Figure 9-6 is generally easy for students. The word "ratio" triggers the general idea, and the problem presents the numbers in the correct order for writing the ratio. The difficulty arises when the numbers are not presented in the correct order and when the word ratio is *not* used. Students also have trouble finding equal ratios. (This problem will be discussed in the section on proportion.) The suggestions that follow focus on the needs of learning disabled students and on ways to supplement standard approaches for introducing ratio to meet those needs.

A man solves 8 puzzles
in 4 hours. What is the
ratio of the number he
can solve to the time it
takes him?

Figure 9-6

Suggested Sequence of Activities and Exercises

1. **Focus.** Figure 9-6 presents a typical introductory ratio problem. When asked to find the ratio, students commonly say "2." To help children focus on the notion of comparing one thing to another, have them underline related parts of the problem using the same color. For example, underline in green everything associated with the first number and everything dealing with the second number in red. Figure 9-7 illustrates this technique.

   Note: Initially, it might be best for the teacher to underline the related parts ahead of time. A follow-up discussion should help the students understand the thought process.

————— = green   - - - - - = red

There are 9 boys and 6 girls
in a classroom. What is the
ratio of girls to boys?

Figure 9-7

2. **Match.** It often is necessary to practice determining the proper ratios for given questions. Even if students understand that a ratio is written in the form of a fraction, number placement is often difficult. A combination card game and puzzle is fun and helpful at this point. Use large index cards (8 × 12) and make puzzle shapes as in Figure 9-8. On the left side of each puzzle piece, write a problem, on the right fill in the ratio. Cut the puzzle pieces apart on the dotted lines. The problem side of the card is placed in a central draw pile, and each player is dealt five ratio cards. The remaining ratio cards are placed face down in a second pile.

   The first player turns over a problem card. If the player already has the correct ratio on a card, a match is made (placed on the board). If not, the player calls for the ratio card. If another player has the requested card, it is given to the caller. Otherwise, the caller draws one ratio card from the pile. When a match is made, the caller puts the pair of cards down on the board. Should an incorrect ratio be requested (the puzzles act as a check), the caller keeps that ratio card and draws another from the pile. The winner is the first person to run out of cards.

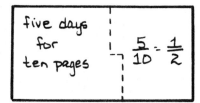

Figure 9-8

3. **Write it out.** Encourage children to write the words as well as the numbers, when setting up a ratio. Seeing and saying the words help give the numbers more meaning (see Figure 9-9).

   Note: At this point, it is unnecessary to simplify (reduce) the ratio. The primary goal is to understand and set up the ratio.

4. **Three ways.** To help students recognize and use the three ways of writing a ratio, post a chart like that shown in Figure 9-10 for students to refer to. The chart is especially helpful to children with language or visual memory difficulties.

We need 12 pencils for 9 students.
What is the ratio of students
to pencils?

$$\frac{-\text{ students}}{-\text{ pencils}} \rightarrow \text{ For every } \underline{\ \ } \text{ students we need } \underline{\ \ } \text{ pencils.}$$

Figure 9-9

3 to 2 = 3 : 2   = $\frac{3}{2}$

Figure 9-10

5. **Practice.** Make a set of 10 cards, numbered 1 to 10. On each card, place groups of common objects that represent ratios like the following: $\frac{2}{3}, \frac{4}{3}, \frac{1}{2}, \frac{1}{4}, \frac{1}{3}, \frac{5}{3}, \frac{5}{6}, \frac{7}{8}, \frac{8}{3}, \frac{3}{4}$. Under each picture also write the ratio to be expressed. Have the students number their papers from 1 to 10. Next to each number, they write the ratio shown on the corresponding card.

   • *Follow-Up:* Write the corresponding ratio on the back of each card. Have students study the pictures and write the ratio to describe each picture, then use the backs of the cards to check the answer.

6. **Color code.** Similarity involves ratio; thus, it is often helpful to use colors to focus attention. Keep a set of pages as in Figure 9-11, with color coding as shown. To aid the transition to noncolor-coded presentations, have the students put in the colors to describe statements about each. In written work, it may help at first to color code statements to match the figures. For children who have trouble processing what they read, this approach helps break the steps down to a manageable size. The focus here, of course, is on recognizing ratios in an applied setting, not on setting up or solving proportions.

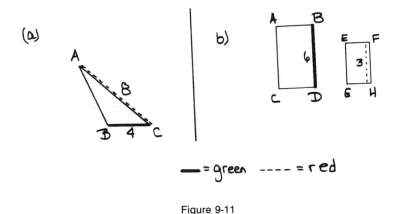

Figure 9-11

Note: Sometimes letters are used to describe the comparison of sides. With many learning disabled children, this can be confusing as it is very abstract. When numbers are assigned to the ratio, as in Figure 9-11, students can more readily internalize the relationship.

PROPORTIONS

Problem area: Difficulty setting up proportions for given situations.

Typical disabilities affecting progress: Difficulty with receptive language, sequencing, abstract reasoning, and closure.

Background: Once they have learned about equivalent fractions and solving equations, most learning disabled students have little difficulty solving proportions that *have already been set up.* (Figure 9-12 illustrates typical approaches students might use.)

However, problems arise when students must independently determine the proportion that applies to a given situation. Consider the example of Figure 9-13. The wording in this problem does not allow the use of key words to set it up. Students must fully understand the concepts of ratio and proportion. Many, including those with the preceding disabilities, *are* able to set up simple ratios and solve proportions. They just need help in getting started, so that they:

• Recognize the need for a proportion in a given situation; and

• Can set up the correct proportion.

a)

| Child is given ↓ | Child uses idea of equivalent fractions and thinks ↓ |

2 pencils for 15¢. If I buy 6 pencils, how much will it cost?

$$\frac{2}{15} = \frac{6}{\square}$$

$$\frac{2 \times 3 = 6}{15 \times 3 = \square} \quad \circ\circ\circ$$

2 x 3 is 6 so multiply 15 by 3, too

b)

Child needs ↓

2 cups of flour to make 3 dozen cookies. I only have $1\frac{1}{4}$ cups of flour. How many cookies can I make?

$$\frac{2}{3} = \frac{1\frac{1}{4}}{\square}$$

Recognizing no easy equivalence, child uses "cross multiply" rule and solves the following equation:

$$2 \times \square = 3 \times 1\frac{1}{4}$$

Figure 9-12

A recipe for 3 dozen cookies uses 2 cups of flour. How many cookies can you make if you only have $1\frac{1}{4}$ cups of flour?

Figure 9-13

Many of these same students need help to develop a better sense about proportion, so they can judge whether results are reasonable. The suggestions which follow may prove helpful in this regard.

Suggested Sequence of Activities and Exercises

Help Students with Computation

1. **Construct a chart.** Help the students learn to set up a chart, like that of Figure 9-14, for proportion problems. Charts like this help them organize their thinking and set up the proportion properly. The sample chart is based on the following problem: "On the map 1 cm equals 80 km. If the distance from Santa Barbara to Los Angeles is about 144 km, how far away are the two cities on the map?" The chart helps students recognize and compare like terms of the written problem.

distance in km	=	distance in cm
80 km	=	1 cm
144 km	=	__ cm

Figure 9-14

2. **Map out an alternative.** It often is effective to present alternative methods to help students solve problems. For example, although proportions can be used to compare prices at a grocery store, it is easier for many to use unit pricing as in Figure 9-15. Most stores display unit pricing labels on the shelves, so children need to learn what the labels mean and how to use them to buy wisely.

Help Students Develop Number Sense

1. **Establish benchmarks.** As a first step, help children sort ratios as "close to 0," "close to $\frac{1}{2}$," "close to 1." For example, in $\frac{80}{144}$ (Figure 9-14) the numerator is about half the denominator, so this ratio is close to $\frac{1}{2}$. If a numerator

Figure 9-15

is very small by comparison, as in $\frac{2}{40}$, the ratio is close to 0. Numerators that are comparatively large in relation to the denominator characterize a ratio "close to" 1, as in $\frac{87}{90}$.

2. **Does my answer make sense?** Encourage students to plug computed elements of a proportion back into the original problem to check whether the number obtained makes sense. To develop this skill, present computed elements—some correct and some *way off*. Students plug the number back into the problem and examine, using ideas from Activity 1, whether both ratios in the proportion are similar. $\frac{80}{144} = \frac{1}{20}$, for example, makes no sense. The first ratio is a little more than half. The second is closer to 0, therefore, it makes no sense to equate them. Exercises like this build good concepts for and intuitions about proportion.

PERCENT EQUIVALENTS

Problem area: Changing percents to decimals or fractions.

Typical disabilities affecting progress: Difficulty with sequencing and visual discrimination.

Background: Generally, when students are introduced to percent, they are shown a hundreds square with part of it shaded. Often the explanation is given that percent means "per one hundred" or "out of one hundred." These examples and explanations are rather easily understood by most students. Quite often, in fact, the basic concept of percent is less difficult for learning disabled children than some of the topics presented up to this point. The difficulty arises when students need to develop good number sense in relation to percent and apply percent to everyday situations. Students who have a good number sense may be able to estimate to solve a problem, making cumbersome computations unnecessary. They also are more likely to judge whether statements or computations involving percent are "reasonable." (Aspects of these issues are discussed in this and the following two sections of this chapter.) When using paper and pencil to solve problems involving percent, it usually is necessary to express a percent either as a fraction or as a decimal. Changing whole number percents to fractions typically is not very difficult for students. Most children readily recognize what to do and remember to put the number itself over 100. Similarly, 2-digit whole number percents are fairly easy to convert to decimals. However, single-digit percents are sometimes more difficult, and it is not uncommon for teachers to see the following: 6% = .6. Even harder is the conversion of percents like that of Figure 9-16 to decimals or fractions. When learning this latter skill, children must think through each step to the point of overlearning. The ideas that follow should help with this and other aspects of instruction related to finding percent equivalents.

Figure 9-16

Suggested Sequence of Activities and Exercises

1. **Fractions first.** As noted in Chapter 6, decimals are often most meaningfully introduced when related to the familiar, *less abstract* fraction notation. Similarly, when converting percents to decimals, it is often preferable first to change the percent to a fraction with the denominator 100. Seeing the two zeros in the denominator often instantly reminds students where to place the decimal point. This approach is particularly effective for helping students avoid the 6% = .6 error cited above. The underscoring technique of Figure 9-17

$$6\% = \frac{6}{100} = .06$$

Figure 9-17

can be used to emphasize the fact that the correct decimal equivalent of a single-digit percent has *two* decimal places.

2. **Make it easier.** Given a percent like $5\frac{1}{2}\%$, students can be instructed to change the $\frac{1}{2}$ to .5 right away. This step makes it easier to change the percent to a fraction. In Figure 9-18, 5.5% is first expressed as a fraction with denominator 100, then changed, as necessary, to eliminate the decimal.

$$5\frac{1}{2}\% = 5.5\% = \frac{5.5}{100} = \frac{55}{1000} = .055$$

Figure 9-18

3. **Chart it.** Using charts as in Figure 9-19 helps students who have trouble with memory sequencing. Such a chart also provides structure. For many students who enter the fifth or sixth grade with an *intuitive* understanding of the rela-

Percent	=	Fraction (Denominator of 100)	=	Decimal	=	Reduced Fraction
50%	=	$\frac{50}{100}$	=	.50	=	$\frac{1}{2}$
8%	=	$\frac{8}{100}$	=	.08	=	$\frac{2}{25}$
$5\frac{1}{2}\% = 5.5\% =$		$\frac{5.5}{100} = \frac{55}{1000}$	=	.055	=	$\frac{11}{200}$

Figure 9-19

tionship of percents to fractions and decimals, this structure is especially important as it helps them begin to realize how the conversions are derived.

4. **Make a book** (a practice activity for two or three players). Provide a deck of 51 cards, 17 showing percents, the remainder giving the fraction or decimal equivalent of each percent. After each player has been dealt five cards, the rest of the deck is placed face down between the players. The object of the game is to make books of three cards: the percent and its fraction and decimal equivalent. If, at a player's turn, there is no book in hand, the top card from the discard pile or from the draw pile is taken. The player discards one card and the next person has a turn. During a player's turn all exposed books can be played. The winner is the one with the most books when one of the players runs out of cards.

PERCENT FORM OF A FRACTION

Problem area: Difficulty changing fractions to percents.

Typical disabilities affecting progress: Difficulty with memory, abstract reasoning, and closure.

Background: It is relatively easy to convert fractions to percents when the denominator is 100. The difficulty arises when the denominator is not 100. The general technique for handling situations like this is illustrated in Figure 9-20: cross-multiply and solve the equation for ×. Most textbooks include problems of this type in the section on proportion. For students with good memory and abstract reasoning skills, this approach is fine. In fact, for students who have closure difficulties, it is sometimes simpler than alternative methods. However, for other learning disabled children who have difficulty solving proportions, the following sequence might be more effective. Because the sequence (a) involves very small learning increments, (b) relates to the familiar process of finding equivalent fractions, and (c) makes adequate provision for overlearning, it has proven helpful to the students with whom we work.

Suggested Sequence of Activities and Exercises

1. **Build prerequisites.** Be sure that the children have adequate understandings and skills associated with naming and writing fractions and their equivalents. Then introduce the concept of percent in the usual manner.

$$(3)(100) = 8x$$

$$300 = 8x$$

$$37\tfrac{1}{2}\% = x$$

— = green

---- = red

Figure 9-20

2. **Easy things first.** Now help the students write percents as fractions (in unreduced form) and fractions (*having a denominator of 100*) as percents.

3. **Review.** Be sure the children can apply the idea of equivalent fractions to reducing given fractions to lowest terms.

4. **Now reduce.** Students should now be able to write percents as fractions in reduced form.

5. **Use what you know.** Next, turn to writing fractions (with the *denominator a factor of 100*) as percents. Help the students use the idea of equivalent fractions, as in Figure 9-21. The children first locate an equivalent fraction having a denominator of 100, then rewrite as a percent.

Figure 9-21

6. **One last step.** Finally, have the students write as percents fractions whose denominators are *not* factors of 100. As before, the students first rewrite the fraction with a denominator of 100. To find this fraction, they must divide (Figure 9-22a) to determine the factor for multiplying numerator and denominator (Figure 9-22b). Then they can rewrite the fraction as a percent as shown.

a) $\dfrac{3}{8} = \dfrac{\square}{100}$

$8\overline{)100} 12\tfrac{1}{2}$

b) $\dfrac{3 \times 12\tfrac{1}{2}}{8 \times 12\tfrac{1}{2}} = \dfrac{37\tfrac{1}{2}}{100} = 37\tfrac{1}{2}\%$

Figure 9-22

Note: Students who have difficulty both with the proportion and with the equivalent fraction approach to writing fractions as percents might be permitted to use a calculator. (This alternative is viable only if the students have adequate visual-perception skills.) Initially, assign fractions that have exact 2-digit decimal equivalents. Review the idea of converting a fraction to a decimal, and allow students to use a calculator to divide the numerator by the denominator. The students can then move the decimal point two places to the right (to show division by 100) and add the % sign in forming the percent equivalent (see Figure 9-23).

Given Fraction		Decimal Form		Percent Equivalent
$\tfrac{1}{4}$	=	.25	=	25%

Figure 9-23

PERCENT IN EVERYDAY SITUATIONS

Problem area: Difficulty using percent to solve problems.

Typical disabilities affecting progress: Difficulty with abstract reasoning, sequencing, visual perception, and short-term memory.

Background: Many learning disabled students intuitively are able to solve problems using the common percents, such as 50 percent, 10 percent, and sometimes 25 percent and 75 percent. They are able to estimate, and some students can calculate mentally with easy percents. However, as they begin to deal with other percents, things become more difficult:

- "What method should be used to solve the problem?"

- "Should a fraction or a decimal equivalent be used?"

- "Now that I've found the answer, does it need to be rounded off?"

Decisions like these must be made, and longer, more complex sequences must be employed. In addition, applying meaning to the final answer is usually difficult. Too often, a student ends up knowing only that x = 20 without being able to relate the number to the original problem. The following are ideas for helping students handle difficulties.

Suggested Sequence of Activities and Exercises

1. **From problem to equation.** Determining the appropriate equation for a given word problem can be the most difficult part. It is often helpful to teach children the vocabulary related to the page and then use the color-coding technique of Figure 9-24 to help them set up the equation. During early work, structuring problems into "one-liners," so that the equation can be written directly beneath the problem, helps students translate the verbal statement into an equation. Children learn, for example, to associate the word *of* with "x" and *is* with "=."

2. **Three easy pieces.** If the children have *memory*, *sequencing*, or *abstract-reasoning* difficulties, provide preformatted pages using the idea of Figure 9-25. Help the students analyze sample problems to recognize that percent situations typically involve *three pieces of information* (refer to the three boxes of Figure 9-25): the

Figure 9-24

Figure 9-25

part, the whole or base, and the percent figure. A percent problem-solving exercise provides two of these pieces of information and requires that the student find the third. The format shown in Figure 9-25 can be used to help solve any of the three types of percent problems:

1. Percent figure missing

2. The "part" missing

3. The "whole" or base missing

Using this approach, it becomes a matter of placing information from the verbal statement into the appropriate boxes and then solving to determine the unknown piece of information. Gradually, the students themselves can learn to format their own papers, when necessary, to solve percent problems. When an answer is found, encourage students to write it above the appropriate box in the problem statement. This step is necessary for some students by relating the answer to the original problem.

3. **Using proportion.** Students with good sequencing, abstract-reasoning, and spatial-organization skills may prefer the proportion method to solve percent problems. The color-coding technique of Figure 9-26a, similar to that discussed earlier, can be used if necessary. Figure 9-26b illustrates how a page can be preformatted for this purpose and kept on file. If the proportion method is used, encourage the students, as suggested in Activity 2, to relate the answer back to the original problem statement.

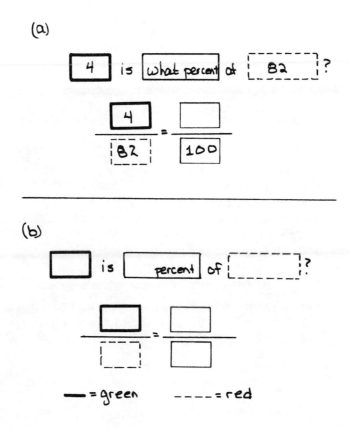

Figure 9-26

NUMBER SENSE FOR PERCENTS

Problem area: Difficulty estimating in practical situations that involve percent.

Typical disabilities affecting progress: Difficulty with abstract reasoning, receptive and expressive language, short-term and sequential memory, visual perception.

Background: An instructional focus on estimation and mental computation in relation to percent situations is receiving renewed interest in school mathematics. In most day-to-day situations, people make quick estimates. When exact answers are required, they typically work out simple percent problems in their heads and use a calculator for more difficult ones. They rarely make paper-and-pencil calculations.

Needed insights, experiences and skills take time to develop. Given this time, sound teacher modeling and systematic instruction based on ideas like those that follow will enable many learning disabled students to develop adequate estimation skills for percent. Actually, many LD students prefer estimation as an alternative to difficult, cumbersome, and easily forgotten rules associated with paper-and-pencil procedures.

Suggested Sequence of Activities and Exercises

1. **"Closer to."** In early work with percents, help students develop intuitions about the relative size of percents. For example, 3%, 12%, and 21% are each "closer to" 0% than to 50% or 100%. If necessary, have students close their eyes as they run a finger on a meter stick from 12 (for example) to the 0 end, and then from 12 to 100, to help develop the notion of "close to." Later, as students complete computational exercises, ask them to identify answers in a given row that are "close to" 50%; 100%; 1%.

2. **Benchmark estimation.** When converting between fractions, decimals and percents, certain "nice" numbers are good benchmarks or points of reference. 1%, 50%, and 100% are good benchmarks, as is the fact that $\frac{1}{2}$ = 50%. 7 out of 15 is pretty close to 7 out of 14: $\frac{1}{2}$ or 50%. The same statement can be made about:

   • 8 out of 17 ($\frac{8}{17}$)

   • 31 out of 67 ($\frac{31}{67}$)

   • 157 out of 298 ($\frac{157}{298}$)

In each of these cases, the first number (numerator) is about half the second (denominator).

Similarly, a very small numerator compared to the denominator is close to 1%, as in $\frac{2}{87}$. A numerator very close to the denominator, as in 49 correct out of 53, is very close to 100%.

Parallel observations can be made in terms of decimals and percents. It is important to verbalize observations like these *often* in order to *role model* appropriate thinking and a good attitude toward percent.

3. **What is likely?** Learning disabled students need opportunities to explore and discuss questions such as the following. (A hand calculator can be used in some instances, *after* the student has offered an opinion, to work out an exact answer in comparison to the initial response.)

   • Can we have 100% attendance at school today? 200%?

   • Can a price increase 40%? 100%? 300%?

   • Can a price decrease 50%? 200%?

   • What does it mean to have 10% unemployment? 10.5% unemployment?

4. **What is meant?** Discuss common occurrences of percents like: Orange juice—100% pure. Paper towels—20% more absorbent. Mixed nuts—less than 50% peanuts. Hamburger—at least 70% lean.

5. **Mentally take 1%, 10%, and 100% of a number.**

100% of $3518 = $3518	100% of $423 = $423
10% of $3518 = $351.80	10% of $423 = $42.30
1% of $3518 = $35.18	1% of $423 = $4.23

   The general pattern of dividing by shifting the decimal point one or two places to the left, as in Figure 9-27, can be noted.

6. **Estimate using 1%, 10%, and 100% of a number.** Three examples of estimating using these "nice" percents are shown in Figure 9-28. Another "nice" number is 50%: half a number.

7. **Lots of ways.** Flexibility is important in estimation. No *one* way is "right." Using 1%, 10%, 50%, and 100%, most percent situations can be estimated with relative ease and accuracy. Two examples follow:

   • *Example 1:* 42.5% of 40 is about 50% of 40, or 20. Accept estimates, regardless of how close they are to the exact answer. Good attitudes, as well as good answers are important. With good attitudes and structured experiences, estimation skills will grow.

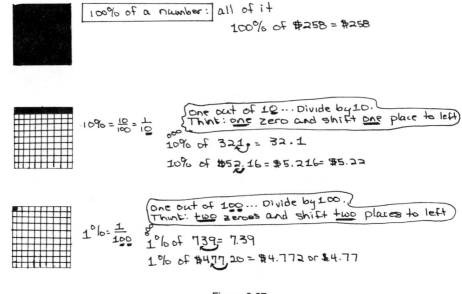

100% of a number: all of it
100% of $258 = $258

$10\% = \frac{10}{100} = \frac{1}{10}$

One out of 10... Divide by 10.
Think: one zero and shift one place to left

10% of 321. = 32.1

10% of $52.16 = $5.216 = $5.22

$1\% = \frac{1}{100}$

One out of 100... Divide by 100.
Think: two zeroes and shift two places to left

1% of 739 = 7.39

1% of $477.20 = $4.772 or $4.77

Figure 9-27

98.4% of $3521   CLOSE TO 100% of it, so just about $3521.

9.5% of $8.75   About 10% of $8.75, $0.88. I'll say about $0.90.

1.2% of $625.   Very close to 1% of $625, $6.25.

Figure 9-28

• *Example 2*: 61% of 847 can be estimated by:
a) Breaking 61% apart (take 50% + 10% + 1% of 847):
50% of 847: about 425
                                   85
                                    9
61% of 847:   500+

b) Approximating 61% as 60% and rounding 847:
60% of 850: 6(10% of 850)
     6 × 85 or 510

c) Or, more simply round 61% to the closest "nice" percent, 50%:
50% of 847 is about 425.

8. **Does it make sense?** As their estimation skills improve, children should routinely be asked to decide whether given estimates make sense. Provide a mix of examples, some correct, others *way off*. For example: Does it make sense to say: "61% of 625=201?" (No. 61% is close to 50%, so the answer is about 300+. The answer cannot be less than 300.) This kind of *thinking*, rooted in number sense and estimation, along with proficiency at using calculators to derive exact answers, is an important goal in mathematics today.

INTEGERS: NEW SYMBOLISM

Problem area: Difficulty associating meaning with abstract representations.

Typical disabilities affecting progress: Difficulty with visual or auditory association, integrative processing, visual perception, and receptive or expressive language.

Background: We use the idea of integers regularly in our everyday lives. We borrow money from a friend and then *we pay it back*. Do we still *owe* money? The temperature *drops* 8°, but then *climbs* 9° the next morning. A salary *increase* means we earn more money, but then we might take a *cut* in salary of $10 when we switch jobs. All of these ideas are familiar to children. Even the learning disabled child has little difficulty comprehending their meaning in context. However, when the same ideas are expressed symbolically using positive or negative integers, many children become confused. Most can readily tell you how much a friend owes them if $4 was borrowed, and they may even use the expression, "I'm $4 in the hole." However, the mathematical representation −4 is not as easily explained, although it may have the same meaning.

Poor visual or auditory association skills coupled with poor integrative processing abilities make it difficult for many students to deal meaningfully with the written integer form. Students are asked to relate an old idea to old signs (+

and −) in a new way using new language. That is, they have to decide what the familiar sign now means: "add" or "positive;" "subtract" or "negative." To complicate matters, new skills and new language are often presented simultaneously. Those with expressive or receptive language deficits may understand the difference between the words (add/positive; subtract/negative), but find it hard to elicit or associate the word with the correct meaning in context. These students require considerable overlearning, consistent verbal and pictorial association, and small learning increments in early work with integers.

The following are suggestions for how to deal with these difficulties during early concept development with integers. The ideas presented can be used to supplement textbook treatments that typically focus on the application of integers to real-life situations. An attempt is made in this and the following four sections to present integers in such a way that learning disabled students can learn and possibly continue on algebra.

Suggested Sequence of Activities and Exercises

1. **Color code.** Children with language deficits often benefit from color-coded pages like that of Figure 9-29. The assumption at this point is that the student understands the vocabulary used. The colors help reinforce understanding by allowing the student to focus directly on the ideas of "more" and "less." Related symbolism is highlighted and associated with the corresponding terminology.

$$7 \text{ miles north} = {}^{O}7$$

$$\text{lose } \$8 = {}^{()}8$$

Figure 9-29

2. **Time out.** To help students develop an automatic association of integers with their use in real-life situations, take time out to build up vocabulary. Exer-

cises like those in Figure 9-30 make it easier for students to focus on the necessary language. A sense of usefulness develops, and the children begin to use the numbers more appropriately. The exercise also serves as a transition to eventually eliminating colors.

Figure 9-30

3. **Number line: Develop good number sense.** As the children begin to use the number line, have them select examples from everyday situations to describe verbally several points on the number line. Figure 9-31 presents a sample exercise.

Figure 9-31

4. **Picture it.** As a class activity, present pictures with related phrases that describe "positive" or "negative" situations. (Figures 9-29 and 9-30 present sample ideas for such situations.) If possible, put the pictures and matching phrases on a ditto with the guide words "positive" and "negative" at the top in two different colors. Discuss the meaning of the two terms and have students underline the key words or phrases to match the color of the guide words.

5. **Point plotting.** As the students begin to plot points in all four quadrants, a color-coded grid, like that of Figure 9-32, often helps with directionality. Ordered pairs are coded according to quadrant, as shown.

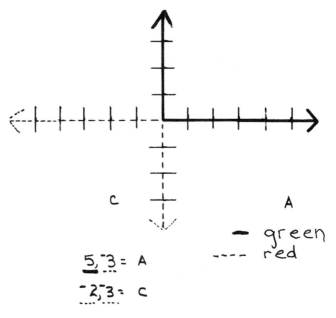

Figure 9-32

INTEGERS: POSITIVE AND NEGATIVE SIGNS

Problem area: Difficulty interpreting signs used with integers.

Typical disabilities affecting progress: Difficulty with visual perception, spatial organization, and closure.

Background: The greatest difficulty in dealing with integers is for many students misreading or misplacing the sign. For this reason, it is essential that the teacher be consistent in the placement of these signs. When signs are to be interpreted as negative or positive, they should be placed in a *raised* position, as in Figure 9-33. When used to denote an operation, the sign should be centered between the two numbers that are involved. Figure 9-34 shows a typical problem that can be very confusing. Does the sign in front of the 8 mean "subtract" or "negative?" The following ideas have proven useful in dealing with problems related to sign interpretation. In our experience, they have helped make computation with integers easier for students.

$^-7$ means "negative seven"

-6 means "subtract six"

Figure 9-33

$7-8$

Figure 9-34

Suggested Sequence of Activities and Exercises

1. **Circle to focus.** Preview the text used and circle the raised signs on the first several pages of the chapter on integers. Adult volunteers can be called upon to help.

2. **Label all numerals.** Some students, especially those with memory difficulties, forget that numbers without signs are assumed to be positive. Therefore, it is not unusual for them to misread the 9 of Figure 9-35 and treat it as a negative integer. For these students, it helps to *label all numerals* until they become more comfortable with integer signs.

$8-9 = 17$

Figure 9-35

3. **Do it first.** Until the children become familiar with the raised positive and negative signs, teach them to circle the signs on a text or worksheet page prior

to carrying out any computation to help focus their attention on the meaning of the signs. When it is time for computation, the bright color or dark circle will serve as a reminder that "this sign means something different."

4. **Use graph paper.** If the students need help to spatially organize their writing of signed numbers, allow them to use graph-paper. Show them how to place the signs and numbers on the lines as in Figure 9-36. Students with severe visual-perception deficits will find this activity difficult. For others, the graph-paper technique simplifies the task of writing integers and computing.

Note: Graph paper with six squares to the inch works well.

Figure 9-36

- *Variation:* For students needing additional assistance to organize their writing spatially, use the format of Figure 9-37a to prepare sheets in advance. The students fill in the problem as shown in Figure 9-37b. The adaptation for vertical alignment of numbers is shown in Figure 9-38.

Figure 9-37

Figure 9-38

5. **Use parentheses.** Often, just inserting parentheses within a problem (as in Figure 9-39) is sufficient to make signs easier to interpret. Parentheses, instead of circles, could be used to mark raised signs on textbook pages, as suggested in Activity 1.

$$9 - (^-3) + (^+4) = 9 + 3 + 4 = 16$$

Figure 9-39

COMPUTATION WITH INTEGERS

Problem area: Difficulty computing with integers.

Typical disabilities affecting progress: Difficulty with visual perception, sequencing, abstract reasoning, and memory.

Background: Assuming that visual perception or spatial deficits do not interfere or that such deficits have been controlled, computing with integers still requires more sequencing and mental regrouping than previous computation involving positive integers. As with all calculation, "easy" problems can be completed more quickly if done mentally. For others, it may be more appropriate to hand compute or use a calculator. A major instructional goal is to help children develop expertise with all three methods and be able to choose appropriately between them.

When teaching any of the computational skills, encourage learning disabled students to proceed step by step through *all* the steps, even when they think they can do the work mentally. It may also be necessary for these students to spend more time practicing than others in order to assure overlearning. Suggestions for how to supplement or reinforce textbook treatment of integer computation for the four operations follow.

Suggested Sequence of Activities and Exercises

Addition

1. **Informal beginnings.** Most textbooks suggest activities involving chips, cards, charged particles, or walk-on number lines to introduce, informally, addition of integers. Generally, it is important to carry out rather than omit these activities for learning disabled students because they help develop the mental

imagery necessary to deal successfully with addition of integers. The following activities are based on the number line. Alternately, the charged particle model might be used, as in Figure 9-40.

Figure 9-40

2. **Different strokes.** Textbook treatments typically present number line or other models in an effort to lead students to verbalize the patterns or "rules" for adding integers. A chart similar to that of Figure 9-41 is provided for reference. Eventually, the students memorize the procedures. If students have abstract-reasoning difficulties, it generally is more helpful to:

- Present the chart and discuss it in conjunction with several examples so that, procedurally, the students can use the chart to solve integer addition problems;

- Have students copy the chart onto a file card for ready reference;

- Have students use the rules to work out a number of problems until they become familiar with the general procedures for adding integers;

- Use a walk-on number line to verify that the sums derived in this manner actually make sense before attempting to memorize the procedural rules.

This last step is usually first in the standard sequence. It is an important tie-in to earlier, informal work.

Addition of Integers

Given problem	What to do	Sign of Sum
positive + positive	Add	+
negative + negative	Add	−
negative + positive or positive + negative	Subtract to find distance between	Sign of the greater addend

Figure 9-41

3. **For other folks.** For other students, such as those with memory or perceptual difficulties, the standard sequence is followed with additional reinforcing measures like: (a) color code signs to emphasize them whenever they appear in integer addition problems; (b) use the graph-paper technique of Figure 9-38 when helpful; and (c) provide kinesthetic/motor involvement in analyzing or verifying the procedural rules for adding integers.

- Allow students to dramatize simple additions, as in Activity 2, on a walk-on number line.

- Have students think of their bodies as number lines. Spreading both arms out, the left arm can represent the negative integers, the right arm the positive ones. The body is the zero. To add a negative 5 to a positive 4, for example, students must pass through 0 and on to negative 1. Doing this for several sample problems helps children *internalize the action* of integer addition. The general technique, when used later for verifying that indeed the "chart (Figure 9-41) always works," strengthens retention of the procedural rules.

- *Variation:* An alternative to arm stretching involves taping a smaller number line from shoulder to shoulder across a child's back. The body midline, then, is the zero. As the teacher dramatizes a simple addition problem by finger movement on the child's back, the student can either (a) close eyes and reverbalize the problem as it is enacted, or (b) with eyes open, mimic the teacher's movements by "finger walking" the addition on a personal number line placed on the desk in front of the child.

Subtraction

Note: Suggestions for successful integer addition have obvious implications for integer subtraction. Informal introductory work is important. Variation of the standard subtraction sequence for students with abstract-reasoning difficulty is similar to that outlined for integer addition. Likewise, the compensatory techniques outlined in Activity 3 of the addition section can be reviewed and adapted to work with integer subtraction. The following ideas, based on the number line model, also deserve special emphasis. Similar activities could be carried out using the charged particle model.

1. **Act it out.** There generally is great value in having students use a walk-on or "body" number line (as in the preceding Activity 3):

   • To solve simple integer subtraction problems (this often results in noting the pattern summarized in the Figure 9-42 "rule" statement); and

   • To verify that given answers, or those obtained by using a calculator, can also be derived by "following the rule."

   To subtract two integers:
   add the 1st integer to
   the opposite of the 2nd.

   Figure 9-42

2. **To the rule.** The following ideas are recommended when carrying out the first suggestion under Activity 1 with students who have no abstract reasoning difficulties.

   • **Use the number line.** A problem like that of Figure 9-43a might be posed and the students cued to think of the related addition problem. "What must be added to $^+4$ to get $^-7$?" Starting at $^+4$ on the number line, the children find that they must take 11 steps in a negative direction to get to $^-7$. The result should be charted along with others obtained in this manner. Using previously solved problems, help the students notice the pattern by grouping like problems, as in Figure 9-43b. Have them verbalize that the pairs $^-7 - {}^+4$ and $^-7 + {}^-4$ have the same answer. Repeat with other similar examples to help students determine the rule: "To subtract

a)

sum   addend   addend
 ↓   ↓   ↓
$^-7 - {}^+4 =$ □

□ $+ {}^+4 =$ $^-7$

□ $= {}^-11$

b)

$^-7 - {}^+4 = {}^-11$

$^-7 + {}^-4 = {}^-11$

Figure 9-43

two integers, the first can be added to the *opposite* of the second." Use the number line to verify the equivalence.

- **Match.** Design worksheets or card-sort activities in which the students solve and then match an integer subtraction problem to an equivalent addition problem. For example:

Solve:

$^-7 - {}^+4 =$ _____ $^-8 + {}^+5 =$ _____

$^+3 - {}^-2 =$ _____ $^-7 + {}^-4 =$ _____

$^-8 - {}^-5 =$ _____ $^+3 + {}^+2 =$ _____

Pair them:

a. $^-7 - {}^+4 =$ _____ and $^-7 + {}^-4 =$ _____

b. _____ $=$ _____ and _____ $=$ _____

c. _____ $=$ _____ and _____ $=$ _____

When all matches are made, the students must use a number line to verify the equivalence of each match contained in a circled statement.

- **Just one step.** Next, give the students integer subtraction problems and instruct them to carry out just the *first step* of each. As in Figure 9-44a, have the students merely rewrite the problem, without solving. (After the papers are checked, the problems can be completed.)

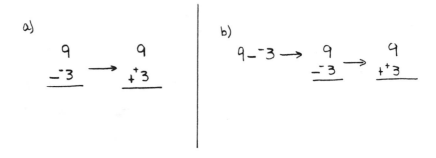

Figure 9-44

Note: Most texts present integer computation horizontally; for many learning disabled students, however, the vertical format is easier. As shown in Figure 9-44b, it may be necessary to help the students rewrite the horizontal form.

3. **Different strokes.** The sequence outlined in Activity 2 starts intuitively with number line moves, notes an equivalent method for finding answers (adding the opposites), then drills on that method. Some students may have difficulty with this more sophisticated, standard method of using the additive inverse to solve integer subtraction problems. For these students:

- **Use number line moves** as before to introduce integer subtraction intuitively. As before, cue the students to think of the related addition problem. Using the example of Figure 9-45a, ask the students, "What must be added to a positive 4 to get negative 7?" The students *rewrite* the problems, as in the second line of Figure 9-45b, to match the question. Starting at ⁺4, children then *move back* to zero and on to negative 7, for a total of 11 spaces in a negative direction. This result (⁻11) is now recorded (Figure 9-45c).

  Note: Either the walk-on or the "body" number line discussed earlier can be used in this activity.

- **Write it out.** To reinforce the subtraction-addition relation and to help students internalize the procedure for subtracting, use the technique of Figure 9-46. (The subtraction sign in the problem is written in a bright color.) Write out the procedure for subtracting as shown. The students solve the problem by filling in the blanks. Later, just put an example at the top of the page as a reminder, but continue to highlight the subtraction signs.

a)

$$^-7 - {}^+4 = \square$$

b)

$$^-7 - {}^+4 = \square$$
$$\square + {}^+4 = {}^-7$$

c)

$$^-7 - {}^+4 = \square$$
$$\square + {}^+4 = {}^-7$$
$$\square = {}^-11$$

Figure 9-45

$$^-4 - {}^-3 = \square$$

What must I add to ___ to get ___?

$$\left. \square + {}^-3 = 4 \right\} \leftarrow \text{student writes this.}$$

Figure 9-46

• **The whole thing.** As the children begin to solve integer subtraction problems independently, encourage them to picture the number line.

Example 1:

$$8 - {}^-3 = \underline{\hspace{1cm}}$$

Child writes: $\underline{\hspace{1cm}} + {}^-3 = 8$.
Child thinks: "Start at ${}^-3$, move forward to 0, then on to 8.
A move of ${}^+11$. $\underline{\hspace{1cm}} = {}^+11$."

Example 2:

$$36 - {}^-25 = \underline{\hspace{1cm}}$$

Child writes: $\underline{\hspace{1cm}} + {}^-25 = 36$.
Child thinks: "Start at ${}^-25$. Move forward to 0, to 36."
(Child now adds 25 and 36 on scrap paper.)
"A move of ${}^+61$. $\underline{\hspace{1cm}} = {}^+61$."

Note: This method does not utilize the traditional rule for subtracting integers—that of adding the opposite (additive inverse). It is based on the addition-subtraction relationship, but it allows children to remain concrete in their thinking. The children are encouraged to picture (or actually make) number line moves *first to zero, then on* to a target number. This two-step process can also be used with larger 2- and 3-digit numbers.

Multiplication and Division

Prerequisite Skills:

For some students, it may be necessary to review briefly the concept of multiplication as repeated addition and remind them that multiplication is commutative.

1. **Products and unlike signs.** Given mastery of the prerequisites, the sign for the product of a positive and a negative number can readily be identified.

   • *Example:*

   $7 \times {}^-6$. "That's seven negative 6s." One could repeatedly add, if necessary, to obtain the $^-42$. And, since multiplication is commutative, $7 \times {}^-6 = {}^-6 \times 7 = 42$.

2. **Products and like signs.** Many students can recognize and continue the pattern to the answers in Figure 9-47a. Each product is 5 less than the one directly above it. Similarly, in Figure 9-47b, each product is 4 less than that directly above it. Further, when the answers are filled in, the students can see how, each time, the product of two negative numbers is always positive. Some students, particularly those with abstract-reasoning difficulties, may not follow the logic of this exercise, but will merely remember that, as long as the signs are the same, the product is positive.

3. **Mail time.** A table like that of Figure 9-48 can also be used as a story line to dramatize the sign patterns for products. Since most students like to get mail, that is positive. No one likes to receive bills; that is negative.

4. **Same as multiplication.** Most students have little difficulty remembering how to handle the signs in division once they are comfortable with multiplication of integers. They are used to relating multiplication and division, so it is easy to remember (and verify) that sign rules for quotient figures are analogous to those for products:

Divisor and Dividend	Quotient
Like signs	Positive
Unlike signs	Negative

Example 1: $^-45 \div 5 = {}^-9$. ("Yes, because $^-9 \times 5 = {}^-45$.")

Example 2: $^-63 \div {}^-7 = 9$. ("Yes, because $9 \times {}^-7 = {}^-63$.")

a)

$$5 \times {}^-5 = {}^-25$$
$$4 \times {}^-5 = {}^-20$$
$$3 \times {}^-5 = {}^-15$$
$$2 \times {}^-5 = {}^-10$$
$$1 \times {}^-5 = \underline{\quad}$$
$$0 \times {}^-5 = \underline{\quad}$$
$${}^-1 \times {}^-5 = \underline{\quad}$$
$${}^-2 \times {}^-5 = \underline{\quad}$$
$${}^-3 \times {}^-5 = \underline{\quad}$$
$${}^-4 \times {}^-5 = \underline{\quad}$$

b)

$$5 \times {}^-4 = {}^-20$$
$$4 \times {}^-4 = {}^-16$$
$$3 \times {}^-4 = {}^-12$$
$$2 \times {}^-4 = {}^-8$$
$$1 \times {}^-4 = \underline{\quad}$$
$$0 \times {}^-4 = \underline{\quad}$$
$${}^-1 \times {}^-4 = \underline{\quad}$$
$${}^-2 \times {}^-4 = \underline{\quad}$$
$${}^-3 \times {}^-4 = \underline{\quad}$$
$${}^-4 \times {}^-4 = \underline{\quad}$$

Figure 9-47

If letters (+) are brought (+) that's positive (+).
If bills (−) are brought (+) that's negative (−).
If letters (+) are taken away (−) that's negative (−).
If bills (−) are taken away (−) that's positive (+).

Figure 9-48

EXPONENTS: BASIC CONCEPT

Problem area: Difficulty understanding, reading, and writing exponents.

Typical disabilities affecting progress: Difficulty with short-term memory, visual perception, expressive language, and abstract reasoning.

Background: Students are introduced to the concept and symbolism of exponents as early as the fifth or sixth grade. At that point, the idea is dealt with basically in conjunction with factoring and primes. As students advance in mathematics, computation involving exponents becomes more commonplace. Mathematical problem-solving applications in a number of fields—including medicine, science, and computer science—regularly use exponents to express both very large and very small numbers. Students with interests in these fields benefit from a firm foundation in exponents.

At the prealgebra level, development of adequate understanding of and skill with exponents is both important and necessary for students planning to continue mathematics in high school. The topic itself is not particularly difficult, except that it introduces new terminology and new notation that can be visually confusing. The following activities suggest ways of making exponents more understandable and usable, especially for those with language deficits. Previewing language and/or providing vocabulary cards may be needed by some students.

Suggested Sequence of Activities and Exercises

1. **Helpful models.** At an intuitive level, *prior* to the textbook introduction of exponents, squares and cubes of various dimensions can be used as in Figure 9-49 to acquaint students with exponential notation and language.

2. **Factors first.** Color coding can be used in the previous activity to help students remember how to read and write exponents. Since an exponent indicates the number of times a number is used as a factor, generally, it is best to have students first write the exponential form from a list of factors (Figure 9-50). This sequence especially seems to help students with expressive-language deficits, as it reinforces the meaning of the numbers used. Figure 9-50 contains an exercise that can be kept on file and used *prior* to the textbook introduction of exponents. The color coding, of course, can extend beyond the second and third powers of the base.

3. **Reverse what's given.** Once students can write the exponential form from the factored form, provide practice translating the exponential form. Color coding again can be used as in Figure 9-51.

4. **I call.** Make a deck of 52 cards. Twenty-six cards should show a number in exponential form, 26 in factored form, as in Figure 9-52. After each child is dealt five cards, the rest of the deck is placed face down between the players. The game is played by making pairs of an exponential card and one with matching factors. In turn, players request one card from the player to the left. If

2×2 <u>square</u>: 2^2 ₀₀₀ (2 <u>squared</u>)

|Also|

3×3 <u>square</u>: 3^2 or °° (3 <u>squared</u>)

4×4 <u>square</u>: 4^2 or °° (4 <u>squared</u>)

10×10 <u>square</u>: 10^2 ₀₀₀ 10 <u>squared</u>

2×2×2 <u>cube</u>: 2^3 ₀₀₀ (2 <u>cubed</u>)

|Also|

3×3×3 <u>cube</u>: 3^3 ₀₀₀ (3 <u>cubed</u>)

4×4×4 <u>cube</u>: 4^3 ₀₀₀ (4 <u>cubed</u>)

10×10×10 <u>cube</u>: 10^3 ₀₀₀ (10 <u>cubed</u>)

Figure 9-49

━━ = green   ---- = red

$4 × 4 × 4 = \underline{\quad}$ ⋯

4

4

Figure 9-50

━━ = green   ---- = red

$4^3 = \square × \square × \square$

Figure 9-51

that player has the requested card, it is given to the caller, who can then lay a pair down. A turn continues until no more pairs can be drawn from the pile, and play continues. The first player to run out of cards wins.

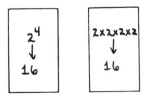

Figure 9-52

5. **New terminology.** For many students, the language involved in exponents is the most difficult. These students have trouble meaningfully associating the words "six to the third power" with any visual image. To help build up the necessary language, provide language drill that is separate from computational drill. Pages such as those shown in Figure 9-53a are useful as they present the new symbolism together with the associated language. Figure 9-53b suggests an alternative exercise that visually reinforces the fact that the exponent is raised.

a)

$$4^{:3} = \underline{\quad} \text{ to the } \ldots \text{power}$$

b) $4^{:3} = \underline{\quad}$ to the ---- power

— = green   ---- = red

Figure 9-53

SCIENTIFIC NOTATION

Problem area: Using exponents for scientific notation.

Typical disabilities affecting progress: Visual perception, figure-ground, sequencing, and closure problems.

Background: Scientific notation is used in many fields to express both very large and very small numbers. The successful conversion of numbers to (or from) scientific notation requires several major prerequisites:

- Strong numeration concepts and skills;

- Ability to multiply and divide by powers of 10;

- Basic understanding of and skill with exponents; and

- Ability to read decimals.

Application of all these isolated understandings and skills when writing numbers in scientific notation requires good reasoning, recall, and sequencing. These are typically weak areas for learning disabled students. In addition, closure or visual-perception deficits can lead to confusion when reading the numbers. Too often, these deficits make it seem as if the student does not understand what to do when, in fact, it really may be a matter of the student losing the place or not being able to recall information. The following suggestions offer ideas for how to handle some of the common problems children face as they deal with scientific notation.

Suggested Sequence of Activities and Exercises

1. **Color highlight.** During early work, for students with figure-ground deficits, it sometimes helps to highlight the digits to be used. Figure 9-54 illustrates two alternatives for color coding digits. Highlighting in this manner helps minimize the chance that students lose their place or misperceive the numbers read.

a) $6{,}240{,}000 = (6.24) \times 10^{6}$

b) $6{,}240{,}000 = (6.24) \times 10^{6}$

— = green   .... = red

Figure 9-54

2. **Use a mask.** Some students need to use a card, as in Figure 9-55, to block out part of the number field while counting digits. Students write the answer, digit by digit, while moving the card.

$$54,800,000 = 5[\qquad\qquad] =$$

$$54[\qquad\qquad] = 54,8[\qquad\qquad]$$

$$\underline{5.48} \times \underline{10}^-$$

Figure 9-55

3. **Help for computation.** When multiplying with scientific notation, color highlight, as in Figure 9-56, to help students apply the distributive law. Otherwise, the visual field can be confusing. Texts can be highlighted as in Figure 9-56a. Pages, formatted as in Figure 9-56c, can be kept on hand for students to use.

a)

$$\left(\underline{3.6} \times \underline{10}^3\right) \times \left(\underline{4.31} \times 10^{-5}\right)$$

b) $\left(3.6 \times 4.31\right) \times \left(10^3 \times 10^{-5}\right)$ ← Student rewrites inside parentheses

c) $\left(\quad \times \quad\right) \times \left(\quad \times \quad\right)$

—— = green   ---- = red

Figure 9-56

CHAPTER

Problem Solving

The National Council of Teachers of Mathematics (NCTM), in *An Agenda for Action* for the 1980s, set goals which called for greater emphasis on problem solving at all levels (National Council, 1980, p. 1). Since then, NCTM has gone on to address these goals by developing *Curriculum and Evaluation Standards for School Mathematics* (1987). This document not only stresses the importance of emphasizing problem solving throughout the mathematics curriculum, but also addresses these needs in relation to a changing society—one in which more calculators and computers are available. Suggestions are also made for changing the focus of instruction and for revising textbook material.

Problem solving is a difficult area to teach and one that is often avoided, especially with learning disabled students. Yet, it is one of the most important areas in mathematics instruction as it affects all aspects of a person's life. Thus, students must feel confident that, when they approach new or difficult situations, they possess the skills necessary to make a reasonable attempt to solve the problem, whether it involves determining if there is enough money to buy something or whether they have enough time to go to a movie with a friend before going to work. Academic and socialization skills often depend on our ability to feel confident about our reasoning skills.

In the past, too often problem solving in the mathematics curriculum placed heavy emphasis on reaching a final answer, rather than on the process of reasoning. The thrust is now changing and school mathematics texts include more problems which stress the process of arriving at an acceptable solution rather than the "right answer." At the lower grade levels, teachers should encourage students to feel comfortable with situations that involve words such as "some" or "a few." In daily life, we talk about going places with "some friends" or "losing a few things." As children progress in math they must become more aware that there are a variety of ways to solve a problem. Strategies such as the following constitute an important component of any mathematics curriculum and rely less on the exact answer than on the procedure:

- Making an organized list;
- Noticing a pattern;
- Analyzing a survey;
- Working a problem backwards;
- Using reasonable guess-and-check tests; and
- Simulating a procedure.

When methods such as these are used, students begin to feel comfortable with different ways of thinking and approaching problems. They learn that sometimes there is no "right" answer, but rather an acceptable variety of answers or methods.

Other important aspects of problem solving include the ability to:

- Recognize whether a problem contains enough information or extraneous information;
- Use a chart or table to obtain needed data;
- Retell a problem in one's own words;

    Note: Children with expressive-language problems may need help with this. For example, rather than being asked to restate a problem they might be allowed to read/hear a variety of restatements and asked to choose the correct one.

- Comfortably estimate and use such an estimate rather than an exact answer.

Teachers must continually use and train a variety of ways to approach problem solving. Even young children can begin to learn reasoning skills, especially if the mathematics curriculum is approached developmentally. Some effective approaches, which can be used at various levels, are summarized as follows:

- Use interesting problems that are within a child's experience. Young children and children with learning disabilities respond best when problem situations are meaningful. "About how long until recess?" Even if the answer is "About two big dots" (as described by one child who looked at an analog clock), students are still learning to "feel" time.

- Encourage and reinforce children's estimates, even if the answers are way off or the approach is not efficient. Help them learn other approaches but remember that, either because of their developmental level or their own learning style, what is efficient for one person may not be efficient for another.

- Pose problem situations orally. This is especially appropriate for first-grade students and children who have trouble reading.

  Note: Providing concrete visual reinforcement for each orally presented problem, *regardless of the student's age,* helps students who have auditory-processing or abstract-reasoning difficulties.

- Calculators and computers serve important functions in our society. If introduced properly at an early age, these tools need not be considered a crutch. Help students learn to use them and to recognize when they offer a more efficient procedure than the use of pencil-and-paper calculation.

- Begin early to encourage children to develop their mental calculation skills. For learning disabled students mental calculation can be difficult, but it does not have to be impossible. Flash pictures, numbers, objects, and the like to young children or students with memory problems and help them concentrate on remembering what they saw *first, second, third.* Other similar, short, repeated activities will help children feel more comfortable about approaching mental calculation.

- Use concrete objects, drawings, and diagrams at all levels of instruction to clarify a problem, find a solution, and verify the answer. Have children act out problems.

- Encourage students to feel comfortable with incorrect answers and teach them to understand that they can learn from errors. Start with a page of solved problems which include incorrect answers. Work with students to locate the wrong answers by talking about unreasonable answers or incorrect digit placement. Especially if introduced at a young age, this approach takes the fear out of making mistakes, teaches students to view mistakes as a learning process, and helps them develop self-confidence.

  Note: Do not use problems which students in the class have solved. The teacher should solve the problems, purposely making mistakes.

- Help students recognize what makes a problem difficult *for them.* Sometimes it is the large numbers, at other times the use of fractions instead of whole numbers. Help children make appropriate substitutions.

- Have children, even very young ones, write (match) mathematical sentences for problems without computing the answers. This emphasizes the importance of the procedure, rather than the correct answer.

  Note: Allow children with expressive-language difficulties to choose the appropriate sentence from several that are provided. Encourage the use of concrete aids, as needed.

- Use open-ended problems (those with more than one solution) to foster creative thinking and to develop a confidence that "people think in different ways."

- Use problems containing too much or too little information and ask students to identify what is still needed or what information is extra.

- Point out to students how mathematics is involved in much of what they do every day. Help them understand that we use math in day-to-day situations like figuring out how long it will take to get to the airport or determining how often to water a plant. Help students learn that we use math all the time and that most of the time the math we use does not involve exact answers.

- Have students make up problems to be solved in class. To offset the tendency to make problems too difficult, require that children be able to solve their own problems or explain why they cannot be solved. This technique has proven highly motivating for some students.

- Help students develop the language and thought process necessary for solving problems. Many mathematics textbooks present sequences like:

  1. Read the problem.
  2. Picture what is happening.
  3. Think: What is the question?
  4. What must you do to answer it (add, subtract, . . .)?
  5. Compute the answer.
  6. Check. Is it reasonable?

  Break down this sequence in steps and help students overlearn each step.

- Encourage children to devise word problems or use manipulatives to describe computation problems. Problems should relate to situations that may come up during the school day or outside school.

- Use problems with words such as "some" or "many" instead of numbers to check if students know when to use each operation. Encourage students to insert low numbers to help determine the operation.

- Use problems without a stated question and encourage students to ask a question about the information. Do this in a small group and work with the students so that each one asks a different question.

- Make sure you understand children's thinking before commenting on the work or marking an answer wrong. Remember, given their thinking or what they saw, their answer may be correct.

- Supplement textbook problems with problems of your own based on situations in the classroom.

- Post a "problem of the week" on the bulletin board.

- In class discussions, ask for alternative suggestions or methods to solving a problem.

- Be sure the children know the mathematics needed to solve assigned problems. For example, if they understand which operation to use but have not memorized the facts involved, allow them to use a cross-out list, as suggested on page 223 in Chapter 5. Work on learning the facts at another time.

Given the emerging broad scope of problem solving in school mathematics, this chapter will focus on the related subskills needed to solve standard 1- or 2-step problems. The techniques suggested apply not only to helping students determine "correct" answers, but also to helping them develop the confidence and ability to solve nonroutine or process problems. Throughout, recommendations are also made to help teachers relate isolated components of problem solving to real-world situations.

PROBLEM SOLVING AND THE LEARNING DISABLED STUDENT

The suggestions in the previous section are important for *all* students. The approach to teaching students with learning disabilities, however, may need to be different and involve more review or skill breakdown. Nonetheless, the ideas are essential for developing a sense of confidence and the "belief that they [all students] have the power to do mathematics and that they have control over their own success or failure" (National Council of Teachers of Mathematics, 1988, p. 26).

Problem-solving situations call upon children to retrieve previously learned skills and apply them in new or varying situations. Knowing basic arithmetic skills vs. knowing when and how to incorporate these skills in new contexts are two completely different tasks. All too often we assume that students understand how to solve a problem if they understand and can carry out the operations involved.

As difficult as it may be for learning disabled students to learn a particular skill, it generally is considerably more difficult for them to decide when and how to *use* that skill in new contexts. Many learning disabled students will develop confidence in their ability to use the problem-solving process if they are provided specific help in:

- decision making

- information use

- vocabulary

- sequencing

- patterning

Because of their importance in the problem-solving process, each of these areas deserves special consideration in a mathematics program for learning disabled students.

Decision Making

All problem solving involves making decisions. Very young children make a decision when they indicate whether the symbol in front of them is a "2" or a "3." They also make decisions when playing a game, such as Bingo, where they must use an understanding of "more" and "less" to decide where to put their chips. As children progress and learn more skills, decision making continues to enter their daily life. Thus, they are confronted not only with deciding what a sign means or whether to regroup, but also with answering such questions as what operation to use, which problem to solve first, or whether they have enough money to buy something.

The decision-making process is complex. It requires (a) strong abstract-reasoning ability; (b) the ability both to receive and express words in a meaningful way; (c) the ability to draw on previously learned concepts and skills; (d) the ability to distinguish among them; and (e) the ability to choose the one that is most appropriate in a given situation.

Information Use

In order to solve problems, students must be able to interpret information accurately and to formulate and express the key ideas involved. They must understand what question/questions are being asked. In addition, they must be able to isolate given information within a problem. In some problems, sorting out irrelevant information is essential. In real-life situations, we are not always told in advance that some of the information is not important. Similarly, on a day-to-day basis, we are not informed about what we need to know in order to solve a problem. We must determine what information is missing. All these requirements demand language—both receptive and expressive. For many children, problem solving is difficult, not because of the computation involved, but because they are unable to use language appropriately. They are unable to express their ideas or associate the words with the appropriate meanings involved.

Vocabulary

Due to the many special problems involved, vocabulary is considered apart from the more general use of language in relation to problem solving. Like reading, mathematics has a vocabulary. Although the vocabulary varies depending on the level of the material, it is still an integral part of the mathematics program. For younger children, the relevant vocabulary involves associating a word with a symbol, as in Figure 10-1, and understanding that word when it is spoken or read. Older students, generally fourth grade and above, must acquire a rapidly expanding vocabulary, including many words with multiple meanings (e.g., "and," "factor," "times," and so on). When new vocabulary is used, many learning disabled students may not automatically know the meaning just from the context. At best, they may know that a familar word does not make sense in its current context.

Figure 10-1

Sequencing

Problem solving requires not only using skills that have previously been taught, but also choosing which previously learned skills are needed and using them in a *properly organized way*. In other words, sequencing skills are important to success in problem solving. Unlike computation where the sequence does not vary, the sequences needed to handle real-life problems can vary from situation to situation. In one instance, it may be necessary to add first and then multiply, whereas, in another, the reverse procedure might be required.

Patterning

Generally, when we think of patterning in mathematics, we think of numbers or shapes that follow a specific order, as in Figure 10-2. Patterning is also part of solving common daily problems. In Chapter 3, the complex patterning needed to count money was addressed. An extension of this type of patterning underlies the ability to decide which of the four basic operations to apply in a given situation. Can students notice and retrieve the similarities and differences between a given problem and those previously worked using a particular operation? (See Figure 10-3.) Some learning disabled students cannot "see" what is laid out from just the words of a problem—that the situation really *fits the pattern* of addition or division. They do not see the similarity between this and previous work with addition, division, or some other operation. Unfortunately, it is often easier for learning disabled students to expresss the differences than to express the similarities between things. In order for them to expand their problem-solving skills it is helpful, and often necessary, that similarities be isolated and that repeated practice focus first on recognizing those similarities.

a)

□ □ △ △ ○ ○ □□

Continue the pattern.

b) 6.7   5.7   4.7 . . .

Continue the pattern.

Figure 10-2

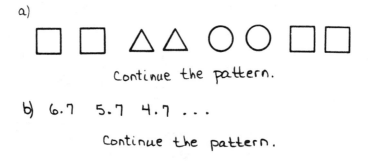

"I will earn $14.25 after working 5 hours. I wonder how much I'll earn each hour."

Hmm! That's like separating a whole group. I'll divide.

Figure 10-3

Decision making, information use, vocabulary, sequencing, and patterning—all are key aspects of the problem-solving process. When certain prerequisite skills, those discussed in the next section, are intact, teachers of learning disabled students can give these aspects of problem solving the attention they deserve.

PREREQUISITE SKILLS FOR EFFICIENT PROBLEM SOLVING

Good problem solvers can estimate, predict, draw conclusions, and use information effectively. Too often these skills are only taught in the reading curriculum. It is important for mathematics teachers to realize that children's abilities to handle these tasks greatly affect their confidence and success in many areas of mathematics, including problem solving. The following are suggestions for how to develop these and other subskills.

1. **Rounding.** Repeated work on understanding the relationship between rounding isolated numbers and problem solving is essential. Too often students view rounding as a computational skill and are unable to apply it. Help them see that rounding a computation, such as that shown in Figure 10-4, is similar to what you might do if you want to make sure you have enough money with you to go to a movie ($6.50), buy a book ($7.45, without tax) and have dinner ($11.00).

Figure 10-4

2. **Choosing efficient methods.** Starting with very young children and those using only manipulatives or single-digit numbers, help students develop an understanding of when use of a calculator is the most efficient way to solve a problem. Using an analog clock, ask students to time how long it takes to solve a problem mentally. Compare the result to the time it takes to solve the same problem using a calculator. "Which is more efficient?"

> *Note 1:* For young children, or those with visual-perceptual problems, use a calculator with large keys, a large display, and large print on the keys.

> *Note 2:* Think developmentally! An approach that is not efficient for an adult or an older child may be efficient for younger students or those with different types of learning disabilities. Children with abstract-reasoning difficulties, for example, may be able to punch the keys on a calculator quickly without understanding what is happening unless they have access to manipulatives or unless they "imagine a picture."

3. **Predicting.** Do a lot of work with blocks, coins, and other real-life objects to help children think about "What might happen if we do this?" Spread some centimeter cubes out on the table and ask the children what might happen if the cubes were all pushed together. Encourage different answers: "They'd be closer together." "I'd be able to carry them easier." "I'd be able to count them easier." All these answers (a) are acceptable, (b) involve predicting, (c) help children recognize different ways of thinking, and (d) develop self-confidence.

4. **Introducing the language of estimation.** Make sure children understand the difference in meaning between such expressions as "I *have* 7 crayons" and "I *have about* 10 crayons." Practice different situations where students describe a picture or event, first using factual words such as "is" and "have" and then estimation words like "about," "nearly," "almost," and so on.

5. **Estimating.** Provide lots of practice estimating an answer ahead of time. Do this in small groups and have students explain how they arrived at their answer. Plot the different answers on a number line and talk about situations where the different estimates would be acceptable. Check estimates using the calculator. The goal of this task is to develop comfort with estimates, as opposed to "correct" estimates and computation.

Rather than presenting an all-encompassing approach, the following pages are intended to stimulate teachers to recognize how often we need to use math to solve a problem. Numerous topics need to be considered, and it is far beyond the scope of this book to address them all. What is needed, however, is more flexibility in approaching different situations and more focus on making children feel comfortable with math as it relates to their own everyday lives.

DETERMINING THE CORRECT OPERATION

Typical disabilities affecting progress: Difficulty with abstract reasoning, visual memory, and receptive or expressive language.

Background: The need to decide whether to add, subtract, multiply, or divide enters many facets of daily life. At the store, we must decide whether the correct change has been given or how much money to give the clerk. Purchasing school supplies requires that we decide when to multiply and when to add. The following activities describe some specific decision-making skills at the computation level. Teachers are encouraged to relate these ideas to more meaningful situations to help students understand the relationship between computation and problem solving and apply their mathematics skills accordingly.

Suggested Sequence of Activities and Exercises

1. **Prerequisites.** Be sure the children have a strong mental picture of each operation. For young children who are still at the concrete level, use objects and follow-up color-coded pages as in Figure 10-5 to help them associate the ideas of subtraction with the number sentence and the subtraction symbol. Review other operations in a similar manner.

   • *Variation:* Relate this activity to their daily lives by having students describe (show) what they do when called upon to share their toys or take playing chips from a box so their friends each have the same amount.

2. **You tell.** In early work with simple number combinations, help students develop reasoning skills by presenting problems with answers, as in Figure 10-6. Have students supply the correct sign. As a preliminary exercise, discuss what the possibilities are. For a page like the one illustrated, help children verbalize that the answers to addition problems have to be larger than the addends involved. Similarly, the answers to subtraction problems must be smaller than what you "start with" (the subtrahend).

   Note: Similar work would be carried out in early work with multiplication and division. Once facts are learned, answers are given spontaneously, and students tend to ignore the real reason for the sign. Given 5, 6 and 30, for example, they will choose the multiplication problem because, "I

Figure 10-5

What's the sign?

$$\begin{array}{r} 4 \\ \square\ 9 \\ \hline 13 \end{array} \qquad \begin{array}{r} 7 \\ \square\ 3 \\ \hline 10 \end{array} \qquad \begin{array}{r} 6 \\ \square\ 4 \\ \hline 2 \end{array}$$

Figure 10-6

know that 5 × 6 = 30." Hence, it is essential to incorporate these exercises early, before children commit facts to memory.

3. **Do it with big numbers.** As the students begin to work with larger numbers, a similar exercise can be used (see Figure 10-7). When using larger numbers, keep the pace fairly quick so the children do not have time to compute. Discuss the numbers involved. Make sure they can tell whether (and why) the answer will be larger or smaller than what you "start with."

$$\begin{array}{r} 463 \\ \square\ 297 \\ \hline 760 \end{array} \qquad \begin{array}{r} 834 \\ \square\ 129 \\ \hline 705 \end{array}$$

Figure 10-7

4. **Special help.** Students with visual-memory or visual-discrimination deficits may have trouble retrieving the correct sign without having the symbols in front of them. For them, keep strips as in Figure 10-8 to be used by students at their desks. As problems are solved, the strip will serve as a visual reminder of the alternatives.

Figure 10-8

5. **Do the easy one first.** Older students who have learned when to use each of the four operations in situations involving whole numbers often have trouble with fractions and decimals when trying to:

- Recognize which operation to use; and

- Carry out the appropriate operation.

For these students, it is helpful to parallel two problems that are solved similarly, but involve different types of numbers. Figure 10-9b shows an equation that gives many middle-school and junior-high students trouble. It is made much simpler when paralleled with that in Figure 10-9a.

a) $9A = 73$

$A = 72 \div 9$

$A = 9\overline{)73} \;\; \begin{smallmatrix}8\\ -72\\ \hline 1\end{smallmatrix} = 8\frac{1}{9}$

$A = 8\frac{1}{9}$

b) $4\frac{1}{2} A = 64$

$A = 64 \div 4\frac{1}{2}$

$A = 64 \div \frac{9}{2}$

$64 \times \frac{2}{9} = \frac{128}{9} = 14\frac{2}{9}$

$A = 14\frac{2}{9}$

Figure 10-9

6. **Tell what to do, then stop.** Follow through on these ideas in verbal problems by having the students:

- Read the problem;

- Picture what is happening;

- Use objects or draw to picture the problem if this helps (similar to work in Activity 1, page 453);

- Think about what is being asked; and

- Tell what to do (add, subtract, multiply, divide).

At first, do not require that the children actually compute. After their papers are checked, the computation can be carried out and the result checked.

DETERMINING WHETHER AN ANSWER IS REASONABLE

Typical disabilities affecting progress: Difficulty with abstract reasoning and closure.

Suggested Sequence of Activities and Exercises

1. **Choose.** Present questions and multiple-choice answers as in Figure 10-10. From the answers, have students select those that are most reasonable. Discuss with them why the other choices "won't work."

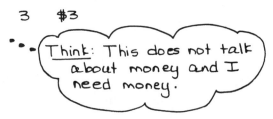

Figure 10-10

2. **Estimate.** Help children estimate answers *before* they compute. Help them get a "ball-park" answer as in Figure 10-11.

- *Follow-Up:* Have the students tell how they arrived at the "ball-park" answer. Hearing how other children derive estimates gives them ideas on how to proceed and makes them more confident about trying it themselves.

$$5\tfrac{1}{4} \times 3\tfrac{2}{3} = 15\tfrac{1}{6}$$

5 × 4 = 20 My answer is pretty far off.

Figure 10-11

3. **The whole thing.** When students arrive at an answer to a written word problem, they must fill in the word the number describes, as in Figure 10-12. Have them read or say the entire sentence as illustrated to determine whether, in context, the answer make sense.

You work 8 hours a day for 6 days. How many hours do you work in all?

I work _____.

Student fills in blanks.

Figure 10-12

MAKING GOOD USE OF INFORMATION

Typical disabilities affecting progress: Difficulty with long-term memory, abstract reasoning, receptive, and expressive language.

Suggested Sequence of Activities and Exercises

1. **"X" what's not needed.** Present problems as in Figure 10-13 and have the students cross out any information that is not needed (in this case, the number of pages). Generally, the assignment is best spread over two days so responses can be checked and discussed before the students actually carry out the computation. For younger students or for initial presentation, highlight the needed items, as in Figure 10-14. As they become more proficient, have the children themselves highlight the items in the question and then in the statement part of the problem.

2. **Just give the data.** Present short "problems" that do not ask a question but merely supply information. Have students determine what they know from this small amount of information. Figure 10-15 illustrates the format for an initial presentation which has proven effective, even with students who have retrieval or expressive-language deficits. The goal, at this point, is to identify what information is supplied and what information will be useful in solving the problem.

Figure 10-13

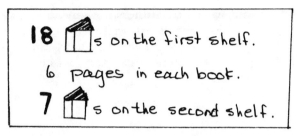

18 ☐s on the first shelf.

6 pages in each book.

7 ☐s on the second shelf.

How many **books** ? ___

Figure 10-14

You have $46.50. You spend $\frac{1}{5}$ of
the money on books. Then you
spend $4.86 for lunch.

<u>Match.</u>

$46.50   cost of lunch

part of
$46.50   money had to
                                 begin with

$4.86   cost of books

Figure 10-15

3. **Tell what's missing.** A similar procedure can be used to help students determine missing information. Initially, present problems where the question asks
for something that cannot be learned from the information given. Highlight
the word in the question that calls for the missing information.

Note: At the verbal level, when manipulatives are not used, this type of
problem can be very difficult, especially for students with learning disabilities.
Check the child's developmental level (see *Prerequisite Skills for Efficient Problem Solving*) *and provide a lot of practice using concrete aids.* Make the transition to written and oral word problems very gradually.

4. **Number word to numeral.** Many children are unable to attach meaning to verbal number names used in some problems. Practice pages like that of Figure 10-16 are often helpful. Initially, the child fills in the numeral named. Later, the appropriate operation can be determined and the computation carried out.

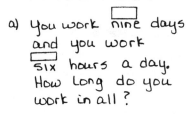

Figure 10-16

5. **Two steps.** Problems involving two steps can be color coded as shown in Figure 10-17 to help associate the necessary information with the correct step. As before, do not require that students compute answers to the problems until they have been checked to be sure that the proper information for each step is available.

   Note: To help develop their independence, encourage students to do their own highlighting prior to solving the problem. This will make them more aware of the thought process involved and the task sequence.

6. **Special help.** Even when the children are better able to identify, in context, numerals in written form, they may still have trouble verbalizing, either aloud or to themselves, what they need to do to solve the problem. To help in such situations, present problems like that of Figure 10-18. Steps for solving the problem are shown in random order, at the right. Seeing the information usually helps children verbalize what needs to be done. Then, step by step, in the spaces provided, they write up the computation in correct order to solve the problem. As the children become more proficient with practice, eliminate showing one or more of the completed steps.

7. **Picture choice.** For younger children a variation of the preceding procedure consists of presenting a choice of pictures as in Figure 10-19. Children choose the picture that best describes the problem. Encourage them to state the completed number sentence orally. With practice, students become more proficient and can be helped to draw their own pictures to describe given problem situations.

You earn $2.25 each hour. You work
for 6 days, 8 hours each day.

1) How long do
you work all
together?
_____ days
_____ hours
↗
(Child fills in
and circles the
correct word.)

2) How much do
you earn? _____

◼ = green
· · · · = red

Figure 10-17

Copy the correct solution for each step in
the right spaces and then solve.

You buy 14 pads
of paper for 3¢
a pad. You sell
them for 5¢ a
pad. What is
your profit?

14 × 5¢

(14 × 5¢) − (14 × 3¢)

14 × 3¢

Step 1   Step 2

Step 3

Figure 10-18

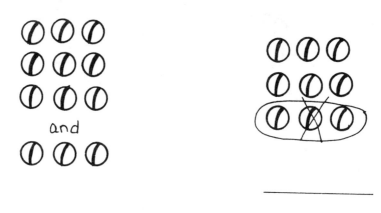

Figure 10-19

MATHEMATICAL MEANING OF WORDS AND SYMBOLS

Typical disabilities affecting progress: Difficulties with closure, abstract reasoning, memory, and receptive language.

Suggested Sequence of Activities and Exercises

1. **Focus.** Help students associate words with numbers and symbols by presenting exercises like those shown in Figure 10-20. Figure 10-20a is used in con-

Cross out all numbers that are not related
to the word in the box.

a) You give [each]
friend ten pencils.

9   1   3   7

We have [many]
books here

0   1   8   43

b) You start with $10.
You [earn] $9.16.

When you earn
money you have
{ more
  less } than when
you started;
therefore when you earn
money you { add (+)
            subtract (−) }.

Figure 10-20

junction with word problems that contain the troublesome terms "each" and "many." The exercise helps students internalize the numerical meaning of the terms. In the first problem, "each" means 1, not 9, 3, or 7. "Many" may mean 8 or 43, but never 0 or 1. The exercise in Figure 10-20b focuses on developing meaning for the term "earn." Similar exercises should be developed for other vocabulary terms that cause students difficulty.

2. **Key words.** Exercises like that of Figure 10-21 help children begin to associate mathematical meaning with words. Key words and their meaning are placed just before each problem and are highlighted within the problem.

return → less { ⊕
                ⊖ }

I have 8 pencils. I return 6 of them.

Now I have ____ pencils.

Figure 10-21a

I have 8 pencils. My friend returns
2 pencils to me. Now I have _____ pencils.

Figure 10-21b

3. **Chart it.** Post a chart, or help students make a personal file, that pairs troublesome terms or symbols with their meaning.

DETERMINING THE CORRECT SEQUENCE

Typical disabilities affecting progress: Difficulty with expressive language, abstract reasoning, short-term memory, spatial and temporal organization, and closure.

Background: In order for students to determine the correct sequence for a problem, they must possess a good understanding of the concepts "before" and "after," regardless of whether the outcome of the problem is an exact numerical answer. Sometimes the best answer does not involve a number. Rather, a decision must be made as to what sequence to follow. The "correct" sequence can vary, however, depending on the situation, and children must feel comfortable with the ideas of "before" and "after" to make these decisions.

Many learning disabled students need specific help with these concepts, even as they get older. Often this means reviewing the ideas prior to problem-solving situations. For example, asking learning disabled students whether they want to see a movie before lunch or after lunch may involve briefly reviewing temporal concepts first. The following activities propose some ways of helping students of all ages in this area. The suggestions are presented in the format of word problems so they can be taught and practiced as skills. The general ideas, however, are meant to be used and transferred to daily situations as they arise.

Suggested Sequence of Activities and Exercises

1. **Before-after.** While most children learn to sequence steps as they mature, many learning disabled students must be taught a thought process to help them determine a given sequence of steps. To this end, it often helps to set up problems with the "before-after" concept clearly presented. This is especially true for situations involving two steps, one of which is not clearly stated (Figure 10-22a). Provide worksheets, as shown, in Figure 10-22b. Ask students to cross out the wrong choice and then solve the problem.

   Note: Prior to the start of the school year, have an aide or adult volunteer preview the textbook and make up pages, as shown, to go along with the problems in the book. If necessary, color code as illustrated in Figure 10-22c.

   - *Variation 1:* Encourage children to think about (predict) what they will have to do before giving them the worksheet. Use coins or other manipulatives, if necessary.

   - *Variation 2:* Present 2- and 3-step problems along with the needed steps, out of sequence. Talk with the children, use manipulatives, and help them determine the correct sequence. Have them cut out the steps, paste them in the correct order, and solve the problem. For some students, especially those with memory problems, this task may be a 2- or 3-part assignment. Use the manipulatives one day; later when they sequence the written words, encourage students to "picture what you did with the coins yesterday." Check the sequencing before they continue.

2. **Color cue.** Various activities in the previous pages have highlighted the effectiveness of color coding as an aid in sequencing. Figure 10-23 shows another way to color code a word problem so students begin to internalize the thought process and procedure for sequencing problems.

3. **Phase out.** As the children begin to develop sequencing skills, randomly list the necessary steps and have them number them in the correct order. If necessary, color code either the word problem *or* the steps, but not both (as in Figure 10-24). When checking the numbering, have the students note alternative sequences that their friends might have chosen. After the sequences have been checked, students can solve the problems.

a) You buy $3\frac{1}{5}$ lb.
of meat at $2.42
per lb. How much
change will you have
left from $10?

b) You buy $3\frac{1}{5}$ lb. of meat at $2.42 per lb.
How much change will you have left from $10?

   Before I can find the change I
      need to know $\begin{cases} \text{how much I spend.} \\ \text{how much meat I buy.} \end{cases}$

c) You buy $3\frac{1}{2}$ lb. of meat at $2.42 per lb.
How much change will you have left
from $10?

   Before I can find the change I
      need to know $\begin{cases} \underline{\text{how much I spend.}} \\ \text{how much meat I buy.} \end{cases}$

Figure 10-22

—— = green   - - - = red

You spend $1.28 per gallon on gasoline.
You travel 48 miles and use 18 gallons
of gasoline per mile. How much does
gasoline cost?

Step 1   Step 2

I need ___ gallons.   I spend ___ in all.

Figure 10-23

You earn $3.22 each hour.
You work 3 hours a day
for 6 days. Then you buy
a book for $2.84. How
much do you have left? _____

_____ amount earned in all
_____ number of hours worked
_____ amount left after buying
the book.

Sentence 1 = black   Sentence 2 = green
Sentence 3 = red

Figure 10-24

RECOGNIZING THE PATTERN OF A PROBLEM

Typical disabilities affecting progress: Difficulty with abstract reasoning and auditory processing.

Suggested Sequence of Activities and Exercises

1. **See the pattern.** Present simple visual problems and have students circle the best solution. Help them notice the pattern of their solutions. In the example of Figure 10-25, the numbers 2, 3, and 5 use multiplication because they involve finding the total when the groups contain the same number.

2. **Word problems now.** As the children become better able to recognize the pattern for applying a given operation, gradually introduce word problems. At first, present assignments in which students use only one operation. Choose different numbers in the problems and help students manipulate concrete aids or draw a picture of the problem, as in Figure 10-25. Rather quickly get to

Figure 10-25

pages of mixed problem types. Throughout, encourage students to look for a pattern: separating groups, finding the total of groups equal in size, and so on. Allow the children to use the concrete aids or to draw a picture of the problem as long as this seems helpful.

3. **Easy one first.** Earlier in this chapter we pointed out that working a parallel problem with whole numbers can help students solve a problem that contains fractions or decimals. A similar technique helps in problem solving. Some students "go blank" when they notice that a word problem contains a fraction or decimal. Giving these students a parallel problem with whole numbers often helps them recognize the general pattern to the solution (add, subtract, multiply, divide), which they then can apply to the original problem with fractions or decimals.

PROBLEM SOLVING IN THE REAL WORLD

Although essential, the activities in the preceding sections are only of value if students can apply and use the basic problem-solving skills in their daily lives. It is hoped that by considering a nonstandard topic (e.g., vocabulary or decision making) as a specific skill and teaching students ways to approach it in structured situations, teachers will make students more aware of how to use these skills in various problem-solving situations. The following are suggestions for applying problem-solving skills to practical, real-world situations.

Suggested Sequence of Activities and Exercises

1. **What works.** Give students opportunities to choose whatever method they want for solving a problem, even if their choice might not be the most efficient. Later, as a separate activity, help them identify more efficient methods.

2. **Each one different.** Present a problem to a small group of students and require that each student solve the problem in a different way. Have students compare their answers. If answers are different, help them see why the various approaches resulted in different solutions. Similarly, help students also see why varying approaches may have achieved the *same* answers.

   Note: It may be necessary to tell some students which method to use. Students who are more confident and possess good expressive language and abstract-reasoning skills may be able to come up with different solutions as a group.

3. **Plan ahead.** Before going on a planned field trip, discuss with students the possible price of things they may want to do or buy. Write the prices on the board and practice rounding off the needed amounts to decide on a reasonable amount of money for students to bring.

4. **What's first.** Have students plan a segment of the morning schedule. Present alternatives which include required subjects as well as free-time activities. List the activities on the board along with the approximate times needed for each. Let children decide on a sequence they think will work.

   Note: The first few times they try this activity, let the students realize that not all sequences will work. Even if it means that not all the work is completed, students will have learned a valuable lesson about sequencing and planning ahead.

   • *Variation:* Some students, especially those with expressive-language, short-term memory, or temporal difficulties, may be helped by having the activities written out on strips and the times noted on pie segments of an analog clock. They can then fill in the clock with the activities as shown in Figure 10-26.

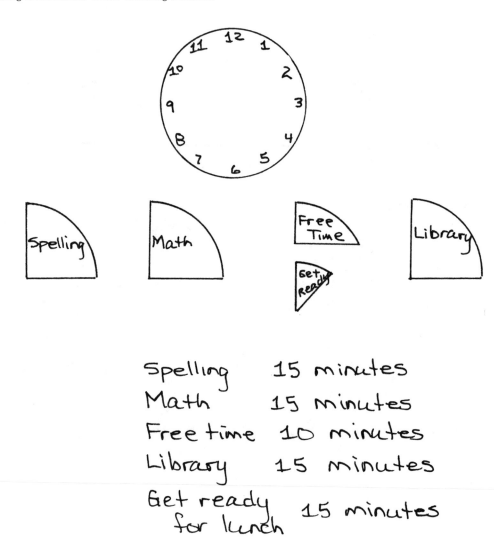

Spelling   15 minutes
Math   15 minutes
Free time   10 minutes
Library   15 minutes
Get ready
   for lunch   15 minutes

Figure 10-26

CHAPTER 11

Mathematics, Microcomputers, and Learning Disabled Students

CURRENT TRENDS

In recent years, due both to improved teacher education and to legislation (PL 94-142), there has been an increased awareness of the need to work more effectively with handicapped students in general and with learning disabled students in particular. As more and more students are being mainstreamed, teachers are striving to provide material which is individualized enough to help these children learn and retain what is presented, while still allowing as much participation within the classroom as is reasonable.

At times, planning and implementation of instruction can be overwhelming. However, with the increased use and availability of the microcomputer, mathematics teachers have a potential helpmate. If used properly, by a teacher who feels comfortable with it, the computer can provide practice, at a slow enough pace for students to process material and overlearn where necessary. For most students, the computer is highly motivating. Students who are reluctant to join in social situations involving a lot of conversation (students with expressive and receptive language difficulties) often can develop improved socialization skills by interacting with a peer at the computer. Finally, a computer's response to mistakes can be less threatening than the personal response of a teacher, peer, or parent.

At present, mathematics teachers appear to use computers most commonly for:

- drill and practice, primarily for basic facts and computation skills;

- tutorial presentation of new or previously learned material;

- developing student understanding of data bases and spreadsheets;

- increasing students' logic, reasoning, and problem-solving skills.

Although the computer can be of tremendous assistance, especially in a mainstreamed classroom, teachers must recognize some of the difficulties learning disabled students may encounter while using the computer. Specifically, consideration of how students' learning disabilities can interfere with successful computer use will help the teacher plan more effectively. The following section addresses specific learning disabilities which have been mentioned throughout the book—this time in terms of their interaction with the computer. At the end of each section suggestions for general remediation techniques are provided. The major disabilities have been subdivided similarly to the overview in Table 1-1 (see Chapter 1). Table 11-1 summarizes the discussion as it is presented in this chapter.

Table 11-1
Learning Disabilities and the Computer

Disability	Problem Area	Ways of Helping

Figure-Ground	Visual
	— size of type
	— amount on screen
	— tracking from
	    — screen to keyboard
	    — screen to paper
	— locating keys on
	    — keyboard
		— use large type
		— skip lines
		— allow enough time
		
		— bold type
		— heavy cursor

	Auditory — use of sound — number of computers in room	— choose programs which reinforce without sound

Table 11-1.   Continued.

Disability	Problem Area	Ways of Helping
Discrimination	Visual — noticing punctuation — too much on screen — line spacing — type of screen reinforcement	— tilt screen — place to side of keyboard — use paper to track — underlining capability — ability to control speed of presentation
	Auditory — misperception of endings	— highlight word/number as said — make tape to match lesson
Spatial Perception	— use of arrow keys — solving multistep problems	— programs with arrow pointing to steps — encourage use of I-J-K-M

Memory	Short/Long Term
	— screen-to-screen retention
	— too much skill/subject isolation
	— keyboard/screen retention
		— ease of returning to
		    — menu
		    — previous frame
		— paper/pencil use

	Visual Memory — lack of realistic pictures — low vocabulary	— preview vocabulary — off-computer activities for keyboard recognition
Language	Receptive Language — difficulty relating word to meaning	— provide visual cues — preview vocabulary
	Expressive Language — difficulty with timed programs	— allow student to determine timing
Abstract Reasoning	— lack of concrete representation	— interactive program — concrete aids — branching capability

LEARNING DISABILITIES AND THE COMPUTER

Most teachers have encountered one or more of the following situations while students are using a computer:

- A student continues to hit a key/keys, randomly, until the screen changes.

- Students are unable to locate the correct response key even though the program only requires the use of, for example, numbers and the *return* key or the *return* key and the *space bar*.

- A student forgets why and how a particular screen was accessed and what the relevance of that screen is to what is being done.

- A student is able to successfully play any available computer game, even if use of basic facts is involved. However, the same student is unable to memorize the facts and successfully integrate their use into everyday experiences.

- A student is confused over the way symbols are represented on the keyboard versus the screen (Figure 11-1).

Figure 11-1

An awareness of problems such as these is important, but even more important is an understanding of why they are occurring and how to handle them. Computer use must not be random. Like any other classroom activity, it must be properly scheduled based on its function at a given time and the student(s) using it.

EFFECT OF LEARNING DISABILITIES ON USING THE COMPUTER

Visual and Auditory Perceptual Problems

Figure-Ground Difficulties

Background: Students with visual figure-ground deficits tend to have trouble keeping their place on the keyboard, especially when they need to look back and forth from the screen to the keyboard. Even those students who seem to "know their way around" a keyboard may have trouble because the keys are close together. Although it may appear helpful for students to learn touch typing, this is not always possible, especially for younger students or for students with fine-motor problems. These students especially have trouble with the number keys and other keys which carry two symbols. Additionally, many programs use small print on the screen, making it still more difficult for students to sort out the information being presented.

Auditory figure-ground difficulties are compounded by the sound from other computers and computer users in the room. Even if no game is being played and the monitor sound is turned off, the mere sound of typing can interfere with these students' thought processes. If a sound factor is added, either to the individual student's program or to that of another child, even more confusion results.

Suggested Sequence of Activities and Exercises

1. **Cover it.** For those programs which only require that a few keys be used for responses, it is often helpful to cover up the remaining keys. For exam-

ple, if only the number keys and perhaps the *space bar* or *return* key[1] are required, cover up the remaining keys as in Figure 11-2.

Note: See Activity 4 (*Hide It*) in Section 2, page 480, for a variation of this activity.

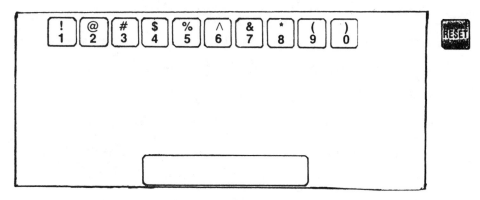

Figure 11-2

2. **Practice it.** Encourage students to look at the keyboard when they are not at the computer. (Remember that the main goal is to increase familiarity with and memory of the keyboard.) Make up a picture of the computer's keyboard and have students practice locating the keys as in Figure 11-3. Initially highlight as shown, but gradually reduce the highlighting. If possible, use paper which is a similar color to the keyboard.

Note: Paper keyboards are commercially available. Be sure you get one that matches your computer so that students do not have to unlearn.

---

[1] The key names used throughout this chapter refer to the Apple microcomputer. This is the computer the authors are most familiar with besides being the most widely used in schools across the country. If your system uses different terms, adjust accordingly.

//// = green   □ = blue   +++ = yellow

Figure 11-3

- *Variation:* Highlight the keyboard by placing removable colored dots on the keys which the child will be using (see Figure 11-4). Leave the other keys alone. In this way, familiarity with the keyboard continues to grow, but progress and use of the computer is not as greatly affected by any deficit area.

Figure 11-4

3. **Time out.** When choosing commercially prepared programs or developing your own, consider programs which allow for teacher or student decision making on timing. Students with figure-ground deficits (as well as other deficits) will be relieved if they do not need to work within a time frame as they search the keyboard.

4. **Hold still.** Select programs in which the location of the problem remains reasonably consistent from screen to screen. In this way, students can practice finding information in a specific location and off-computer work becomes easier to arrange (see Activity 5).

> **Note:** Consistency of problem location is even more important when students begin to use timed programs. There is less chance for them to lose their place if they know to look in the same place each time.

5. **There it is.** Preview a program with a student by providing worksheets as in Figure 11-5. Discuss the sheet and use it with the actual program so students become more aware of their eye movement. Help them realize how they locate the problem on the worksheet and what it "feels" like to find it on both the worksheet and the monitor.

6. **Block it.** Allow students to use earphones, even for games which depend on a bell or another type of sound. In this way, the sound of the other computers will not interfere as much, allowing students to more easily attend to what is required.

Visual Discrimination Difficulties

Background. Students with visual-discrimination difficulties who often misread numbers on a written or typed page tend to have similar problems when using a computer. The clarity of the print on the screen, the color of the monitor, and the size of the print all play a part in how well a child can discern the material on the screen. Children with visual-discrimination problems may have an especially difficult time with decimal numbers as it is often hard for them to "see" the decimal point. Even using the arrow keys can be confusing as these students try to figure out which way the arrows go. Frequently, there is too much on the screen, the text is too close together, the type is too small, and the clarity of the color or monochrome background interferes with a child's perception of material. Additionally, often the graphics which accompany the text are unclear in spite of recent improvements in this area.

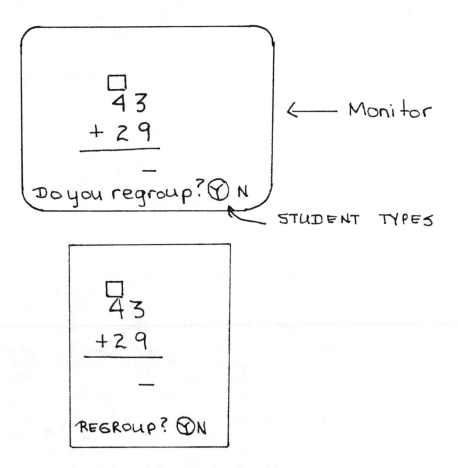

Figure 11-5

Suggested Sequence of Activities and Exercises

1. **Look closely.** Preview the programs students will be using to notice any oddly shaped words or letters. For example, many programs result in an "m" that looks something like that in Figure 11-6 or a "+" that is hard to read. Check

Figure 11-6

the documentation for examples of the pictures used on the screen. If presented, make copies so students can become familiar with them before using the program. Play matching games, make flash cards, or devise other means of acquainting students with hard-to-read visuals.

2. **Go for big.** Use programs with large numbers. The examples in Figure 11-7 represent two math programs currently on the market which both offer good presentations. However, the one in Figure 11-7a is far easier for most students to use simply because the numbers are larger and clearer.

3. **Highlight it.** If a program with smaller print must be used, assist students by providing a tachistoscopic card. It is easiest to use the card with a program that always places the numbers in the same location. This allows the card to be attached to the monitor, as in Figure 11-8.

4. **Hide it.** Some students have trouble using the number keys because there are two symbols on each (see Activity 1 on page 475). Because of the size of the symbols, students may spend unnecessary time (a) trying to separate the symbols and (b) trying to figure out which number they want. Since, generally, the goal is to locate the correct number, it is often helpful to use removable stickers with numbers on them to cover the keys.

   Note: Be sure the numbers on the stickers closely resemble the keyboard numbers, as in Figure 11-9.

5. **Consistency, please.** Use programs where the screen format does not vary greatly from screen to screen. This enables students to learn to focus their eyes more easily. In addition, off-computer activities can help students know what to expect when they go the computer.

a)

b)

Figure 11-7

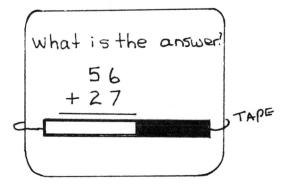

Figure 11-8

Removable COLORED
STICKERS WITH
NUMBERS WRITTEN
ON THEM

Figure 11-9

6. **Find it.** Make flash cards of "key" computer words students need in order to load and run a program. If possible, make worksheets of some of the screens that involve these words and have students practice locating the words on the worksheet. Then have them locate the words on the keyboard and the monitor several times prior to running the program. Provide an acetate overlay which has a heavy line on it so students can place the card on the screen with the heavy line under the word.

Auditory Discrimination

Background: Students with auditory-discrimination problems encounter difficulties using computers even when no voice synthesizer is involved. For example, students who misperceive endings on words or have trouble discriminating between the difference in ending sounds for numbers, such as between "nineteen" and "ninety," may encounter those same problems when using the computer. Unfortunately, it often may not be noticed if there is no teacher-student interaction at the time. For example, a student attempting to solve a computation problem as shown in Figure 11-10 might run into problems. Depending on how "friendly" the computer feedback is when a mistake is made, frustration may occur.

Suggested Sequence of Activities and Exercises

1. **Preview it.** Particularly when students are solving computation problems involving teen numbers, it may help to preview the work. Choose programs where the presentation order of problems can be previewed, either on screen or in the documentation, and practice with the student ahead of time. Have students read the problems to you and match or otherwise associate the individual numbers with written words. In this way, students are learning a method of checking themselves which can be helpful when they use the program independently.

2. **Tape it.** Choose programs which allow the teacher to determine the sequence of presentation. At the beginning of the school year, have an aide or volunteer tape problems from a particular program. Students can use the tape when working with the program and when a teacher or peer is unavailable to monitor the work.

Figure 11-10

- *Variation:* Break the computer use into two or three sessions. Initially, have students call up each problem and read the computation into a tape recorder. Next, at their desks, students listen to the tape and write the problem on paper. After the teacher, an aide, or a *trusted* peer has checked the numbers, the student should use the program.

3. **Pair up.** Encourage students to work with a peer. Ask both students to read the problem aloud as they are solving it.

4. **Sequence it.** Ideally, choose computational programs which allow the student to key in the regrouping number first, as in Figure 11-11a. (Unfortunately, such programs are not widely available.) If a computer must be used for this type of computation, even though the program calls for typing in the regrouped digit second, choose a program that at least asks the student to think about whether or not regrouping is needed.

   Note: Students with visual-discrimination problems should not use computer programs to solve these problems if they are required to type in the solution from right to left (see Figure 11-11b).

Spatial and Temporal Difficulties.
Background: Much current software allows use of the arrow keys to move the cursor around the screen. The idea behind this is sound; however, it often is defeated by the location of the keys on the keyboard. Frequently, the keys have no actual relationship to space unless the student is looking at the arrows (see Figure 11-12).

a)

```
    1
   7 5
 + 1 9
 ───────
    -
```

TYPE THE ANSWER.

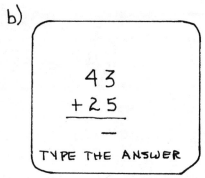

b)

```
  4 3
 + 2 5
 ───────
   -
```

TYPE THE ANSWER

Figure 11-11

Figure 11-12

Concepts such as "up," "down," or "behind," which are already difficult for some students to comprehend, become especially confusing on a computer monitor, where their meaning has a different orientation (Figure 11-13a) than on a piece of paper (Figure 11-13b) or on any object which is parallel to the ground. Moreover, the ability to involve children motorically is limited because their hands and the keyboard are in a different plane than the monitor, making it hard to help them feel the direction. This confusion is compounded by the fact that accessing the "next" screen or the one "before" usually involves using the CONTROL key and some letter, but often not a related letter such as "N" for "next" or "B" for "before."

Figure 11-13

As discussed in other parts of this book, a sense of time is difficult for most children, and especially for learning disabled students. Therefore, even if other skill areas are strong, these students' poor sense of time makes it hard for them to effectively react under a time pressure without specific assistance.

Suggested Sequence of Activities and Exercises

1. **Stretch yourself.** While allowing the use of the arrow keys, many programs also provide for cursor movement through use of the I, J, K, M keys or

some other combination. These keys can be helpful for some students because they more closely replicate movement in space. However, it may be necessary to practice these movements in an off-computer activity. Start by placing direction arrows on removable stickers. Put the stickers on a large paper keyboard—one that is larger than the actual keyboard, as in Figure 11-14. Practice with students, or pair them with a peer, by saying "Move the cursor up;" or "Move the cursor towards the left."

a)

b)

Figure 11-14

- *Variation:* For younger children, start by covering keys which are in a similar position but farther apart on the keyboard, as in Figure 11-14b, thereby requiring more arm movement. Gradually, transition students to using the correct keys before they go to the computer.

2. **See it.** Help students see the correct direction by placing removable stickers on the monitor. The color of the stickers on the monitor should match the color of the stickers on the keys (see Figure 11-15).

Figure 11-15

3. **Compare it.** Use a program in which the cursor movement is directed by one of the keys previously described. Pair two students and have one of them place a finger on the "up" arrow or the "I" key. Stand behind the students and run your finger up the child's back while saying "Feel the 'up' direction; now feel 'up' on the computer." Run your finger on the child's back again while having them depress the key they are pointing to *while looking at the screen.* Do this several times with both students, then have them practice with each other for a while.

4. **Look for it.** Several programs help develop spatial awareness. Have students practice with these programs by following spatial directions. Preferably, the design should be printed or at least saved to a disk so their work can be evaluated. Start with programs which use common words such as "right," "left," "up," and "down."

5. **aMAZING.** Some commercial programs involve mazes that are not too complex. Initially, students will be reluctant to use them, but with teacher assistance, reduced timing, and clearly defined lines on the screen they usually begin to enjoy these games.

6. **See the time.** Some programs have on-screen clocks or timing bars at the bottom of the screen. Have students start by using programs like this and help them notice the movement of the clock or bar. In this way, they can begin to "feel" the time and use it to help pace themselves.

> *Note:* It is not easy to teach time and the effort may not be worth it for many students. Children with visual-perceptual problems may find these on-screen aids too confusing.

Memory Problems

Short- and Long-Term Memory Problems

Background: In many ways the computer can help build retention because it can be "patient" and can provide the overlearning which is essential to many students. At the same time, however, some students encounter unexpected problems because they are only able to access a certain amount of information at any one time. Since the screen holds relatively little information, even though previous screens may be easily accessed, students must flip continually between screens. If access to previous screens is not possible, the problem is further compounded.

The continual need to look back and forth between the screen and the keyboard is often problematic for students with memory deficits, especially if they are unfamilar with the keyboard or lose their place easily. These students may forget what they are looking for while their eyes move from screen to keyboard and back to the screen again. Worse, while they are searching the keyboard for the correct key, the action may take place on the screen. Having missed it, by the time these children look at the screen they no longer know what they are supposed to be looking for.

Commercial programs which do not allow for teacher or student entry of curriculum-related information may cause "skill-subject isolation." Specifically, students learn certain material in class, such as basic facts or percent conversions. The sequence and presentation of these facts is controlled to meet the students' needs. When these students use a computer program to help them practice the facts or convert percents, they may be faced with a variety of material, only some of which is related to what they are studying.

Suggested Sequence of Activities and Exercises

1. **Help.** Increasingly, programs are providing help screens, rather than requiring students to access previous screens or start all over if they forget. If placed properly, these screens and of-screen calculators can be important aids.

2. **I've seen that.** Choose programs which allow for entry of curriculum-related material. In that way, overlearning can be achieved, and skills which have been addressed in class can be reinforced, including approaches to problem solving.

3. **Picture it.** When the screen format remains fairly constant throughout a program, preview the screens and draw pictures of the format for students to use at their desks.

4. **New words.** As part of students' ongoing vocabulary development include key computer words such as "return," "control," "delete," and so on. Make flash cards, play concentration or matching games, making sure that the words are written as on the computer. For example, on Apple computers the major words are written in lower case. Although instructions usually refer to the "control" key as "ctrl" students must learn to refer to the correct key whenever they see "ctrl."

> *Note:* If students use different models of computers choose a separate color for each and write key word names in the color which matches the computer. Some students find it easier to recall the variation in words by associating the words with a color.

Visual Memory

Background: The need for visual aids to reinforce learning or to assist with recall is as important when students are using a computer as when they work out of a workbook or read a book. Realistic, clear pictures and graphics are essential. For example, a program designed to develop money skills should involve clear, simulated coins and bills, as well as the opportunity to use real coins while solving problems.

As noted earlier, many students need to be able to associate unfamiliar words, or words presented in a new context, with a mental picture. Computer programs can be especially helpful along these lines if their graphics are easily distinguished and associated.

Students with visual-memory deficits may find it especially difficult to become familiar with the keyboard since there is no pattern (alphabetic) to the key location and nothing concrete for them to use to help recall the key placement.

Suggested Sequence of Activities and Exercises

1. **That's it.** Keyboard activities are helpful when students are trying to remember the key location for a specific program. Highlight worksheets as shown in Figure 11-16 to assist recalling which keys are associated with which program. Make flash cards or concentration games for students to play with each other as off-computer activities.

2. **Preview it.** (See Activity 1 on page 483.) The goal of this activity is to allow a student to use the computer independently, at least to start up a program. Therefore, although it is preferable that students be able to read certain key computer words in varying contexts, students with visual-memory problems may need to repeatedly practice these words in isolation. In addition, they may also need the cards to locate the words immediately before using the program.

Language Difficulties

Expressive and Receptive Language Difficulties

Background: Much of the time spent using the computer involves responses which are elicited by the on-screen presentation. Often, to score a correct response, an answer must be supplied with a minimum amount of cueing. If the information being presented is related to the student's experience, responding is easier. However, for students with language difficulties the task can be confusing, especially if a time limit is involved. Timed situations for these students make eliciting or comprehending information more difficult.

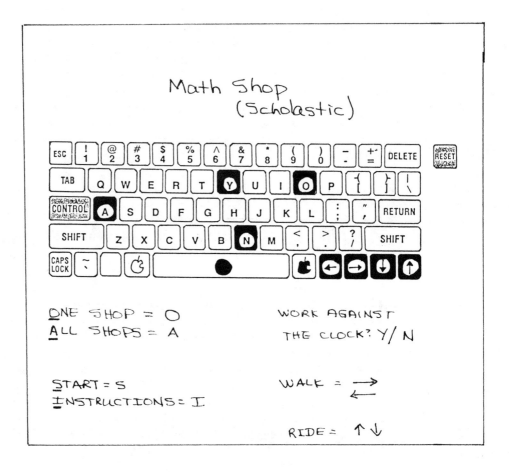

Figure 11-16

Suggested Sequence of Activities and Exercises

1. **Study it.** Even programs which require only a minimal amount of reading usually involve some reading skills if only to be able to access a particular game or section. Before having a child use the program, preview it and make a list of the essential words the student should be able to recognize to run the program independently. Put each word on an individually numbered 3×5 card *in the same order* as the words will appear when the program is loaded. Make sure the child can read the words before using the program. As the program is running, children need not worry about "all the other words," but can search for the key word to tell them what to do.

2. **Crossword puzzle.** At the beginning of the school year make keyboard crossword puzzles as in Figure 11-17. Have an aide, parent, or student assist. Use crayons to lightly color certain keys (on paper keyboards) and write the crossword number on the key. When using the puzzles, students fill in the word in the correct crossword puzzle box. Make different crossword puzzles to match different computer games.

3. **Let's play a game.** A variation of "Old Maid" can be played by two or three children. Make cards as in Figure 11-18. Each student starts with seven cards; the rest of the cards are placed face down in the middle of the table. Students take turns requesting cards based on the cards they are holding. In Figure 11-18a the child holding the keyboard with the "return" key highlighted would ask for a card that has the corresponding word on it. In Figure 11-18b the next child requests a keyboard on which the "control" key is highlighted.

   Note: Allow students to keep paper keyboards in front of them to assist with language requirements as needed.

Reasoning Skills

Abstract Reasoning

Background: The computer can serve as an effective tool for developing reasoning, logic, and problem-solving skills, yet many students find computers mystical. For example, computers are not concrete enough for children who have trouble drawing conclusions. "How does it remember so much?" "How does the disk know what to do?" "Why does 'return' mean that it is the computer's turn?" These and many other questions are very reasonable for any child, even adults, to ask. Much can be done to help gain an understanding of these concepts. In reality,

Figure 11-17

a)

b)

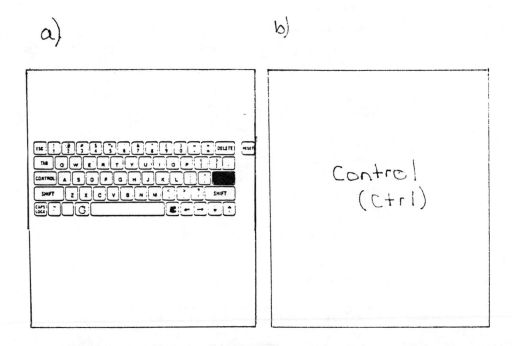

Figure 11-18

however, most teachers working with elementary-school students have neither the expertise nor the time to explain what happens.

At the very basic level of mathematics, where we teach students one-to-one correspondence or use very simple shapes and matching exercises, much of the computer's pictorial representation is good. Still, many students need concrete aids, and often computer timing factors or the nature of a given program do not allow for use of concrete aids. As the material becomes more complex, pictorial representations decrease and students must rely more and more on processes containing symbols only. Some good programs are available, however. For example, programs explaining the concepts of fractions, decimal and place value. Often, however, explanations are placed on separate disks or are not integrated with symbolic work. Therefore, students who need to transition slowly, and require a great deal of overlearning, are unable to access previous information as needed.

Suggested Sequence of Activities and Exercises

1. **Is it gone?** Help students sort out the mystery of a computer by comparing it to a book. Have them find a problem on a page in their book and circle it. Close the book. "Did the problem go away or is it waiting for us to look at it again?" Compare this procedure to the way a computer works by showing a program which provides easy access to previous screens. Help students see that "out of sight" is *not* "out of mind."

2. **Real things, please.** As much as possible, encourage (require) the use of concrete aids and manipulatives with the programs students use. In many instances, this means that the time limits must be eliminated.

PROGRAM CONSIDERATIONS WITH REGARD TO LEARNING DISABILITIES

General Considerations

Teachers, students, and administrators are still becoming accustomed to the changing environment of computer use. Part of this exploration involves ongoing evaluation of the type of software that is needed. As with the more traditional type of learning tools, such as textbooks and workbooks, a wide variety of needs must be considered when choosing/using a computer with students. No one piece of software can meet all needs. Before addressing specific learning disabilities, some general areas must be considered. The following suggestions are based on what is currently available, especially in commercial software.

Choose programs which allow for the use of curriculum-related material.[2] Computers can be of tremendous help in developing problem-solving skills, building retention, and extending abstract reasoning, but only if the material presented is relevant and sequenced according to the students' needs. Therefore, select programs where:

---

[2] Authoring systems, which would allow for complete curriculum integration, are not considered here. Although they are ideal, if good, we recognize that most teachers do not have the time to implement them effectively. Instead, we have tried to emphasize ways in which teachers can use materials that are available on the market.

1. Teacher-made word problems can be entered which follow the desired sequence, allow for proper reading level, and provide the option of either an on-screen calculator or use of a real calculator for students who need to work on problem solving and fact retention separately.

2. Basic facts can be entered according to the sequence described in Chapter 4. (Too many programs use the traditional, less appropriate method of "tables of.")

3. The time needed to respond can vary and is under the control of the teacher and/or the student. In this way, if help screens, on-screen calculators, or other aids are not available, such tools can still be used.

4. The presentation of basic facts and computation can be either horizontal or vertical.

5. Students can easily access help screens or previous screens.

6. Spelling errors are accepted, or the computer can at least be programmed so that it recognizes spelling variations. (Remember, language is an important and often neglected component in mathematics instruction.) A tic-tac-toe game where a student is required to type in the correct word (seventeen) for a number (How much is one ten and seven ones?) should not penalize the student for misspelling 17 (sevintene).

7. Student input is automatically recorded so that the teacher can check the work at a later date if direct observation is not possible. Ideally, a print-out (paper or screen) should be available, similar to Figure 11-19. Too often students work independently at the computer while the teacher is occupied with other students. As a result, there is no way immediately to evaluate their work.

8. Computer response is helpful and can be under the teacher's control. For example, a program involving basic facts might present the correct answer

You have learned:
how to subtract with borrowing
how to multiply with carrying

You need to work on:
basic facts
making change
using decimal points
combining coins

Figure 11-19

immediately following an error; or to develop fraction concepts the computer may offer various types of help. ("Do you want to see a picture?" "Shall I [the computer] help you?" "Did you mean to type that key?") In the former case, correct rather than wrong answers are being reinforced. In the latter instance, problem solving is being reinforced.

9. The letters and numbers are clear and large enough for students to read easily.

10. Students have the opportunity to review incorrect or difficult problems.

11. The "working" division sign ($\overline{)}$) is used rather than either a / or the ÷.

12. Fractions are presented in vertical format with a horizontal fraction bar rather than with a slash.

13. Branching is possible, depending on the student's level. The option to branch (go) to another level—either to a more advanced one or to review—should be part of the program. It should, however, be under the control of the teacher and/or student, rather than being automatically determined by the computer.

Specific Suggestions

The following is a description of various programs selected for specific learning disabilities. In no way is it meant to be an endorsement (advertisement) for any one program or publisher, nor is the listing meant to be complete. The software market is changing constantly and teacher input is being incorporated into the design and development of software. The purpose of this section is, rather, to help teachers learn to evaluate the needs of the student in light of both learning disabilities and specific programs.

No one software program can meet all needs, and some are better suited than others to particular curriculum goals and specific learning disabilities. Even the most highly rated program, in terms of ease of use, teacher utility, and content may not be equally useful to all students. Proper integration of computers into the ongoing instructional schedule requires an understanding of the relationship between curriculum goals and the affect of learning disabilities on successful use of computers. Additionally, teachers must evaluate the strengths and weaknesses of individual programs in light of student needs.

Note: A dash (–) in front of a program means that the user can customize it to some extent in order to meet specific curriculum needs.

Type of Learning Disability: *Figure-Ground*

Considerations for determining the effectiveness of programs for students with figure-ground difficulties include:

- Amount and size of the print on the screen;

- Ability to track material on the screen, either by using a cursor within the program or by using teacher-made tachistoscopic materials;

- Amount of key searching needed in order to work the program. The goal is to allow the student to focus more on the screen and less on going back and forth between keyboard and screen;

- Whether teacher/student can adjust time factors;

- Consistency of screen format;

- Whether sound is available but optional.

Program	Publisher
– *Tic Tac Show*	Scholastic
– *Grammar Examiner*	Designware
– *Create-Lessons*	Hartley
– *FasTrack Quizzer*	Designware
– *Wiz Works*	DLM
– *MathBlaster Plus*	Davidson

Note: Provided the users make up their own gameboards, *Grammar Examiner* is a good program for students with figure-ground deficits, especially if a color monitor is available. However, using the gameboards provided on the program can be horribly confusing, difficult to follow, and long. Although written with the intent of teaching grammar, this program can be adapted to language-related math work; it will accept the use of numbers.

Type of Learning Disability: *Discrimination*

Considerations for determining the effectiveness of programs for students with discrimination difficulties include:

- Size and spacing of numbers and words on the screen;

- Method used to focus students' attention on the task;

- Type of reinforcement used;

- Clarity of monitor, especially color monitors.

Program	Publisher
– *Match Wits*	CBS
– *Square Pairs*	Scholastic

– *MathBlaster Plus*	Davidson
– *Arcademic Drill Builders*	DLM
Clock	Hartley
Addition Magician	Learning Company
– *Create/Lessons*	Hartley

Type of Learning Disability: *Spatial*

Considerations for determining the effectiveness of programs for students with spatial difficulties include:

- How material on the screen deals with directionality;

- Whether a minimal number of keys can be used to work the program and whether the keys are kinesthetically/visually related to the intended direction;

- How the program deals with movement in space—visual or temporal;

- Whether off-computer activities can be used to help students understand the difference in directions between using a screen (vertical) and paper and pencil (different orientation).

Program	**Publisher**
Clock	Hartley
Darts	Apple
Peanuts Mazes	Random House
Fences (Part of *Microzine #5*)	Scholastic
Bumble Plot	Learning Company
– *Turtle Tracks*	Scholastic
Addition Magician	Learning Company
– *Tangrams*	Milliken

Type of Learning Disability: *Memory Difficulties*

Considerations for determining the effectiveness of programs for students with memory difficulties include:

- Teacher/student ability to control the time limits within the program;

- Whether repetition of material, if needed, is possible, especially after an error or at the end of the program for review;

- Whether the presentation method of the material (i.e., random or sequential) can be controlled by the teacher;

- Whether curriculum-related material can be entered into the program;

- Whether the teacher can preview some of the material so off-computer material can be used prior to or while students use the computer.

Program	Publisher
– *Match Wits*	CBS
– *Square Pairs*	Scholastic
– *Mystery Match* (part of *Math Rabbit*)	Learning Company
Success with Math	Mindscape
– *Long Division Made Easy*	Spinfex
– *Subtraction Made Easy*	Spinfex
– *MathBlaster Plus*	Davidson
– *Arcademic Drill Builders*	DLM
– *Magic Cash Register*	Avant Garde

Note: The Spinfex programs are good for students with memory problems who need a slow-paced review that sequences steps and gives students as much time as they need. At the same time, however, these programs may be difficult for students with figure-ground or other visual-perceptual problems. (The numbers that appear on the screen are small and placed close together.)

Type of Learning Disability: *Receptive and Expressive Language*

Considerations for determining the effectiveness of programs for students with expressive-language difficulties include:

- Ability to use a multiple-choice format;

- Interactive ability with curriculum-related material;

- Ability to control (remove) the time limits within the program;

- Ability to access previous screens;

- Provisions for previewing vocabulary;

- Consistency of format.

Program	Publisher
– *Word Attack*	Davidson
– *Tic Tac Show*	Scholastic
– *Arcademic Drill Builders*	DLM
– *FasTrack Quizzer*	Designware

Clock	Hartley
Addition Magician	Learning Company
– *Clowns Counting Program*	
and *Mystery Match* (part of	
Math Rabbit)	Learning Company
– *Magic Cash Register*	Avant Garde

Type of Learning Disability: *Abstract Reasoning*

Considerations for determining the effectiveness of programs for students with abstract-reasoning difficulties include:

- Ability to interact with the program using concrete aids;

- Use of representative visual cues on the screen;

- Ease of accessibility between screens;

- Provisions for teacher preview of vocabulary;

- Ability to add help screens for curriculum-related material.

Program	**Publisher**
– *Magic Cash Register*	Avant Garde
– *Create/Lessons*	Hartley
Math Shop	Scholastic
– *Math Word Problems*	Weekly Reader
– *Tightrope* (part of *Math Rabbit*)	Learning Company
The Factory	Sunburst

RECOMMENDATIONS FOR SOFTWARE DEVELOPMENT

The following section presents ideas for both publishers and teachers to consider with regard to developing software for students with learning disabilities. Even if teachers have the ability to develop software, they may have neither the time nor the interest to do so. However, since much software is part of the public domain and can, therefore, be adjusted relatively easily to meet individual needs, we felt that a discussion of certain programming and software development issues were in order. Additionally, teaching assistants, parents, or students who are "computer whizzes" may be able to implement many of the following ideas into both commercial and public domain software or authoring systems.

Sequence

When selecting or developing programs it is not only important to consider the relevance of the content to the ongoing curriculum, but also the sequence of the content presentation. As noted throughout this book, learning disabled students often need altered sequences of traditional instructional presentations in order to learn and retain information. For example, a child who requires a great deal of overlearning but who tends to perseverate would not benefit from a computation program that only presented computation problems without regrouping. Yet, this same child might not be ready to solve problems with regrouping. Instead, an intermediate step might be helpful where the child learns to differentiate between problems that require regrouping and those that do not. If the teacher can insert a decision-making section/option into a computation program, the student has an opportunity to acquire the necessary skills without being impeded by a learning disability. (An example of one such idea is shown in Figure 11-20.)

$$73 \\ + 19 \qquad\qquad 64 \\ + 21$$

REGROUP ? : Y N   Regroup? Y N

(If regrouping is needed, the computer goes on to the next problem.)

Figure 11-20

Other content-related suggestions include:

1. Allowing for teacher input at various points within the program so that a student can review as needed.

2. Changing the format of computation programs so that the teacher is able to:

   a. Determine the sequence of presentation.

   b. Substitute numbers within the problems without changing the basic structure (i.e., the basic structure of no regrouping would remain, but the basic facts could be changed as a child learned various clusters according to the sequence suggested in Chapter 4).

3. Allowing for curriculum-related information to be entered at selected points, depending on student needs.

4. Providing help screens which can be used by the teacher. The information included in a help screen can be based on teacher assessment of a student's work.

5. Formatting programs so that work can be saved on a separate disk. Then, if students need to stop before completing a program they need not begin all over again unless that is preferable.

Response Format

Learning disabled students respond to information in various ways, depending on their specific disabilities. In order to instruct these students effectively, special education teachers must be able to clearly determine the goal of particular assignment and then control the environment to the extent necessary. Only in this way will students learn the information without being held back due to learning deficits. For example, a student with expressive-language difficulties may enjoy and benefit from using a computer if a multiple-choice format is available, while another student would do fine if required to provide an answer without language cues. Programs with a format choice have the potential of not only being more individualized but allowing two students, with differing learning disabilities, to work together. Some suggestions along these lines include:

1. Games which allow the teacher to choose whether a student has to type in an entire answer (Figure 11-21a) or select from choices by typing in a number only (Figure 11-21b) allow for broader use. Students with figure-ground, visual-discrimination, or expressive-language deficits might benefit from the second format, whereas students strong in these areas but working on building up their memory might do better with the former.

   Note: Figure 11-21b calls for use of a number rather than a letter because less of the keyboard is involved. This feature enables students with figure-ground or discrimination problems to successfully use the program.

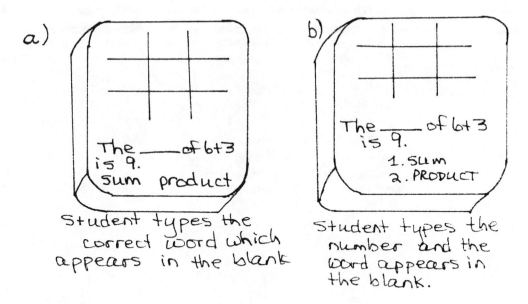

a)

The ____ of 6+3
is 9.
sum   product

Student types the
correct word which
appears in the blank

b)

The ____ of 6+3
is 9.
1. sum
2. PRODUCT

Student types the
number and the
word appears in
the blank.

Figure 11-21

2. Computer response to student input should involve some evaluation on the student's part. A student with figure-ground difficulties or perceptual deficits may type in the wrong answer unknowingly. Before the computer immediately responds to the input, a question might be asked such as, "Are you sure that is the answer you want?" At the very least, some time should elapse before the computer responds to the answer.

Time Factors

For many students, time restrictions greatly inhibit progress. For example, students with language difficulties need time to process information. Figure-ground deficits may mean a student needs more time to locate the keys on the keyboard. Memory problems affect the student's speed. If there is no way to alter the built-in timing, many, otherwise good, programs lose their effectiveness.

1. The teacher should easily be able to control the time factor of any program. This means being able to set the allotted time prior to a student

using the program. In some cases, it also means allowing the student to control the timing, within certain parameters, as the material is mastered. For example, prior to a student beginning a program, the teacher could set the time to a certain speed and then establish parameters within which the student may increase or decrease the time. While working on the program at different levels which have been predetermined by the teacher, the student has a choice of how to handle the time factor.

2. As they develop the confidence to work within a timed setting, some students would benefit from "seeing" the elapsed time. In this way, they are helped to develop a sense about different lengths of time and learn to adjust them to different activities. An example of a type of screen is shown in Figure 11-22.

Figure 11-22

3. It should be possible to save timing changes for individual students so the same time structure can be used during a subsequent session. This feature would also allow another student to begin/continue at a different level without interfering with the work of other students.

Computation

In developing programs which are meant to teach either basic facts or computational skills, the following factors must be considered. For example, the presentation order of the facts is essential to avoid students feeling as if they have to learn 100 (or 90) isolated facts for each of the four operations. The method by which the problem is presented (horizontal or vertical) and by which the student enters the digits in a computation problem is also important both in terms of specific learning disabilities and in terms of understanding a concept. In addition, the location and size of the material on the screen are critical.

1. When a student is required to solve computational problems on the monitor, the presentation should appear in a vertical position with input from right to left, except where regrouping is involved. (See Chapter 5.)

   Note: In Chapter 5 a left-to-right sequence was described that is often needed for students with severe reversal problems. Maybe some day the left-to-right option for computation problems will also be available on computers.

2. For those programs which do not allow for vertical presentation of problems:

   a. The teacher should be able to preview the problems and the order in which they are presented so that the student has paper and pencil available to solve the problem, if needed.

   b. An on-screen calculator should be presented, or at least be available. The student uses it by typing in the numbers from the keyboard. Perhaps keying numbers into the on-screen calculator could cause the numbers to be placed correctly on the screen as in Figure 11-23.

   c. Ideally, the program will allow for a well-spaced print-out of the problems so that the student has a worksheet.

3. If regrouping is involved, the student should:

   a. Be required to decide whether or not to regroup. If no regrouping is involved, a certain key can be designated to push so the problem can move along.

   b. Be required to enter the answer so that the "regrouped digit" is entered first.

4. Numbers should be sufficiently large and centered well enough on the screen so they are easily read. Not only will this reduce the problems encountered

Figure 11-23

by students with perceptual problems, it also will keep the numbers from appearing to "jump out" at you.

5. When solving division problems, even short division, the option of using either division sign ($\overline{)}$ or ÷) should be available so that the teacher can determine ahead of time which sign the student will use.

6. It is not always advisable to have students solve a page with mixed operations. However, the option should be available to the teacher ahead of time.

7. Fraction problems should use the horizontal bar instead of a slanted line, and computation should be presented vertically.

Branching Capabilities

Ideally, the computer should be an integral, related tool of the overall curriculum. As such, computers must enable users to retain the material presented without becoming bored or stagnating at a certain level. These are the same requirements that apply to any classroom instruction. To ensure that the computer meets these criteria, the following branching options must be available.

1. The computer must perform ongoing evaluation so that, as a student reaches mastery or continues to make errors, appropriate branching can occur.

2. The teacher should be able to exert some control over this branching by:

   a. Accessing the student's input and noting the sequence in which the information was answered as well as the number of times it took for the student to get the correct answer.

   b. Predetermining at what points the computer should decide when and where to branch.

3. The scope and sequence of the material presented in the software should be available either in the printed documentation or on a disk. This allows the teacher to:

   a. Decide whether a particular program serves the purposes of the curriculum.

   b. Decide how and when to have the computer branch to another part and when review is needed.

   c. Develop off-computer activities that are related to the material used in the program.

   d. Develop materials that the student can use while working on the computer.

Reading Level

The reading level should be controlled to the extent possible, especially when dealing with computation and word problems. Usually it is not possible to eliminate all reading demands from a program. At a minimum, language is typically needed to give instructions. However, software publishers are encouraged to consider the following recommendations.

1. In addition to the intended age and/or grade level, it would also help to delineate the reading level of the software program on the outside of the box. The age descriptions on the box frequently refer more to interest level rather than actual reading level.

2. Make directions as simple as possible, written in clear, large print, with generous space between the lines. An ongoing help line at the bottom

of each screen would benefit students by reminding them of what to do in order to (a) return to the menu, (b) correct an error, or (c) receive help. If this feature is not possible, a simplified card containing the most basic user information should be included in the documentation. Such a card can easily be kept at the student's side while working.

3. To the extent possible, representative icons should be used to assist in understanding the directions.

4. Include a glossary of words which the student needs to understand to use a program successfully. This would also allow some off-computer activities to be developed prior to actual use of the program.

5. Programs aimed at developing word problem-solving skills should specify both the interest and the reading level on the outside of the box and in the documentation.

6. On-screen help boxes with vocabulary and definitions or representative examples would assist students as they read the problems and possibly encounter words with which they are unfamiliar.

7. Software which is programmed to accept teacher-developed word problems are most helpful. The shell program could be written and published in such a way that the teacher could determine:

   a. Reading level and material.

   b. Number of steps in the problem.

   c. Types of problems presented.

   d. Help given in solving the problems:

      • Steps listed in order

      • Steps listed, out of order

      • Things to consider prior to solving

   e. Order in which the problems are presented (sequential or random).

Teacher Utility

One of the important advantages of having computers in the classroom is their potential for individualizing instruction. It is especially important, therefore, that the classroom teacher has some control over the software while also being aware of how the student uses the software without having to be present at all times.

Note: Even though it is not realistic to expect teachers to watch students at the computer continuously, too often no monitoring takes place. In order to evaluate the usefulness of a given activity, there must be time for teachers to see how students are interacting with and responding to the computer. Otherwise, the computer simply becomes busy work.

To enhance computer utility for teachers, the following should be considered:

1. The utility section must be easily accessible to the teacher but not to the student. In some instances, it is helpful for students to be able to access part of the utility section, but the record keeping and error analysis should be open only to the student with the assistance of the teacher.

2. Automatic recordkeeping should start as soon as a student signs on the computer by entering a name.

3. A paper print-out showing the following information would help in assessing student progress:

   • Number of problems attempted;

   • A copy of: the problems
      the numbers keyed in to derive the answers
      the final answers;

   • Percent correct.

4. If correct answers involve words, rather than numbers, the program should allow for the teacher to include a spell checker—one which permits inclusion of "odd" spellings. Often, students with learning disabilities have trouble with spelling. If the answer to a math problem depends on correctly spelled words, there is no way to measure math ability. At the very least, the program should accept spelling errors. Most teachers, however, are more familiar with the types of errors their students make than are software developers, hence the advantage of flexibility in this area.

General Recommendations

As we become more and more sophisticated in our approach to teaching and to integrating computers into instruction, our knowledge of what comprises useful software will also improve. The ideas in the preceding discussion apply to particular areas of learning and software. The following points are more general.

1. It is important that the student be able to read what is on the screen. To that end, the type must be large. Just as some word processors offer a variation in the number of columns, math software should allow for varying size of type and perhaps even boldness of the type.

2. When solving word problems the student should be required to include a word answer along with the correct computation. If spelling is a problem, the student should be presented with choices from which one answer must be selected. Figure 11-24 presents one suggestion for younger students or those who have difficulty with the keyboard.

Figure 11-24

3. The spacing between numbers and between words should be clear. At the very least, double spacing should be available to make it easier to read the material on the screen.

4. The use of underlining, arrows, and cursors to help focus attention is essential to many students. Screens change quickly and many learning disabled students need help to refocus their attention on the correct place on the screen.

5. When graphics are included, many children, though enjoying and benefitting from them, nevertheless have trouble keeping their orientation. Therefore, these students need assistance, in terms of cursors and appropriate time limits, to locate the problem or the answer amidst the graphics.

6. Much software benefits from and/or requires color monitors. If this is the case, it is important that the color monitor be very clear and the type size of the numbers and letters be large enough so the images are not blurred.

7. The area in which students solve the problems should be centrally located on the screen. If more than one problem is present on the screen or if an area is reserved for computation, the program should allow the teacher to spatially organize the workspace for students who would otherwise be overwhelmed.

8. Many programs provide off-computer activities. These should include activities focusing on the directions needed to work through material. This would make the student familiar with the keyboard as it relates to a particular piece of software.

REFERENCES

National Council of Supervisors of Mathematics. (1988). *Twelve components of essential mathematics*. Minneapolis, MN: National Council of Supervisors of Mathematics.

National Council of Teachers of Mathematics. (1989). *Curriculum and evaluation standards for school mathematics*. Reston, VA: National Council of Teachers of Mathematics.

Thornton, C. A. (1989). *Teaching basic facts: Addition and subtraction*; and *Teaching basic facts in the intermediate grades*. Pacific Grove, CA: Midwest Publications.

Tucker, B. F. (1983, Winter). Diagnosing for big ideas. *Focus on Learning Problems in Mathematics, 5*, 23–32.

INDEX

ABOUT THE AUTHORS

Nancy S. Bley is Academic Coordinator at Park Century School in Los Angeles, California, where she has been a staff member since 1976. Park Century is a private school specializing in individualized one-to-one programs for learning disabled children. In addition to her work at Park Century, she maintains a private practice working with learning disabled children and has taught *Diagnosis and Remediation of Mathematical Difficulties to Students with Learning Disabilities* at UCLA Extension. Prior to working at Park Century, Bley taught math in Chicago at the elementary- and high-school levels. She has presented at numerous conferences, including the Association for Children and Adults with Learning Disabilities, the Council for Learning Disabilities, Computer Using Educators, and the Research Council for Diagnostic and Prescriptive Mathematics. Bley has published articles in various areas of learning disabilities and currently is especially interested in computer use with learning disabled students.

Carol A. Thornton is a professor in the Department of Mathematics at Illinois State University, Normal, Illinois. Thornton has 10 years' teaching experience in public schools and has started and directed a clinic for children with severe learning difficulties in mathematics. She is also an elementary-school mathematics textbook author and has published an instructional money kit and several series of books for special education and regular class students. Primary among her publications are teacher resource and instructional materials related to helping children master basic arithmetic facts. In addition to her publications, Thornton has developed a special education filmstrip and a videotape on computational skills. Finally, she has been a speaker and workshop leader at numerous state, regional, and national meetings, and has received several grants related to mathematics education for the learning disabled as well as other exceptional and regular class students.